FULLY UPDATED FOR THE NEW GRE GENERAL TEST

BOB MILLER'S MATH for the NEW GRE®

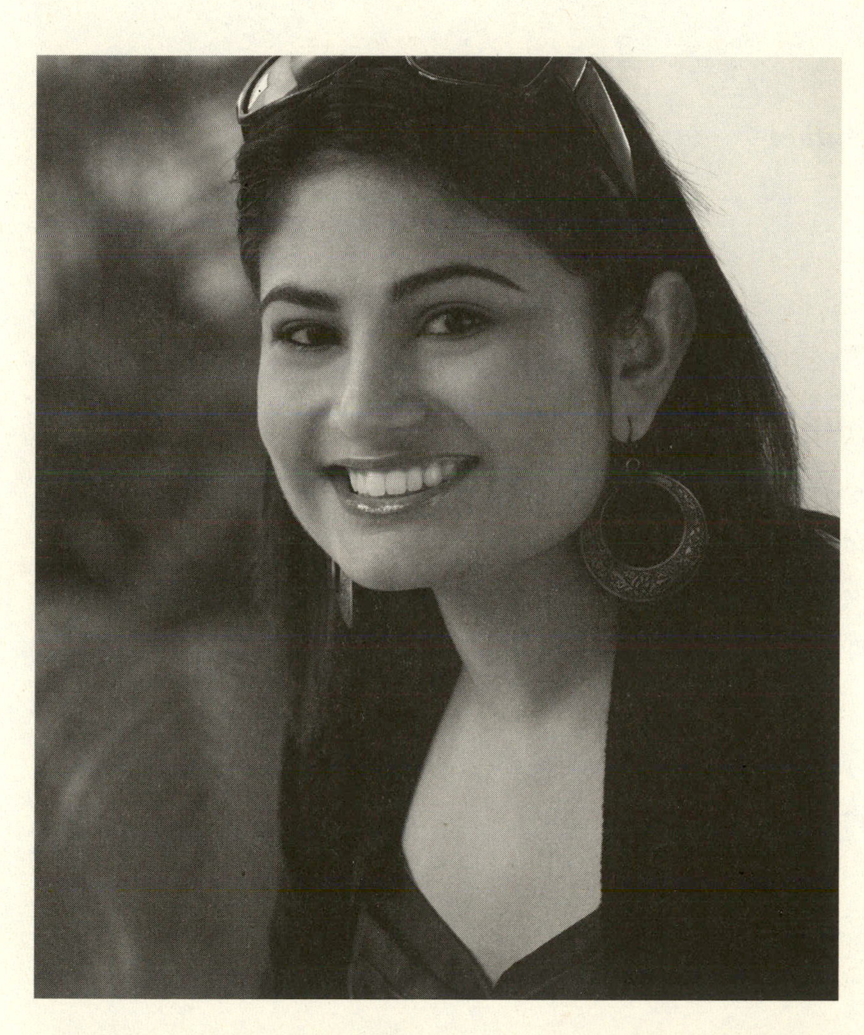

Bob Miller
Former Lecturer in Mathematics
City College of New York
New York, NY

Research & Education Association
Visit our website at: www.rea.com

Planet Friendly Publishing
✔ Made in the United States
✔ Printed on Recycled Paper
Text: 10% Cover: 10%
Learn more: www.greenedition.org

At REA we're committed to producing books in an Earth-friendly manner and to helping our customers make greener choices.

Manufacturing books in the United States ensures compliance with strict environmental laws and eliminates the need for international freight shipping, a major contributor to global air pollution.

And printing on recycled paper helps minimize our consumption of trees, water and fossil fuels. This book was printed on paper made with **10% post-consumer waste.** According to Environmental Defense's Paper Calculator, by using this innovative paper instead of conventional papers, we achieved the following environmental benefits:

Courier Corporation, the manufacturer of this book, owns the Green Edition Trademark.

Trees Saved: 12 • Air Emissions Eliminated: 3,484 pounds
Water Saved: 6,225 gallons • Solid Waste Eliminated: 1,016 pounds

For more information on our environmental practices, please visit us online at **www.rea.com/green**

Research & Education Association
61 Ethel Road West
Piscataway, New Jersey 08854
E-mail: info@rea.com

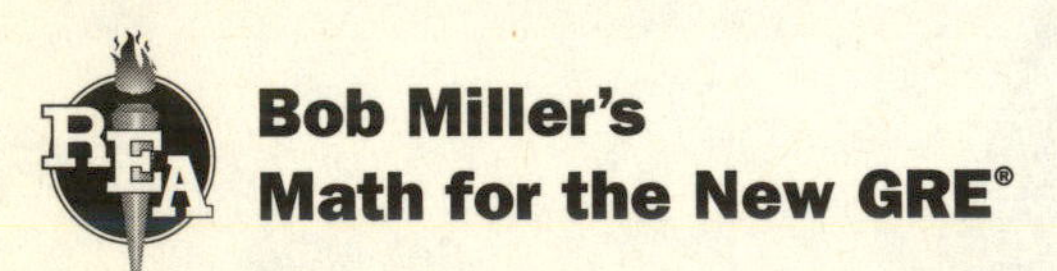

Printed in the United States of America

Library of Congress Control Number 2011929513

ISBN-13: 978-0-7386-0902-7
ISBN-10: 0-7386-0902-1

G11

TABLE OF CONTENTS

ACKNOWLEDGMENTS

I have many people to thank.

I thank my wife, Marlene, who makes life worth living, who is truly the wind under my wings.

I thank the rest of my family: children Sheryl and Eric and their spouses Glenn and Wanda (who are also like my children); grandchildren Kira, Evan, Sean, Sarah, Ethan, and Noah; my brother Jerry, and my parents, Cele and Lee, and my in-law parents, Edith and Siebeth.

I thank Larry Kling, Michael Reynolds, and Mel Friedman for making this book possible.

I thank Martin Levine for making my whole writing career possible.

I have been negligent in thanking my great math teachers of the past. I thank Mr. Douglas Heagle, Mr. Alexander Lasaka, Mr. Joseph Joerg, and Ms. Arloeen Griswold, the best math teacher I ever had, of George W. Hewlett High School; Ms. Helen Bowker of Woodmere Junior High; and Professor Pinchus Mendelssohn and Professor George Bachman of Polytechnic University. The death of Professor Bachman was an extraordinary loss to our country. In a country that produces too few advanced degrees in math, every year two or three of his students would receive a Ph.D. in math, with more receiving their M.S. His teaching and writings were clear and memorable. He wrote four books and numerous papers on subjects that had never been written about or had been written so poorly that nobody could understand the material.

As usual, the last three thanks go to three terrific people: a great friend, Gary Pitkofsky; another terrific friend and fellow lecturer, David Schwinger; and my cousin, Keith Robin Ellis, the sharer of our dreams.

Bob Miller

DEDICATION

To my wife, Marlene. I dedicate this book and everything else I ever do to you.
I love you very, very much.

BIOGRAPHY

I received my B.S. in the Unified Honors Program sponsored by the Ford Foundation and my M.S. in math from N.Y.U. Polytechnic University. After the first class I taught, as a substitute for a full professor, one student said to another upon leaving the classroom, "At least we have someone who can teach the stuff." I was hooked forever on teaching. Since then, I have taught at C.U.N.Y., Westfield State College, Rutgers, and Poly. No matter how I feel, I always feel a lot better when I teach. I always feel great when students tell me they used to hate math or couldn't do math and now they like it more and can do it better.

My main blessing is my family. I have a fantastic wife in Marlene. My kids are wonderful: daughter Sheryl, son Eric, son-in-law Glenn, and daughter-in-law Wanda. My grandchildren are terrific: Kira, Evan, Sean, Sarah, Ethan, and Noah. My hobbies are golf, bowling, bridge, crossword puzzles, and Sudoku. My ultimate goals are to write a book to help parents teach their kids math, a high school text that will advance our kids' math abilities, and a calculus text students can actually understand.

To me, teaching is always a great joy. I hope that I can give some of that joy to you. I do know this book will help you get the score you need to get into the graduate school of your choice.

I really like GRE questions. I like all kinds of puzzles, both mathematical and word. To me the GRE is a game. If you win, you win the graduate school of your choice. Good luck!!!!!

OTHER BOOKS

Bob Miller's Math for the GMAT, Third Edition
Bob Miller's Math for the Accuplacer
Bob Miller's Math for the ACT
Bob Miller's Math for the TABE
Bob Miller's Basic Math and Pre-Algebra for the Clueless, Second Edition
Bob Miller's Algebra for the Clueless, Second Edition
Bob Miller's Geometry for the Clueless, Second Edition
Bob Miller's Math SAT for the Clueless, Second Edition
Bob Miller's Pre-Calc with Trig for the Clueless, Third Edition
Bob Miller's High School Calc for the Clueless
Bob Miller's Calc 1 for the Clueless, Second Edition
Bob Miller's Calc 2 for the Clueless, Second Edition
Bob Miller's Calc 3 for the Clueless

ABOUT RESEARCH & EDUCATION ASSOCIATION

Founded in 1959, Research & Education Association (REA) is dedicated to publishing the finest and most effective educational materials—including software, study guides, and test preps—for students in middle school, high school, college, graduate school, and beyond.

REA's test preparation series includes books and software for all academic levels in almost all disciplines. REA publishes test preps for students who have not yet entered high school, as well as high school students preparing to enter college. Students from countries around the world seeking to attend college in the United States will find the assistance they need in REA's publications. For college students seeking advanced degrees, REA publishes test preps for many major graduate school admission examinations in a wide variety of disciplines, including engineering, law, and medicine. Students at every level, in every field, with every ambition can find what they are looking for among REA's publications.

REA's publications and educational materials are highly regarded and continually receive an unprecedented amount of praise from professionals, instructors, librarians, parents, and students. Our authors are as diverse as the subject matter represented in the books we publish. They are well known in their respective disciplines and serve on the faculties of prestigious colleges and universities throughout the United States and Canada.

Today, REA's wide-ranging catalog is a leading resource for teachers, students, and professionals.

We invite you to visit us at *www.rea.com* to find out how "REA is making the world smarter."

REA ACKNOWLEDGMENTS

In addition to our author, we would like to thank Larry B. Kling, Vice President, Editorial, for his overall direction; Pam Weston, Publisher, for setting the quality standards for production integrity and managing the publication to completion; Michael Reynolds, Managing Editor, for project management; Mel Friedman, Lead Mathematics Editor, for technical review; Weymouth Design, for designing our cover; and S4Carlisle Publishing Services, for typesetting this edition. Back cover photo by Eric L. Miller.

INTRODUCTION

Hi! My name is Bob Miller, and this is the introduction to a book that will help you do great on the quantitative section of the New GRE. This book will help you achieve your goal—getting admitted to the graduate school of your choice. It is important to know that a perfect score is not necessary. You only need a score that is high enough to get you into the school of your choice. ETS has changed the score scale from 130 to 170, in units of one. Therefore, a score of 169 is possible.

This book gives you everything you need to master math on the GRE revised General Test. All the topics in this book are covered in a way most readers have found easy to understand and sometimes even enjoyable. The kinds of questions on the GRE quantitative section are approximately 10% arithmetic, 40% algebra, 15% geometry, and 35% data analysis. (No advanced math such as trig or calculus or geometric proofs will be found on this test.) However, I've found great variation from test to test in the past. Some of the topics overlap each other. So even these percentages are very approximate. This book teaches you the topics you need, has many questions that are worked out in detail for you, and provides many other review questions and answers.

According to ETS, the test consists of either two or three math sections (one is an ungraded field test). There are 20 questions in each section on the computer-based test and 25 questions on each section on the paper-and-pencil test, with a time limit of 35 minutes. A calculator is provided for both the computer-based and paper-and-pencil versions—a major change. It is a simple calculator with only addition, subtraction, multiplication, division, and square root keys. There are memory keys and a special key on the computer—a button that will allow you to directly transfer your answer to the answer sheet.

On either version of the test, you may return to any question in a section. On the computerized version, you can add a check to problems and come back to them, changing answers if you choose. Once a section is finished, however, you cannot go back. Some advice: Never change an answer unless you are 100% sure the new answer is correct. On the last test I took, I went against my own advice and went from a correct answer to a wrong one!

There will be four types of questions. The first is the standard (single-answer) multiple-choice question, about 45% of the test (again, percentages are very approximate). The second is a multiple-answer multiple choice, which accounts for about 10% of the questions. The third is numeric entry, again about 10% of the test. The last is quantitative comparisons, about 35% of the test. Let's talk about each type.

The first multiple-choice type is the one with which you are most familiar. There are five possible answers. You are to pick the correct answer and fill in the oval.

Question: If $2a = 3b = 4c = 20$, what is the value of $9abc$?

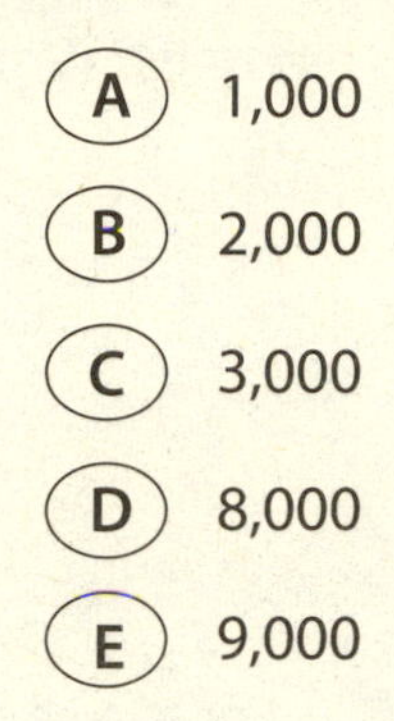

Answer: $(2a)(3b)(4c) = 24abc = (20)^3$ the $= 8{,}000$. Then $abc = \frac{8{,}000}{24} = 333\frac{1}{3}$.

Thus, $9abc = (9)\left(333\frac{1}{3}\right) = 3{,}000$.

The next type is the new multiple-answer multiple-choice question, with three to six answer choices. One or more of the answers will be correct, and you must fill in *all* the correct boxes. No credit will be given unless all the correct boxes are filled in. There must be at least one correct answer, but it is possible that all the answers might be correct. If a question requires two correct answers, you will get credit only if you fill in *both* correct answers.

Question: If $3 < x < 7$, and x is an integer, then x might be

Answer: (D) and (E) are the correct answers. Choices (A) and (B) are obviously wrong; for choice (C), 3 is not greater than 3; for choice (F), $2\pi \approx 6.28$ but it is not an integer!

The third kind of question is the numeric entry. In plain English, this means to fill in the blank(s). The paper version and computer version are very different. On the computerized version, a rectangular blank must be filled in. If there is a fraction, there will be a rectangle, a fractional bar, and another rectangle under the bar.

Fractions on either version of the test do not have to be reduced to be correct. The paper version has a grid to fill in. Any place on the grid with the correct answer will be correct. Beware that on this part of the test, you must give the answer exactly as the question asks. For example, suppose the answer was calculated to be 45.2%. If the rectangular box has a % sign after it, you must put only 45.2 in the box. On the gridded test 45.2 must be filled in.

Question: A jar has 7 red balls and 3 orange balls. Two balls are drawn, one at a time, without replacement. What is the probability of selecting two red balls? Write your answer as a fraction.

Answer: $\frac{7}{15}$ The probability for selecting the first red ball is $\frac{7}{10}$. For the second selection, there are nine balls left, of which six are red. So the probability of selecting a second red ball is $\frac{6}{9}=\frac{2}{3}$. Therefore, the required probability is $\frac{7}{10}\times\frac{2}{3}=\frac{14}{30}=\frac{7}{15}$. (Examples of other acceptable answers are $\frac{14}{30}$ and $\frac{42}{90}$.)

An answer of 0.452, the same answer as a decimal, will be marked wrong. If the problem asks you to round off the answer to the nearest integer, you must put 45. All other answers are incorrect. You must give exactly the answer asked for!

The last question type is quantitative comparison. Your answer is actually the answer to "how do these two quantities compare?" Your answer choices are:

- (A) if Quantity A is greater.
- (B) if Quantity B is greater.
- (C) if the two Quantities are equal.
- (D) if the relationship cannot be determined from the information given.

Here's an example. (Fill in the correct oval.)

Quantity A	**Quantity B**
(45678–87654)	(87654–45678)

The answer is B. You do not have to do the problem. You only need to know that B is larger because B is positive and A is negative. I always found these problems the easiest because you don't have to work many of them out. Hints about this section: If A and B have only numbers, the answer is never D. The answer can always be determined. If there are only letters, the answer can only be C or D. If given more specific information about where the unknown numbers are (as an example, say, $x > 4$ and $y > 6$) or there is a mix of numbers and letters, any answer is possible.

With the New GRE, ETS is giving more real-life situations. This doesn't change the nature of the problem. It only changes the location of the problem from a zoo to a factory. The math remains the same.

I tried to write this book as I wished my books had been written when I was a student. Good luck on the New GRE.

Bob Miller

STUDY PLAN

HOW TO USE THIS BOOK

If you need an extra boost of math prep before you feel confident enough to tackle the math portion of the GRE revised General Test, this book is for you!

Depending on where you are on your educational pathway, some of you haven't seen math in a very long time. Maybe that's why you chose this test prep—for its easy-to-understand math practice and reinforcement. As you read through this book you may find that you know the material in some of the chapters pretty well—and others, not so much. Those are the areas on which you'll need to focus.

Before you pick up your pencil and start studying, read the introduction and become familiar with the math portion of the GRE. Make sure you understand how the test is conducted, and know the type and style of questions that will be asked.

Every day, devote at least an hour (or perhaps two hours, depending on your math skills) to studying the math concepts presented in this book. At first—just like starting an exercise plan—it will be hard. But after a few days, studying will become a natural part of your routine. Find a study routine that works for you and stick to it! Some people like to get up early and study for an hour or two before going to work or class. Others might choose to study on their lunch hour, at the library, or at home. Whatever schedule you choose, make a commitment to study every day—even on weekends.

Go through each chapter and try some of the practice problems. If you find them to be very easy, skip to the next chapter. Whenever you find a chapter that is not so easy, take your time and study the chapter in detail. After you have gone through the chapters that you think give you the most trouble, go back and study the remaining chapters. Practical math tips are included in all the chapters, and they will help you solve math problems quickly and more easily.

When you have a good grasp of the material, try the first practice test. Give yourself plenty of time and work in a quiet place where you won't be disturbed. After you've finished the practice test, check your answers. If you find there are some types of questions (such as quadrilaterals) that you constantly get wrong, restudy the appropriate review chapter and practice problems.

After you've finished restudying any areas of weakness, repeat the process with the remaining two practice tests. Keep reviewing the math topics that give you trouble until you feel comfortable with the material. In just a matter of weeks, your math skills will improve and you'll be ready for the GRE!

SUGGESTED STUDY PLAN

"You don't need to follow any study plan except your own. Only you know how and when you study best. So work through this book at your own pace and take as much time as you need in each chapter. But if you want some guidelines, try this 4-week Study Plan. For those of you crunched for time, condense this into a 2-week schedule by combining weeks 1 and 2 together, and weeks 3 and 4 together."

Week	Activity
1	Read the introduction. Take Practice Test 1 to determine your strengths and weaknesses. Give yourself a block of time after school or work, on a weekend, or at another convenient time to take the exam. You will need to concentrate, so take the practice test at a time and place where you will not be disturbed. When you take the test, try to do your best, even on sections where you may be confused. After you have finished the test, record your scores. This will help you track your progress as you study. Later in the week, study the answers for the questions you answered incorrectly. In the cases where you erred, find out why. Take notes and pay attention to sections where you missed a lot of questions. You will need to spend more time reviewing the related material.
2	Make a firm commitment to study for at least an hour a day, every day, for the next few weeks. It may seem hard to find time in your busy schedule, but remember: the more you study, the better prepared you will be for the GRE General Test. This week, study review chapters 1 through 7. Do the practice exercises and check your answers for each section of the review. Pace yourself and make sure you understand the basics before moving on to the more difficult chapters. If you find yourself in need of extra review or clarification on a topic, you may want to consult your math textbook or ask a classmate or professor for additional help.

Week	Activity
3	Keep working your way through the review chapters and practice problems. This week focus your study on chapters 8 through 14. Take your time and make sure you're familiar with all the math formulas and rules presented in the review. Pay close attention to the examples and exercises; they will show you how to solve the types of questions you will encounter on the actual GRE exam. After you've completed the review chapters, take Practice Test 2. Record your score and see how well you did. After you've evaluated your test results, go back through each chapter and brush up on the topics you need to review. Later this week, study the answers for any questions you answered incorrectly. Make sure you understand why you answered the question wrong, so you can improve your test-taking skills.
4	After a day or two of additional study to reinforce any areas of weakness, take Practice Test 3. Don't rush! Remember what you've learned and answer every question to the best of your ability. How much has your score improved since you took the first practice exam? After the test, thoroughly review all the explanations for the questions you answered incorrectly. Later in the week, go back and review any questions you answered wrong on the previous practice tests. Spend time studying the answer explanations and re-read the relevant chapters for extra review. If you feel you need extra GRE math practice, why not review your notes during your lunch hour or at the end of the day?

Congratulations! You've worked hard and you're ready for the math portion of the GRE General Test!

CHAPTER 1: *The Basics*

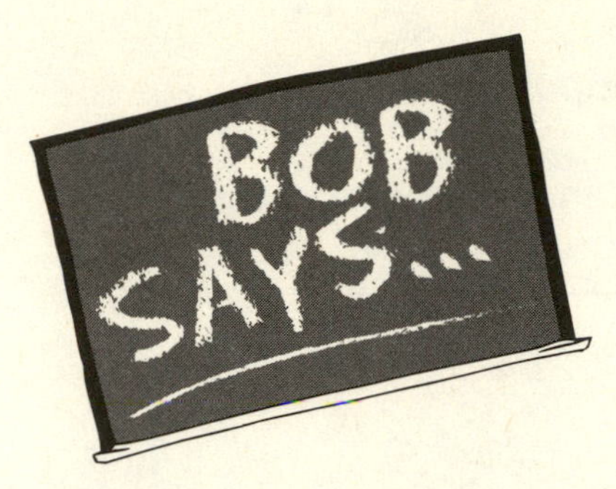

"All math begins with whole numbers. Master them and you will begin to speak the language of math."

Let's begin at the beginning. The GRE works only with **real numbers**, numbers that can be written as decimals. However, it does not always say "numbers." Let 's get specific.

NUMBERS

Whole numbers: 0, 1, 2, 3, 4, ...

Integers: 0, ±1, ±2, ±3, ±4, ..., where ±3 stands for both +3 and −3.

Positive integers are integers that are greater than 0. In symbols, $x > 0$, x is an integer.

Negative integers are integers that are less than 0. In symbols, $x < 0$, x is an integer.

Even integers: 0, ±2, ±4, ±6, ...

Odd integers: ±1, ±3, ±5, ±7, ...

Inequalities

For any numbers represented by a, b, c, or d on the number line:

−6 −5 −4 −3 −2 −1 0 1 2 3 4 5 6

We say $c > d$ (c is greater than d) if c is to the right of d on the number line.

We say $d < c$ (d is less than c) if d is to the left of c on the number line.

$c > d$ is equivalent to $d < c$.

$a \leq b$ means $a < b$ or $a = b$; likewise, $a \geq b$ means $a > b$ or $a = b$.

Example 1: Tell whether the following inequalities are true:

a. $4 \leq 7$ **b.** $9 \leq 9$ **c.** $7 \leq 2$.

Solution: **a.** $4 \leq 7$ is true, since $4 < 7$;

b. $9 \leq 9$ is true, since $9 = 9$;

c. $7 \leq 2$ is false, since $7 > 2$.

Example 2: Graph all integers between −4 and 5.

Solution:

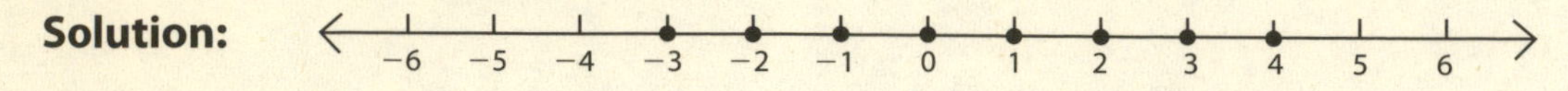

Notice that the word "between" does *not* include the endpoints.

Example 3: Graph all the multiples of 5 between 20 and 40 inclusive.

Solution:

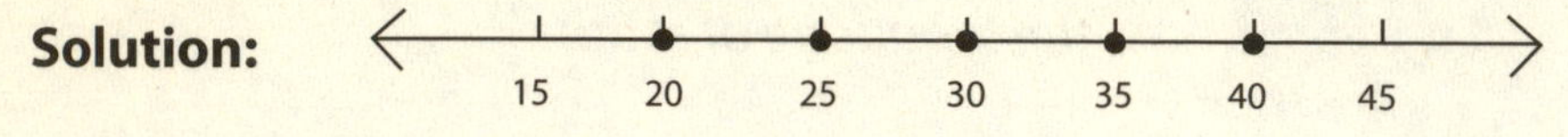

Notice that "inclusive" means to include the endpoints.

Odd and Even Numbers

Here are some facts about odd and even integers that you should know.

- The sum of two even integers is even.
- The sum of two odd integers is even.
- The sum of an even integer and an odd integer is odd.
- The product of two even integers is even.
- The product of two odd integers is odd.
- The product of an even integer and an odd integer is even.
- If n is even, n^2 is even. If n^2 is even and n is an integer, then n is even.
- If n is odd, n^2 is odd. If n^2 is odd and n is an integer, then n is odd.

OPERATIONS ON NUMBERS

Product is the answer in multiplication; **quotient** is the answer in division; **sum** is the answer in addition; and **difference** is the answer in subtraction.

Since $3 \times 4 = 12$, 3 and 4 are said to be **factors** or **divisors** of 12, and 12 is both a **multiple** of 3 and a **multiple** of 4.

A prime is a positive integer with exactly two distinct factors, itself and 1. The number 1 is not a prime since only $1 \times 1 = 1$. It might be a good idea to memorize the first eight primes:

2, 3, 5, 7, 11, 13, 17, and 19.

The number 4 has more than two factors: 1, 2, and 4. Numbers with more than two factors are called **composites**. The number 28 is a **perfect** number since if you add the factors less than 28, they add to 28.

Example 4: Write all the factors of 28.

Solution: 1, 2, 4, 7, 14, and 28.

Example 5: Write 28 as the product of prime factors.

Solution: $28 = 2 \times 2 \times 7$.

Example 6: Find all the primes between 70 and 80.

Solution: 71, 73, 79. How do we find this easily? First, since 2 is the only even prime, we only have to check the odd numbers. Next, we have to know the divisibility rules:

- A number is divisible by 2 if it ends in an even number. We don't need this here because then it can't be prime.
- A number is divisible by 3 (or 9) if the sum of the digits is divisible by 3 (or 9). For example, 456 is divisible by 3 since the sum of the digits is 15, which is divisible by 3 (it's not divisible by 9, but that's okay).
- A number is divisible by 4 if the last two digits are divisible by 4. For example, 3,936 is divisible by 4 since 36 is divisible by 4.
- A number is divisible by 5 if the last digit is 0 or 5.
- The rule for 6 is a combination of the rules for 2 and 3.
- It is easier to divide by 7 than to learn the rule for 7.
- A number is divisible by 8 if the last *three* digits are divisible by 8.
- A number is divisible by 10 if it ends in a zero, as you know.
- A number is divisible by 11 if the difference between the sum of the even-place digits (2nd, 4th, 6th, etc.) and the sum of the odd-place digits (1st, 3rd, 5th, etc.) is a multiple of 11. For example, for the number 928,193,926: the sum of the odd digits (9, 8, 9, 9, and 6) is 41; the sum of the even digits (2, 1, 3, 2) is 8; and $41 - 8$ is 33, which is divisible by 11. So 928,193,926 is divisible by 11.

That was a long digression!!!!! Let's get back to example 6.

We only have to check 71, 73, 75, 77, and 79. 75 is not a prime since it ends in a 5. 77 is not a prime since it is divisible by 7. To see if the other three are prime, for any number less than 100, you have to divide by the primes 2, 3, 5, and 7 only. You will quickly find they are primes.

Rules for Operations on Numbers

Note *( ) are called parentheses (singular: parenthesis); [ ] are called brackets; { } are called braces.*

Rules for adding signed numbers

1. If all the signs are the same, add the numbers and use that sign.
2. If two signs are different, subtract them, and use the sign of the larger numeral.

Example 7:

a. $3 + 7 + 2 + 4 = +16$

b. $-3 - 5 - 7 - 9 = -24$

c. $5 - 9 + 11 - 14 = 16 - 23 = -7$

d. $2 - 6 + 11 - 1 = 13 - 7 = +6$

Rules for multiplying and dividing signed numbers

Look at the minus signs only.

1. Odd number of minus signs—the answer is minus.
2. Even number of minus signs—the answer is plus.

Example 8: $\dfrac{(-4)(-2)(-6)}{(-2)(+3)(-1)} =$

Solution: Five minus signs, so the answer is minus, -8.

Rule for subtracting signed numbers

The sign $(-)$ means subtract. Change the problem to an addition problem.

Example 9: **a.** $(-6) - (-4) = (-6) + (+4) = -2$

b. $(-6) - (+2) = (-6) + (-2) = -8$, since it is now an adding problem.

Order of Operations

In doing a problem like this, $4 + 5 \times 6$, the **order of operations** tells us whether to multiply or add first:

1. If given letters, substitute in parentheses the value of each letter.
2. Do operations in parentheses, inside ones first, and then the tops and bottoms of fractions.
3. Do exponents next. (Chapter 3 discusses exponents in more detail.)
4. Do multiplications and divisions, left to right as they occur.
5. The last step is adding and subtracting. Left to right is usually the safest way.

Example 10: $4 + 5 \times 6 =$

Solution: $4 + 30 = 34$

Example 11: $(4 + 5)6 =$

Solution: $(9)(6) = 54$

Example 12: $1{,}000 \div 2 \times 4 =$

Solution: $(500)(4) = 2{,}000$

Example 13: $1{,}000 \div (2 \times 4) =$

Solution: $1{,}000 \div 8 = 125$

Example 14: $4[3 + 2(5 - 1)] =$

Solution: $4[3 + 2(4)] = 4[3 + 8] = 4(11) = 44$

Example 15: $\dfrac{3^4 - 1^{10}}{4 - 10 \times 2} =$

Solution: $\dfrac{81 - 1}{4 - 20} = \dfrac{80}{-16} = -5$

Example 16: If $x = -3$ and $y = -4$, find the value:

a. $7 - 5x - x^2$

b. $xy^2 - (xy)^2$

Solutions:

a. $7 - 5x - x^2 = 7 - 5(-3) - (-3)^2 = 7 + 15 - 9 = 13$

b. $xy^2 - (xy)^2 = (-3)(-4)^2 - ((-3)(-4))^2 = (-3)(16) - (12)^2$
$= -48 - 144 = -192$

Before we get to the exercises, let's talk about ways to describe a group of numbers (data).

DESCRIBING DATA

Four of the measures that describe data are used on the GRE. The first three are measures of central tendency; the fourth, the range, measures the span of the data. Chapter 14 discusses these measures in more detail.

Mean: Also called average. Add up the numbers and divide by how many numbers you have added up.

Median: Middle number. Put the numbers in numeric order and see which one is in the middle. If there are two "middle" numbers, take the average of them. This happens with an even number of data points.

Mode: Most common. Which number(s) appears the most times? A set with two modes is called bimodal. There can actually be any number of modes, including that everything is a mode.

Range: Highest number minus the lowest number.

Example 17: Find the mean, median, mode, and range for 5, 6, 9, 11, 12, 12, and 14.

Solutions: Mean: $\frac{5+6+9+11+12+12+14}{7} = \frac{69}{7} = 9\frac{6}{7}$

Median: 11

Mode: 12

Range: $14 - 5 = 9$

Example 18: Find the mean, median, mode, and range for 4, 4, 7, 10, 20, 20.

Solutions: Mean: $\frac{4+4+7+10+20+20}{6} = \frac{65}{6} = 10\frac{5}{6}$

Median: For an even number of points, it is the mean of the middle two:

$$\frac{7+10}{2} = 8.5$$

Mode: There are two: 4 and 20 (blackbirds?)

Range: $20 - 4 = 16$

Example 19: Jim received grades of 83 and 92 on two tests. What grade must the third test be in order to have an average (mean) of 90.

Solution: There are two methods.

Method 1: To get a 90 average on three tests Jim needs $3(90) = 270$ points. So far, he has $83 + 92 = 175$ points. So, Jim needs $270 - 175 = 95$ points on the third test.

Method 2 (my favorite): 83 is -7 from 90. 92 is $+ 2$ from 90, and $- 7 + 2 = -5$ from the desired 90 average. Jim needs $90 + 5 = 95$ points on the third test. (Jim needs to "make up" the 5-point deficit, so add it to the average of 90.)

EXERCISES

Finally, after a long introduction, we get to some exercises.

The GRE has four types of questions.

The first type is quantitative comparison with two Quantities, A and B. You must compare the value in each.

The second type is multiple-choice, for which there is one correct answer among the five answer choices that are labeled A, B, C, D, and E.

The third type is numeric entry, for which you are given a box in which you must supply a numerical value. In some cases, you will be given two boxes that represent the numerator and denominator of a fraction. The fraction need not be reduced, but you must insert an integer in each box.

The fourth type is multiple-answer multiple-choice, for which you must select all correct answers from a list of answer choices. In this type of question, there is at least one correct answer and as many as all correct answers.

For the first type, compare the two quantities in Quantity A and Quantity B and choose:

A. if the quantity in Quantity A is greater

B. if the quantity in Quantity B is greater

C. if the two quantities are equal

D. if the relationship cannot be determined from the information given

Let's do some comparison exercises.

	Quantity A	Quantity B
Exercise 1:	(1,234,567)(2,345,678)	(1,234,568)(2,345,677)
Exercise 2:	$\frac{94 \times 357 \times 10 \times 9 \times 8 \times 7}{7 \times 3 \times 2}$	$\frac{7 \times 4 \times 3 \times 2 \times 357 \times 94}{9 \times 8 \times 7}$
Exercise 3:	$x - 1$	$x + 1$
Exercise 4:	x	$\frac{1}{x}$
Exercise 5:	$(-1)^{1,000,000}$	$(-1)^{2,000,000}$
Exercise 6:	$(-2)^{2,222}$	$(-2)^{2,223}$
Exercise 7:	$(-3)^8$	-3^8
Exercise 8:	$(59.123456789)^2$	3,600
Exercise 9: $n > 0$, n even	even prime factors of n	prime factors of $2n$
Exercise 10: p, q primes	prime factors of pq	prime factors of $2pq$

Let's look at the answers.

Answer 1: The correct answer is (B). The number in Quantity A can be written as (1,234,567)(2,345,677 + 1) = (1,234,567)(2,345,677) + 1,234,567. The number in Quantity B can be written as (1,234,567 + 1)(2,345,677) = (1,234,567)(2,345,677) + 2,345,677. Since 2,345,677 > 1,234,567, the number in Quantity B is larger.

Answer 2: Now here's a problem for which we never want to do any arithmetic. We don't have to. On each side, cross off all the sevens, 357, and 94. We then get $\frac{10 \times 9 \times 8}{3 \times 2}$ and $\frac{4 \times 3 \times 2}{9 \times 8}$. The left number is greater than 1 and the other is less than 1. The answer is (A).

Answer 3: Cancel x on both sides. The answer is (B).

Answer 4: Let $x = 1, 3,$ and $\frac{1}{2}$. The answer is (D).

Answer 5: The correct answer is (C). The number -1 raised to any even power is 1.

Answer 6: The correct answer is (A). Any negative number raised to an even power is a positive number. Any negative number raised to an odd power is a negative number.

Answer 7: The correct answer is (A). Again, any negative number raised to an even power is a positive number, whereas choice B is the negative of a positive number raised to an even power.

Answer 8: The correct answer is (B). Since $59.123456789 < 60$, then $(59.123456789)^2$ must be $< (60)^2$, which is 3,600.

Answer 9: The correct answer is (C). If n is even, multiplying by 2 doesn't change the prime factors. They are the same.

Answer 10: This is not the same as Example 9. If p or $q = 2$, then A and B are the same. If p and q are both odd, multiplying by 2 increases Quantity B by 1 (because 2 is another prime factor). The answer is (D), you can't tell!

The second type of question on the GRE is the multiple-choice question.

Q **Let's do some multiple-choice questions.**

Exercise 11: If $x = -5$, the value of $-3 - 4x - x^2$ is

A. -48

B. -8

C. 2

D. 13

E. 4

Exercise 12: $-0(2) - \frac{0}{2} - 2 =$

A. 0

B. -2

C. -4

D. -6

E. Undefined

Exercise 13: The scores on three tests were 90, 91, and 98. What does the score on the fourth test have to be in order to get exactly a 95 average (mean)?

A. 97
B. 98
C. 99
D. 100
E. Not possible

Exercise 14: On a true-false test, 20 students scored 90, and 30 students scored 100. The sum of the mean, median, and mode is

A. 300
B. 296
C. 295
D. 294
E. 275

Exercise 15: If m and n are odd integers, which of the following is odd?

A. $mn + 3$
B. $m^2 + (n + 2)^2$
C. $mn + m + n$
D. $(m + 1)(n - 2)$
E. $m^4 + m^3 + m^2 + m$

Exercise 16: If $m + 3$ is a multiple of 4, which of these is also a multiple of 4?

A. $m - 3$
B. m
C. $m + 4$
D. $m + 9$
E. $m + 11$

Exercise 17: If p and q are primes, which one *can't* be a prime?

A. pq
B. $p + q$
C. $pq + 2$
D. $2pq + 1$
E. $p^2 + q^2$

Exercise 18: The sum of the first n positive integers is p. In terms of n and p, what is the sum of the next n positive integers?

A. np
B. $n + p$
C. $n^2 + p$
D. $n + p^2$
E. $2n + 2p$

Exercise 19: Let p be prime, with $20p$ divisible by 6; p could be

A. 3
B. 4
C. 5
D. 6
E. 7

Exercise 20: Given that r is a factor of s and that s is a factor of t, which of the following are multiples of r? Indicate *all* correct choices.

A. s^2
B. t^2
C. $t - s$
D. $s + t + st$
E. $s^2 + t^2$

Exercise 21: Given that a is an odd number and b is an even number, which of the following are odd numbers? Indicate *all* correct choices.

A. $ab + 7$
B. $a + b + ab$
C. $3a + b + b^2$
D. $6a + 7b + 8$
E. $a^2 + b^2 + (a + b)^2$
F. $(a + b + 1)^{10}$

Exercise 22: Thus far, Sue has test scores of 75, 84, and 96, and she will take one more test. Her final grade will be a B if her test average is between 80 and 89, inclusive. Which of the following grades on her last test will earn her a grade of B? Indicate *all* correct choices.

A. 60
B. 70
C. 80
D. 90
E. 95
F. 100

For Exercises 23 and 24, use the following list of numbers: 98, 99, 98, 97, 96, 95.

Exercise 23: To the nearest integer, what is the value of the mean?

Exercise 24: What is the value of the median?

Exercise 25: What is the sum of all positive factors of 28 that are less than 28?

Exercise 26: 50% of 0.5 is twice what number?

Let's look at the answers.

Answer 11: The correct answer is (B). $-3 - 4(-5) - (-5)^2 = -3 + 20 - 25 = -8$.

Answer 12: The correct answer is (B). $0 - 0 - 2 = -2$.

Answer 13: The correct answer is (E). $95(4) = 380$ points; $90 + 91 + 98 = 279$ points. The fourth test would have to be $380 - 279 = 101$.

Answer 14: The correct answer is (B). The median is 100; the mode is 100; for the mean we can use 2 and 3 instead of 20 and 30 since the ratio is the same:

$$\frac{2(90) + 3(100)}{5} = 96.$$

Answer 15: Only (C); it's the sum of three odd integers. All of the other answer choices are even.

Answer 16: The correct answer is (E). If $m + 3$ is a multiple of 4, then $m + 3 + 8$ is a multiple of 4 since 8 is a multiple of 4.

Answer 17: The correct answer is (A). By substituting proper primes, all the others might be prime.

Answer 18: The correct answer is (C). Say $n = 5$; $p = 1 + 2 + 3 + 4 + 5$. The next five are $(1 + 5) + (2 + 5) + (3 + 5) + (4 + 5) + (5 + 5) = p + n^2$.

Answer 19: The correct answer is (A). 3 and 6 will work, but only 3 is a prime.

Answer 20: The correct answers are (A), (B), (C), (D), and (E). Since r is a factor of s, we can write $s = ar$, where a is a constant. Similarly, s is a factor of t, so $t = bs$ for some constant b. For answer choice (A), $s^2 = (ar)^2 = (a^2r)(r)$, which means that s^2 is a multiple of r. For answer choice (B), $t^2 = (bs)^2 = b^2a^2r^2 = (b^2a^2r)(r)$, which means that t^2 is a multiple of r. For answer choice (C), $t - s = (bs - ar = bar - ar = (ba - a)(r)$, which means that $t - s$ is a multiple of r. For answer choice (D), $s + t + st = ar + bs + (ar)(bs) = ar + bar + arbs = (r)(a + ba + abs)$, which means that $s + t + st$ is a multiple of r. Finally, $s^2 + t^2 = a^2r^2 + b^2s^2 = a^2r^2 + b^2a^2r^2 = (r)(a^2r + b^2a^2r)$, which means that $s^2 + t^2$ is a multiple of r.

You could also use numerical substitution to verify that each answer option is correct. For example, let $r = 4$, $s = 12$, and $t = 48$.

Answer 21: The correct answers are (A), (B), and (C). For answer choice (A), (odd)(even) + 7 = even + 7 = odd. For answer choice (B), odd + even + (odd)(even) = odd + even + even = odd. For answer choice (C), (3)(odd) + even + (even)(even) = odd + even + even = odd. In a similar manner, it can be shown that each of answer choices (D), (E), and (F) represents an even number. Another way to check these results is to use a numerical substitution, such as $a = 5$ and $b = 8$.

Answer 22: The correct answers are (B), (C), (D), (E), and (F). Her total number of points must be between (80)(4) = 320 and (89)(4) = 356, inclusive. Thus far, her point total is 75 + 84 + 96 = 255. This means that she needs between 320 − 255 = 65 and 356 − 255 = 101, inclusive, on her final test.

Answer 23: The correct answer is 97. The mean equals

$$\frac{98 + 99 + 98 + 97 + 96 + 95}{6} = \frac{583}{6} = 97.1\overline{6},$$

which is 97 when rounded to the nearest integer.

Answer 24: The correct answer is 97.5. Arranged in ascending order, the numbers appear as 95, 96, 97, 98, 98, 99. The median is the mean of the third and fourth numbers, which is $\frac{97 + 98}{2} = 97.5$. (Do *not* round off this answer to 98!)

Answer 25: The correct answer is 28. The positive factors of 28, not including the number 28, are 1, 2, 4, 7, and 14, whose sum is 28. (A number whose proper factors add up to the number itself is called a perfect number. Six is another example of a perfect number, since its proper factors are 1, 2, and 3.)

Answer 26: The correct answer is 0.125. Fifty percent of 0.5 = (0.50)(0.5) = 0.25. Let x represent the missing number. Then 0.25 = $2x$, which means that $x = \frac{0.25}{2} = 0.125$.

Let's do some exercises on numeric entry.

Example 27: Linda eats one-half of her roast beef sandwich at 11:00 AM. At 12:00 noon, she eats one-third of the remainder of her sandwich. What fraction of her sandwich has not been eaten?

Example 28: Marlene has a jug of 20 gallons of a water solution that contains 40% salt. How many gallons of pure water should she add so that the solution contains only 25% salt?

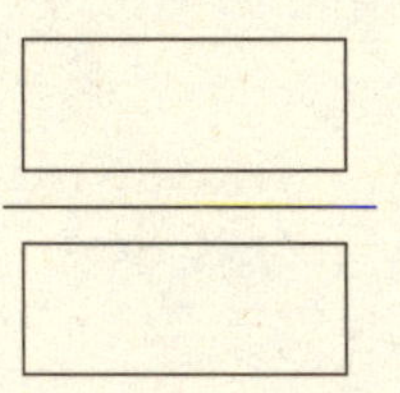

Example 29: Bob travels at a constant rate for 40 minutes from his home to a business meeting. On the return trip, he travels the same route for 30 minutes. If his average speed on the return trip is 15 miles per hour faster than his trip going to the meeting, how many miles apart are his home and the location of the meeting?

Let's look at the answers and explanations

Answer 27: The correct answer is $\frac{1}{3}$. After 11:00 AM, $1-\frac{1}{2}=\frac{1}{2}$ of her sandwich remains not eaten. At 12:00 noon she eats $\frac{1}{3}\times\frac{1}{2}=\frac{1}{6}$ of her sandwich. So far, Linda has eaten $\frac{1}{2}+\frac{1}{6}=\frac{4}{6}=\frac{2}{3}$ of her sandwich. Thus, $1-\frac{2}{3}=\frac{1}{3}$ of her sandwich still remains not eaten.

Answer 28: The correct answer is 12. Let x represent the number of gallons of pure water to be added. The amount of salt in the original jug is $(20)(0.40) = 8$ gallons. When Marlene adds x gallons of pure water, the amount of salt in the final jug is still 8 gallons. This final jug will contain $20 + x$ gallons of water and salt for which the salt content represents 25%. Then $8 = (0.25)(20 + x)$. This equation becomes $8 = 5 + 0.25x$. Then $3 = 0.25x$, which leads to $x = 12$.

Answer 29: The correct answer is 30 miles. Let x represent Bob's speed in miles per hour for the trip going to the meeting and let $x + 15$ represent his speed in miles per hour on the return trip. We'll change 40 minutes to $\frac{2}{3}$ hour and change 30 minutes to $\frac{1}{2}$ hour. Since the distances are equal, $\frac{2}{3}x = \frac{1}{2}(x+15)$. Then $\frac{2}{3}x = \frac{1}{2}x + \frac{15}{2}$. Multiply this equation by 6 to get $4x = 3x + 45$, which means that $x = 45$. This means that his speed going to the meeting was 45 miles per hour, so the distance he traveled was $(45)(\frac{2}{3}) = 30$ miles. (Note that we could have also used his speed of $45 + 15 = 60$ miles per hour on the return trip. The distance would be $(60)(\frac{1}{2}) = 30$ miles.)

Let's do some exercises on multiple-answer multiple-choice.

Example 30: Shawn's favorite number is a prime that is a factor of 42. Which of the following could represent his favorite number?

Indicate all correct answers.

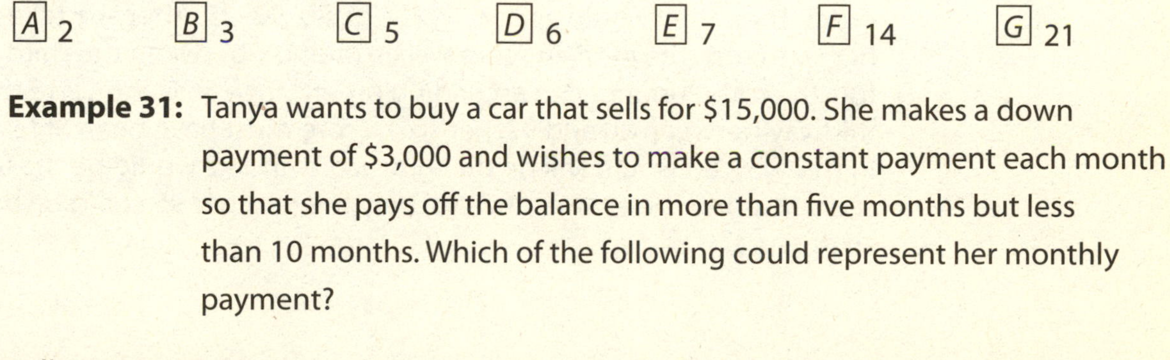

A 2 B 3 C 5 D 6 E 7 F 14 G 21

Example 31: Tanya wants to buy a car that sells for $15,000. She makes a down payment of $3,000 and wishes to make a constant payment each month so that she pays off the balance in more than five months but less than 10 months. Which of the following could represent her monthly payment?

Indicate all correct answers.

A $1,000 B $1,100 C $1,200 D $1,500 E $2,000 F $2,400

Example 32: Melissa has test scores of 80, 75, 92, 63, and 95. After she took her sixth test, her median test score was 86. Which of the following could have been her sixth test score?

Indicate all correct answers.

[A] 80 [B] 84 [C] 85 [D] 88 [E] 90 [F] 95

A Let's look at the answers and explanations.

Answer 30: The correct answers are A, B, and E. Each of 2, 3, and 7 is both a prime number and divides evenly into 42. The number 5 is wrong because it does not divide evenly into 42. Each of the numbers 14 and 21 is wrong because they are not primes.

Answer 31: The correct answers are D and E. After Tanya makes her down payment of $3,000, her balance is $12,000. If she were to pay off this amount in five months, her monthly payment would be $\frac{\$12{,}000}{10} = \$2{,}400$. If she were to pay off the balance in ten months, her monthly payment would be $\frac{\$12{,}000}{10} = \$1{,}200$. Therefore, we require an amount that is between $1,200 and $2,400. Note that if she makes a payment of $1,500 each month, the $12,000 would be paid off in eight months; if she elects to make a payment of $2,000 each month, the balance would be paid off in six months.

Answer 32: The only correct answer is F. First, arrange the test scores in ascending order. Then they would appear as 63, 75, 80, 92, 95. After she takes her sixth test, the median score will lie midway between the third and fourth scores, arranged in ascending order. Since 86 is the score that lies midway between 80 and 92, her sixth score must have been at least 92. In this way, 80 would still be the third score and 92 would be the fourth score. Among the answer choices, only the number 95 could be her sixth score.

CHAPTER 2: *Decimals, Fractions, and Percentages*

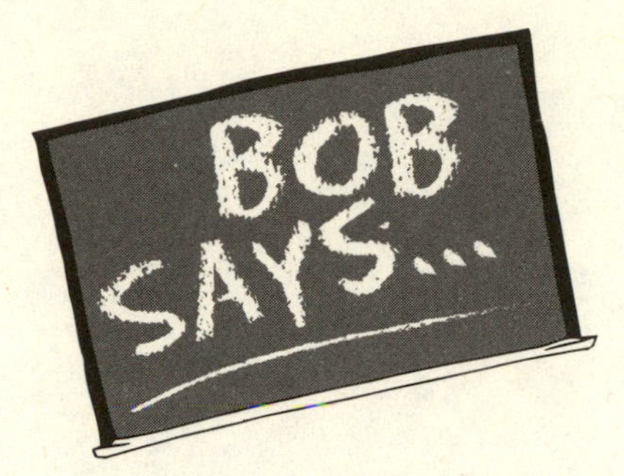

"One must master the parts as well as the whole to fully understand."

Let's start with decimals.

DECIMALS

Rule 1: When adding or subtracting, line up the decimal points.

Example 1: Add: 3.1416 + 234.72 + 86

Solution:

$$\begin{array}{r} 3.1416 \\ 234.72 \\ +\ 86. \\ \hline 323.8616 \end{array}$$

Example 2: Subtract: 56.7 − 8.82

Solution:

$$\begin{array}{r} 56.70 \\ -\ 8.82 \\ \hline 47.88 \end{array}$$

Rule 2: In multiplying numbers, count the number of decimal places and add them. In the product, this will be the number of decimal places for the decimal.

Example 3: Multiply: $45.67 \times .987$

Solution:

$$\begin{array}{rl} 45.67 & \text{(2 places)} \\ \times \quad .987 & \text{(3 places)} \\ \hline 45.07629 & \text{(5 places)} \end{array}$$

If you're curious, the reason it's five places is that if you multiply hundredths by thousandths, you get hundred-thousandths, which is five places. Fortunately, the GRE does not ask you to do pure long multiplications like this.

Rule 3: When you divide, move the decimal point in the divisor and the dividend the same number of places.

$$\text{Divisor}\overset{\displaystyle\text{Quotient}}{\overline{\smash{\big)}\text{Dividend}}}$$

Example 4: Show why $.004\overline{\smash{\big)}23.1} = 4\overset{\displaystyle 5{,}775.}{\overline{\smash{\big)}23{,}100.}}$

Solution: Why is this true? If we write the division as a fraction, it would be $\frac{23.1}{.004}$. Multiplying the numerator and denominator by 1,000, we get $\frac{23.1}{.004} = \frac{23.1 \times 1{,}000}{.004 \times 1{,}000} = \frac{23{,}100}{4}$. When you multiply by 1, the fraction doesn't change. Since $\frac{1{,}000}{1{,}000} = 1$, the fraction is the same.

Rule 4: When reading a number with a decimal, read the whole part, only say the word "and" when you reach the decimal point, then read the part after the decimal point as if it were a whole number, and say the last decimal place. Whew!

Example 5:

Number	Read
4.3	Four and three tenths
2,006.73	Two-thousand six and seventy-three hundredths
1,000,017.009	One million seventeen and nine thousandths

Let's do some exercises.

Exercise 1: Select the smallest:

A. .04
B. .0401
C. .04001
D. .04444
E. .041

	Quantity A	Quantity B
Exercise 2:	$(0.000004)^2$	$\sqrt{0.000004}$
Exercise 3:	$(4.1111)^3$	$\sqrt[3]{4.1111}$

Let's look at the answers.

Answer 1: The correct answer is (A). All choices have the same tenths (0) and hundredths (4) digits. The rest of the places of (A) are zero.

Answer 2: The correct answer is (B). The square of a decimal number between 0 and 1 results in a smaller number, whereas the square root of this type of number results in a larger number. Thus, $(0.000004)^2 < 0.000004$ and $\sqrt{0.000004} > 0.000004$.

Answer 3: The correct answer is (A). Cubing a number greater than 1 results in a larger number, whereas the cube root of this type of number results in a smaller number. Thus, $(4.1111)^3 > 4.1111$ and $\sqrt[3]{4.1111} < 4.1111$.

Now, let's go over fractions.

FRACTIONS

The top of a fraction is called the **numerator**; the bottom is the **denominator**.

Rule 1: If the bottoms of a fraction are the same, the bigger the top, the bigger the fraction.

Example 6: Suppose I am a smart first grader. Can you explain to me which is bigger, $\frac{3}{5}$ or $\frac{4}{5}$?

Solution: Suppose we have a pizza pie. Then $\frac{3}{5}$ means we divide a pie into 5 equal parts, and I get 3. And $\frac{4}{5}$ means I get 4 pieces out of 5. So $\frac{3}{5} < \frac{4}{5}$.

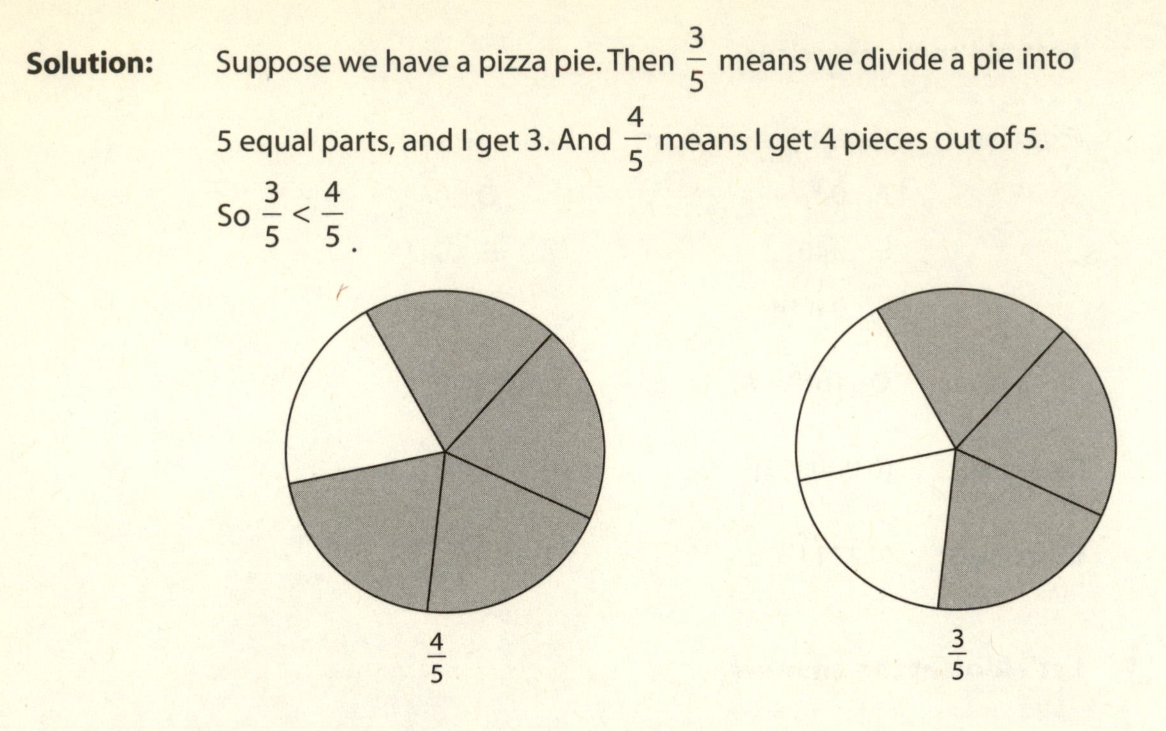

Rule 2: If the tops of two fractions are the same, the bigger the bottom, the smaller the fraction.

Example 7: Which fraction, $\frac{3}{5}$ or $\frac{3}{4}$, is bigger?

Solution: Use another pizza pie example. In comparing $\frac{3}{5}$ and $\frac{3}{4}$, we get the same number of pieces (3). However, if the pie is divided into 4, the pieces are bigger, so $\frac{3}{5} < \frac{3}{4}$.

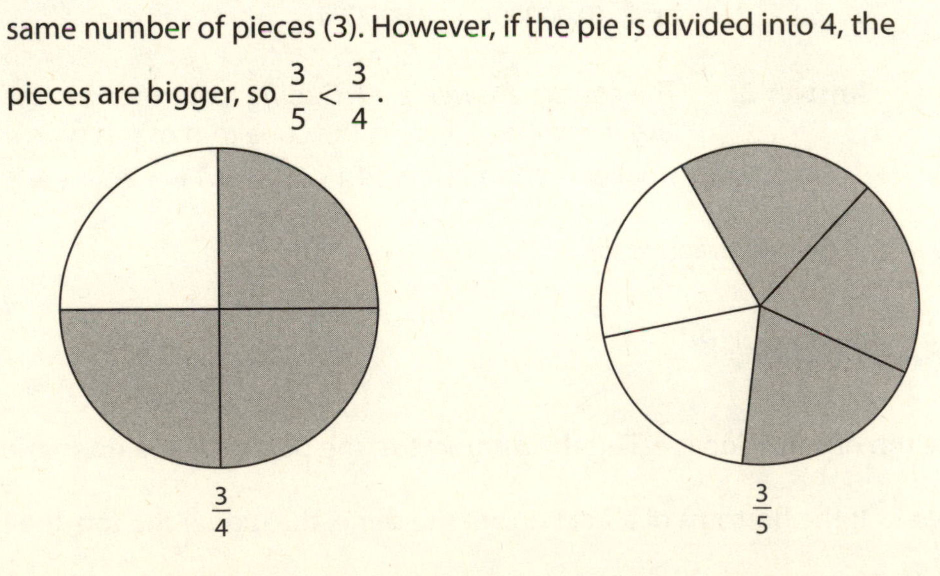

Rule 3: If the tops and bottoms are different, find the Least Common Denominator (LCD) and compare the tops.

Before we get into this section, the teacher in me (and maybe purist in you) must tell you we really are talking about rational numbers, not fractions. There are two definitions:

Definition 1: A **rational** number is any integer divided by an integer, with the denominator not equaling zero.

Definition 2: A **rational** number is any repeating or terminating decimal.

Note *Technically, $\frac{\pi}{6}$ is a fraction but not a rational number. We will use the term "fraction" here instead of rational number. If it is negative, we will say "negative fraction." Note the following facts about fractions:*

$3 < 4$, but $-3 > -4$. Similarly, $\frac{3}{5} < \frac{4}{5}$, but $-\frac{3}{5} > -\frac{4}{5}$. We will do more of this later.

- A fraction is >1 if the numerator is bigger than the denominator.
- A fraction is <1 if the numerator is less than the denominator.
- A fraction is $<\frac{1}{2}$ if the bottom is more than twice the top.
- To double a fraction, either double the top or halve the bottom.
- Adding the same number top and bottom to a fraction makes it closer to 1.

Q Let's do some more exercises.

	Quantity A	**Quantity B**
Exercise 4:	$\frac{1}{6}$	$\left(\frac{1}{0.0006}\right)^2$
Exercise 5:	$\frac{1/7{,}777}{1/6{,}666}$	$\frac{1/6{,}666}{1/7{,}777}$
Exercise 6:	$\left(-\frac{1}{2}\right)^{236}$	$\left(-\frac{3}{2}\right)^{239}$
Exercise 7: $m, n > 2$	$\frac{m}{n}$	$\frac{m+1}{n+1}$

Let's look at the answers:

Answer 4: The correct answer is (B). 0.0006 is less than 1, so the fraction in parentheses is much larger than 1. Squaring this value increases the number. The number $\frac{1}{6}$ is less than 1.

Answer 5: The correct answer is (B). $\frac{1/7{,}777}{1/6{,}666} = \frac{1}{7{,}777} \times \frac{6{,}666}{1} = \frac{6{,}666}{7{,}777}$, which is less than 1. But, $\frac{1/6{,}666}{1/7{,}777} = \frac{1}{6{,}666} \times \frac{7{,}777}{1} = \frac{7{,}777}{6{,}666}$, which is greater than 1.

Answer 6: The correct answer is (A). The value of choice (A) is positive, whereas the value of choice (B) is negative. Whenever a negative number is raised to an even integer, the result is a positive number. If a negative number is raised to an odd integer, the result is a negative number.

Answer 7: The answer is (D), you can't tell. Substitute some numbers for m and n to see that this is so:

If $m < n$, $\frac{3}{4} < \frac{3+1}{4+1} = \frac{4}{5}$

If $m = n$, $\frac{6}{6} = \frac{6+1}{6+1} = \frac{7}{7}$

If $m > n$, $\frac{5}{4} > \frac{5+1}{4+1} = \frac{6}{5}$.

Adding and Subtracting Fractions

If the denominators are the same, add or subtract the tops, keep the bottom the same, and reduce if necessary.

$$\frac{7}{43} + \frac{11}{43} - \frac{2}{43} = \frac{16}{43}$$

$$\frac{2}{9} + \frac{4}{9} = \frac{6}{9} = \frac{2}{3}$$

$$\frac{a}{m} + \frac{b}{m} - \frac{c}{m} = \frac{a+b-c}{m}$$

There is much more to talk about if the denominators are unlike.

The quickest way to add (or subtract) fractions with different denominators, especially if they contain letters or the denominators are small, is to multiply each fraction by the LCD. The LCD is really just the least common multiple, LCM. This consists of three words: *multiple*, *common*, and *least*.

Example 8: What is the LCM of 6 and 8?

Solution: **Multiples** of 6 are 6, 12, 18, 24, 30, 36,42, 48, 54, 60, 66, 72, 78,. . .
Multiples of 8 are 8, 16, 24, 32, 40, 48, 56, 64, 72, 80,. . .
Common multiples of 6 and 8 are 24, 48, 72, 96, 120,. . .
The **least common multiple** of 6 and 8 is 24.

When adding or subtracting fractions, multiply the top and bottom of each fraction by the LCM divided by the denominator:

$$\frac{a}{b}-\frac{x}{y}=\left(\frac{a}{b}\times\frac{y}{y}\right)-\left(\frac{x}{y}\times\frac{b}{b}\right)=\frac{ay}{by}-\frac{bx}{by}=\frac{ay-bx}{by}$$

$$\frac{7}{20}-\frac{3}{11}=\left(\frac{7}{20}\times\frac{11}{11}\right)-\left(\frac{3}{11}\times\frac{20}{20}\right)=\frac{7(11)-3(20)}{20(11)}=\frac{17}{220}$$

Example 9: Add $\frac{5}{6}+\frac{3}{8}+\frac{2}{9}$.

Solution: To find the LCD, take multiples of the largest denominator, 9, and see which one is also a multiple of the others (6 and 8): 9, 18, 27, 36, 45, 54, 63, 72. The LCD is 72, so we have:

$$\frac{5}{6}=\frac{5}{6}\times\frac{12}{12}=\frac{60}{72}$$

$$\frac{3}{8}=\frac{3}{8}\times\frac{9}{9}=\frac{27}{72}$$

$$\frac{2}{9}=\frac{2}{9}\times\frac{8}{8}=\frac{16}{72}$$

Adding these, we get $\frac{103}{72}$, or $1\frac{31}{72}$. You may have to add fractions like this on the GRE.

You will not have to add fractions like the next example, ones with a large LCD. However, this is the technique to use when adding algebraic fractions. That is why the next example is here.

Example 10: Add $\frac{3}{100}+\frac{5}{48}+\frac{4}{135}$.

Solution: What is the LCD? We can find it by breaking the denominators into primes.

$100 = 2 \times 2 \times 5 \times 5$

$48 = 2 \times 2 \times 2 \times 2 \times 3$

$135 = 3 \times 3 \times 3 \times 5$

The LCD is the product of the most number of times a prime occurs in any one denominator. The LCD is thus $2 \times 2 \times 2 \times 2 \times 3 \times 3 \times 3 \times 5 \times 5$.

Then multiply the top numbers (numerators) by "what's missing":

$$\frac{3}{100}=\frac{3}{2\times2\times5\times5}=\frac{3(2\times2\times3\times3\times3)}{2\times2\times2\times2\times3\times3\times3\times5\times5}=\frac{324}{10,800}$$

$$\frac{5}{48}=\frac{5}{2\times2\times2\times2\times3}=\frac{5(3\times3\times5\times5)}{2\times2\times2\times2\times3\times3\times3\times5\times5}=\frac{1125}{10,800}$$

$$\frac{4}{135}=\frac{4}{3\times3\times3\times5}=\frac{4(2\times2\times2\times2\times5)}{2\times2\times2\times2\times3\times3\times3\times5\times5}=\frac{320}{10,800}$$

Adding the numerators, we get 1,769, so the total is $\frac{1,769}{10,800}$. We now must reduce this, if possible. It's not that bad because the only prime factors of 10,800 are 2, 3, and 5. Clearly, 2 and 5 are not factors of 1,769, but $1 + 7 + 6 + 9 = 23$, so 1,769 is not divisible by 3. So $\frac{1,769}{10,800}$, is the final answer.

Incidentally, a trick in multiplying these kinds of numbers is to try and multiply by ten. Rearranging the denominator, we get $5 \times 2 \times 5 \times 2 \times 3 \times 3 \times 3 \times 2 \times 2$. In your head, you say as you multiply, 10, 100, 300, 900, 2,700, 5,400, 10,800.

Multiplication of Fractions

To multiply fractions, multiply the numerators and multiply the denominators, reducing as you go. With multiplication, it is *not* necessary to have the same denominators.

$$\frac{3}{7} \times \frac{4}{11} = \frac{12}{77}$$

$$\frac{a}{b} \times \frac{c}{d} = \frac{a \times c}{b \times d}$$

$$\frac{50}{15} \times \frac{27}{8} = \frac{\overset{25}{\cancel{50}}}{15} \times \frac{27}{\underset{4}{\cancel{8}}} = \frac{25}{\underset{5}{\cancel{15}}} \times \frac{\overset{9}{\cancel{27}}}{4} = \frac{\overset{5}{\cancel{25}}}{\underset{1}{\cancel{5}}} \times \frac{9}{4} = \frac{5}{1} \times \frac{9}{4} = \frac{45}{4}\text{, or } 11\frac{1}{4}$$

To **invert** a fraction means to turn it upside down. The new fraction is called the **reciprocal** of the original fraction.

The reciprocal of $\frac{2}{3}$ is $\frac{3}{2}$. The reciprocal of -5 is $-\frac{1}{5}$. The reciprocal of a is $\frac{1}{a}$ if $a \neq 0$.

Division of Fractions

To divide fractions, invert the second fraction and multiply, reducing if necessary. For example,

$$\frac{3}{4} \div \frac{11}{5} = \frac{3}{4} \times \frac{5}{11} = \frac{15}{44}$$

$$\frac{m}{n} \div \frac{p}{q} = \frac{m}{n} \times \frac{q}{p} = \frac{m \times q}{n \times p}$$

$$\frac{1}{4} \div 5 = \frac{1}{4} \times \frac{1}{5} = \frac{1}{20}$$

Example 11: Problem / Solution

	Problem	Solution
a.	$\frac{7}{9} - \frac{3}{22} =$	$\frac{127}{198}$
b.	$\frac{3}{4} + \frac{5}{6} - \frac{1}{8} =$	$\frac{35}{24}$, or $1\frac{11}{24}$

c. $\frac{3}{10}+\frac{2}{15}-\frac{4}{5}=$ $\frac{-11}{30}$

d. $\frac{1}{4}+\frac{1}{8}+\frac{7}{16}=$ $\frac{13}{16}$

e. $2+\frac{2}{3}+\frac{2}{9}+\frac{2}{27}=$ $2\frac{26}{27}$, or $\frac{80}{27}$

f. $\frac{5}{24}-\frac{7}{18}=$ $-\frac{13}{72}$

g. $\frac{10}{99}-\frac{9}{100}$ $\frac{109}{9{,}900}$

h. $\frac{5}{36}+\frac{5}{27}+\frac{7}{24}=$ $\frac{133}{216}$

i. $\frac{2}{45}+\frac{1}{375}+\frac{8}{27}=$ $\frac{1{,}159}{3{,}375}$

j. $\frac{3}{10{,}000}+\frac{1}{180}+\frac{5}{12}=$ $\frac{38{,}027}{90{,}000}$

k. $\frac{7}{9}\times\frac{5}{3}=$ $\frac{35}{27}$, or $1\frac{8}{27}$

l. $\frac{11}{12}\div\frac{9}{11}=$ $\frac{121}{108}$, or $1\frac{13}{108}$

m. $\frac{5}{9}\times\frac{6}{7}=$ $\frac{10}{21}$

n. $\frac{12}{13}\div\frac{8}{39}=$ $\frac{9}{2}$, or $4\frac{1}{2}$

o. $\frac{4}{9}\times\frac{63}{122}=$ $\frac{14}{61}$

p. $\frac{10}{12}\div\frac{15}{40}=$ $\frac{20}{9}$, or $2\frac{2}{9}$

q. $\frac{100}{350}\times\frac{49}{8}=$ $\frac{7}{4}$, or $1\frac{3}{4}$

r. $\frac{2}{3} \div 12 =$ $\frac{1}{18}$

s. $\frac{2}{3} \times \frac{3}{4} \times \frac{4}{5} \times \frac{5}{6} \times \frac{6}{7} =$ $\frac{2}{7}$

t. $\frac{5}{8} \times \frac{7}{6} \div \frac{35}{24} =$ $\frac{1}{2}$

Notice all the cancellations in the problems above.

Changing from Decimals to Fractions and Back

To change from a decimal to a fraction, you read it and write it.

Example 12: Change 4.37 to a fraction.

Solution: You read it as 4 and 37 hundredths: $4\frac{37}{100} = \frac{437}{100}$, if necessary. That's it.

Example 13: Change to decimals:

a. $\frac{7}{4}$ b. $\frac{1}{6}$

Solution: For the fractions on the GRE, the decimal will either terminate or repeat.

a. Divide 4 into 7.0000: $7.0000 \div 4 = 1.75$

b. Divide 6 into 1.0000: $1.0000 \div 6 = .1666\ldots = .1\overline{6}$

The bar over the six means it repeats forever; for example, $.3454545\ldots = .3\overline{45}$. This means 45 repeats forever, but not the 3.

PERCENTAGES

% means hundredths: $1\% = \frac{1}{100} = .01$.

Follow these rules to change between percentages and decimals and fractions:

Rule 1: To change a percentage to a decimal, move the decimal point two places to the left and drop the % sign.

Rule 2: To change a decimal to a percentage, move the decimal point two places to the right and add a % sign.

Rule 3: To change from a percentage to a fraction, divide by 100% and simplify, or change the % sign to $\frac{1}{100}$ and multiply.

Rule 4: To change a fraction to a percentage, first change to a decimal, and then to a percentage.

Example 14: Change 12%, 4%, and 0.7% to decimals.

Solution: 12% = 12.% = .12; 4% = 4.% = .04; 0.7% = 0.007.

Example 15: Change 0.734, 0.2, and 34 to percentages.

Solutions: 0.734 = 73.4%; 0.2= 20%; 34 = 34. = 3,400%.

Example 16: Change 42% to a fraction.

Solution: $42\% = \frac{42\%}{100\%} = \frac{21}{50}$, or $42\% = 42 \times \frac{1}{100} = \frac{42}{100} = \frac{21}{50}$

Example 17: Change $\frac{7}{4}$ to a percentage.

Solution: $\frac{7}{4} = 1.75 = 175\%$

Two hundred years ago, when I was in elementary school, we had to learn the following decimal, fraction, percent equivalents. It may be in your best interest to memorize the following. At worst, it will help you when you go shopping to see if you get the correct discounts.

Fraction	**Decimal**	**Percentage**	**Fraction**	**Decimal**	**Percentage**
$\frac{1}{10}$	0.1	10%	$\frac{3}{10}$	0.3	30%
$\frac{1}{8}$	0.125	$12\frac{1}{2}\%$	$\frac{1}{3}$	0.3333...	$33\frac{1}{3}\%$
$\frac{1}{6}$	0.1666...	$16\frac{2}{3}\%$	$\frac{3}{8}$	0.375	$37\frac{1}{2}\%$
$\frac{1}{5}$	0.2	20%	$\frac{2}{5}$	0.4	40%
$\frac{1}{4}$	0.25	25%	$\frac{1}{2}$	0.5	50%

Fraction	Decimal	Percentage	Fraction	Decimal	Percentage
$\frac{3}{5}$	0.6	60%	$\frac{5}{6}$	0.8333...	$83\frac{1}{3}\%$
$\frac{5}{8}$	0.625	$62\frac{1}{2}\%$	$\frac{7}{8}$	0.875	$87\frac{1}{2}\%$
$\frac{2}{3}$	0.6666...	$66\frac{2}{3}\%$	$\frac{9}{10}$	0.9	90%
$\frac{7}{10}$	0.7	70%	1	1.0	100%
$\frac{3}{4}$	0.75	75%	$1\frac{1}{2}$	1.5	150%
$\frac{4}{5}$	0.8	80%	2	2.0	200%

If you are good at doing percentage problems, skip this next section. Otherwise, here's a really easy way do percentage problems. Make the following pyramid:

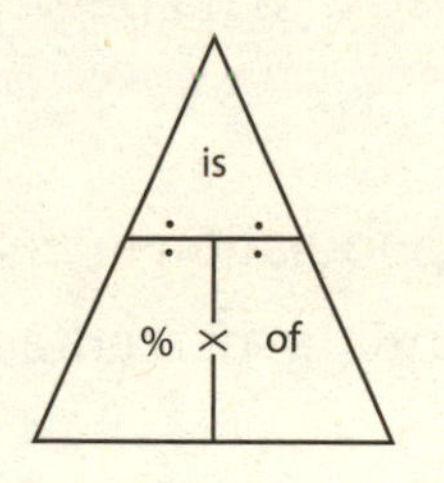

Example 18: What is 12% of 1.3?

Solution:

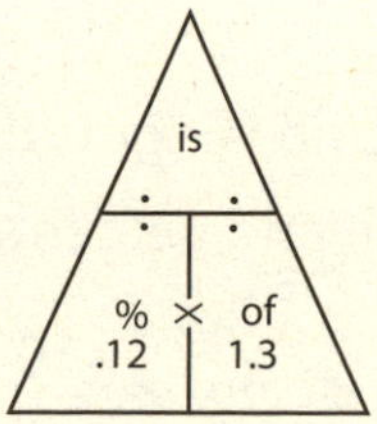

Put .12 in the % box (always change to a decimal in this box) and 1.3 in the "of" box. It tells you to multiply $.12 \times 1.3 = .156$. That's all there is to it.

Example 19: 8% of what is 32?

Solution:

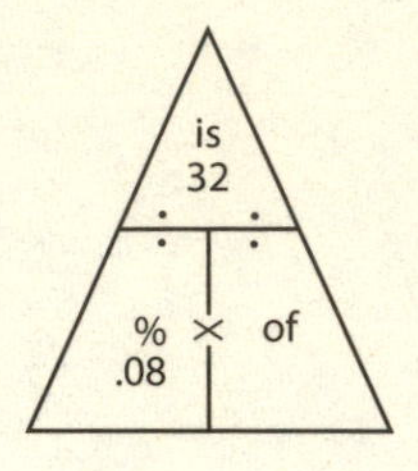

.08 goes in the % box. 32 goes in the "is" box. $32 \div .08 = 400$.

Example 20: 9 is what % of 8?

Solution:

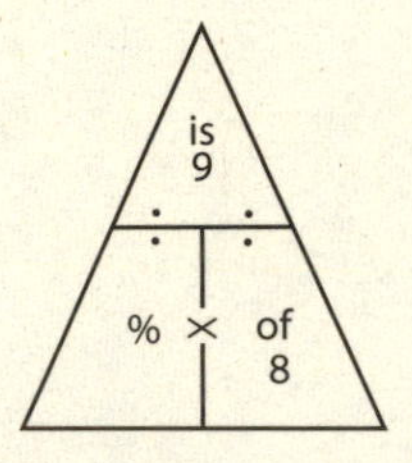

9 goes in the "is" box. 8 goes in the "of" box. $9 \div 8 \times 100\% = 112.5\%$. The goal is to be able to do percentage problems without using the pyramid.

Example 21: In ten years, the population increases from 20,000 to 23,000. Find the actual increase and the percentage increase.

Solution: The actual increase is $23{,}000 - 20{,}000 = 3{,}000$.

The percentage increase is $\frac{3{,}000}{20{,}000} \times 100\% = 15\%$ increase.

Example 22: The cost of producing widgets decreased from 60 cents to 50 cents. Find the actual decrease and percentage decrease.

Solution: $60 - 50 = 10$ cent decrease; $\frac{10}{60} = 16\frac{2}{3}\%$ decrease.

Note *Percentage increases and decreases are figured on the original amount.*

Example 23: The cost of a $2,000 large-screen TV set is decreased by 30%. If there is 7% sales tax, how much do you pay?

Solution: $2,000 $\times$ .30 = $600 discount. $2,000 − $600 = $1,400 cost.

$1,400 $\times$ .07 is $98. The total price is $1,400 + $98 = $1,498.

Note *If you took 70% of $2,000 (100% – 30%), you would immediately get the cost.*

There is an interesting story about why women wear miniskirts in London, England. It seems that the sales tax is 12½% on clothes! But children's clothes are tax exempt. A girl's dress is any dress where the skirt is less than 24 inches, so that is why women in London wear miniskirts!

Let's do some exercises.

Exercise 8: The product of 2 and $\frac{1}{89}$ is

A. $2\frac{1}{89}$

B. $1\frac{88}{89}$

C. 172

D. $\frac{2}{89}$

E. $\frac{1}{172}$

Exercise 9: $\frac{1}{50}$ of 2% of .02 is

A. .08

B. .008

C. .0008

D. .000008

E. .00000008

Exercise 10: 30% of 20% of a number is the same as 40% of what percentage of the same number?

A. 10

B. $12\frac{1}{2}$

C. 15

D. 18

E. Can't be determined without the number

Exercise 11: A fraction between $\frac{3}{43}$ and $\frac{4}{43}$ is

A. $\frac{1}{9}$

B. $\frac{3}{28}$

C. $\frac{5}{47}$

D. $\frac{7}{86}$

E. $\frac{9}{1,849}$

Exercise 12: The reciprocal of $2-\frac{3}{4}$ is

A. $\frac{1}{2}-\frac{4}{3}$

B. $-\frac{5}{4}$

C. $-\frac{4}{5}$

D. $\frac{5}{4}$

E. $\frac{4}{5}$

Exercise 13: A price increase of 20% followed by a decrease of 20% means the price is

A. Up 4%

B. Up 2%

C. The original price

D. Down 2%

E. Down 4%

Exercise 14: A price decreases 20% followed by a 20% increase. The final price is

A. Up 4%

B. Up 2 %

C. The original price

D. Down 2%

E. Down 4%

		Quantity A	Quantity B
Exercise 15:		The mean of $\frac{1}{4}$ and $\frac{1}{8}$	$\frac{1}{6}$
Exercise 16:		Holiday discount of 50% followed by another 20% discount	65% discount
Exercise 17:		$\frac{2}{3}$ of $37\frac{1}{2}\%$	$33\frac{1}{3}\%$ of $\frac{3}{4}$
Exercise 18:		A 10% discount followed by a 10% charge to send item	Original price
Exercise 19:	$8 \le x \le 10$, $4 \le y \le 6$	Largest value of $\frac{x}{y}$	2.5

Exercise 20: Which of the following fractions reduce to $\frac{3}{4}$? Indicate *all* correct choices.

A. $\frac{33}{44}$

B. $\frac{10}{15}$

C. $\frac{15}{20}$

D. $\frac{3,000,000}{4,000,000}$

E. $\frac{21}{28}$

F. $\frac{19}{30}$

Exercise 21: Which of the following are equivalent to $\frac{1}{25}$? Indicate *all* correct choices.

A. 0.25

B. 0.04

C. 40%

D. 4%

E. $\frac{63}{189}$

F. $\frac{0.5}{12.5}$

Exercise 22: An item that is priced at \$249 is initially discounted by 40%, then the new price is discounted by 15%. What is the final price of the item?

Exercise 23: A \$200 television is sold in a state with a 6% sales tax. The store plans to have a sale so that the final price of the television, with tax included, will be \$200. To the nearest cent, what will be the sale price of the television before the tax is applied?

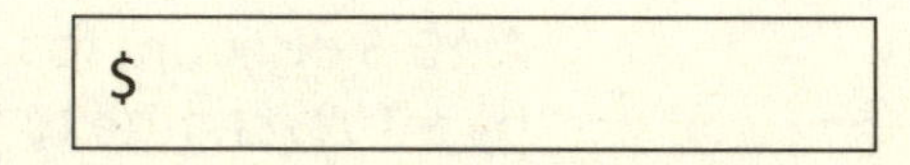

Exercise 24: Refer to Exercise 23. To the nearest hundredth of one percent, what is the percent discount?

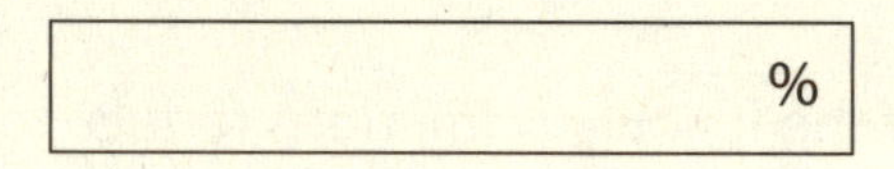

Let's look at the answers.

Answer 8: The correct answer is (D). $\frac{2}{1} \times \frac{1}{89} = \frac{2}{89}$.

Answer 9: The correct answer is (D). $.02 \times .02 \times .02 = .000008$.

Answer 10: The correct answer is (C). You can forget the number and forget the percentages. $(30)(20) = (40)(?)$. $? = 15$.

Answer 11: The correct answer is (D). $\frac{3}{43} = \frac{6}{86}$; $\frac{4}{43} = \frac{8}{86}$; between is $\frac{7}{86}$.

As another example like this one, to get nine fractions between $\frac{3}{43}$ and $\frac{4}{43}$, multiply both fractions, top and bottom, by 10, and the fractions in between would be $\frac{31}{430}$, $\frac{32}{430}$, $\frac{33}{430}$, etc.

Answer 12: The correct answer is (E). $2-\frac{3}{4}=\frac{5}{4}$. Its reciprocal is $\frac{4}{5}$.

Answers 13 and 14: The correct answer is (E) for both. Suppose you have \$100. Increased by 20%, you have \$120. But another 20% less (now on a larger amount) is \$24 less. We are at \$96, down 4%. Suppose we take 20% off first. We are at \$80. 20% up (now on a smaller amount) is \$16. We are again at \$96 or again down 4%.

Answer 15: The correct answer is (A). $\frac{1}{2}\left(\frac{2}{8}+\frac{1}{8}\right)=\frac{3}{16}>\frac{1}{6}$.

Answer 16: The correct answer is (B). Suppose you spend \$100. A 50% discount puts you at \$50. A further discount of 20% (\$10) means you pay \$40, or a 60% discount. That is why the January sales advertise 50% followed by 20%. It sounds like 70%, but it really is 60%.

Answer 17: The correct answer is (C). $\frac{2}{3}\times\frac{3}{8}=\frac{1}{3}\times\frac{3}{4}=\frac{1}{4}$.

Answer 18: The answer is (B). This is similar to Example 13.

Answer 19: The correct answer is (C). The largest value of a fraction occurs when we have the largest top and smallest bottom. It occurs when $x = 10$, and $y = 4$; $\frac{10}{4}=2.5$.

Answer 20: The correct answers are (A), (C), (D), and (E). Choice (B) reduces to $\frac{2}{3}$, and choice (F) is already reduced.

Answer 21: The correct answers are (B), (D), and (F). Choice (A) reduces to $\frac{1}{4}$, choice (C) reduces to $\frac{2}{5}$, and choice (E) reduces to $\frac{1}{3}$.

Answer 22: The correct answer is 126.99. After the discount of 40%, the item would sell for (\$249)(0.60) = \$149.40. After a discount of 15% on \$149.40, the final price is (\$149.40)(0.85) = \$126.99. (Note that the dollar sign is already shown outside the box, so it should *not* be placed inside the box.)

Answer 23: The correct answer is 188.68. Let x represent the sale price (without the tax). Then $x + 0.06x = \$200$. This equation simplifies to $1.06x = \$200$. Thus, $x = \frac{\$200}{1.06} \approx \$188.68$, rounded to the nearest cent. (Note that the dollar sign is already shown outside the box, so it should *not* be placed inside the box.)

Answer 24: The correct answer is 5.66. The sale price was approximately \$188.68, so $\$200 - \$188.68 = \$11.32$. The percent discount becomes $\frac{\$11.32}{\$200} = 0.0566 = 5.66\%$. Put 5.66 inside the box. (Note that the percent sign is already shown outside the box, so it should *not* be placed inside the box.)

Let's do some algebra now.

CHAPTER 3: *Exponents*

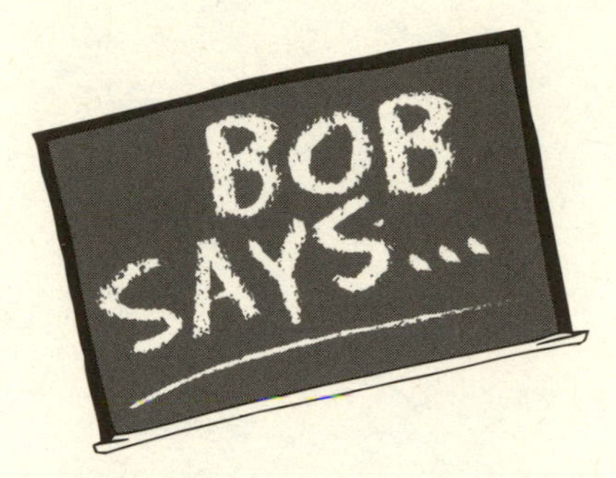

"The power of exponents will bring you strength and knowledge."

Exponents are a very popular topic on the GRE. They are a good test of knowledge and thinking, are short to write, and it is relatively easy to make up new problems. Let's review some basic rules of exponents.

Rule	Examples
1. $x^m x^n = x^{m+n}$	$x^6x^4x = x^{11}$ and $(x^6y^7)(x^4y^{10}) = x^{10}y^{17}$
2. $\frac{x^m}{x^n} = x^{m-n} = \frac{1}{x^{n-m}}$	$\frac{x^8}{x^6} = x^2$, $\frac{x^3}{x^7} = \frac{1}{x^4}$, and $\frac{x^4y^5z^9}{x^9y^2z^9} = \frac{y^3}{x^5}$
3. $(x^m)^n = x^{mn}$	$(x^5)^7 = x^{35}$
4. $(xy)^n = x^ny^n$	$(xy)^3 = x^3y^3$ and $(x^7y^3)^{10} = x^{70}y^{30}$
5. $\left(\frac{x}{y}\right)^n = \frac{x^n}{y^n}$	$\left(\frac{x}{y}\right)^6 = \frac{x^6}{y^6}$ and $\left(\frac{y^4}{z^5}\right)^3 = \frac{y^{12}}{z^{15}}$

You should also recall the following:

Rule	Examples
1. $x^{-n} = \frac{1}{x^n}$ and $\frac{1}{x^{-m}} = x^m$	$2^{-3} = \frac{1}{2^3} = \frac{1}{8}$, $\frac{1}{4^{-3}} = 4^3 = 64$, $\frac{x^{-4}y^{-5}z^6}{x^{-6}y^4z^{-1}} = \frac{x^6z^6z^1}{x^4y^4y^5} = \frac{x^2z^7}{y^9}$, and $\left(\frac{x^3}{y^{-4}}\right)^{-2} = \left(\frac{y^{-4}}{x^3}\right)^2 = \frac{y^{-8}}{x^6} = \frac{1}{x^6y^8}$
2. $x^0 = 1, x \neq 0$; 0^0 is indeterminate	$(7ab^7)^0 = 1$ and $7x^0 = 7(1) = 7$

It might pay to remember the following:

$2^3 = 8$	$2^4 = 16$	$2^5 = 32$	$2^6 = 64$
$2^7 = 128$	$2^8 = 256$	$2^9 = 512$	$2^{10} = 1{,}024$
$3^3 = 27$	$4^3 = 64$	$5^3 = 125$	$6^3 = 216$

Here are some exponential examples.

Example 1: Simplify the following:

Problem	Solution
a. $(-3a^4bc^6)(-5ab^7c^{10})(-100a^{100}b^{200}c^{2,000}) =$	$-1{,}500a^{105}b^{208}c^{1,016}$
b. $(10ab^4c^7)^3 =$	$1{,}000a^3b^{12}c^{21}$
c. $(4x^6)^2(10x^3)^3 =$	$16{,}000x^{21}$
d. $((2b^4)^3)^2 =$	$64b^{24}$
e. $(-b^6)^{101}$	$-b^{606}$
f. $(-ab^8)^{202} =$	$+a^{202}b^{1,616}$
g. $\dfrac{24e^9f^7g^5}{72e^9f^{11}g^7} =$	$\dfrac{1}{3f^4g^2}$
h. $\dfrac{(x^4)^3}{x^4} =$	x^8
i. $\left(\dfrac{m^3n^4}{m^7n}\right)^5 =$	$\dfrac{n^{15}}{m^{20}}$
j. $\left(\dfrac{(p^4)^3}{(p^6)^5}\right)^{10} =$	$\dfrac{1}{p^{180}}$
k. $(-10a^{-4}b^5c^{-2})(4a^{-7}b^{-1}) =$	$\dfrac{-40b^4}{a^{11}c^2}$
l. $(3ab^{-3}c^4)^{-3} =$	$\dfrac{b^9}{27a^3c^{12}}$

m. $(3x^4)^{-4}\left(\left(\frac{1}{9x^8}\right)^{-1}\right)^2 =$ $\quad 1$

n. $(2x^{-4})^2(3x^{-3})^{-2} =$ $\quad \frac{4}{9x^2}$

o. $\left(\frac{(2y^3)^{-2}}{(4x^{-5})}\right)^{-2} =$ $\quad \frac{256y^{12}}{x^{10}}$

Also recall the following facts for reciprocals:

If $0 < x < 1$, then $\frac{1}{x} > 1$, and if $x > 1$, then $0 < \frac{1}{x} < 1$.

If $-1 < x < 0$, then $\frac{1}{x} < -1$, and if $x < -1$, then $-1 < \frac{1}{x} < 0$.

In addition, use these hints for doing comparisons:

- If there are only numbers in the problem, the answer is never (D) (you can't tell because you lack information).
- If there are only letters in the problem, the answer is almost always (C) or (D), as we see in Exercise 1.
- If there are only letters, the more specific the value of the letter (such as $1 < x < 3$), the more likely the answer is (A) or (B).
- If there are both letters and numbers in the comparison, the answer could be anything.

Q **Let's try some exercises.**

	Quantity A	**Quantity B**
Exercise 1:	x	x^2
Exercise 2: $-32 < x < -7$	x^2	x^3
Exercise 3: $-1 < x < 0$	$\frac{-1}{x^3}$	$\frac{-1}{x^4}$
Exercise 4: $a, b \neq 0$	$(3ab^2)^3$	$3a^2b^6$
Exercise 5: $x < 0$	x	$\frac{-1}{x^3}$
Exercise 6:	$3a^2b^6$	$3(ab^3)^2$
Exercise 7:	3^{-2}	$\frac{-1}{9}$

Exercise 8: $x^2 = y^2$ x^2 xy

Exercise 9: $0 < x < 1$: Arrange in order from smallest to largest: x, x^2, x^3.

A. $x < x^2 < x^3$
B. $x < x^3 < x^2$
C. $x^2 < x < x^3$
D. $x^3 < x^2 < x$
E. $x^3 < x < x^2$

Exercise 10: $-1 < x < 0$: Arrange in order from largest to smallest: x^2, x^3, x^4

A. $x^4 > x^3 > x^2$
B. $x^4 > x^2 > x^3$
C. $x^3 > x^4 > x^2$
D. $x^2 > x^3 > x^4$
E. $x^2 > x^4 > x^3$

Exercise 11: $0 < x < 1$.

I: $x > \frac{1}{x^2}$

II: $\frac{1}{x^2} > \frac{1}{x^4}$

III: $x - 1 > \frac{1}{x-1}$

Which statement(s) is always true?

A. None
B. Statement I
C. Statement II
D. Statement III
E. All

Exercise 12: $(5ab^3)^3$

A. $15ab^6$
B. $75ab+6$
C. $125ab^9$
D. $125a^3b^6$
E. $125a^3b^9$

Exercise 13: $\frac{(2x^5)^3(3x^{10})^2}{6x^{15}}$

A. 1
B. x^{20}
C. $2x^{20}$
D. $12x^{20}$
E. $12x^{210}$

Exercise 14: $\left(\frac{12x^6}{24x^9}\right)^3$

A. $1{,}728x^{27}$

B. $\frac{1}{1728x^{27}}$

C. $\frac{1}{6x^9}$

D. $\frac{1}{8x^9}$

E. $\frac{1}{8x^{27}}$

Exercise 15: $\frac{(4x^4)^3}{(8x^6)^2}$

A. $\frac{1}{2}$

B. 1

C. $\frac{1}{2}x^{28}$

D. x^{28}

E. $\frac{1}{2x}$

Exercise 16: $-1 \le x \le 5$. Where is x^2 located?

A. $-1 \le x^2 \le 5$

B. $0 \le x^2 \le 25$

C. $1 \le x^2 \le 5$

D. $1 \le x^2 \le 10$

E. $1 \le x^2 \le 25$

Exercise 17: $2^m + 2^m =$

A. 2^{m+1}

B. 2^{m+2}

C. 2^{m+4}

D. 2^{m2}

E. 4^m

Exercise 18: $\frac{m^{-5}n^6p^{-2}}{m^{-3}n^9p^0} =$

A. $m^2n^3p^2$

B. $\frac{1}{m^2n^3}$

C. $\frac{m^2}{n^3p^2}$

D. $\frac{1}{m^2n^3p^2}$

E. None of these

Exercise 19: If $8^{2n+1} = 2^{n+18}$; $n =$

A. 3

B. 7

C. 10

D. 13

E. 17

Exercise 20: $p = 4^n$; $4p =$

A. 4^{n+1}

B. 4^{n+2}

C. 3^{n+4}

D. 16^p

E. 64^p

Exercise 21: Which of the following are equivalent to $\frac{(a^3 \times a^4)^2 + (a^8 \times a^6)}{2}$? Indicate *all* correct choices.

A. $a^7 + a^7$

B. $a^7 \times a^7$

C. $(a^7)^7$

D. $\frac{a^{28}}{a^2}$

E. $(a^7)^2$

F. $a^{28} - a^{14}$

Exercise 22: Which of the following are equivalent to $2^{22} \times 2^{22}$? Indicate *all* correct choices.

A. 2×2^{22}

B. 2^{44}

C. 2^{484}

D. 4^{22}

E. 4^{44}

F. 4^{484}

Exercise 23: Which of the following are equivalent to $\frac{1}{9^{-3}}$? Indicate *all* correct choices.

A. -729

B. 729

C. $(9^{-6})^{-\frac{1}{2}}$

D. $10^3 - 271$

E. $-\frac{1}{27}$

F. 27

Exercise 24: Express the value of $99 + 99^0 + 100^{-1}$ as a ratio of integers.

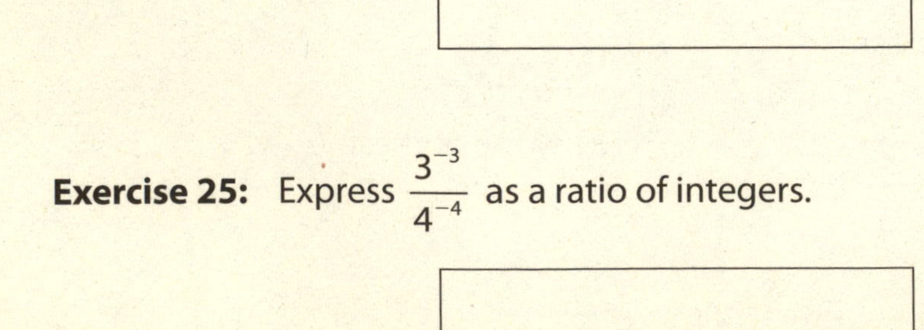

Exercise 25: Express $\frac{3^{-3}}{4^{-4}}$ as a ratio of integers.

Let's look at the answers.

Answer 1: The answer is (D); you can't tell. It is essential that you know why:

If $x > 1$, then $x^2 > x$, since $4^2 > 4$.

If $x = 1$, then $x^2 = x$, since $1^2 = 1$.

If $0 < x < 1$, then $x > x^2$, since $\frac{1}{2} > \left(\frac{1}{2}\right)^2 = \frac{1}{4}$!!

If $x = 0$, then $x = x^2$, since $0 = 0^2$.

If $x < 0$, then $x^2 > x$, since the square of a negative number is a positive number.

Answer 2: The answer is (A). (A) is always positive, and (B) is always negative.

Answer 3: The answer is (A). This exercise is similar to exercise 2.

Answer 4: The answer is (D). (A) multiplied out is $27a^3b^6$. Say $a = 2$; then (A) is definitely bigger than (B). But if $a = -3$, (A) is negative and (B) is positive.

Answer 5: The answer is (B) since (B) > 0 and (A) < 0.

Answer 6: The answer is (C). They are equal.

Answer 7: The answer is (A). $3^{-2} = \frac{1}{9}$; a negative exponent means reciprocal, not necessarily less than 0.

Answer 8: The answer is (D); you can't tell. It depends on whether y is positive or negative.

Answer 9: The answer is (D). If $0 < x < 1$, the higher the power, the smaller the number.

Answer 10: The answer is (E). Take, for example, $x = -\frac{1}{2}$. $\left(-\frac{1}{2}\right)^2 = \frac{1}{4}$; $\left(-\frac{1}{2}\right)^3 = -\frac{1}{8}$; $\left(-\frac{1}{2}\right)^4 = \frac{1}{16}$. Be careful! This exercise asks for largest to smallest. Notice that x^3 has to be the smallest because it is the only negative number, so the answer choices are cut to two, (B) and (E).

Answer 11: The answer is (D).

Statement I: $0 < x < 1$; so $\frac{1}{x} > 1$ and $\frac{1}{x^2} > 1$ also. Let $x = \frac{1}{2}$; then $\frac{1}{x^2} = \frac{1}{\frac{1}{4}} = 4$. Statement I is false.

Statement II: $x^2 > x^4$; so $\frac{1}{x^2} < \frac{1}{x^4}$. Statement II is false.

Statement III: $0 < x < 1$; so $-1 < x - 1 < 0$; this means $\frac{1}{x-1} < -1$. Statement III is true.

Answer 12: The answer is (E). $5^3a^3(b^3)^3 = 125a^3b^9$.

Answer 13: The answer is (D). $\left(\frac{8 \times 9}{6}\right)x^{15+20-15} = 12x^{20}$.

Answer 14: The answer is (D). $\left(\frac{1}{2x^3}\right)^3 = \frac{1}{8x^9}$.

Answer 15: The answer is (B). The numerator and denominator of the fraction each equal $64x^{12}$.

Answer 16: The answer is (B). This is very tricky. 0 is between -1 and 5, and $0^2 = 0$.

Answer 17: The answer is (A). This is one of the few truly hard problems because it is an addition problem.

$2^m + 2^m = (1)(2^m) + (1)(2^m) = (2)(2^m) = 2^1 2^m = 2^{m+1}$.

Similarly, $3^m + 3^m + 3^m = 3^{m+1}$ and four 4^m terms added equal 4^{m+1}.

Answer 18: The answer is (D). $\frac{m^{-5}n^6p^{-2}}{m^{-3}n^9p^0} = \frac{m^3n^6}{m^5n^9p^2} = \frac{1}{m^2n^3p^2}$.

Answer 19: The answer is (A). $8^{2n+1} = (2^3)^{2n+1} = 2^{n+18}$. By the property of 1 to 1 (if you care), if the bases are equal, the exponents must be equal. $3(2n+1) = n + 18$; $n = 3$.

Answer 20: The answer is (A). $p = 4^n$; $4p = 4(4^n) = 4^1 4^n = 4^{n+1}$.

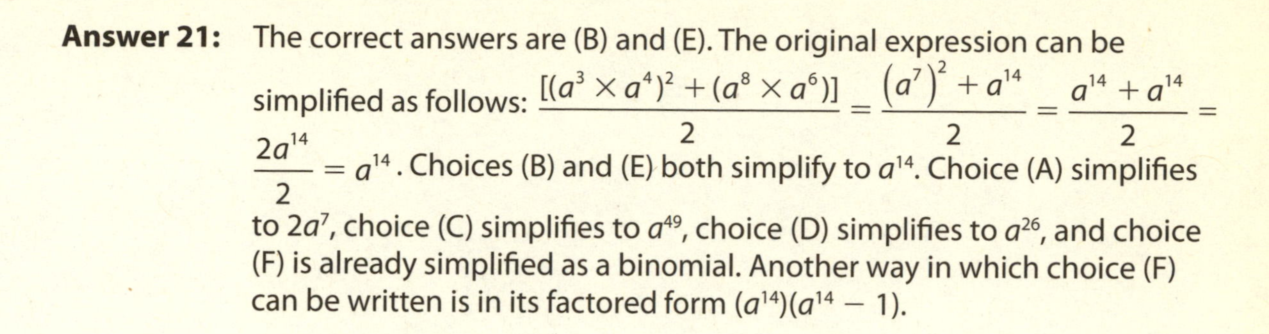

Answer 21: The correct answers are (B) and (E). The original expression can be simplified as follows: $\frac{[(a^3 \times a^4)^2 + (a^8 \times a^6)]}{2} = \frac{(a^7)^2 + a^{14}}{2} = \frac{a^{14} + a^{14}}{2} = \frac{2a^{14}}{2} = a^{14}$. Choices (B) and (E) both simplify to a^{14}. Choice (A) simplifies to $2a^7$, choice (C) simplifies to a^{49}, choice (D) simplifies to a^{26}, and choice (F) is already simplified as a binomial. Another way in which choice (F) can be written is in its factored form $(a^{14})(a^{14} - 1)$.

Answer 22: The correct answers are (B) and (D). The original expression simplifies to $(2^{22})^2 = 2^{44}$. Note that $2^{22} \times 2^{22}$ can also be expressed as $(2 \times 2)^{22} = 4^{22}$. Choice (A) simplifies to 2^{23}, choice (C) is obviously wrong, choice (E) can be written as $(2^2)^{44} = 2^{88}$, and choice (F) can be written as $(2^2)^{484} = 2^{968}$.

Answer 23: The correct answers are (B), (C), and (D). The original expression can be written as $9^3 = 729$. Note that in choice (C), the multiplication rule is applied to the exponents whenever an exponent is raised to an exponent. Also, note that in choice (D), $10^3 = 1000$.

Answer 24: The correct answer is $\frac{10{,}001}{100}$. $99 + 99^0 + 100^{-1} = 99 + 1 + \frac{1}{100} = 100\frac{1}{100} = \frac{10{,}001}{100}$. Note that the answer need not be in reduced form (but *must* show integers in both numerator and denominator). Other acceptable answers would be $\frac{20{,}002}{200}$, $\frac{30{,}003}{300}$, etc.

Answer 25: The correct answer is $\frac{256}{27}$ because $\frac{3^{-3}}{4^{-4}} = \frac{1/3^3}{1/4^4} = \frac{4^4}{3^3} = \frac{256}{27}$. Note that any integral multiplier of the numerator and denominator would be acceptable, so another answer could be $\frac{2{,}560}{270}$.

Now let's go to a radical chapter.

CHAPTER 4: ***Square Roots***

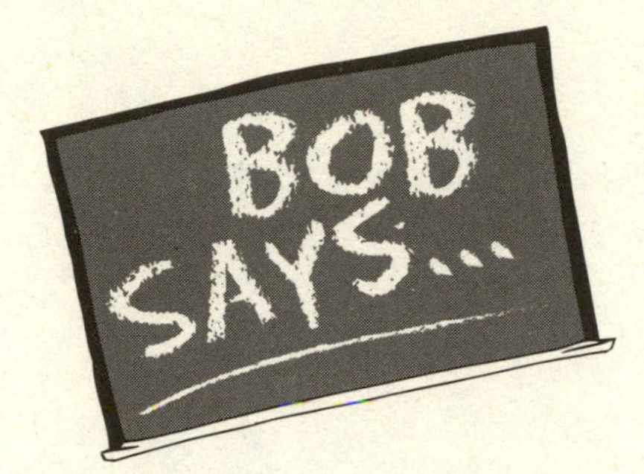

"We must go to the root of the problem to be enlightened."

The square root symbol ($\sqrt{\ }$) is probably the one symbol most people actually like, even for people who don't like math. How else can you explain the square root symbol on a business calculator? I have yet to find a use for it. Here are some basic facts about square roots that you should know.

1. You should know the following square roots:

   $\sqrt{0} = 0$ $\quad\sqrt{1} = 1$ $\quad\sqrt{4} = 2$ $\quad\sqrt{9} = 3$ $\quad\sqrt{16} = 4$ $\quad\sqrt{25} = 5$

   $\sqrt{36} = 6$ $\quad\sqrt{49} = 7$ $\quad\sqrt{64} = 8$ $\quad\sqrt{81} = 9$ $\quad\sqrt{100} = 10$

   The numbers under the *radicals* (square root signs) are called *perfect squares* because their square roots are whole numbers.

2. $\sqrt{2} \approx 1.4$ (actually it is 1.414...), and $\sqrt{3} \approx 1.73$ (actually it is 1.732..., the year George Washington was born).

3. $\sqrt{\frac{a}{b}} = \frac{\sqrt{a}}{\sqrt{b}}$, so $\quad\sqrt{\frac{25}{9}} = \frac{5}{3}$ $\quad\sqrt{\frac{7}{36}} = \frac{\sqrt{7}}{6}$ $\quad\sqrt{\frac{45}{20}} = \sqrt{\frac{9}{4}} = \frac{3}{2}$

4. A method of simplification involves finding all the prime factors:

   $\sqrt{200} = \sqrt{(2)(2)(2)(5)(5)} = (2)(5)\sqrt{2} = 10\sqrt{2}$

5. Adding and subtracting radicals involves combining like radicals:

   $4\sqrt{7} + 5\sqrt{11} + 6\sqrt{7} - 9\sqrt{11} = 10\sqrt{7} - 4\sqrt{11}$

6. Multiplication of radicals follows this rule:

   $a\sqrt{b} \times c\sqrt{d} = ac\sqrt{bd}$

   Therefore, $3\sqrt{13} \times 10\sqrt{7} = 30\sqrt{91}$ and

   $10\sqrt{8} \times 3\sqrt{10} = 10 \times 3\sqrt{2 \times 2 \times 2 \times 2 \times 5} = 10 \times 3 \times 2 \times 2\sqrt{5} = 120\sqrt{5}$

7. If a radical appears in the denominator of a fraction, rationalize the denominator by multiplying both numerator and denominator by the radical:
$\frac{20}{7\sqrt{5}} = \frac{20}{7\sqrt{5}} \times \frac{\sqrt{5}}{\sqrt{5}} = \frac{20\sqrt{5}}{35} = \frac{4\sqrt{5}}{7}$ and $\frac{7}{\sqrt{45}} = \frac{7}{3\sqrt{5}} \times \frac{\sqrt{5}}{\sqrt{5}} = \frac{7\sqrt{5}}{15}$

8. If $c, d > 0$, $\sqrt{c} + \sqrt{d} > \sqrt{c+d}$. Why? If you square the right side, you get $c + d$. If you square the left side you get $c + d +$ the middle term $(2\sqrt{cd})$.

9. The square root varies according to the value of the radicand:

   If $a > 1$, $a > \sqrt{a}$. For example, $9 > \sqrt{9}$.

   If $a = 1$, $a = \sqrt{a}$ since the square root of 1 is 1.

   If $0 < a < 1$, $a > \sqrt{a}$. When you take the square root of a positive number, it becomes closer to 1. So $\sqrt{\frac{1}{4}} = \frac{1}{2} > \frac{1}{4}$.

   If $a = 0$, $a = \sqrt{a}$ since the square root of 0 is 0.

   If $a > 0$ and $\sqrt{a} < 1$, then $\frac{1}{\sqrt{a}} > 1$. Also, if $\sqrt{a} > 1$, then $\frac{1}{a} < 1$.

10. The square root of a negative number is imaginary. The New GRE does not bother with imaginary numbers.

Note *$\sqrt{9} = 3$, $-\sqrt{9} = -3$, but $\sqrt{-9}$ is imaginary. The equation $x^2 = 9$ has two solutions, $\pm\sqrt{9}$, or ± 3, which stands for both $+3$ and -3.*

The GRE often uses square roots in comparison problems.

Let's try some exercises.

Exercise 1: $\left(\sqrt{12} + \sqrt{27}\right)^2 =$

A. 15

B. 39

C. 75

D. 225

E. 675

Exercise 2: Suppose $0 < a < 1$.

I: $a^2 > \sqrt{a}$

II: $\sqrt{a} > \sqrt{a^3}$

III: $\sqrt{a} > \frac{1}{\sqrt{a^7}}$

A. Statement I is correct.

B. Statement II is correct.

C. Statement III is correct.

D. Statements I and III are correct.

E. Statements II and III are correct.

	Quantity A	Quantity B
Exercise 3:	$\frac{1}{\sqrt{c}}$	$\frac{\sqrt{c}}{c}$
Exercise 4: $c > 0$	$\sqrt{c} + 2$	$\sqrt{c + 4}$
Exercise 5: $c > 0$	$\sqrt{c}$	$\frac{1}{\sqrt{c}}$
Exercise 6: $0 < d < 1$	$\sqrt{d} + 1$	$\frac{1}{\sqrt{d} + 1}$
Exercise 7:	999.98	$\sqrt{1,000,003}$

Exercise 8: $0 < m < 1$. Arrange in order, smallest to largest, $a = \frac{1}{m}$, $b = \frac{1}{m^2}$, $c = \frac{1}{\sqrt{m}}$.

A. $a < b < c$

B. $a < c < b$

C. $b < c < a$

D. $b < a < c$

E. $c < a < b$

Exercise 9: Express the value of $\frac{\sqrt{4,846.608}}{\sqrt{2,423.304}}$ to the nearest thousandth.

Exercise 10: Which of the following are equivalent to $\sqrt{3}$? Indicate *all* correct choices.

A. $\dfrac{1}{1/\sqrt{3}}$

B. $\dfrac{3}{\sqrt{3}}$

C. $\dfrac{\sqrt{42}}{\sqrt{39}}$

D. $\sqrt{14}-\sqrt{11}$

E. $\sqrt[4]{81}$

F. 1.73

Exercise 11: Which *three* of the following have equivalent values?

A. 4^2

B. 2^4

C. $15^0 + 15^1$

D. $\sqrt{64^2}$

E. $\dfrac{256}{4}$

F. $2 - 18$

Let's look at the answers.

Answer 1: The answer is (C). $\sqrt{12} = \sqrt{2\times2\times3} = 2\sqrt{3}$ and $\sqrt{27} = \sqrt{3\times3\times3} = 3\sqrt{3}$. Adding, we get $5\sqrt{3}$. Squaring, we get $25\sqrt{9} = 25\times3 = 75$.

Answer 2: The answer to the question is (B). Let's look at the statements one by one.

Statement I: If you square a number between 0 and 1, you make it closer to 0. If you take the square root of the same number, you make it closer to 1. Statement I is wrong.

Statement II: From the previous chapter, if $0 < a < 1$, $a > a^3$. So are its square roots. So statement II is true.

Statement III: $\sqrt{a} < 1$. $a^7 < 1$. So $\sqrt{a^7} < 1$. Then $\dfrac{1}{\sqrt{a^7}} > 1$. Statement III is false.

Answer 3: The answer is (C). Quantity B is just Quantity A rationalized.

Answer 4: The answer is (A). Since $\sqrt{4} = 2$, and $c > 0$, we know $\sqrt{x}+\sqrt{y} > \sqrt{x+y}$, or $\sqrt{c}+\sqrt{4} > \sqrt{c+4}$.

Answer 5: The answer is (D) since we don't know if $c < 1$, $c = 1$, or $c > 1$, and the answer is different for each case.

Answer 6: The answer is (A). $\sqrt{d}+1>1$; so $\frac{1}{\sqrt{d}+1}<1$.

Answer 7: The answer is (B). We observe that 999.38 is less than 1,000. Since $(1{,}000)^2 = 1{,}000{,}000$, it follows that $\sqrt{1{,}000{,}003}$ is slightly larger than 1,000.

Answer 8: The answer is (E). If we take $m=\frac{1}{4}$, we see that $\sqrt{m}>m>m^2$. That makes $\frac{1}{\sqrt{m}}<\frac{1}{m}<\frac{1}{m^2}$, or $c<a<b$.

Answer 9: The correct answer is 1.414. We observe that 4,846.608 is twice 2,423.304, so that $\frac{\sqrt{4{,}846.608}}{\sqrt{2{,}423.304}}=\sqrt{2}$. To the nearest thousandth, $\sqrt{2}$ equals 1.414.

Answer 10: The correct answers are (A) and (B). Choice (C) can be simplified to $\sqrt{\frac{42}{39}}=\sqrt{\frac{14}{13}}$, choice (D) cannot be simplified, and choice (E) can be simplified to 3. Choice (F) may look correct, but it is only an approximation; it is *not* the *equivalent* of $\sqrt{3}$.

Answer 11: The correct answers are (A), (B), and (C), each of which has a value of 16. The values of (D), (E), and (F) are 64, 64, and -16, respectively.

Let's talk briefly about cube roots and fourth roots.

We have learned that $\sqrt{a}=b$ if $b^2=a$. For example, $\sqrt{81}=9$ since $9^2=81$. A similar definition applies to other roots. We denote $\sqrt[3]{a}$ as the cube root of a. If $\sqrt[3]{a}=b$, then $b^3=a$. For example, since $5^3=125$, we can write $\sqrt[3]{125}=5$. Likewise, $\left(\frac{1}{2}\right)^3=\frac{1}{2}\times\frac{1}{2}\times\frac{1}{2}=\frac{1}{8}$, so we can write $\sqrt[3]{\frac{1}{8}}=\frac{1}{2}$. Note that negative numbers may also be used for cube roots. As an example, $(-4)^3=-64$, so $\sqrt[3]{-64}=-4$.

The symbol $\sqrt[4]{a}$ refers to the fourth root of a. If $\sqrt[4]{a}=b$, then $b^4=a$. For example, since $2^4=16$, we can write $\sqrt[4]{16}=2$. Likewise, $\sqrt[4]{\frac{1}{81}}=\frac{1}{3}$, since $\left(\frac{1}{3}\right)^4=\frac{1}{81}$.

A few other information pieces that you should know are the following:

1. Even though both $5^2=25$ and $(-5)^2=25$, the symbol $\sqrt{25}$ refers to only the *positive* square root of 25, which is 5. We use the expression $-\sqrt{25}$ to denote -5. The situation is similar with fourth roots of numbers; that is $\sqrt[4]{16}=2$ and $-\sqrt[4]{16}=-2$.

2. Square roots and fourth roots of negative numbers, such as $\sqrt{-16}$, are not real numbers and will *not* appear on this test.
3. All roots of zero equal 0.
4. If $a > b > 1$, then $\sqrt[n]{a} > \sqrt[n]{b}$. For example, $\sqrt[3]{9} > \sqrt[3]{7}$ because $9 > 7$.
5. If $0 < a < 1$, then $\sqrt[n]{a} > a$. For example, $\sqrt{\frac{1}{2}} > \frac{1}{2}$ because $0 < \frac{1}{2} < 1$. You can use your calculator to evaluate $\sqrt{\frac{1}{2}}$ as approximately 0.71 to see that this is so.

Our last discussion for this chapter deals with fractional exponents, both positive and negative. Given $x^{\frac{p}{r}}$, its value is computed as either $\sqrt[r]{x^p}$ or, equivalently, as $\left(\sqrt[n]{x}\right)^p$. Normally, the latter of these two expressions is easier to compute. For example, to evaluate $8^{\frac{5}{3}}$, it is easier to write $\left(\sqrt[3]{8}\right)^5 = 2^5 = 32$. If we were to compute $8^{\frac{5}{3}}$ by using $\sqrt[3]{8^5}$, we would have to simplify $\sqrt[3]{32,768}$, which would be more difficult.

Now consider an expression such as $4^{-\frac{7}{2}}$. Using our knowledge of negative exponents, we can write $4^{-\frac{7}{2}}$ as $\frac{1}{4^{\frac{7}{2}}}$, which becomes $\frac{1}{\left(\sqrt{4}\right)^7}$. The square root of 4 is 2, and $2^7 = 128$. So the final answer is $\frac{1}{128}$.

As a second example of negative fractional exponents, consider the expression $\frac{5}{64^{-\frac{1}{3}}}$, which can be evaluated as follows: $\frac{5}{64^{-\frac{1}{3}}} = (5)(64^{\frac{1}{3}}) = (5)(\sqrt[3]{64}) = (5)(4) = 20$.

Let's try some exercises.

Exercise 12: What is the value of $\frac{100^{\frac{3}{2}}}{16^{\frac{5}{4}}}$?

Exercise 13: What is the value of $\frac{27^{-\frac{2}{3}}}{4^{-\frac{3}{2}}}$?

A **Let's look at the answers.**

Answer 12: The correct answer is $\frac{125}{4}$. Here are the steps:

$$\frac{100^{\frac{3}{2}}}{16^{\frac{5}{4}}} = \frac{\left(\sqrt{100}\right)^3}{\left(\sqrt[4]{16}\right)^5} = \frac{10^3}{2^5} = \frac{1{,}000}{32} = \frac{125}{4}$$. Note that either $\frac{1{,}000}{32}$ or $\frac{125}{4}$ would be an acceptable answer.

Answer 13: The correct answer is $\frac{8}{9}$. The first step would be to rewrite the given problem with positive exponents as $\frac{4^{\frac{3}{2}}}{27^{\frac{2}{3}}}$. Then $\frac{4^{\frac{3}{2}}}{27^{\frac{2}{3}}} = \frac{\left(\sqrt{4}\right)^3}{\left(\sqrt[3]{27}\right)^2} = \frac{2^3}{3^2} = \frac{8}{9}$.

Notice that with these exercises, just knowing the properties of square roots will help you avoid much and sometimes all of the arithmetic.

CHAPTER 5: *Algebraic Manipulations*

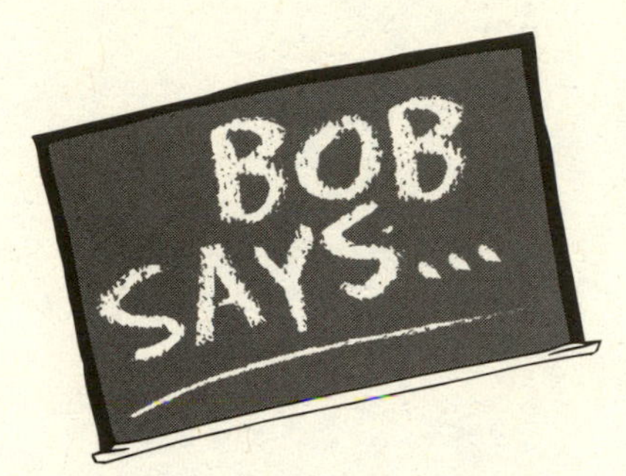

"Along our journey, we must learn to do. It will help us to become truly happy."

Algebraic manipulative skills such as those in this chapter are areas that high school courses have tended to de-emphasize since 1985. It is necessary to show you how to do these problems and give you extra problems to practice. Of course, included will be the kind of questions the GRE asks.

COMBINING LIKE TERMS

Like terms are terms with the same letter combination (or no letter). The same letters must also have the same exponents.

Example 1: Are the following terms like or unlike:

a. $4x$ and $-5x$

b. $4x$ and $4x^2$

c. xy^2 and x^2y

Solutions:

a. $4x$ and $-5x$ are like terms even though their numerical coefficients are different.

b. $4x$ and $4x^2$ are unlike terms

c. xy^2 and x^2y are unlike; $xy^2 = xyy$ and $x^2y = xxy$.

Combining like terms means adding or subtracting their numerical coefficients; exponents are unchanged. Unlike terms cannot be combined.

Example 2: Simplify:

Problem	Solution
a. $3m + 4m + m =$	$8m$
b. $8m + 2n + 7m - 7n =$	$15m - 5n$
c. $3x^2 + 4x - 5 - 7x^2 - 4x + 8 =$	$-4x^2 + 3$

DISTRIBUTIVE LAW

The **Distributive Law** states:

$$a(x + y) = ax + ay$$

Example 3: Perform the indicated operations:

Problem	Solution
a. $4(3x - 7) =$	$12x - 28$
b. $5(2a - 5b + 3c) =$	$10a - 25b + 15c$
c. $3x^4(7x^3 - 4x - 1) =$	$21x^7 - 12x^5 - 3x^4$
d. $4(3x - 7) - 5(4x - 2) =$	$12x - 28 - 20x + 10 = -8x - 18$

BINOMIAL PRODUCTS

A **binomial** is a two-term expression, such as $x + 2$. We use the **FOIL method** to multiply a binomial by a binomial. FOIL is an acronym for First, Outer, Inner, Last. This means to multiply the first two terms, then the outer terms, then the inner terms, and finally the last two terms.

Example 4: Multiply $(x + 4)(x + 6)$.

Solution:

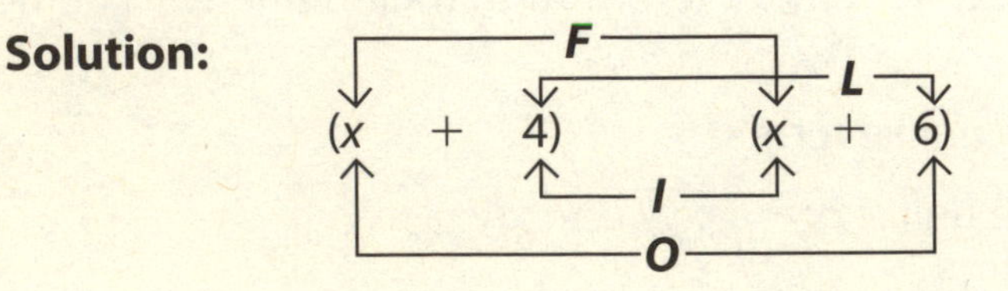

Multiplying, we get $x^2 + 6x + 4x + 24 = x^2 + 10x + 24$.

Example 5: Perform the indicated multiplications:

Problem	Solution
a. $(x + 7)(x + 4) =$	$x^2 + 4x + 7x + 28 = x^2 + 11x + 28$
b. $(x - 5)(x - 2) =$	$x^2 - 7x + 10$
c. $(x + 6)(x - 3) =$	$x^2 + 3x - 18$
d. $(x + 6)(x - 8) =$	$x^2 - 2x - 48$
e. $(x + 5)(x - 5) =$	$x^2 - 5x + 5x - 25 = x^2 - 25$
f. $(x + 5)^2 =$	$(x + 5)(x + 5) = x^2 + 10x + 25$
g. $(x - 10)^2 =$	$x^2 - 20x + 100$
h. $(2x + 5)(3x - 10) =$	$6x^2 - 5x - 50$
i. $3(x + 4)(x + 5) =$	$3(x^2 + 9x + 20) = 3x^2 + 27x + 60$
j. $7(4x + 3)(4x - 3) =$	$7(16x^2 - 9) = 112x^2 - 63$

You should know the following common binomial products:

$$(a + b)(a - b) = a^2 - b^2$$

$$(a - b)(a - b) = a^2 - 2ab + b^2$$

$$(a + b)(a + b) = a^2 + 2ab + b^2$$

Note *For a perfect square $(a + b)^2$, the first term of the resulting trinomial is the first term squared (a^2), and the third term of the resulting trinomial is the last term squared (b^2). The middle term is twice the product of the two terms of the binomial ($2ab$), so*

$$(a + b)^2 = a^2 + 2ab + b^2$$

Example 6: Perform the indicated multiplications:

Problem	Solution
a. $(a + 4)(a + 7)$	$a^2 + 11a + 28$
b. $(b + 5)(b + 6)$	$b^2 + 11b + 30$
c. $(c + 1)(c + 9)$	$c^2 + 10c + 9$
d. $(d + 4)(d + 8)$	$d^2 + 12d + 32$
e. $(e + 11)(e + 10)$	$e^2 + 21e + 110$
f. $(f - 6)(f - 2)$	$f^2 - 8f + 12$
g. $(g - 10)(g - 20)$	$g^2 - 30g + 200$

h. $(h - 4)(h - 3)$	$h^2 - 7h + 12$
i. $(i - 1)(i - 7)$	$i^2 - 8i + 7$
j. $(j - 3)(j - 5)$	$j^2 - 8j + 15$
k. $(k + 5)(k - 2)$	$k^2 + 3k - 10$
l. $(m + 5)(m - 8)$	$m^2 - 3m - 40$
m. $(n - 6)(n + 2)$	$n^2 - 4n - 12$
n. $(p - 8)(p + 10)$	$p^2 + 2p - 80$
o. $(q - 5r)(q + 2r)$	$q^2 - 3qr - 10r^2$
p. $(s + 3)^2$	$s^2 + 6s + 9$
q. $(t - 4)^2$	$t^2 - 8t + 16$
r. $(3u + 5)^2$	$9u^2 + 30u + 25$
s. $(5v - 4)^2$	$25v^2 - 40v + 16$
t. $(ax + by)^2$	$a^2x^2 + 2abxy + b^2y^2$
u. $(be - ma)^2$	$b^2e^2 - 2\ beam + m^2a^2$
v. $(w + x)(w - x)$	$w^2 - x^2$
w. $(a - 11)(a + 11)$	$a^2 - 121$
x. $(am - 7)(am + 7)$	$a^2m^2 - 49$
y. $(a^2b + c)(a^2b - c)$	$a^4b^2 - c^2$
z. $3(x + 5)(x - 2)$	$3x^2 + 9x - 30$
aa. $-4(2x - 5)(3x - 4)$	$-24x^2 + 92x - 80$
bb. $x(2x - 5)(4x + 7)$	$8x^3 - 6x^2 - 35x$
cc. $5(x - 5)(x + 5)$	$5x^2 - 125$

Let's do some exercises.

	Quantity A	Quantity B
Exercise 1:	$6(2x + 2)$	$2(6x + 6)$
Exercise 2:	$x(2x + 3)$	$2(x^2 + 2x)$

		Quantity A	Quantity B
Exercise 3:	$x^2 + y^2 = 20, xy = -6$	$(x + y)^2$	10
Exercise 4:		$(x + y)^2$	$(x - y)^2 + 4xy$

Exercise 5: $x^2 - y^2 = 24. 3(x + y)(x - y) =$

A. 8
B. 24
C. 27
D. 72
E. 13,824

Exercise 6: $x + y = m; x - y = \frac{1}{m}; x^2 - y^2 =$

A. m^2
B. m
C. 1
D. $\frac{1}{m}$
E. $\frac{1}{m^2}$

Exercise 7: $\left(x + \frac{1}{x}\right)^2 = 64;\ x^2 + \frac{1}{x^2} =$

A. 9
B. 62
C. 64
D. 65
E. 66

Let's look at the answers.

Answer 1: The answer is (C). They both equal $12x + 12$.

Answer 2: The answer is (D) since we don't have a value for x. The answer depends on whether x is negative, zero, or positive, or whether $3x > 4x$, $3x = 4x$, or $3x < 4x$.

Answer 3: The answer is (B). $(x + y)^2 =$ (rearranging the terms) $x^2 + y^2 + 2xy = 20 + 2(-6) = 8$, and $8 < 10$.

Answer 4: The answer is (C). They both equal $x^2 + 2xy + y^2$.

Answer 5: The answer is (D). $3(x + y)(x - y) = 3(x^2 - y^2) = 3(24) = 72$.

Answer 6: The answer is (C). $(x + y)(x - y) = x^2 - y^2 = \frac{m}{1} \times \frac{1}{m} = 1$.

Answer 7: The answer is (B). $\left(x + \frac{1}{x}\right)\left(x + \frac{1}{x}\right) = x^2 + 2(x)\left(\frac{1}{x}\right) + \frac{1}{x^2} = x^2 + \frac{1}{x^2} + 2 = 64$. So $x^2 + \frac{1}{x^2} = 64 - 2 = 62$.

Let's go on to factoring.

FACTORING

Factoring is the reverse of the distributive law. There are three types of factoring that you need to know: largest common factor, difference of two squares, and trinomial factorization.

If the distributive law says $x(y + z) = xy + xz$, then taking out the largest common factor says $xy + xy = x(y + z)$. Let's demonstrate a few factoring examples.

Example 7: Factor:

Problem	Answer	Explanation
a. $4x + 6y - 8$	$2(2x + 3y - 4)$	2 is the largest common factor.
b. $8ax + 12ay - 40az$	$4a(2x + 3y - 10z)$	4 is the largest common factor; a is also a common factor.
c. $10a^4y^6z^3 - 15a^7y$	$5a^4y(2y^5z^3 - 3a^3)$	The largest common factor and the lowest power of each common variable is factored out, giving you a^4 and y. However, z is not factored out because it is not in either term.
d. $x^4y - xy^3 + xy$	$xy(x^3 - y^2 + 1)$	Factor out the lowest power of each common variable. Three terms in the original give three terms in parentheses. Note that $1 \times xy = xy$.
e. $9by + 12be + 4ye$	prime	Some expressions cannot be factored.

Difference of Two Squares

Since $(a + b)(a - b) = a^2 - b^2$, factoring tells us that $a^2 - b^2 = (a + b)(a - b)$.

Example 8:

Problem	Answer	Explanation
a. $x^2 - 25$	$(x + 5)(x - 5)$ or $(x - 5)(x + 5)$	Either order is OK.
b. $x^2 - 121$	$(x + 11)(x - 11)$	
c. $9a^2 - 25b^2$	$(3a + 5b)(3a - 5b)$	
d. $5a^3 - 20a$	$5a(a^2 - 4) = 5a(a + 2)(a - 2)$	Factor out largest common factor first, then use the difference of two squares.
e. $x^4 - y^4$	$(x^2 + y^2)(x^2 - y^2) =$ $(x^2 + y^2)(x + y)(x - y)$	This is the difference of two squares where the square roots in the factors are also squares. Sum of two squares doesn't factor, but use the difference of two squares again.

Example 9: Factor completely:

Problem	Solution
a. $12am + 18an$	$6a(2m + 3n)$
b. $6at - 18st + 4as$	$2(3at - 9st + 2as)$
c. $10ax + 15ae - 16ex$	Prime
d. $18a^5c^6 - 27a^3c^8$	$9a^3c^6(2a^2 - 3c^2)$
e. $25a^4b^7c^9 - 75a^8b^9c^{10}$	$25a^4b^7c^9(1 - 3a^4b^2c)$
f. $a^4b^5 + a^7b - ab$	$ab(a^3b^4 + a^6 - 1)$
g. $9 - x^2$	$(3 + x)(3 - x)$
h. $x^4 - 36y^2$	$(x^2 + 6y)(x^2 - 6y)$
i. $2x^3 - 98x$	$2x(x + 7)(x - 7)$
j. $a^4 - 81b^2$	$(a^2 + 9b)(a^2 - 9b)$
k. $x^2 - 49y^6$	$(x + 7y^3)(x - 7y^3)$
l. $5z^2 - 25$	$5(z^2 - 5)$
m. $a^4 - c^8$	$(a^2 + c^4)(a + c^2)(a - c^2)$
n. $2a^9 - 32a$	$2a(a^4 + 4)(a^2 - 2)(a^2 + 2)$

 **Let's do some exercises.**

Exercise 8: Which of the following are equivalent to $(x + 6)^2$? Indicate *all* correct choices.

A. $x^2 + 6x + 12$

B. $x^2 + 12x + 36$

C. $x^2 + 36$

D. $(x - 6)^2 + 24x$

E. $x(x + 6) + 6(x + 6)$

Exercise 9: Which of the following are equivalent to $-6x - 3$? Indicate *all* correct answers.

A. $4(x - 6) - 5(2x - 5)$

B. $-6(x - 3) - 31$

C. $3(x - 2) - 9(x - \frac{1}{3})$

D. $x(x + 5) - x(x + 11) - 3$

E. $12x - (5 + 6x) + 8$

Let's look at the answers.

Answer 8: The correct answers are (B), (D), and (E). The expression $(x + 6)^2$ is equivalent to $x^2 + 6x + 6x + 36 = x^2 + 12x + 36$, which is the expression in choice (B). Choice (D) can be expanded as follows: $(x - 6)^2 + 24x = x^2 - 6x - 6x + 36 + 24x = x^2 + 12x + 36$. Choice (E) can be expanded as follows: $x(x + 6) + 6(x + 6) = x^2 + 6x + 6x + 36 = x^2 + 12x + 36$.

Answer 9: The correct answers are (C) and (D). For choice (C), $3(x - 2) - 9(x - \frac{1}{3}) = 3x - 6 - 9x + 3 = -6x - 3$. For choice (D), $x(x + 5) - x(x + 11) - 3 = x^2 + 5x - x^2 - 11x - 3 = -6x - 3$. Choice (A) simplifies to $-6x + 1$; choice (B) simplifies to $-6x - 13$; and choice (E) simplifies to $6x + 3$.

Later in this chapter and in later chapters, we will see more GRE comparison questions. For now, let's do trinomial factoring.

Factoring Trinomials

Factoring trinomials is a puzzle, a game that is rarely done well in high school and even more rarely practiced. Let's learn the factoring game.

First, let's rewrite the first four problems and solutions found in Example 5 (see page 57) backward and look at them.

A. $x^2 + 11x + 28 = (x + 7)(x + 4)$

B. $x^2 - 7x + 10 = (x - 5)(x - 2)$

C. $x^2 + 3x - 18 = (x + 6)(x - 3)$

D. $x^2 - 2x - 48 = (x + 6)(x - 8)$

Each term starts with x^2 ($= +1x^2$), so the first sign is $+$. We'll call the sign in front of the x term the middle sign, and we'll call the sign in front of the number term the last sign.

Let's look at **A** and **B** above to state some rules of the game:

1. If the last sign (in the trinomial) is $+$, then both signs (in the parentheses) must be the same. The reason? $(+) \times (+) = +$, and $(-) \times (-) = +$.
2. Only if the last sign is $+$, look at the sign of the middle term. If it is $+$, both factors have a $+$ sign (as in **A**); if it is $-$, both factors have a $-$ sign (as in **B**).
3. If the last sign is $-$, the signs in the two factors must be different.

Now, let's play the game,

Example 10: Factor: $x^2 - 16x + 15$.

Solution:

1. The last sign, "+", means both signs are the same. The middle sign, "−", means both are $-$.
2. The only factors of x^2 are $(x)(x)$. Look at the number term 15. The factors of 15 are (3)(5) and (1)(15). So $(x - 5)(x - 3)$ and $(x - 15)(x - 1)$ are the only possibilities. We have chosen the first and last terms to be correct, so we only do the middle term. The first, $-8x$, is wrong; the second, $-16x$, is correct.
3. The answer is $(x - 15)(x - 1)$. If neither worked, the trinomial couldn't be factored.

Example 11: Factor completely: $x^2 - 4x - 21$.

Solution:

1. Last sign negative means the signs in the factors are different.
2. $x^2 = x(x)$ and the factors of 21 are 7 and 3, or 1 and 21. We want the pair that totals the middle number, so 7 and 3 are correct; 7 gets the minus sign!
3. The answer is $(x - 7)(x + 3)$.

Note *If you multiply the inner and outer terms and get the right number but the wrong sign, both signs in the parentheses must be changed.*

The game gets more complicated if the coefficient of x^2 is not 1.

Example 12: Factor completely: $4x^2 + 4x - 15$.

Solution:

1. Last sign is $-$, so the signs of the factors must be different.
2. The factors of $4x^2$ are $(4x)(x)$ or $(2x)(2x)$.
3. The factors of -15 are 3 and 15 or 1 and 15. Let's write out all the possibilities and the resulting middle terms. We are looking for terms whose difference is $4x$.

   $(4x \_ 3)(x \_ 5)$; middle terms are $3x$ and $20x$, no way to get $4x$.

   $(4x \_ 5)(x \_ 3)$; middle terms are $5x$ and $12x$, and again, there is no way to get $4x$.

   $(4x \_ 15)(x \_ 1)$; middle terms are $15x$ and $4x$, wrong.

   $(4x \_ 1)(x \_ 15)$; middle terms are $1x$ and $60x$, the next county.

   $(2x \_ 1)(2x \_ 15)$; middle terms are $2x$ and $30x$, wrong again!

   $(2x \_ 3)(2x \_ 5)$; middle terms are $6x$ and $10x$, correct, whew!

4. The minus sign goes in front of the 3 and the plus sign goes in front of the 5. The answer is $(2x - 3)(2x + 5)$.

Example 13: Factor completely: $3x^2 + 15x + 12$

Solution: Take out the common factor first.

$3x^2 + 15x + 12 = 3(x^2 + 5x + 4) = 3(x + 4)(x + 1)$.

Example 14: Factor completely; coefficients may be integers only.

Problem	Solution
a. $x^2 + 11x + 24$	$(x + 3)(x + 8)$
b. $x^2 - 11x - 12$	$(x - 12)(x + 1)$
c. $x^2 + 5x - 6$	$(x + 6)(x - 1)$
d. $x^2 - 20x + 100$	$(x - 10)^2$
e. $x^2 - x - 2$	$(x - 2)(x + 1)$

f. $x^2 - 15x + 56$ $(x - 7)(x - 8)$

g. $x^2 + 8x + 16$ $(x + 4)^2$

h. $x^2 - 6x + 16$ $(x - 8)(x + 2)$

i. $x^2 - 17x + 42$ $(x - 14)(x - 3)$

j. $x^2 + 5xy + 6y^2$ $(x + 2y)(x + 3y)$

k. $3x^2 - 6x - 9$ $3(x - 3)(x + 1)$

l. $4x^2 + 16x - 20$ $4(x + 5)(x - 1)$

m. $x^3 - 12x^2 + 35x$ $x(x - 7)(x - 5)$

n. $2x^8 + 8x^7 + 6x^6$ $2x^6(x + 3)(x + 1)$

o. $x^4 - 10x^2 + 9$ $(x + 3)(x - 3)(x + 1)(x - 1)$

p. $x^4 - 8x^2 - 9$ $(x^2 + 1)(x + 3)(x - 3)$

q. $2x^2 - 5x + 3$ $(2x - 3)(x - 1)$

r. $2x^2 + 5x - 3$ $(2x - 1)(x + 3)$

s. $5x^2 - 11x + 2$ $(5x - 1)(x - 2)$

t. $9x^2 + 21x - 8$ $(3x + 8)(3x - 1)$

u. $3x^2 - 8x - 3$ $(3x + 1)(x - 3)$

v. $6x^2 - 13x + 6$ $(3x - 2)(2x - 3)$

w. $6x^2 + 35x - 6$ $(6x - 1)(x + 6)$

x. $9x^2 + 71x - 8$ $(9x - 1)(x + 8)$

y. $9x^4 + 24x^3 + 12x^2$ $3x^2(3x + 2)(x + 2)$

Q **Let's do a couple of exercises.**

Exercise 10: $x^2 + 5x + 4 = 27$; $3(x + 1)(x + 4) =$

A. 9

B. 24

C. 30

D. 81

E. 243

	Quantity A	Quantity B
Exercise 11: $x^2 + 11x + 24 = 0$	$x^2 + 11x$	24

Let's look at the answers.

Answer 10: The answer is (D). $x^2 + 5x + 4 = (x + 1)(x + 4) = 27$; $3(x + 1) \times (x + 4) = 3(27) = 81$.

Answer 11: The answer is (B). It looks like you have to factor but you don't. $(x^2 + 11x) + 24 = 0$; so $x^2 + 11x$ has to equal -24!

Again, later on, we will have more problems involving trinomial factoring.

ALGEBRAIC FRACTIONS

Except for adding and subtracting, the techniques for algebraic fractions are easy to understand. They must be practiced, however.

Reducing Fractions

Factor the top and bottom; cancel factors that are the same.

Example 15: Reduce the following fractions:

Problem	Solution
a. $\dfrac{x^2 - 9}{x^2 - 3x}$	$\dfrac{(x+3)(x-3)}{x(x-3)} = \dfrac{x+3}{x}$
b. $\dfrac{2x^3 + 10x^2 + 8x}{x^4 + x^3}$	$\dfrac{2x(x+4)(x+1)}{x^3(x+1)} = \dfrac{2(x+4)}{x^2}$
c. $\dfrac{x-9}{9-x}$	$\dfrac{(x-9)}{-1(x-9)} = -1$

Let's do some more exercises.

	Quantity A	Quantity B
Exercise 12:	$\dfrac{16x+4}{4}$	$4x$
Exercise 13:	$\dfrac{x^2-16}{x-4}$	$2x+4$
Exercise 14:	$\dfrac{2x^2+10x+12}{2x+6}$	x

Let's look at the answers.

Answer 12: The answer is (A). $\dfrac{16x+4}{4}=\dfrac{4(4x+1)}{4}=4x+1>4x$. Alternatively, $\dfrac{16x+4}{4}=\dfrac{16x}{4}+\dfrac{4}{4}=4x+1$.

Answer 13: The answer is (D). $\dfrac{(x+4)(x-4)}{x-4}=x+4$. Comparing $x+4$ to $2x+4$ or x to $2x$ is impossible, since we don't know if $x>0$, $x=0$, or $x<0$.

Answer 14: The answer is (A). $\dfrac{2(x+2)(x+3)}{2(x+3)}=\dfrac{2(x+2)}{2}=x+2>x$.

Multiplication and Division of Fractions

Algebraic fractions use the same principle as multiplication and division of numerical fractions except we factor all tops and bottoms, canceling one factor in any top with its equivalent in any bottom. In a division problem, we must remember to invert the second fraction first and then multiply.

Example 16: $\dfrac{x^2-25}{(x+5)^3}\times\dfrac{x^3+x^2}{x^2-4x-5}=$

Solution: $\dfrac{(x+5)(x-5)}{(x+5)(x+5)(x+5)}\times\dfrac{x^2(x+1)}{(x-5)(x+1)}=\dfrac{x^2}{(x+5)^2}$

Example 17: $\dfrac{x^4+4x^2}{x^6} \div \dfrac{x^4-16}{x^2+3x-10} =$

Solution: $\dfrac{x^2(x^2+4)}{x^6} \times \dfrac{(x+5)(x-2)}{(x^2+4)(x-2)(x+2)} = \dfrac{x+5}{x^4(x+2)}$

Adding and Subtracting Algebraic Fractions

It might be time to review the section in Chapter 2 on adding and subtracting fractions. Follow these steps:

1. If the bottoms are the same, add the tops, reducing if necessary.
2. If the bottoms are different, factor the denominators.
3. The LCD is the product of the most number of times a prime appears in any one denominator.
4. Multiply top and bottom by "what's missing."
5. Add (subtract) and simplify the numerators; reduce, if possible.

Example 18: $\dfrac{x}{36-x^2} - \dfrac{6}{36-x^2} =$

Solution: $\dfrac{x-6}{36-x^2} = \dfrac{x-6}{(6-x)(6+x)} = \dfrac{-1}{x+6}$

Example 19: $\dfrac{5}{12xy^3} + \dfrac{9}{8x^2y} =$

Solution: $\dfrac{5}{2\times2\times3xyyy} + \dfrac{9}{2\times2\times2xxy} = \dfrac{5(2x)}{2\times2\times2\times3xxyyy} +$

$\dfrac{9(3yy)}{2\times2\times2\times3xxyyy} = \dfrac{10x+27y^2}{24x^2y^3}$

Example 20: $\dfrac{2}{x^2+4x+4} + \dfrac{3}{x^2+x+6} =$

Solution: $\dfrac{2}{(x+2)(x+2)} + \dfrac{3}{(x+2)(x+3)} = \dfrac{2(x+3)}{(x+2)(x+2)(x+3)} +$

$\dfrac{3(x+2)}{(x+2)(x+3)(x+2)} = \dfrac{5x+12}{(x+2)(x+2)(x+3)}$

Simplifying Complex Fractions

This is a topic you can expect the GRE to cover quite a bit. Some examples will help you to understand how to simplify complex fractions.

Example 21: Simplify $\dfrac{2-\frac{5}{6}}{\frac{2}{3}+\frac{7}{8}}$

Solution: Find the LCD of all the terms (24) and multiply each term by it.

$$\frac{\frac{2}{1}\times\frac{24}{1}-\frac{5}{6}\times\frac{24}{1}}{\frac{2}{3}\times\frac{24}{1}+\frac{7}{8}\times\frac{24}{1}}=\frac{48-20}{16+21}=\frac{28}{37}$$

Note *When you multiply each term by 24, all the fractions disappear except for the major one.*

Example 22: Simplify $\dfrac{\frac{1}{y^2}-\frac{1}{z^2}}{\frac{1}{y}-\frac{1}{z}}$

Solution: The LCD is y^2z^2.

$$\frac{\frac{1}{y^2}\times\frac{y^2z^2}{1}-\frac{1}{z^2}\times\frac{y^2z^2}{1}}{\frac{1}{y}\times\frac{y^2z^2}{1}-\frac{1}{z}\times\frac{y^2z^2}{1}}=\frac{z^2-y^2}{yz^2-y^2z}=\frac{(z-y)(z+y)}{yz(z-y)}=\frac{z+y}{yz}$$

This is my favorite problem in the whole world because it is relatively short but calls on lots of skills. I've noticed it's a favorite of a number of other authors.

Example 23: Simplify $\dfrac{1-\frac{25}{x^2}}{1-\frac{10}{x}+\frac{25}{x^2}}$

Solution: The LCD is x^2.

$$\frac{x^2\left(1-\frac{25}{x^2}\right)}{x^2\left(1-\frac{10}{x}+\frac{25}{x^2}\right)}=\frac{x^2-25}{x^2-10x+25}=\frac{(x+5)(x-5)}{(x-5)(x-5)}=\frac{x+5}{x-5}$$

Let's do some more exercises.

Exercise 15: The reciprocal of $2 - \frac{1}{4}$ is

A. $\frac{1}{2} - 4$

B. $-\frac{4}{7}$

C. $-\frac{4}{9}$

D. $\frac{4}{9}$

E. $\frac{4}{7}$

Exercise 16: $x, y, z > 0.\ x + \dfrac{1}{y + \frac{1}{z}} =$

A. $\dfrac{x+y}{z}$

B. $\dfrac{xyz + y + z}{yz}$

C. $\dfrac{xz + yz + 1}{yz}$

D. $\dfrac{x+y+z}{xyz+1}$

E. $\dfrac{xyz + x + z}{yz + 1}$

Exercise 17: $y = \frac{1}{x}$. Then $\dfrac{1-x}{1-y} =$

A. $-x$

B. x

C. 1

D. $(1 - x)$

E. $(x - 1)$

	Quantity A	**Quantity B**
Exercise 18:	$\dfrac{1}{6 + \dfrac{1}{3 + \frac{1}{2}}}$	$\dfrac{1}{2 + \dfrac{1}{5 + \frac{1}{4}}}$
Exercise 19:	$\dfrac{5}{3 - \frac{3}{2}} + \dfrac{5}{\frac{3}{2} - 3}$	0

Let's look at the answers.

Answer 15: The answer is (E). $2-\frac{1}{4}=\frac{7}{4}$. Its reciprocal is $\frac{4}{7}$.

Answer 16: The answer is (E).

$$x+\frac{z\times 1}{z\left(y+\frac{1}{z}\right)}=\frac{x}{1}+\frac{z}{yz+1}=\frac{x}{1}\times\frac{yz+1}{yz+1}+\frac{z}{yz+1}=\frac{xyz+x+z}{yz+1}.$$

Answer 17: The answer is (A). $\frac{1-x}{1-y}=\frac{1-x}{1-\frac{1}{x}}=\frac{x(1-x)}{x\left(1-\frac{1}{x}\right)}=\frac{x(1-x)}{(x-1)}=-x$ since $\frac{1-x}{x-1}=-1$. The secret of this problem is *not* to multiply out the top.

Answer 18: The answer is (B). This looks like Exercise 16, and it can be done that way. However, there is a much easier way. Fraction A is $\frac{1}{6+m}$, where $0<m<1$. So $\frac{1}{7}<A<\frac{1}{6}$. Fraction B is $\frac{1}{2+n}$, where $0<n<1$. So $\frac{1}{3}<B<\frac{1}{2}$. B is larger. Again, the idea is to do as little arithmetic as possible.

Answer 19: The answer is (C). Again, the problem looks like simplifying a complex fraction. However, the first fraction in A is the negative of the second fraction. When added, the sum is 0.

RELATIONS AND FUNCTIONS

The new GRE contains questions on the topics of relations and functions. A **relation** is any general set of ordered pairs (x, y). Although x and y may represent any quantities, our discussion here is restricted to real numbers. For example, three relations, identified as sets A, B, and C, could be $A = \{(1, 3), (1, 4), (5, 9), (2, 7)\}$, $B = \{(4, 8), (6, 8), (7, 3)\}$, and $C = \{(0, 0), (2, 5)\}$. Note that the number of elements in sets A, B, and C is 4, 3, and 2, respectively.

A **function** is a set of ordered pairs (x, y) such that for each x value there is exactly one y value. This means that every function must be a relation, but not vice versa.

Therefore, sets B and C shown above qualify as functions. In set B, although the y value of 8 is repeated, it is associated with two different x values. But set A is not a function because the x value of 1 is matched with two different y values, namely 3 and 4.

For every relation (as well as every function), the set of x values is called the **domain** and the set of y values is called the **range**. Thus, the domain of set A is {1, 5, 2} and the range of set B is {8, 3}.

There are several notes about sets that we should mention.

1. In writing the elements of a set, order is not important. Set {8, 3} is equivalent to {3, 8}. But be careful! The ordered pair (1, 2) is *not* identical to (2, 1).
2. It is not necessary to repeat elements of a set. Thus, {2, 3, 4, 3, 4, 6} is equivalent to {2, 3, 4, 6}. Both sets contain four elements.
3. For any given relation, a domain and range may contain common elements, as shown in set C above. Both domain and range contain 0.
4. Pictorially, a relation is a function if and only if no vertical line crosses its graph more than once. If a vertical line crosses the graph twice, then the two points of intersection would have the same x values but different y values. This would violate the definition of a function.
5. A function is often written in terms of the domain. The most commonly used letters to designate a function are f, g, h, F, G, and H. As an example, given the function described as $y = 2x - 1$, we could write $f(x) = 2x - 1$. Then the notation $f(3)$ would symbolize the y value when $x = 3$. For this example, $f(3) = (2)(3) - 1 = 5$. So, the ordered pair (3, 5) lies on the graph of $f(x)$.

Q Let's do some exercises.

Exercise 20: If $F(x) = x^2 + 3x + 10$, and the domain is {5, 4, 0}, what is the sum of all the range values?

Exercise 21: Which of the following represent functions? Indicate *all* correct answers.

A. {(0, 4), (4, 0), (0, −4)}

B. {(1, 1), (2, 3), (1, 2)}

C. {(8, 5), (8, 1)}

D. {(2, 5), (5, 7), (7, 2), (5, 3)}

E. {(0, 0), (0, 2)}

F. {(4, 6), (5, 6), (9, 6)}

Exercise 22: Given that $f(x) = x^2 + 5x + 6$, then $f(x) = 2$ for which values of x? Indicate *all* correct answers.

A. −4

B. −3

C. −2

D. −1

E. 0

F. 20

For Exercises 23, 24, $f(x) = \dfrac{x^2 - 5x - 6}{x^3 + 3x^2 + 2x}$.

Exercise 23: For which values of x does $f(x) = 0$? Indicate *all* correct answers.

A. -6
B. -3
C. -1
D. 0
E. 1
F. 3
G. 6

Exercise 24: For which values of x is $f(x)$ undefined? Indicate *all* correct answers.

A. -3
B. -2
C. -1
D. 0
E. 1
F. 2
G. 3

Exercise 25: Given $g(x) = 2x^2 + 3x + 4$, what is the value of $g\left(\dfrac{1}{4}\right)$?

Exercise 26: Given $h(x) = 2x^2 + 5x + 3$, what is the product of the zeros of $h(x)$?

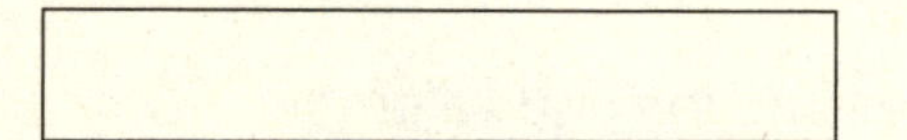

Let's look at the answers.

Answer 20: The correct answer is 98. We need to calculate the sum $F(5) + F(4) + F(0)$. $F(5) = 5^2 + (3)(5) + 10 = 25 + 15 + 10 = 50$, $F(4) = 4^2 + (3)(4) + 10 = 16 + 12 + 10 = 38$, and $F(0) = 0^2 + (3)(0) + 10 = 10$. The sum of 50, 38, and 10 is 98.

Answer 21: The correct answer is (F). Each of the domain values 4, 5, and 9 correspond to exactly one range value. In answer choice (F), it happens that the only range value is 6. In each of the other answer choices, there is a domain value that corresponds to two different range values. For example, in answer choice (A), the x value of 0 corresponds to y values of 4 and -4. In answer choice (B), the x value of 1 corresponds to y values of 1 and 2. In answer choice (D), the x value of 5 corresponds to y values of 7 and 3. Each of the answer choices (C) and (E) shows only a single x value that corresponds to two different y values.

Answer 22: The correct answers are (A) and (D). By substitution, $2 = x^2 + 5x + 6$, which becomes $0 = x^2 + 5x + 4$. Then, by factoring, we get $0 = (x + 1)(x + 4)$, which means that $x + 1 = 0$ or $x + 4 = 0$. Therefore, $x = -1$ or $x = -4$ only.

Answer 23: The correct answers are (C) and (G). If $f(x) = 0$, then the numerator must be zero. So $x^2 - 5x - 6 = 0$, which becomes $(x - 6)(x + 1) = 0$. Either $x - 6 = 0$ or $x + 1 = 0$. Thus, $x = 6$ or $x = -1$.

Answer 24: The correct answers are (B), (C), and (D). If the denominator is zero, then the function is undefined. This means that $x^3 + 3x^2 + 2x = 0$. So $(x)(x + 1)(x + 2) = 0$, which implies that $x = 0$, $x + 1 = 0$, or $x + 2 = 0$. Thus, the three solutions are 0, -1, or -2.

Answer 25: The correct answer is $\frac{39}{8}$. By substitution, $g\left(\frac{1}{4}\right) = 2\left(\frac{1}{4}\right)^2 + 3\left(\frac{1}{4}\right) + 4 = 2\left(\frac{1}{16}\right) + \frac{3}{4} + 4 = \frac{1}{8} + \frac{3}{4} + 4 = 4\frac{7}{8}$. You can change $4\frac{7}{8}$ to its improper fraction equivalent of $\frac{39}{8}$.

Answer 26: The correct answer is $\frac{3}{2}$. The zeros of $h(x)$ are found by solving $0 = 2x^2 + 5x + 3$. By factoring, we get $(2x + 3)(x + 1) = 0$. Then either $2x + 3 = 0$ or $x + 1 = 0$. Thus, the two solutions are $-\frac{3}{2}$ and -1, and their product is $\frac{3}{2}$.

TRANSFORMATIONS

A **family of functions** refers to a basic function, such as $f(x) = x$, and all related functions. For $f(x) = x$, the related functions would include equations such as $f(x) = x - 7$, $f(x) = 3x$, and $f(x) = 4x + 11$. The process by which we discover related functions, given a specific basic function, is called a **transformation**.

The first transformation for our discussion involves the change from $f(x)$ to $f(x) + k$, where k is a constant. For example, using $f(x) = x$, let the function $g(x) = f(x) + 5 = x + 5$. The graphs of the two functions are shown below.

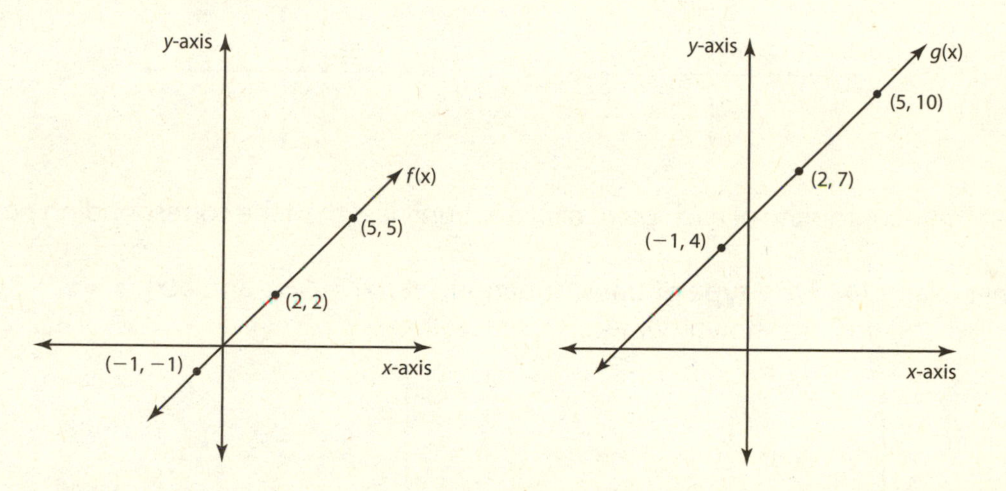

In this example, notice that the y-coordinate of each point of $g(x)$ is 5 units larger than the corresponding y-coordinate of each point of $f(x)$.

For another example of this type of transformation, let $f(x) = x^3$ and $g(x) = x^3 - 2$. The graphs of these two functions are shown below.

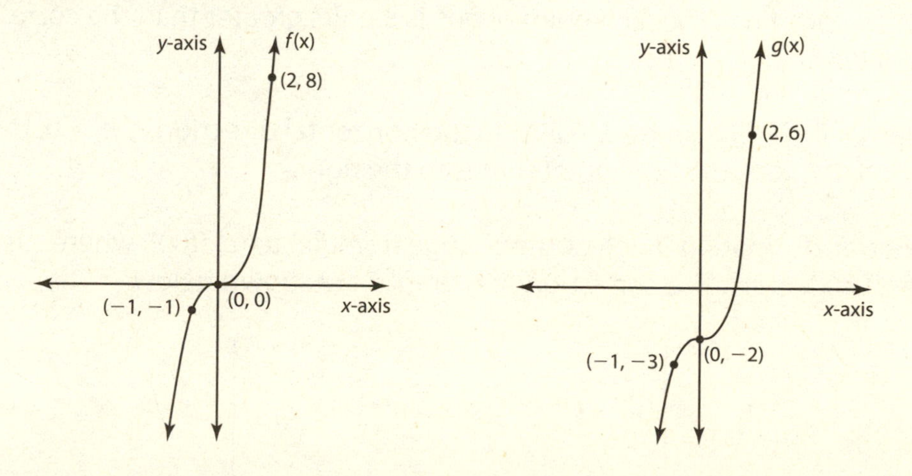

For this example, the y-coordinate of each point of $g(x)$ is 2 units less than the corresponding y-coordinate of $f(x)$.

Thus, the graph of $g(x) = f(x) + k$ is shifted k units in the vertical direction. If $k > 0$, the vertical shift is upward; if $k < 0$, the vertical shift is downward.

A second type of transformation involves the change from $f(x)$ to $f(x + h)$, where h is a constant. For example, let $f(x) = x^4$ and let $g(x) = (x + 1)^4$. Each of these functions is graphed below.

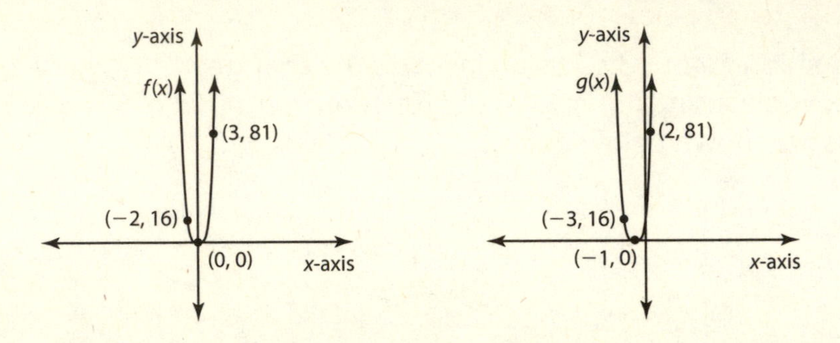

Notice that the x-coordinate of each point of $g(x)$ is 1 unit less than the corresponding point of $f(x)$.

For another example of this type of transformation, let $f(x) = \sqrt{x}$ and $g(x) = \sqrt{x - 3}$. The graphs of $f(x)$ and $g(x)$ are shown below.

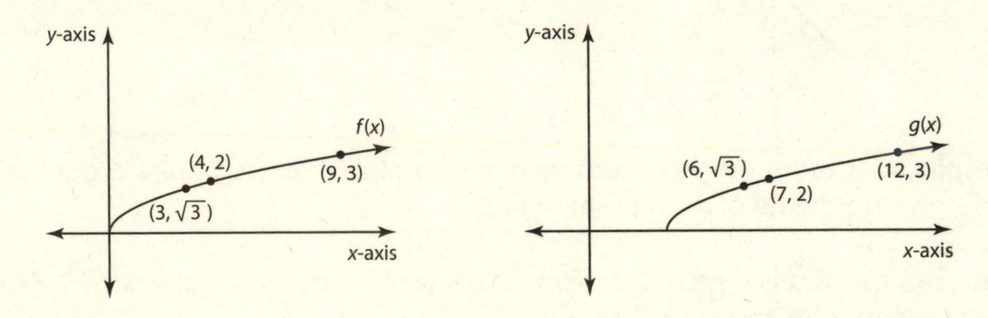

Notice that the x-coordinate of each point of $g(x)$ is 3 units greater than the corresponding x-coordinate of $f(x)$.

Thus, the graph of $f(x + h)$ is shifted h units in the horizontal direction. If $h > 0$, the horizontal shift is to the left; if $h < 0$, the horizontal shift is to the right.

A third type of transformation involves the change from $f(x)$ to $(c)(f(x))$, where c is a constant. Let $f(x) = x^2$ and $g(x) = 3x^2$. The corresponding graphs are shown below.

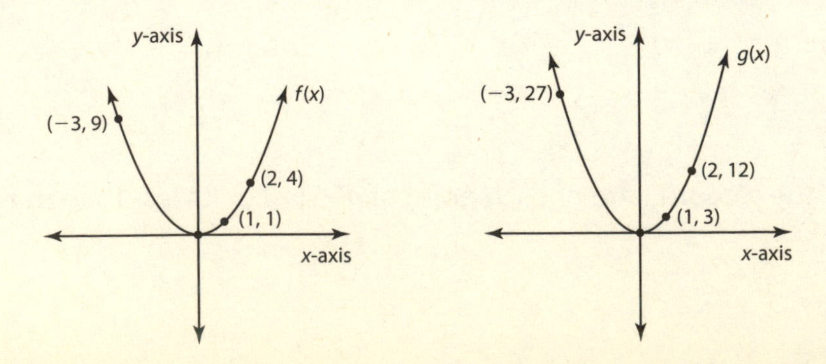

Notice that the y-coordinate of each point of $g(x)$ is three times as large as the corresponding y-coordinate of $f(x)$.

For another example, in which c is a negative number, let $f(x) = \frac{1}{x}$ and $g(x) = \frac{-5}{x}$. A few selected points are shown below for each graph.

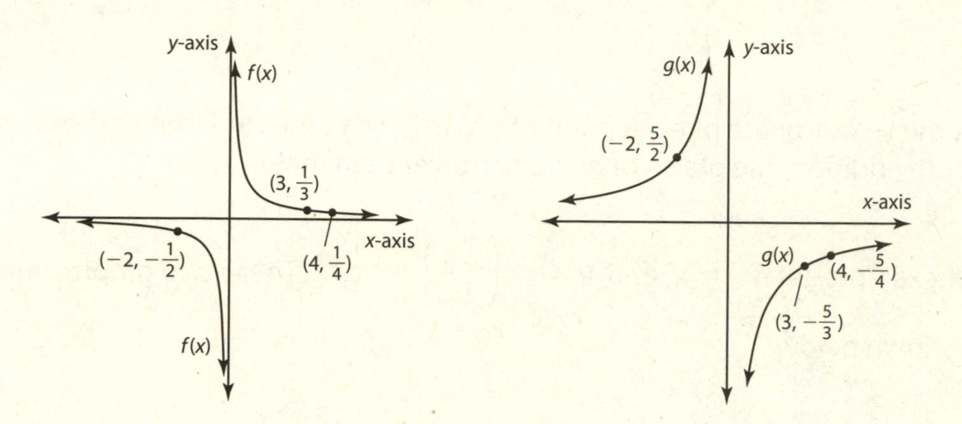

Notice that the y-coordinate of each point of $g(x)$ is negative five times as large as the corresponding point of $f(x)$.

As a special case of this type of transformation, consider the value of c to be -1. Then we would compare the graph of $f(x)$ with that of $(-1)(f(x))$. We would discover that the graph of $(-1)(f(x))$ would be the reflection of the graph of $f(x)$ over the x-axis. For example, the graphs of $f(x) = \frac{1}{x}$ and $g(x) = \frac{-1}{x}$ are shown below.

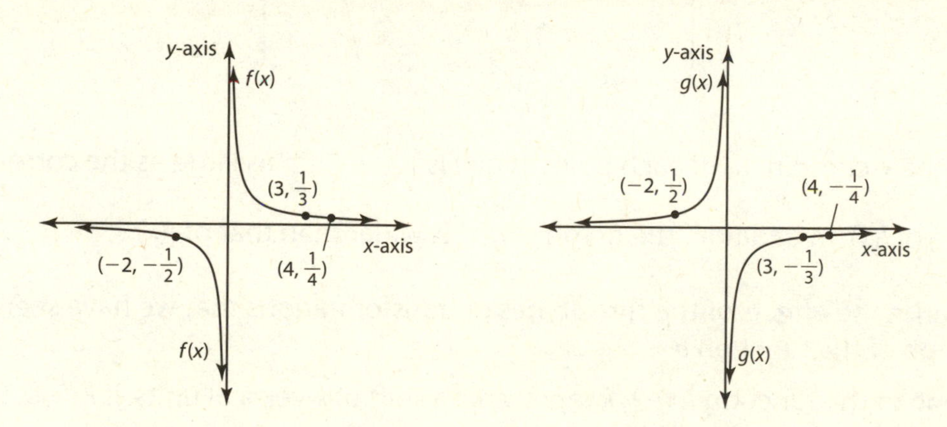

The fourth (and last) type of transformation that we will discuss involves the change from $f(x)$ to $f(bx)$, where b is a constant. For example, let $f(x) = x^2$ and $g(x) = (2x)^2 = 4x^2$. These two functions are shown on the next page.

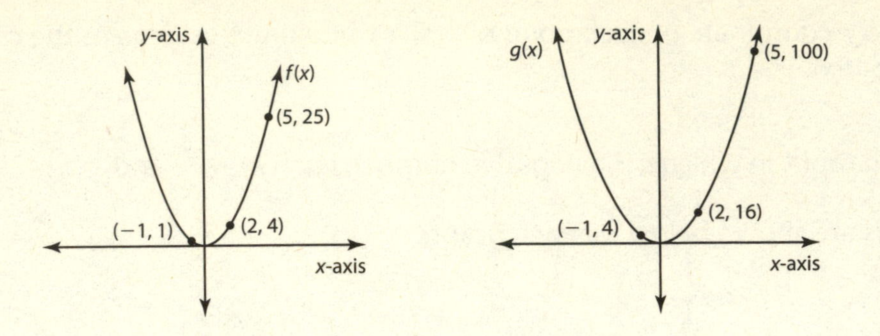

Notice that the y-coordinate of each point of $g(x)$ is $2^2 = 4$ times as large as the corresponding point of $f(x)$. In addition, the graph of $g(x)$ is narrower than that of $f(x)$.

For another example, let $f(x) = x^3$ and $g(x) = \left(\frac{1}{2}x\right)^3 = \frac{1}{8}x^3$. These two graphs, with selected points, are shown below.

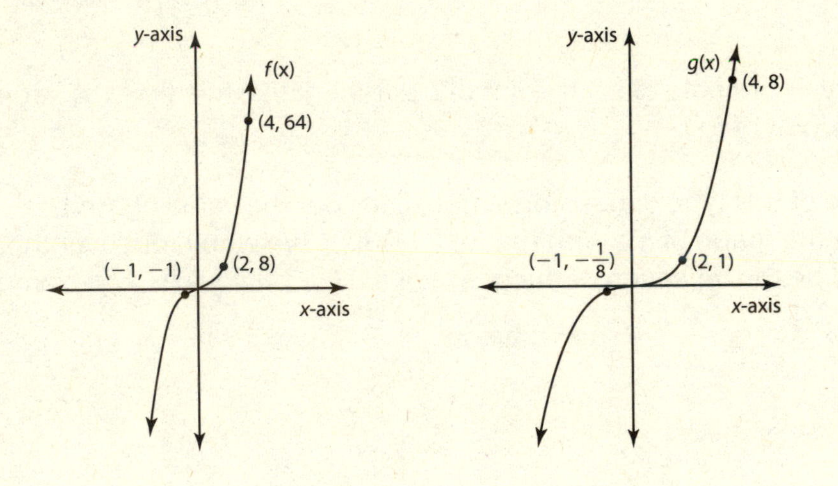

Notice that the y-coordinate of each point of $g(x)$ is $\left(\frac{1}{2}\right)^3 = \frac{1}{8}$ as large as the corresponding y-coordinate of $f(x)$. In addition, the graph of $g(x)$ is wider than that of $f(x)$.

Let's summarize the effects of the three types of transformations that we have seen. We start with the graph of the function $f(x)$.

1. The graph of the function $f(x) + k$ represents a shift of k vertical units. If $k > 0$, the shift is upward; if $k < 0$, the shift is downward.
2. The graph of the function $f(x + h)$ represents a shift of h horizontal units. If $h > 0$, the shift is to the left; if $h < 0$, the shift is to the right.

3. For the graph of the function $(c)(f(x))$, and for a given x value, the y-coordinate of each point is c times the corresponding y-coordinate of $f(x)$. In particular, if $c = -1$, the graph of $(c)(f(x))$ is a reflection across the x-axis of the graph of $f(x)$.
4. For the graph of the function $f(bx)$, and for a given x value, the y-coordinate of each point is b^n times the corresponding y-coordinate of $f(x)$, where the letter n represents the degree of $f(x)$. As an example, if the degree of $f(x)$ is 2 and $b = 5$, each y-coordinate of $f(x)$ would be multiplied by $5^2 = 25$ for a given x value. In addition, if $|b| > 1$, the graph of $f(bx)$ is narrower than that of $f(x)$. If $|b| < 1$, then the graph of $f(bx)$ is wider than that of $f(x)$.

Q **Let's do a few exercises on transformations.**

Exercise 27: Each point of the graph of the function $f(x) = x^5$ is shifted 6 units to the left to create the graph of the function $g(x)$. Which of the following describes $g(x)$?

A. $x^5 + 6$

B. $x^5 - 6$

C. $(x + 6)^5$

D. $(x - 6)^5$

E. $6x^5$

Exercise 28: Each point of the graph of $f(x) = \frac{1}{x}$ is shifted 8 units downward to create the graph of $g(x)$. Which of the following describes $g(x)$?

A. $\frac{8}{x}$

B. $\frac{1}{8x}$

C. $\frac{1}{x} + 8$

D. $\frac{1}{x - 8}$

E. $\frac{1}{x} - 8$

Exercise 29: Each point of the graph of $f(x) = x^2$ is shifted 5 units to the right and 1 unit upward to create the graph of $g(x)$. Which of the following describes $g(x)$?

A. $(x - 5)^2 + 1$

B. $(x - 5) - 1$

C. $5x^2 - 1$

D. $(x + 5)^2 - 1$

E. $(x + 5)^2 + 1$

Exercise 30: Given the functions $f(x) = x^4$ and $g(x) = (3x)^4$, which statements are true concerning their graphs? Indicate *all* correct answers.

A. $g(x)$ is narrower than $f(x)$.

B. $g(x)$ is wider than $f(x)$.

C. $g(x)$ represents a shift of 3 units to the right of each point of $f(x)$.

D. $g(x)$ represents a shift of 3 units to the left of each point of $f(x)$.

E. For a given x value, each y-coordinate of $g(x)$ is 12 times as large as the corresponding y-coordinate of $f(x)$.

F. For a given x value, each y-coordinate of $g(x)$ is 81 times as large as the corresponding y-coordinate of $f(x)$.

Exercise 31: Given the graph of $f(x) = x^2$, which of the following describe graphs of functions that are wider than $f(x)$? Indicate *all* correct answers.

A. $g(x) = 7x^2$

B. $g(x) = (x + 4)^2$

C. $g(x) = (x - 9)^2$

D. $g(x) = \frac{1}{3}x^2$

E. $g(x) = (4x)^2$

F. $g(x) = (0.6x)^2$

Let's look at the answers.

Answer 27: The answer is (C). The function $f(x + h)$, where $h > 0$, represents a shift of h units to the left. Since $h = 6$, the shift is 6 units to the left.

Answer 28: The answer is (E). The function $f(x) + k$, where $k < 0$, represents a shift of k units downward. Since $k = -8$, the shift is 8 units downward.

Answer 29: The answer is (A). The function $f(x + h) + k$, where $h < 0$ and $k > 0$ represents a shift of h units to the right and k units upward. Since $h = -5$ and $k = 1$, the shift is 5 units to the right and 1 unit upward.

Answer 30: The correct answers are (A) and (F). We can write $g(x) = (3x)^4 = 81x^4$. The graph of the function $g(bx)$, where $|b| > 1$, is narrower than that of the graph of $g(x)$. In addition, for any given x value, the y-coordinate of $g(x)$ is $3^4 = 81$ times as large as the corresponding y-coordinate of $f(x)$.

Answer 31: The correct answers are (D) and (F). The graph of a function in the form $f(bx)$ will be wider than the graph of $f(x)$ whenever $|b| < 1$. In answer choice (D), $b = \frac{1}{3}$; in answer choice (F), $b = (0.6)^2 = 0.36$.

Absolute Value Function

Two important functions that utilize the concepts of transformations are the absolute value function and the parabola.

The **absolute value function**, denoted as $f(x) = |x|$, is defined as follows:

$f(x) = \begin{cases} x, & \text{if } x \geq 0 \\ -x, & \text{if } x < 0 \end{cases}$. The graph of $f(x) = |x|$ is shown below, with selected points.

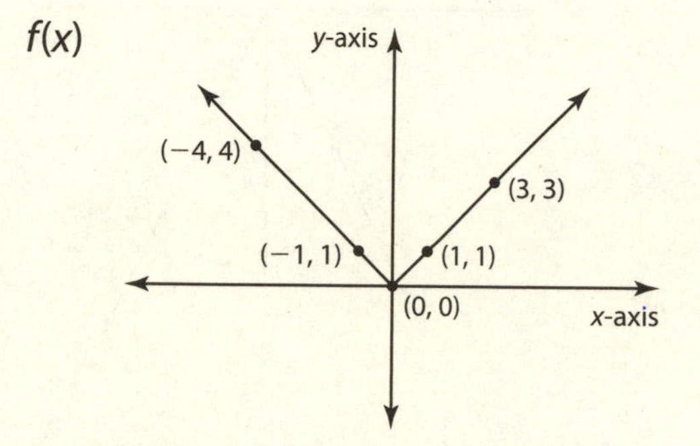

Now consider the function $g(x) = |x| - 4$, whose graph is shown below.

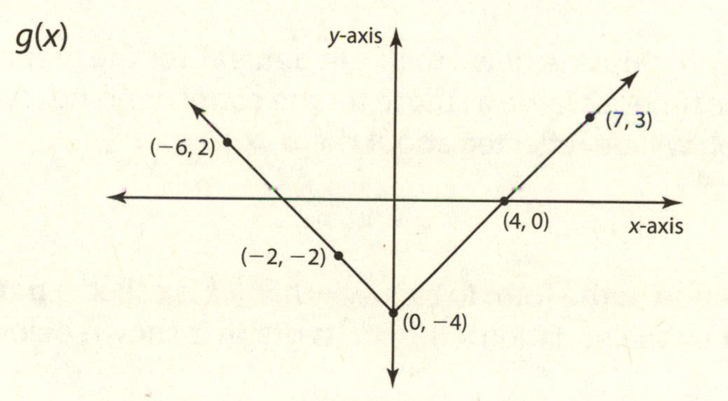

Although we have chosen a different set of x values for the points shown in the above two graphs, notice that the graph of $f(x)$ has been shifted 4 units downward to create the graph of $g(x)$.

In general, the graph of $g(x) = |x| + k$ will represent a vertical shift of k units from the graph of $f(x)$. If $k > 0$, the shift is upward; if $k < 0$, the shift is downward.

Let's consider the function $g(x) = |x + 3|$, whose graph is shown below.

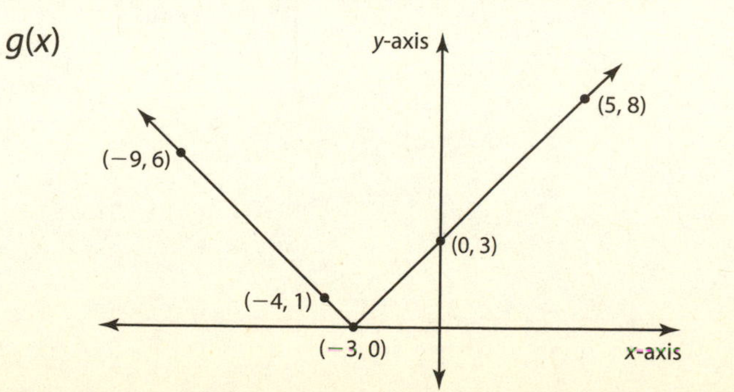

We notice that the graph of $g(x)$ is shifted 3 units to the left of $f(x) = |x|$. In general, the graph of $g(x) = |x + h|$ will be shifted horizontally h units from the graph of $f(x) = |x|$. If $h > 0$, the shift will be to the left; if $h < 0$, the shift will be to the right.

As our third illustration of transformations involving the absolute value function, consider the graph of $g(x) = (-2)(|x|)$, shown below.

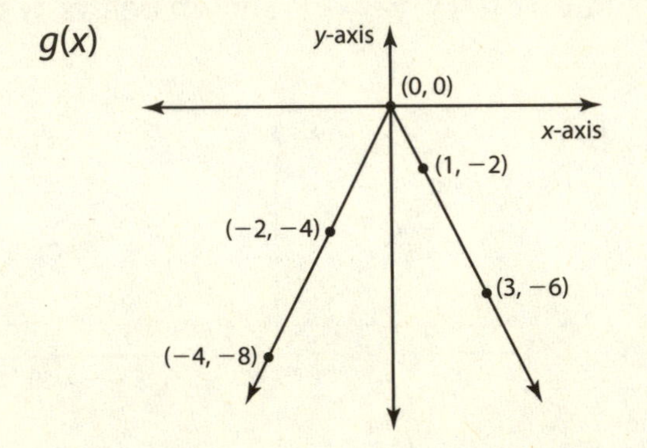

When compared to the graph of $f(x) = |x|$, we observe that the y-coordinate of each point (for a specified x value) is twice as large as the corresponding y-coordinate of $f(x)$.

Note also that the graph is upside down to $f(x)$. In general, for the graph of $g(x) = (c)(|x|)$, the y-coordinates will be c times as large as those for the corresponding x values of $f(x)$. In addition, if $c < 0$, the graph will be reflected about the x-axis.

Parabolas

The graph of any function in the form $f(x) = a(x - h)^2 + k$ is called a **parabola**. Let's first look at the parabola given by the equation $f(x) = x^2$. Its graph is shown below, with selected points.

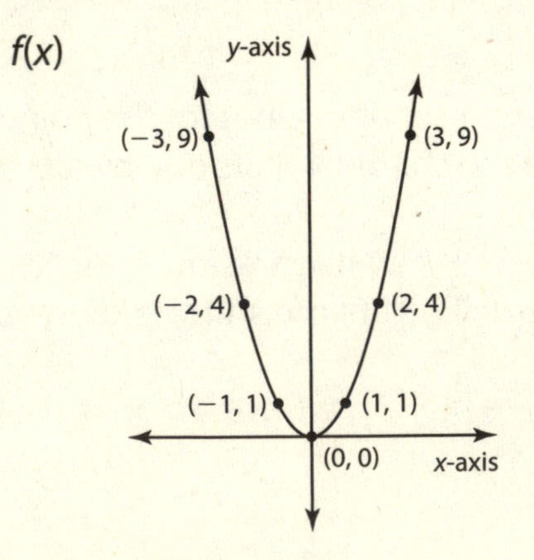

Now let's consider the function $g(x) = x^2 + 3$, whose graph is shown below.

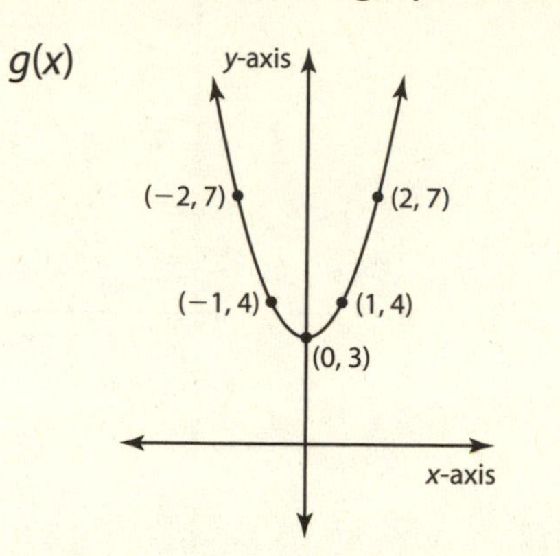

When compared to the graph of $f(x) = x^2$, we notice that it has been shifted 3 units upward. This result should come as no surprise, based on our previous discussions of the sections on transformations and absolute value functions. The point (0, 0) is called the vertex. For the graph of each parabola, the **vertex** represents either the highest or the lowest point.

We now consider the function $g(x) = (x + 2)^2$, which we will graph by using the five x values of −4, −3, −2, −1, and 0. The corresponding y values are found, and the graph is plotted as shown below.

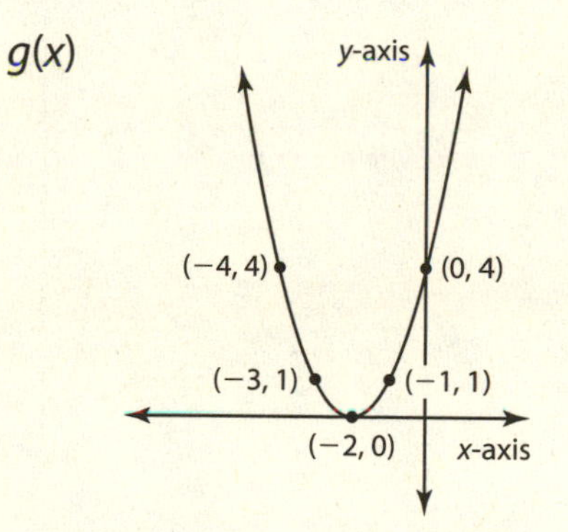

This graph represents a shift of 2 horizontal units to the left from the graph of $f(x)$.

Suppose we are given the function $g(x) = 2(x - 1)^2 - 5$. If we use the x values of, −1, 0, 1, 2, and 3, we determine the corresponding y values of 3, −3, −5, −3, and 3, respectively. The graph of $g(x)$ is shown below. Note that the vertex is located at (1, −5), or is shifted 1 unit to the right and 5 units down from the graph of $f(x) = x^2$. Also, the graph is half as wide as that for $f(x)$, corresponding to the coefficient 2 at the beginning of the function.

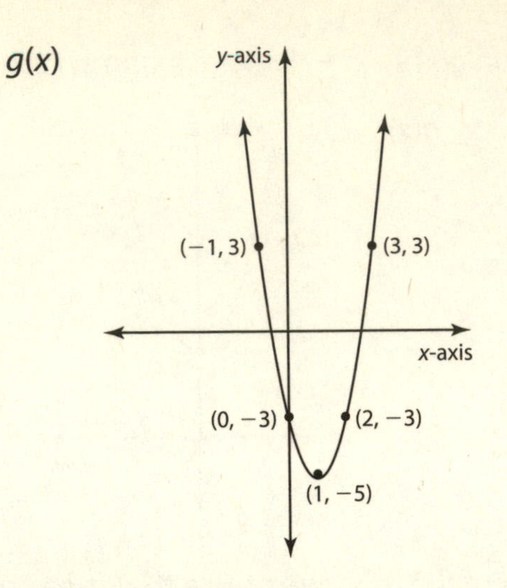

For our next graph, let's consider the function $g(x) = -1(x + 4)^2 - 2$. We'll use the x values of $-7, -6, -4, -2$, and -1. The corresponding y values are $-11, -6, -2, -6$, and -11, respectively. The graph is shown below.

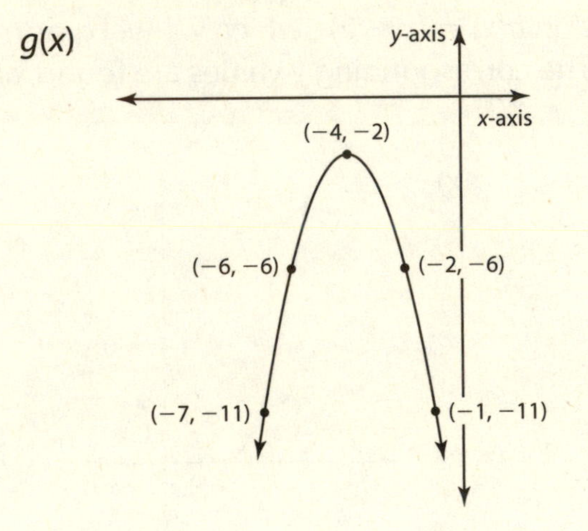

Notice that the vertex is located at $(-4, -2)$ and that this graph appears "upside down" from the graph of $f(x)$ because the coefficient of x^2 is negative. Thus, the vertex is the highest point of the graph.

The next illustrative graph of a parabola is for the function $g(x) = -3(x - 2)^2 + 1$. Using the x values of 0, 1, 2, 3, and 4, the corresponding y values are $-11, -2, 1, -2$, and -11, respectively. The graph appears below.

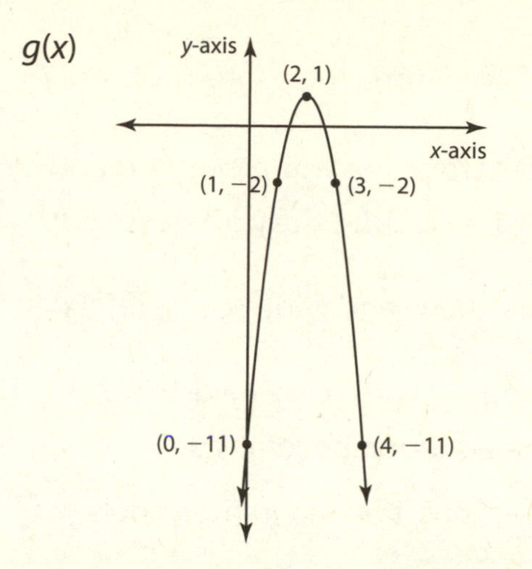

Similar to the previous graph, we observe that the vertex, which is located at (2, 1), is the highest point.

The following rules govern the graph of a parabola given the form $f(x) = a(x - h)^2 + k$, where a, h, and k are constants.

1. The vertex is located at (h, k).
2. The vertex is the highest point of the graph if $a < 0$.
3. The vertex is the lowest point of the graph if $a > 0$.
4. The larger the absolute value of a, the narrower the graph.

Sometimes the equation of a parabola is given in the form $f(x) = ax^2 + bx + c$, where a, b, and c are constants and $a \neq 0$. In this form, we can easily locate the y-intercept and any x-intercepts. The y-intercept is found by assigning the value 0 to x. The x-intercepts (if they exist) are found by replacing $f(x)$ with 0 and then solving for x.

Example 24: What are the x- and y-intercepts for $f(x) = 9 - x^2$?

Solution: To find the x-intercepts, we write $0 = 9 - x^2$, which can be factored as $0 = (3 - x)(3 + x)$. The solutions are thus $3 - x = 0$ or $3 + x = 0$, or $x = 3$ or -3, which means that the x-intercepts are (3, 0) and (−3, 0). The y-intercept is found by replacing x with 0, which leads to $9 - 0^2 = 9$. Therefore, the y-intercept is (0, 9).

Example 25: What are the x- and y-intercepts for $f(x) = 2x^2 + 3x + 1$?

Solution: To find the x-intercept, replace $f(x)$ with 0, so that $0 = 2x^2 + 3x + 1$. Factoring the right side of this equation, we get $0 = (2x + 1)(x + 1)$. Then either $2x + 1 = 0$ or $x + 1 = 0$, which means that $x = -\frac{1}{2}$ or

$x = -1$. Therefore, the x-intercepts are $(-\frac{1}{2}, 0)$ and $(-1, 0)$. The y-coordinate of the y-intercept is found by substituting $x = 0$: $(2)(0)^2 + (3)(0) + 1 = 1$. Thus, the y-intercept is $(0, 1)$.

Example 26: What are the x- and y-intercepts for $f(x) = 9x^2 + 12x + 4$?

Solution: Replacing $f(x)$ with 0, we have $0 = 9x^2 + 12x + 4$. By factoring the right side, the equation becomes $0 = (3x + 2)^2$. Then $3x + 2 = 0$, so $x = -\frac{2}{3}$. Thus, the only x-intercept is $(-\frac{2}{3}, 0)$. The y-intercept is found by replacing x by 0: $(9)(0) - (12)(0) + 4 = 4$. Thus, the y-intercept is $(0, 4)$.

Let's try some exercises on the absolute value function and on the parabola.

Exercise 32: Given the function $f(x) = |x|$, the function $g(x)$ is created by moving each point of $f(x)$ 10 units downward. Which of the following correctly describes $g(x)$?

A. $|x - 10|$

B. $|x + 10|$

C. $\frac{1}{10}|x|$

D. $|x| - 10$

E. $|x| + 10$

Exercise 33: Given the function $f(x) = |x|$, the function $h(x)$ is created by moving each point of $f(x)$ 9 units to the left and 7 units upward. Which of the following correctly describes $h(x)$?

A. $9|x| + 7$

B. $|x + 7| + 9$

C. $|x - 9| + 7$

D. $|x - 7| + 9$

E. $|x + 9| + 7$

Exercise 34: Which of the following functions lie *completely* above the x-axis, and do *not* touch it? Indicate *all* correct answers.

A. $g(x) = |x - 4| + 1$

B. $g(x) = |x - 3|$

C. $g(x) = |x + 5| + 8$

D. $g(x) = |x + 7| - 2$

E. $g(x) = (4)(|x - 10|) + 3$

F. $g(x) = (5)(|x - 12|) - 6$

Exercise 35: The graph of which of the following functions contains exactly one x-intercept? Indicate *all* correct answers.

A. $f(x) = 4x^2 - 28x + 49$

B. $f(x) = 9x^2 + 6x + 1$

C. $f(x) = x^2 - 10x + 24$

D. $f(x) = 25x^2 - 4$

E. $f(x) = 16x^2 - 24x + 9$

F. $f(x) = x^2 + 20x + 100$

Exercise 36: What is the *smaller* of the x-coordinates of the two x-intercepts for the graph of $f(x) = 2x^2 + 3x - 5$?

Exercise 37: What is the product of the x-coordinates of the two x-intercepts for the graph of $f(x) = 3x^2 + 19x + 20$? Be sure to write your answer as a ratio of integers.

Let's look at the answers.

Answer 32: The answer is (D). The graph of $f(x) + k$ represents a vertical transformation of the graph of $f(x)$. If the transformation is 10 units downward, $k = -10$.

Answer 33: The answer is (E). The graph of $f(x + h) + k$ represents a horizontal shift of h units and a vertical shift of k units. If $h > 0$, the shift is to the left. If $k > 0$, the shift is upward. For this exercise, $h = 9$ and $k = 7$.

Answer 34: The correct answers are (A), (C), and (E). The vertices for these graphs are (4, 1), (−5, 8), and (10, 3), respectively. Each of these vertices lies above the x-axis. Since each vertex represents the lowest point of the corresponding graph, the graphs do not cross the x-axis. Note that answer choice (B) is wrong because the vertex (3, 0) lies on the x-axis.

Answer 35: The correct answers are (A), (B), (E), and (F). The factored forms of these answer choices are: $f(x) = 2x - 7)^2$; $f(x) = (3x + 1)^2$; $f(x) = (4x - 3)^2$; and $f(x) = (x + 10)^2$, respectively. Consequently, each of these choices has only one x-intercept. The x-intercepts for answer choices (A), (B), (E), and (F) are $(\frac{7}{2}, 0)$, $(-\frac{1}{3}, 0)$, $(\frac{3}{4}, 0)$, and $(-10, 0)$, respectively. Answer choices (C) and (D) both contain two x-intercepts.

Answer 36: The correct answer is -2.5. Substituting 0 for $f(x)$ and factoring the right side, we have $0 = (2x + 5)(x - 1)$. This leads to the equations $2x + 5 = 0$ and $x - 1 = 0$. Thus, the two x-coordinates of the x-intercepts are -2.5 and 1, of which the smaller value is -2.5.

Answer 37: The correct answer is $\frac{20}{3}$. Substituting 0 for $f(x)$ and factoring the right side, we have $0 = (3x + 4)(x + 5)$. Then $3x + 4 = 0$ or $x + 5 = 0$. The two x values are $-\frac{4}{3}$ and -5, so the product is $(-\frac{4}{3})(-5) = \frac{20}{3}$.

CHAPTER 6: *First-Degree and Quadratic Equations and Inequalities*

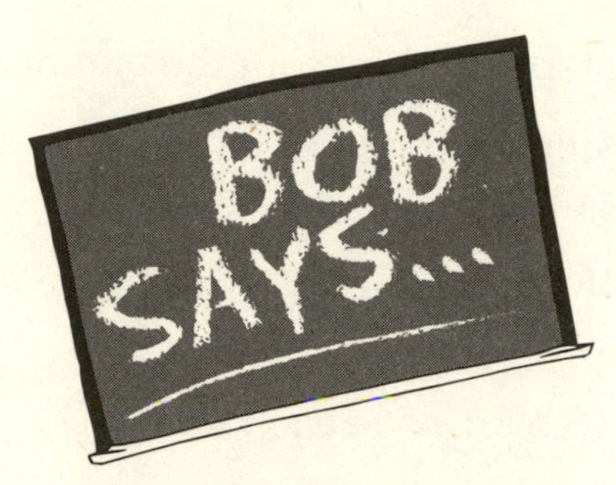

"The equations here are the equations for life. Master them, and it will bring you joy."

FIRST-DEGREE EQUATIONS

In high school, the topic of first-degree equations was probably the most popular of all. The GRE asks questions that are usually not too long and usually not too tricky. To review, here are the steps to solving first-degree equations. If you get good at these, you will know when to use the steps in another order.

To solve for x, follow these steps:

1. Multiply by the LCD to get rid of fractions. Cross-multiply if there are only two fractions.
2. If the "x" term appears only on the right, switch the sides.
3. Multiply out all parentheses by using the distributive law.
4. On each side, combine like terms.
5. Add the opposite of the x term on the right to each side.
6. Add the opposite of the non-x term(s) on the left to each side.
7. Factor out the x. This step occurs only if there is more than one letter in a problem.
8. Divide each side by the whole coefficient of x, including the sign.

Believe it or not, it took a long time to get the phrasing of this list just right.

Note *The* ***opposite*** *of a term is the same term with its opposite sign. So the opposite of* $3x$ *is* $-3x$*, the opposite of* $-7y$ *is* $+7y$*, and the opposite of 0 is 0. The technical name for "opposite" is* ***additive inverse.***

Let's do some examples.

Example 1: Solve for x: $7x - 2 = 10x + 13$

Solution: Steps 1–4 are not present.

$7x - 2 = 10x + 13$	Step 5: Add $-10x$ to each side.
$-3x - 2 = +13$	Step 6: Add $+2$ to each side.
$-3x = 15$	Step 8: Divide each side by -3.
$x = -5$	Solution.

Example 2: Solve for x: $7 = 2(3x - 5) - 4(x - 6)$

Solution:

$7 = 2(3x - 5) - 4(x - 6)$	No Step 1. Step 2: Switch sides.
$2(3x - 5) - 4(x - 6) = 7$	Step 3: Multiply out the parentheses.
$6x - 10 - 4x + 24 = 7$	Step 4: Combine like terms on each side.
$2x + 14 = 7$	No Step 5. Step 6: Add -14 to each side.
$2x = -7$	Step 8: Divide each side by 2.
$x = -\frac{7}{2}$	The answer doesn't have to be an integer.

Example 3: Solve for x: $\frac{x}{4} + \frac{x}{6} = 1$

Solution:

$\frac{x}{4} + \frac{x}{6} = 1$	Step 1: Multiply each term by 12.
$3x + 2x = 12$	Step 4: Combine like terms.
$5x = 12$	Step 8: Divide each side by 5.
$x = \frac{12}{5}$	Solution.

Example 4: Solve for x: $y = \frac{3x - 5}{x - 7}$

Solution:

Write $y = \frac{y}{1}$: $\frac{y}{1} = \frac{3x - 5}{x - 7}$	Step 1: Cross-multiply.
$(x - 7)y = 1(3x - 5)$	Step 3: Distribute.
$xy - 7y = 3x - 5$	Step 5: Add $-3x$ to each side.
$xy - 3x - 7y = -5$	Step 6: Add $7y$ to each side.
$xy - 3x = 7y - 5$	Step 7: Factor out the x from the left.
$x(y - 3) = 7y - 5$	Step 8: Divide each side by $y - 3$.
$x = \frac{7y - 5}{y - 3}$	Solution.

Let's do some exercises.

Exercise 1: $2x - 6 = 4; x + 3 =$

A. 5

B. 6

C. 7

D. 8

E. 9

Exercise 2: $x - 9 = 9 - x; x =$

A. 0

B. 4.5

C. 9

D. 13.5

E. 18

Exercise 3: $4x - 17 = 32; 12x - 51 =$

A. $12\frac{1}{4}$

B. $36\frac{3}{4}$

C. 64

D. 96

E. 288

Exercise 4: $\frac{xy}{y - x} = 1; x =$

A. $\frac{1}{2}$

B. 1

C. $\frac{y}{y+1}$

D. $\frac{y}{y-1}$

E. $\frac{y}{1-y}$

Let's look at the answers.

Answer 1: The answer is (D). $x = 5$, but the question asks for $x + 3 = 8$.

Note *Tests such as the GRE often ask for x + something instead of just x. Be careful—give what the test wants.*

Answer 2: The answer is (C). $2x = 18; x = 9$. It actually can be solved just by looking, since $9 - 9 = 9 - 9$ (or $0 = 0$).

Answer 3: The answer is (D). We do not need to solve this equation if we recognize that $12x - 51 = 3(4x - 17) = 3(32) = 96$.

Answer 4: The answer is (C). By cross-multiplying, we get $xy = y - x$. Then $xy + x = y$, which factors to $x(y + 1) = y$. Therefore, $x = \frac{y}{y+1}$.

LINEAR INEQUALITIES

To review some facts about inequalities:

$a < b$ (read, "a is less than b") means a is to the left of b on the number line.

$a > b$ (read, "a is greater than b") means a is to the right of b on the number line.

$x > y$ is the same as $y < x$.

The notation $x \geq y$ (read, "x is greater than or equal to y") means $x > y$ or $x = y$.

Similarly, $x \leq y$ (read, "x is less than or equal to y"), means $x < y$ or $x = y$.

We solve linear inequalities ($<, >, \leq, \geq$) the same way we solve linear equalities, except when we multiply or divide by a negative, the order reverses.

Example 5: Solve for x: $6x + 2 < 3x + 10$

Solution: $3x < 8$, so $x < \frac{8}{3}$.

The inequality does not switch because both sides are divided by a positive number (3).

Example 6: Solve for x: $-2(x - 3) \leq 4x - 3 - 7$

Solution: $-2x + 6 \leq 4x - 10$, or $-6x \leq -16$. Thus, $x \geq \frac{-16}{-6} = \frac{8}{3}$.

Here the inequality switches because we divided both sides by a negative number (-6).

Example 7: Solve for x: $8 > \frac{x-2}{-3} \geq 5$

Solution: We multiply through by -3, and both inequalities switch. We get $-24 < x - 2 \leq -15$. If we add 2 to each part to get a value for x alone, the final answer is $-22 < x \leq -13$.

Now, let's do some more exercises.

Exercise 5: If $3x + 4 > 17$, $3x + 7 >$

A. $\frac{13}{3}$

B. $\frac{22}{3}$

C. 14

D. 17

E. 20

Exercise 6: If $3x + 4y < 5$; $x <$

A. $5 - 4y - 3$

B. $\frac{5}{4}y - 3$

C. $\frac{5}{12}y$

D. $\frac{5 - 4y}{3}$

E. $\frac{5}{3} - 4y$

Exercise 7: $x > 0$ and $y > 0$. The number of ordered pairs of whole numbers (x, y) such that $2x + 3y < 9$ is

A. 1

B. 2

C. 3

D. 4

E. 5

Let's look at the answers.

Answer 5: The answer is (E). We don't actually have to solve this one. $3x + 7 = (3x + 4) + 3 > 17 + 3$, or 20.

Answer 6: The answer is (D). $3x + 4y < 5$ is the same as $3x < 5 - 4y$. Dividing by 3, we get $\frac{5 - 4y}{3}$.

Answer 7: The answer is (C). We must substitute numbers. (1,1) is okay since $2(1) + 3(1) < 9$; (2,1) is okay since $2(2) + 3(1) < 9$; (1,2) is okay since $2(1) + 3(2) < 9$. And that's all.

We will do more on ordered pairs later in the book. As we already have seen, some questions overlap more than one topic.

ABSOLUTE VALUE EQUALITIES

Absolute value is the magnitude, without regard to sign. You should know the following facts about absolute value:

$|3| = 3$, $|-7| = 7$ and $|0| = 0$

$|u| = 6$ means that $u = 6$ or -6.

$|u| = 0$ always means $u = 0$.

$|u| = -17$ has no solutions since the absolute value is never negative.

Example 8: Solve for x: $|2x - 5| = 7$

Solution: Either $2x - 5 = 7$ or $2x - 5 = -7$. So $x = 6$ or $x = -1$.

Note *This kind of problem always has two answers.*

Example 9: Solve for x: $|5x + 11| = 0$.

Solution: $5x + 11 = 0; x = -\frac{11}{5}$.

Note *This type of problem (absolute value equals 0) always has one answer.*

Those of you with some math background know there is a lot more to absolute value. This section and the next, however, are all you need for the GRE.

Q Let's do a few more exercises.

Exercise 8: $|2x + 1| = |x + 5|; x =$

A. -2
B. 0
C. 4
D. 4 and -2
E. 0 and 4

Exercise 9: $|x - y| = |y - x|$. This statement is true:

A. For no values
B. Only if $x = y = 0$
C. Only if $x = y$
D. Only for all integers
E. For all real numbers

Exercise 10: If $4|2x+3| = 11$, then $8|2x+3|+5 =$

A. $\frac{11}{4}$

B. $\frac{31}{4}$

C. 22

D. 27

E. 110

Let's look at the answers.

Answer 8: The answer is (D). $2x + 1 = x + 5$ or $2x + 1 = -(x + 5)$.

Answer 9: The answer is (E).

Answer 10: The answer is (D). We don't have to solve this at all. If $4|2x+3| = 11$, then $8|2x+3| = 2(11) = 22$. Adding 5, we get 27.

ABSOLUTE VALUE INEQUALITIES

If we talk about integers $|u| \leq 3$, we have $u = -3, -2, -1, 0, 1, 2,$ and 3. So $|u| \leq a$ means $-a \leq u \leq a$, where $a > 0$.

Example 10: Solve for x: $|2x-3| < 11$

Solution: $-11 < 2x - 3 < 11$. Adding 3 to each piece means $-8 < 2x < 14$. Dividing by 2 gives $-4 < x < 7$.

If we talk about integers $|u| \geq 4$, we have $u = 4, 5, 6, \ldots$ and $-4, -5, -6, \ldots$ So $|u| \geq a$ means $u \geq a$ or $u \leq -a$, $a > 0$.

Example 11: Solve for x: $|x-7| > 4$.

Solution: $x - 7 > 4$ or $x - 7 < -4$. The two parts of the answer are $x > 11$ or $x < 3$.

Let's do some more exercises.

Exercise 11: If $5 \leq |x| \leq 5$, $x =$

A. 0

B. 5

C. -5 and 5

D. no values

E. all values

Exercise 12: $|x-5| \geq -5$ if $x =$

A. 0
B. 5
C. −5 and 5
D. no values
E. all values

Exercise 13: $|x+5| \leq -5$ if $x =$

A. 0
B. 5
C. −5 and 5
D. no values
E. all values

Let's look at the answers.

Answer 11: The answer is (C).

Answer 12: The answer is (E). The absolute value is always greater than any negative number because it is always greater than or equal to zero.

Answer 13: The answer is (D). The absolute value can't be less than a negative number.

QUADRATIC EQUATIONS

Quadratic equations, equations involving the square of the variable, can be solved in three principal ways: factoring, taking the square root, and using the quadratic formula. Another name for the solution of any equation is a **root**.

Solving Quadratics by Factoring

Solving quadratic equations by factoring is based on the fact that if $a \times b = 0$, then either $a = 0$ or $b = 0$.

Example 12: Solve for all values of x: $x(x-3)(x+7)(2x+1)(3x-5)(ax+b)(cx-d) = 0$.

Solution: Setting each factor equal to 0 (better if you can do it just by looking), we get $x = 0, 3, -7, -\frac{1}{2}, \frac{5}{3}, -\frac{b}{a}$, and $\frac{d}{c}$.

Solving Quadratics by Taking the Square Root

If the equation is of the form $x^2 = c$, with no x term, we just take the square root: $x = \pm\sqrt{c}$.

Note *Remember that* $\sqrt{9} = 3$, $-\sqrt{9} = -3$, $\sqrt{-9}$ *is not real, and if* $x^2 = 9$, *then* $x = \pm 3$*!*

Example 13: Solve for all values of x:

a. $x^2 - 7 = 0$

b. $ax^2 - b = c$, where $a, b, c > 0$.

Solutions:

a. $x^2 = 7$; $x = \pm\sqrt{7}$

b. $ax^2 = b + c$; $x^2 = \frac{b+c}{a}$, so $x = \pm\sqrt{\frac{b+c}{a}}$, or $\pm\frac{\sqrt{a(b+c)}}{a}$

Solving Quadratics by Using the Quadratic Formula

The quadratic formula states that if $ax^2 + bx + c = 0$, then

$$x = \frac{-b \pm \sqrt{b^2 - 4ac}}{2a},$$

where a is the coefficient of the x^2 term, b is the coefficient of the x term, and c is the number term.

Example 14: Solve $3x^2 - 5x + 2 = 0$ by using the quadratic formula.

Solution: $a = 3, b = -5, c = 2$. $x = \frac{-(-5) \pm \sqrt{(-5)^2 - 4(3)(2)}}{2(3)} = \frac{5 \pm 1}{6}$.

x_1 (read, "x sub one," the first answer) $= \frac{5+1}{6} = 1$; x_2 (read, "x sub two," the second answer) $= \frac{5-1}{6} = \frac{2}{3}$.

Example 15: Solve $3x^2 - 5x + 2 = 0$ by factoring.

Solution: This is the same problem as Example 14. $3x^2 - 5x + 2 = (3x - 2)(x - 1) = 0$, so $x = 1, \frac{2}{3}$.

Factoring is preferred; using the quadratic formula takes too long.

Before we go to the next set of exercises, I suppose most of you know the quadratic formula, but few have seen it shown to be true. The teacher in me has to show you, even if you don't care.

$$ax^2 + bx + c = 0$$

The coefficient of x^2 must be 1.

$$x^2 + \frac{b}{a}x = \frac{-c}{a}$$

Complete the square; this means taking half the coefficient of x, squaring it, adding it to both sides.

$$x^2 + \frac{b}{a}x + \left(\frac{b}{2a}\right)^2 = \left(\frac{b}{2a}\right)^2 - \frac{c}{a}$$

Take the square root of both sides.

$$\left(x + \frac{b}{2a}\right)^2 = \frac{b^2}{4a^2} - \frac{c}{a}$$

$$= \frac{b^2}{4a^2} - \frac{4ac}{4a^2}$$

$$= \frac{b^2 - 4ac}{4a^2}$$

$$x + \frac{b}{2a} = \frac{\pm\sqrt{b^2 - 4ac}}{\sqrt{4a^2}}$$

$$= \frac{\pm\sqrt{b^2 - 4ac}}{2a}$$

Solve for x and simplify.

$$x = -\frac{b}{2a}\frac{\pm\sqrt{b^2 - 4ac}}{2a} \text{ or}$$

$$= \frac{-b \pm \sqrt{b^2 - 4ac}}{2a}$$

$$\text{So } x = \frac{-b \pm \sqrt{b^2 - 4ac}}{2a}$$

The formula is really true. You should have questioned it in high school. I hope college has taught you to question everything.

Let's do some exercises.

		Quantity A	Quantity B
Exercise 14:	$x^2 + 5x - 6 = 0$	The sum of the two roots.	0
Exercise 15:	$x^2 = 11$	Minimum root	-4
Exercise 16:	$\frac{x^2 - 9}{x^2 - 25}$	Maximum value to make fraction = 0	4
Exercise 17:	$\frac{x^2 - 9}{x^2 - 25}$	Minimum value to make fraction undefined	0
Exercise 18:	$x^3 - 4x^2 - 7x + 28 = 0$	$x^3 - 4x^2$	$7x - 28$
Exercise 19:	$\frac{x - 4}{x - 3} = \frac{x - 2}{x}$	Root of this equation	0

Exercise 20: What values of x are solutions to $(x - 3)^2 = 25$? Indicate *all* correct answers.

A. -5
B. -2
C. 3
D. 5
E. 8
F. 11

Exercise 21: If $|x - 5| < 3$, which of the following could be values of x? Include *all* correct answers.

A. -2
B. 2
C. 5
D. 8
E. 11
F. 17

Exercise 22: If $2x^2 + 5x - 7 = 0$, which of the following statements are true concerning the two solutions? Indicate all correct answers.

A. They are not real numbers.
B. They are identical.
C. They are real numbers.
D. They are rational numbers.
E. They are both integers.

Exercise 23: What values of x are solutions of $2x^2 + 5x + 1 = 0$? Indicate *all* correct answers.

A. $\frac{-5-\sqrt{17}}{4}$

B. $\frac{5-\sqrt{17}}{4}$

C. $\frac{-5+\sqrt{17}}{4}$

D. $\frac{5+\sqrt{17}}{4}$

E. Two rational solutions

Exercise 24: What values of x are solutions of $\frac{x+3}{x+4} = \frac{2x+6}{x}$? Indicate *all* correct answers.

A. -10

B. -8

C. -3

D. -0.8

E. 2

F. 7

Exercise 25: What values of x are solutions of $3x^2 - 7 = 0$? Indicate *all* correct answers.

A. $\pm\sqrt{21}$

B. $\frac{\pm\sqrt{21}}{21}$

C. $\pm\sqrt{\frac{7}{3}}$

D. $\pm\frac{\sqrt{21}}{3}$

E. $\pm\frac{\sqrt{21}}{7}$

F. $\pm\sqrt{147}$

Exercise 26: What is the product of the solutions of $|x - 4| = 2$?

Exercise 27: What is the sum of the roots of $5x^2 - 3x - 2 = 0$? Write your answer with integers in both numerator and denominator.

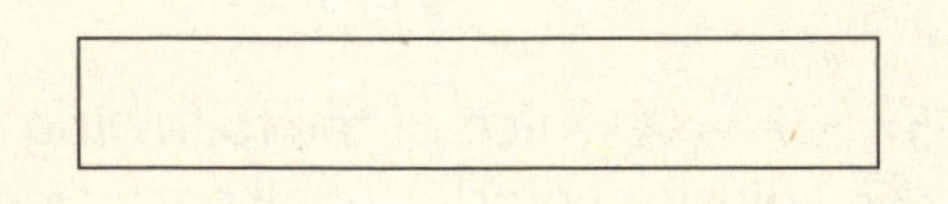

Let's look at the answers.

Answer 14: The answer is (B). $(x + 6)(x - 1) = 0$; the roots are -6 and $+1$. The sum is less than 0.

Answer 15: The answer is (A). $-\sqrt{11} > -\sqrt{16} = -4$.

Answer 16: The answer is (B). For the fraction to equal 0, the top must equal 0, so $x = 3 < 4$.

Answer 17: The answer is (B). For the fraction to be undefined, the bottom must equal 0; the minimum value is $-5 < 0$.

Answer 18: The answer is (C). Move the last two terms to the other side of the equation.

Answer 19: The answer is (A). Cross-multiplying, we get $x(x - 4) = (x - 3)(x - 2)$. Canceling the x^2 terms, we get $-4x = -5x + 6$. So $x = 6 > 0$.

Answer 20: The correct answers are (B) and (E). Taking the square root of both sides of the equation, we get $x - 3 = \pm 5$. If $x - 3 = -5$, then $x = -2$. If $x - 3 = 5$, then $x = 8$.

Answer 21: The only correct answer is (C). $|x - 5| < 3$ is equivalent to $-3 < x - 5 < 3$. Add 5 to each of the three parts of the inequality to get $2 < x < 8$. Thus, the solution includes any number between 2 and 8, but not including 2 and 8.

Answer 22: The correct answers are (C) and (D). The left side of the equation can be factored as $(2x + 7)(x - 1)$. If $2x + 7 = 0$, $x = -3.5$. If $x - 1 = 0$, $x = 1$. The numbers -3.5 and 1 are real and rational. Note that -3.5 is not an integer.

Answer 23: The correct answers are (A) and (C). Use the quadratic formula to find the solutions. Given $ax^2 + bx + c = 0$, the solutions are $x = \dfrac{-b \pm \sqrt{b^2 - 4ac}}{2a}$.

Thus, $x = \dfrac{-5 \pm \sqrt{5^2 - (4)(2)(1)}}{2(2)} = \dfrac{-5 \pm \sqrt{25 - 8}}{4} = \dfrac{-5 - \sqrt{17}}{4}$

or $\dfrac{-5 + \sqrt{17}}{4}$.

Answer 24: The correct answers are (B) and (C). Cross-multiplying yields $(x)(x + 3) = (x + 4)(2x + 6)$, which becomes $x^2 + 3x = 2x^2 + 6x + 8x + 24$. This equation can now be simplified to $0 = x^2 + 11x + 24$. Then $0 = (x + 8)(x + 3)$, so $x = -8$ or $x = -3$.

Answer 25: The correct answers are (C) and (D). Since $3x^2 - 7 = 0$, $3x^2 = 7$. Then $x^2 = \frac{7}{3}$, which means that $x = \pm\sqrt{\frac{7}{3}}$. By rationalizing the denominator, $\pm\sqrt{\frac{7}{3}}$ can be written as $x = \pm\sqrt{\frac{7}{3} \times \frac{3}{3}} = \pm\frac{\sqrt{21}}{\sqrt{9}} = \pm\frac{\sqrt{21}}{3}$.

Answer 26: The correct answer is 12. The equation $|x - 4| = 2$ implies that either $x - 4 = 2$ or $x - 4 = -2$. The two solutions are 6 and 2, and their product is 12.

Answer 27: The correct answer is $\frac{3}{5}$. The left side of the equation $5x^2 - 3x - 2 = 0$ can be factored as $(5x + 2)(x - 1)$. Then $5x + 2 = 0$ or $x - 1 = 0$. The two roots are $-\frac{2}{5}$ and 1, so their sum is $\frac{3}{5}$. Note that any equivalent fraction may be used, such as $\frac{6}{10}$. A shortcut would be to recognize that the sum of the roots of a quadratic equation in the form $ax^2 + bx + c = 0$ is $-\frac{b}{a}$. In this exercise, $b = -3$ and $a = 5$.

Now let's go to a chapter that discusses word problems, which are important to the GRE and thus to you.

CHAPTER 7: *Word Problems in One Unknown*

"It is necessary to study the words of math. Only then can you truly understand all."

I consider this section the most important section of the book. Although the book is filled with skills that may be on the GRE, most of the questions will not be pure math questions but will have words that you must interpret and then do some math. Unfortunately, most high schools have de-emphasized these kinds of problems. In this chapter, I will try to make these dreaded "word problems" easy to understand.

First, we'll look at the words you'll need to know. Next, we'll go over the more likely problems to show up on the GRE. We'll then go over the other types of word problems. Finally, we'll review some common measurements.

BASICS

As we know, the answer in **addition** is the **sum**. Other words that indicate addition are **plus**, **more**, **more than**, **increase**, and **increased by**. You can write all sums in any order since addition is commutative.

The answer in **multiplication** is the **product**. Another word that is used is **times**. Sometimes the word **of** indicates multiplication, as we shall see shortly. **Double** means to multiply by two, and **triple** means to multiply by three. Since multiplication is also commutative, we can write any product in any order.

Division's answer is called the **quotient**. Another phrase that is used is **divided by**.

The answer in **subtraction** is called the **difference**. Subtraction can present a reading problem because $4 - 6 \neq 6 - 4$, so we must be careful to subtract in the correct order. Example 1 shows how some subtraction phrases are translated into algebraic expressions.

Example 1:

Phrases	Expressions
a. The difference between 9 and 5	$9 - 5$
The difference between *m* and *n*	$m - n$
b. Five minus two	$5 - 2$
m minus *n*	$m - n$
c. Seven decreased by three	$7 - 3$
m decreased by *n*	$m - n$
d. Nine diminished by four	$9 - 4$
m diminished by *n*	$m - n$
e. Three from five	$5 - 3$
m from *n*	$n - m$
f. Ten less two	$10 - 2$
m less *n*	$m - n$
g. Ten less than two;	$2 - 10$
m less than *n*	$n - m$

Notice in phrases **f** and **g** of Example 1 how just one word makes a difference: *a* less *b* means $a - b$; a less than *b* means $b - a$. *a* is less than *b* means $a < b$. You must read carefully!

The following words usually indicate an equal sign: *is, am, are, was, were, the same as, equal to.*

You also must know the following phrases for inequalities: at least ($\geq$), not more than ($\leq$), over ($>$), and under ($<$).

Example 2: Write the following in symbols:

Problem	Solution
a. *m* times the sum of *q* and *r*	$m(q + r)$
b. Six less the product of *x* and *y*	$6 - xy$
c. The difference between *c* and *d* divided by *f*	$\frac{c - d}{f}$
d. *b* less than the quotient of *r* divided by *s*	$\frac{r}{s} - b$
e. The sum of *d* and *g* is the same as the product of *h* and *r*	$d + g = hr$

Example 3:	Phrases	Expressions
	a. x is at least y	$x \geq y$
	b. Zeb's age n is not more than 21	$n \leq 21$
	c. Let l = my age; I am over 30 years old	$l > 30$
	d. Let p = most people, since most people are under seven feet tall	$p < 7$

Warning: The word "number" does not necessarily mean an integer or even necessarily a positive number.

RATIOS

Comparing two numbers is called a **ratio**. The ratio of 3 to 5 is written two ways: $\frac{3}{5}$ or 3:5 (say "the ratio of 3 to 5").

Example 4: Find the ratio of 5 ounces to 2 pounds.

Solution: The ratio is $\frac{5}{32}$, since 16 ounces are in a pound.

Example 5: A board is cut into two pieces that are in the ratio of 3 to 4. If the board is 56 inches long, how long is the longer piece?

Solution: If the pieces are in the ratio 3:4, we let one piece equal $3x$ and the other $4x$. The equation, then, is $3x + 4x = 56$; so $x = 8$; and the longer piece is $4x = 32$.

I have asked this problem many, many times. Almost no one has ever gotten it correct—not because it is difficult, but because no one does problems like this anymore.

CONSECUTIVE INTEGERS

If there are any "fun" word problems, they would have to do with consecutive integers. Let's recall the following facts about integers, most of which you know without having to even think about them:

Integers: $-3, -2, -1, 0, 1, 2, 3, 4, \ldots$

Evens: $-6, -4, -2, 0, 2, 4, 6, 8, \ldots$

Odds: $-5, -3, -1, 1, 3, 5, 7, \ldots$

If we let x = integer, then $x + 1$ represents the next consecutive integer, and $x + 2$ represents the next consecutive integer after that. Then $x + (x + 1) + (x + 2) = 3x + 3$ is the sum of three consecutive integers, where x is the smallest and $x + 2$ is the largest in the group.

If $y =$ an even integer, then $y + 2$ is the next consecutive even integer; $y + 4$ and $y + 6$ are the next consecutive integers after that. Then the sum of four consecutive even integers is $y + (y + 2) + (y + 4) + (y + 6) = 4y + 12$.

Similarly, if z is an odd integer, the next three odd integers are $z + 2$, $z + 4$, and $z + 6$. This is the same as for even integers, except we start out letting z be odd instead of even.

Example 6: The sum of three consecutive integers is twice the smallest. What is the smallest integer?

Solution: We have $x + (x + 1) + (x + 2) = 2x$, which simplifies to $3x + 3 = 2x$. So $x = -3$. The integers are -3, -2, and -1; and the smallest is -3. Notice that integers can be negative!

Most consecutive integer problems are done by using tricks, as the next few examples show.

Example 7: The sum of five consecutive even integers is 210. What is the sum of the smallest two?

Solution: If you have an odd number of consecutive, consecutive even, or consecutive odd integers, the middle number is the average (the mean). So the middle number is given by $\frac{210}{5} = 42$. Once you know that, count backward and forward to get the others. The five numbers are 38, 40, 42, 44, and 46. The sum of the two smallest is $38 + 40 = 78$.

Example 8: The sum of four consecutive integers is -50. What is the sum of the two largest?

Solution: Dividing -50 by 4, we get -12.5. The four consecutive integers are the closest integers to -12.5, namely -14, -13, -12, and -11. The sum of the two largest, -12 and -11, is -23.

AGE

Similar to consecutive integer problems are age problems. We just have to think about it logically.

Example 9: p years ago, Mary was q years old; in r years, she will be how many years old?

Solution: The secret is age now. If Mary was q years old p years ago, now she is $p + q$; so r years in the future, she will be $p + q + r$. If necessary, substitute numbers for p, q, and r to see how this works.

SPEED

We are familiar with speed being given in miles per hour (mph), so it is easy to remember that speed $= \frac{\text{distance}}{\text{time}}$, or $r = \frac{d}{t}$, where r stands for rate (the speed). Use this relationship, or the equivalent ones, $d = rt$ or $t = \frac{d}{r}$, to do word problems involving speed.

Example 10: Sue drives for 2 hours at 60 mph and 3 hours at 70 mph. What is her average speed?

Solution: Sue's average speed for the whole trip is given by $r = \frac{d}{t}$, where d is the total distance and t is the total time. Note that her average speed is *not* the average of the speeds. Use $d = rt$ for each part of her trip to get the total distance. The total distance is $60(2) + 70(3) = 330$ miles. The total time is 5 hours. So Sue's average speed is $r = \frac{330}{5} = 66$ mph.

Example 11: Don goes 40 mph in one direction and returns at 60 mph. What is his average speed?

Solution: Notice that the problem doesn't tell the distance. It doesn't have to; the distance in each direction is the same, since it is a round trip. We can take any distance, so let's choose 120 miles, the LCM of 40 and 60. Then the time going is $\frac{120}{40} = 3$ hours, and the time returning is $\frac{120}{60} = 2$ hours. The average speed is the total distance divided by the total time, $\frac{2(120)}{3+2} = \frac{240}{5} = 48$ mph.

We actually don't have to choose a number for the distance, however. We could use x. Just for learning's sake, we will do this same problem (Example 11) using x as the distance. The time going is $\frac{x}{40}$, and the time returning is $\frac{x}{60}$. Then we have:

$$\text{Total speed} = \frac{\text{total distance}}{\text{total time}} = \frac{2x}{\frac{x}{40} + \frac{x}{60}} = \frac{120(2x)}{120(\frac{x}{40} + \frac{x}{60})} = \frac{240x}{5x} = 48 \text{ mph}$$

Example 12: A plane leaves Indianapolis traveling west. A plane traveling 30 mph faster leaves Indianapolis going east. After two hours the planes are 2,000 miles apart. What is the speed of the faster plane?

Solution: A chart and a picture are best for problems like this.

	r	t	d
W	x	2	$2x$
E	$x + 30$	2	$2(x + 30)$

We let $x =$ the speed of the plane going west; then $x + 30$ is the speed of the eastern-going plane. The time for each is 2 hours. Since $rt = d$, the distances are as shown in the above chart. According to the picture, $2x + 2(x + 30) = 2{,}000$. So $x = 485$; $x + 30 = 515$ mph.

The problem is the same if the planes are starting at the ends and flying toward each other.

Example 13: A car leaves Chicago at 2 p.m. going west. A second car leaves Chicago at 5 p.m., going 30 mph faster. At 7 p.m., the faster car hits the slower one. The accident occurred after how many miles?

Solution: Again, let's construct a chart and picture.

	r	t	d
Slower	x	5	$5x$
Faster	$x + 30$	2	$2(x + 30)$

Chicago
$5x$
$2(x + 30)$

The rate of the slower car is x, and the time of the slower car is 7 p.m.–2 p.m., or 5 hours. The rate of the faster car is $x + 30$; and its time is 7 p.m.–5 p.m., or 2 hours. When they crashed, their distances were equal, so $5x = 2(x + 30)$. Then $x = 20$; and the total distance is 5(20) or $2(20 + 30) = 100$ miles.

Let's do some basic exercises.

Exercise 1: Four more than a number is seven less than triple the number. The number is

A. 4

B. 5.5

C. 7

D. 9

E. 11

Exercise 2: Mike must have at least an 80 average but less than a 90 average to get a B. If he received 98, 92, and 75 on the first three tests, which of these grades will give him a B?

A. 42
B. 54
C. 66
D. 98
E. 100

Exercise 3: Nine less than a number is the same as the difference between nine and the number. The number is

A. 18
B. 9
C. 0
D. 29
E. All numbers are correct.

Exercise 4: Seven consecutive odd numbers total -77. The sum of the largest three is

A. -21
B. -27
C. -33
D. -39
E. -45

Exercise 5: For three consecutive integers, the sum of the squares of the first two equals the square of the largest. There are two sets of answers. The sum of all six integers is

A. 0
B. 3
C. 6
D. 12
E. 24

Exercise 6: Ed goes 20 mph in one direction and 50 mph on the return trip. His average speed is

A. 25 mph
B. $27\frac{2}{7}$ mph
C. $28\frac{4}{7}$ mph
D. 30 mph
E. $30\frac{6}{7}$ mph

Exercise 7: The angles of a triangle are in the ratio of 3:5:7. The largest angle is

A. 12°
B. 36°
C. 60°
D. 84°
E. 108°

		Quantity A	**Quantity B**
Exercise 8:	y is greater than 4 less than twice x	y	$2x - 6$

Exercise 9: b years in the future, I will be c years old. How old was I six years in the past?

A. $b - c - 6$
B. $c - b - 6$
C. $c - b + 6$
D. $b - c + 6$
E. $b + c - 6$

Exercise 10: Meg is six times as old as Peg. In 15 years, Meg will be three times as old as Peg. Meg's age now is

A. 10
B. 25
C. 60
D. 75
E. 90

Exercise 11: A fraction, when reduced, is $\frac{2}{3}$. If 6 is added to the numerator and 14 is added to the denominator, the fraction reduces to $\frac{3}{5}$. The sum of the original numerator and denominator is

A. 60
B. 70
C. 80
D. 90
E. 100

Let's look at the answers.

Answer 1: The answer is (B). Let's break this one down into small pieces. Four more than a number is written as $n + 4$ (or $4 + n$). Seven less than triple the number is $3n - 7$ (the only correct way). "Is" means equals, so the equation is $n + 4 = 3n - 7$. Solving, we get $n = 55$.

Answer 2: The answer is (C). The "setup" to do this problem is $80 \leq \frac{(98+92+75+x)}{4} < 90$. However, $80(4) = 320$ total points for a minimum, and it must be less than $90(4) = 360$ points. So far, Mike has $98 + 92 + 75 = 265$ points; $265 + 66 = 331$ points. (Note that choices (D) or (E) will result in a grade of A, and I'm sure Mike wouldn't object to that.)

Answer 3: The answer is (B). $x - 9 = 9 - x; x = 9$.

Answer 4: The answer is (A). The middle one is $-\frac{77}{7} = -11$. The three largest ones are thus $-9, -7, -5$, and their sum is -21.

Answer 5: The answer is (D). $x^2 + (x + 1)^2 = (x + 2)^2$, which simplifies to $x^2 - 2x - 3 = 0$; $(x - 3)(x + 1) = 0$. The solution set is $x = 3$ or $x = -1$. For $x = 3$, the integers are 3, 4, 5; for $x = -1$, the integers are $-1, 0, 1$. The sum of all six is $3 + 4 + 5 + (-1) + 0 + 1 = 12$.

Answer 6: The answer is (C). If we assume a 100-mile distance, the original trip was 5 hours, and the return trip was 2 hours. $r = \frac{d}{t} = \frac{200}{7} = 28\frac{4}{7}$ mph.

Answer 7: The answer is (D). $3x + 5x + 7x = 180°$, so $x = 12°$. The largest angle is $7x = 84°$.

Answer 8: The answer is (A). Since $y > 2x - 4$ and $2x - 4 > 2x - 6$ (because $-4 > -6$), then $y > 2x - 6$.

Answer 9: The answer is (B). My age now is $c - b$, so six years ago it was $(c - b) - 6$.

Answer 10:

	Age now	Age in 15 years
Peg	x	$x + 15$
Meg	$6x$	$6x + 15$

The answer is (C). We let x = Peg's (the younger one's) age. Meg's age is thus $6x$. In 15 years, Meg's age $(6x + 15)$ will be (equals) three times Peg's age $(3(x+15))$. So the equation is $6x + 15 = 3x + 45$, and $x = 10$. Meg's age now is $6x = 60$.

Answer 11: The answer is (A). The fraction can be written as $\frac{2x}{3x}$. So $\frac{2x+6}{3x+14} = \frac{3}{5}$.

By cross-multiplying, we get $5(2x + 6) = 3(3x + 14)$, so $x = 12$. $2x = 24$ and $3x = 36$, and their sum is $24 + 36 = 60$.

WORK

The basic idea of work problems is that if a job can be done in x hours, then for each hour, the amount that is done is $\frac{1}{x}$ of the job. In 4 hours, for example, a job that takes 6 hours to do is $\frac{4}{6} = \frac{2}{3}$ done. The whole job done is represented by the number 1.

Example 14: Rob can do a job in 8 hours and Nan can do the same job in 4 hours. Together, they can do the job in how many hours?

Solution: I always say there are two answers to this problem. The first is that they start watching TV and the job never gets done. However, this is how to do the real problem. If a job can be done in 8 hours, then the part done in one hour is $\frac{1}{8}$; in three hours, it is $\frac{3}{8}$; and in x hours, it is $\frac{x}{8}$. The part done in x hours by Rob is $\frac{x}{8}$, and similarly, the part done by Nan in x hours is $\frac{x}{4}$. The part done by Rob plus the part done by Nan is the whole job, so $\frac{x}{8} + \frac{x}{4} = 1$. Thus, $x = 2\frac{2}{3}$. It would take them $2\frac{2}{3}$ hours to do the job together.

Example 15: Sandy takes twice as long to do a job as Randy. They finish the job together in 3 hours. How long would it take Randy to do the job alone?

Solution: The number of hours it takes Randy is x hours, so he does $\frac{3}{x}$ of the job in 3 hours. Sandy takes $2x$ hours to do the job, so she does $\frac{3}{2x}$ of the job in 3 hours. Therefore, $\frac{3}{x} + \frac{3}{2x} = 1$ is the equation representing the work done in three hours. Multiplying by $2x$, we get $6 + 3 = 2x$, or $x = 4.5$. It would take Randy 4.5 hours to do the job alone.

MIXTURES

These kinds of problems are easier done with charts. The columns are cost per pound, the number of pounds, and the total cost.

Example 16: Walnuts selling at $6.00 a pound are mixed with 24 pounds of almonds at $9.00 a pound to give a mixture selling at $7.00 a pound. How many pounds of walnuts are used?

Solution: We set up a chart for the cost.

	Cost/Pound ×	Number of Pounds =	Total Cost
Walnuts	6	x	$6x$
Almonds	9	24	216
Mixture	7	$x + 24$	$7(x + 24)$

We let x equal the number of pounds of walnuts. The total pounds of walnuts plus the total pounds of almonds is the total weight of the mixture. The equation for the cost of the walnuts plus the cost of the almonds is the cost of the mixture: $6x + 216 = 7(x + 24)$, so $x = 48$ pounds of walnuts.

Coin problems are just like mixture problems, except we are working with money, not nuts and bolts (or walnuts and almonds).

Example 17: There are 40 coins in nickels and dimes totaling $2.80. How many nickels are there?

Solution:

	Value/Coin ×	Number of Coins =	Total Value
Nickels	5	x	$5x$
Dimes	10	$40 - x$	$10(40 - x)$
Mixture	—	40	280

The problem is done in pennies. The total number of coins is 40. If there are x nickels, there are $40 - x$ dimes. The value of x nickels is $5x$. The value of $40 - x$ dimes is $10(40 - x)$. The values of nickels plus dimes is the total value: $5x + 400 - 10x = 280$, so $x = 24$ nickels.

Let's do some more exercises.

Exercise 12: The value of d dimes and q quarters in pennies is

A. $d + q$

B. dq

C. $250\,dq$

D. $10d + 25q$

E. $35dq$

Exercise 13: Water is poured into a tank at the same time a pipe is opened that drains the tank. If the tank is filled in 10 hours and the tank can empty in 15 hours, and the tank starts empty, how many hours does it take to fill the tank?

A. 20

B. 30

C. 40

D. 60

E. 120

Exercise 14: Adult tickets cost $10 and children's tickets cost $5. If 100 tickets are sold and $800 is taken in, how many adult tickets are sold?

A. 50

B. 60

C. 70

D. 75

E. 80

Exercise 15: Sid is twice as old as Rex. Ten years ago, Sid was four times as old as Rex. How old is Sid today?

A. 5

B. 10

C. 20

D. 30

E. 60

Exercise 16: The number of quarters is four more than twice the number of dimes. If the total is $7.00, how many dimes are there?

A. 10

B. 16

C. 20

D. 24

E. 34

Exercise 17: Fred leaves Fort Worth by car traveling north. Two hours later, Jim also leaves Fort Worth going north, but 20 mph slower. After six more hours, they are 300 miles apart. Fred's speed is

A. 60 mph
B. 70 mph
C. 80 mph
D. 90 mph
E. 100 mph

Exercise 18: Deb can do a job alone in 6 hours. After working alone for two hours, she is joined by Sue who can do the job alone in 8 hours. They work together and finish the job. How many hours did Deb work?

A. $3\frac{3}{7}$
B. 4
C. $4\frac{2}{7}$
D. $4\frac{1}{2}$
E. 5

Exercise 19: Given three consecutive integers, the sum of the squares of the first two equals the square of the largest. What is the sum of these three integers? Indicate *all* correct answers.

A. 0
B. 3
C. 6
D. 12
E. 24
F. 30

Exercise 20: The product of three consecutive even integers is six times the product of the two smaller integers. What is the smallest integer? Indicate *all* correct answers.

A. −2
B. 0
C. 2
D. 4
E. 12
F. 24

Exercise 21: Working alone, John can do a job in six hours. He will be joined by Eric because the job must be completed within a maximum of two hours. Which of the following could represent the number of hours that Eric would require, if working alone? Indicate *all* correct answers.

A. 2.5
B. 3
C. 3.5
D. 4
E. 4.5
F. 5

Exercise 22: How many liters of a mixture that contains 40% alcohol must be mixed with pure alcohol in order to produce a mixture of 12 liters that contains 60% alcohol?

Exercise 23: At a local movie theater, adult tickets cost \$6 each and children's tickets cost \$2 each. If 70 tickets were sold for \$200, how many adult tickets were sold?

Exercise 24: One of two planes was flying 40 miles per hour faster than the other plane. The planes flew in opposite directions from the same location at the same time. After three hours, they were 3,000 miles apart. What was the speed, in miles per hour, of the slower plane?

A **Let's look at the answers.**

Answer 12: The answer is (D). Dimes are 10 cents each, and the value is $10d$. Similarly, the value of quarters is $25q$.

Answer 13: The answer is (B). $\frac{x}{10} - \frac{x}{15} = 1$. We use a minus sign because it empties. Solving, we get $x = 30$.

Answer 14: The answer is (B).

	Value/ Tickets	× Number of Tickets	= Total Value
Adult	10	x	$10x$
Child	5	$100 - x$	$5(100 - x)$
Mixture	—	100	800

As the chart indicates, this is similar to the mixture problem, Example 16 in this chapter. The equation is $10x + 500 - 5x = 800$, so $x = 60$.

Answer 15: The answer is (D).

	Age now	Age 10 years ago
Sid	$2x$	$2x - 10$
Rex	x	$x - 10$

According to the chart and the problem, $2x - 10 = 4(x - 10)$, so $x = 15$. Sid's age is $2x = 30$.

Answer 16: We could use a chart like the one for Example 17, but it probably is unnecessary. We have x dimes and $(2x + 4)$ quarters. The equation is $10x + 25(2x + 4) = 700$, so $x = 10$. The answer is (A).

Answer 17: The answer is (D).

	r ×	t =	d
Fred	x	8	$8x$
Jim	$x - 20$	6	$6(x - 20)$

Fred goes at x mph for 8 hours. Jim goes at $x - 20$ mph for 6 hours. Since they are going in the same direction, we get $8x - 6(x - 20) = 300$, or $x = 90$. Notice that 300 is the *difference* in their distances, not the distance they traveled, so we use subtraction.

Answer 18: The answer is (C). Deb can do the job in 6 hours; her part is $\frac{x}{6}$. Sue worked two hours less and can do the job in 8 hours; her part is $\frac{x-2}{8}$. The equation is $\frac{x}{6} + \frac{x-2}{8} = 1$, so $x = 2\frac{2}{7}$. Deb spent $2\frac{2}{7}$ hours working with Sue, plus the 2 hours she worked alone, or $4\frac{2}{7}$ hours total.

Answer 19: The correct answers are (A) and (D). Let x, $x + 1$, and $x + 2$ represent the three consecutive integers. Then $x^2 + (x + 1)^2 = (x + 2)^2$. Removing the parentheses, this equation becomes $x^2 + x^2 + 2x + 1 = x^2 + 4x + 4$. By combining similar terms, the equation simplifies to $x^2 - 2x - 3 = 0$. Then, factoring the left side leads to $(x + 1)(x - 3) = 0$. This means $x + 1 = 0$ or $x - 3 = 0$. Thus, $x = -1$ or $x = 3$. If $x = -1$, the three integers are -1, 0, and 1, so their sum is 0. If $x = 3$, the three integers are 3, 4, and 5, so their sum is 12.

Answer 20: The correct answers are (A), (B), and (C). Let x, $x + 2$, and $x + 4$ represent the three consecutive even integers. Then $(x)(x + 2)(x + 4) = (6x)(x + 2)$. Rewrite this equation as $(x)(x + 2)(x + 4) - (6x)(x + 2) = 0$ and factor out $(x)(x + 2)$. Then we get $(x)(x + 2)(x + 4 - 6) = 0$, which is simply $(x)(x + 2)(x - 2) = 0$. This implies that $x = 0$, -2, or 2. As a check, the three sets of consecutive even integers are (i) 0, 2, 4; (ii) -2, 0, 2; and (iii) 2, 4, 6. Each set will satisfy the given conditions.

Answer 21: The correct answers are (A) and (B). Let x represent the number of hours that Eric needs, working alone. If the job takes exactly two hours, then $\frac{2}{6} + \frac{2}{x} = 1$. Subtract $\frac{2}{6}$ from each side to get $\frac{2}{x} = \frac{4}{6}$. Then $x = 3$. Thus, Eric can take no longer than 3 hours when working alone.

Answer 22: The correct answer is 8. Let x represent the number of liters of the 40% alcohol mixture. Then $12 - x$ represents the number of liters of pure alcohol. The number of liters of alcohol in the first mixture added to the number of liters of alcohol in the second mixture must equal the number of liters of alcohol in the combined mixture. Then $0.40x + (1.00)(12 - x) = (0.60)(12)$, which becomes $0.40x + 12 - x = 7.20$. Combining similar terms, we get $-0.60x = -4.80$. Finally, $x = \frac{-4.80}{-0.60} = 8$.

Answer 23: The correct answer is 15. Let x represent the number of adult tickets, so that $70 - x$ represents the number of children's tickets. The revenue from the sale of all adult tickets is $6x$, and the revenue from the sale of all children's tickets is $2(70 - x)$. Then $6x + 2(70 - x) = 200$, which expands to $6x + 140 - 2x = 200$. This equation simplifies to $4x = 60$, so $x = 15$.

Answer 24: The answer is 480. The two rates are x and $x + 40$, where x is the rate of the slower plane. The planes fly for three hours each in opposite directions, so the sum of their distances is 3,000 miles. Then $3x + 3(x + 40) = 3{,}000$, which expands to $3x + 3x + 120 = 3{,}000$. Combining similar terms, we get $6x = 2{,}880$. Thus, $x = 480$.

INTEREST

Our next topic deals with interest that one earns on money that is invested. When money is deposited into a bank account, this initial deposit is called the **principal**. As time progresses, the principal is increased by an amount called the **interest**. The sum of principal and interest is called the **final amount**, often referred to simply as the amount. The interest is almost always expressed as an annual percent.

Simple Interest

Simple interest is calculated on the original principal only, and does not include accumulated interest from prior periods. The formula to use is $I = PRT$, where I = interest, P = principal, R = annual rate, and T = time in years.

Example 18: Jill invests \$1,500 into an account that pays an annual rate of 5% simple interest. How much interest will she earn over a period of three years?

Solution: $I = PRT = (\$1{,}500)(0.05)(3) = \$225$.

Example 19: Ron invests \$900 into an account that pays an annual rate of 8% simple interest. What will be his final amount after three months?

Solution: Change 8% to 0.08 and change 3 months to $\frac{3}{12} = \frac{1}{4}$ year. Then the interest he will earn is $(\$900)(0.08)(\frac{1}{4}) = \$18$. The final amount, A, is the sum of the principal and interest ($A = P + I$). Thus, his final amount is \$900 + \$18 = \$918.

Example 20: Nadine invested \$2,000 into an account that paid a simple interest annual rate. After four years, she earned \$520 in interest. What percent interest did the account pay?

Solution: Let R represent the unknown rate. Then \$520 = (\$2,000)(R)(4). This equation simplifies to \$520 = \$8,000R, which means that $R = \frac{\$520}{\$8,000} = 0.065$. Since the rate is usually expressed as a percentage, our answer is 6.5%.

Example 21: Arthur invests \$1,200 into an account that pays a simple interest annual rate of 4%. How many years will be needed in order for this account to grow to \$1,560?

Solution: First, we calculate the interest to be earned as \$1,560 − \$1,200 = \$360. Let T represent the number of years. Then \$360 = (\$1,200)(0.04)(T), which simplifies to \$360 = \$48T. Thus, $T = \frac{\$360}{\$48} = 7.5$ years.

Compound Interest

With compound interest, money that is deposited grows faster. After each compounding period, the new (and larger) amount then earns interest over the next period. As an example, suppose that \$500 is deposited into an account that pays 4% compounded annually. After one year, the interest is (\$500)(0.04) = \$20, and thus the amount after one year is \$520. During the second year, the interest becomes (\$520)(0.04) = \$20.80. So, after the second year, the amount becomes \$520 + \$20.80 = \$540.80. Notice that the interest earned during the first year was \$20, but the interest earned during the second year was \$20.80. In fact, the interest earned each year will continue to grow.

The formula for compound interest is $A = P\left(1 + \frac{R}{n}\right)^{nt}$, where A = final amount, P = principal, R = annual percent rate, t = number of years, and n = number of compounding periods per year.

Example 22: Tim invests \$1,800 into an account that pays at the rate of 7%, compounded annually. What will be his final amount after five years?

Solution: $A = (\$1,800)\left(1 + \frac{0.07}{1}\right)^{(1)(5)} = (\$1,800)(1.07)^5 \approx \$2,524.59$.

Example 23: Amanda invests \$2,500 into an account that pays at the rate of 6% compounded semi-annually. How much interest will she earn after $3\frac{1}{2}$ years?

Solution: We'll find the (final) amount first: $A = (\$2,500)\left(1 + \frac{0.06}{2}\right)^{(2)(3.5)} =$ $\$2,500)(1.03)^7 \approx \$3,074.68$. As with simple interest, the interest earned is the difference between the amount and the principal. Thus, her earned interest will be \$3,074.68 − \$2,500 = \$574.68.

Example 24: Six years ago, Joanne invested money into an account that paid at the rate of 5% compounded quarterly (four times per year). She now has an amount of \$4,311. To the nearest dollar, what was her initial amount (principal)?

Solution: Let P represent the principal. Then $\$4,311 = (P)\left(1 + \frac{0.05}{4}\right)^{(4)(6)} =$ $(P)(1.0125)^{24}$. Thus, $P = \frac{\$4,311}{(1.0125)^{24}} \approx \frac{\$4,311}{1.34735} \approx \$3,200$.

Q Let's try a few exercises on both types of interest.

Read each problem carefully to decide whether you should use the simple interest formula or the compound interest formula.

Exercise 25: Roger invests \$3,500 into an account that pays at the rate of 12%, compounded quarterly. To the nearest dollar, how much interest will he earn after two years?

Exercise 26: Tina invests \$5,000 into an account that pays at the rate of 9% compounded annually. To the nearest dollar, what will be her final amount after three years?

Exercise 27: Viola invests \$1,600 into an account that pays an annual rate of 4.5% simple interest. What will be her final amount after 21 months?

Exercise 28: Frank invested \$6,200 into an account that paid a simple-interest annual rate. After five years, he had a final amount of \$8,835. What percent interest did the account pay?

Exercise 29: A certain bank pays at an interest rate of 13% compounded semi-annually. Marlene wishes to have a final amount of \$20,000 after five years. To the nearest dollar, how much money must she invest in this bank?

Let's look at the answers.

Answer 25: The correct answer is 934. Since this question involves compound interest, we use $A = (\$3,500)\left(1+\frac{0.12}{4}\right)^{(4)(2)} = (\$3,500)(1.03)^8 \approx \$4,434$. Thus, the interest earned is \$4,434 − \$3,500 = \$934.

Answer 26: The correct answer is 6,475. This question involves compound interest, so $A = (\$5,000)\left(1+\frac{0.09}{1}\right)^{(1)(3)} = (\$5,000)(1.09)^3 \approx \$6,475$.

Answer 27: The correct answer is 1,726. Change 21 months to $\frac{21}{12} = 1.75$ years. The simple interest becomes (\$1,600)(0.045)(1.75) = \$126. Thus, the final amount is \$1,600 + \$126 = \$1,726.

Answer 28: The correct answer is 8.5. The interest that Frank earned was \$8,835 − \$6,200 = \$2,635. Let R represent the unknown rate. Now, using the simple interest formula, we have \$2,635 = (\$6,200)(R)(5), which simplifies to \$2,635 = \$31,000R. Thus, $R = \frac{\$2,635}{\$31,000} = 0.085$. Finally, change 0.085 to its percent equivalent of 8.5%.

Answer 29: The correct answer is 10,655. Let P represent the unknown quantity to be invested, which is the principal. Then $\$20,000 = (P)\left(1+\frac{0.13}{2}\right)^{(2)(5)}$, which simplifies to \$20,000 = (P)$(1.065)^{10}$. The approximate value of $(1.065)^{10}$ is 1.877, so $P = \frac{\$20,000}{1.877} \approx \$10,655$.

MEASUREMENTS

You might want to review some basic measurements and how to convert a few.

Linear: 12 inches = 1 foot; 3 feet = 1 yard; 5,280 feet = 1 mile.

Liquid: 8 ounces = 1 cup; 2 cups = 1 pint; 2 pints = 1 quart; 4 quarts = 1 gallon

Weight: 16 ounces = 1 pound; 2,000 pounds = 1 ton.

Dry measure: 2 pints = 1 quart; 8 quarts = 1 peck; 4 pecks = 1 bushel. If I love you, a bushel and a peck, it would be 5 pecks or 40 dry quarts.

Metric: 1,000 grams in a kilogram; 1,000 liters in a kiloliter; 1,000 meters in a kilometer;

1,000 millimeters = 1 meter; 100 centimeters = 1 meter; 10 millimeters = 1 centimeter

When doing conversions, we pay particular attention to the units, canceling them when doing the multiplications. A good guide is: To go from large to small, multiply; from small to large, divide (or multiply by the reciprocal).

Example 25: Change 30 kilograms 20 grams to milligrams.

Solution: This is going from large to small, so multiply by the conversions:

$$\frac{30 \text{ kg}}{1} \times \frac{1{,}000 \text{ g}}{1 \text{ kg}} \times \frac{1{,}000 \text{ mg}}{1 \text{ g}} + \frac{20 \text{ g}}{1} \times \frac{1{,}000 \text{ mg}}{1 \text{ g}} = 30{,}020{,}000 \text{ mg}.$$

Notice how the measurements (g, kg) cancel.

Example 26: Change 90 miles per hour into feet per second.

Solution: Now we are going from small to large, so multiply by the reciprocals (same as dividing); to change from miles to feet, though, we are going from large to small, so just multiply by $\frac{5{,}280 \text{ feet}}{1 \text{ mile}}$:

$$\frac{90 \text{ miles}}{\text{hour}} \times \frac{1 \text{ hour}}{60 \text{ minutes}} \times \frac{1 \text{ minute}}{60 \text{ seconds}} \times \frac{5{,}280 \text{ feet}}{1 \text{ mile}} = \frac{132 \text{ feet}}{\text{sec}}$$

Note *Each fraction after the first is equivalent to 1. When you multiply by 1, the value doesn't change. Again, the measurements cancel, and you wind up with feet per second.*

CHAPTER 8: *Working with Two or More Unknowns*

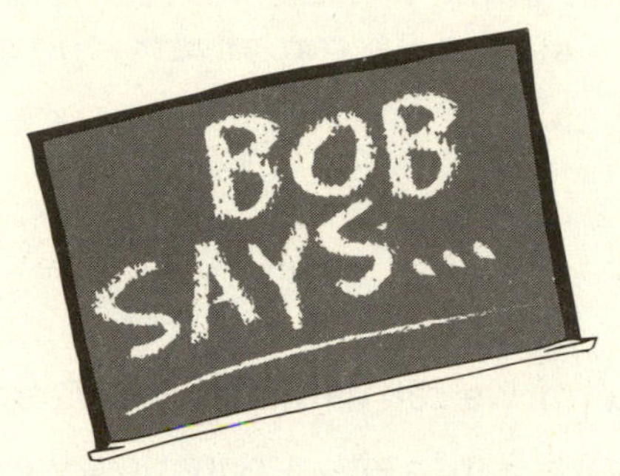

"Understanding more complex problems will be gratifying to you."

SOLVING SIMULTANEOUS EQUATIONS

We can solve two equations in two unknowns, also known as **simultaneous equations**, in five basic ways. Only two are practical for this exam: **substitution** and **elimination**. Sometimes we use a combination of these two.

Substitution

In substitution, we find an unknown with a coefficient of 1, solve for that variable, and substitute it in the other equation.

Example 1: Solve for x and y:

$$3x + 4y = 4 \quad (1)$$
$$x - 5y = 14 \quad (2)$$

Solution: In equation (2) $x = 5y + 14$. Substituting this into equation (1), we get $3(5y + 14) + 4y = 4$. Solving, we get $y = -2$; $x = 5y + 14 = 5(-2) + 14 = 4$. The answer is $x = 4$ and $y = -2$.

Example 2: Solve for x and y:

$$3x + y = 14 \quad (1)$$
$$2x + 5y = 18 \quad (2)$$

Solution: In equation (1), we solve for y: $y = 14 - 3x$, and substitute it into equation (2). Equation (2) then becomes $2x + 5(14 - 3x) = 18$. Solving this equation, we get $2x + 70 - 15x = 18$, or $-13x = -52$. So $x = 4$. Since $y = 14 - 3x$, $y = 14 - 3(4) = 2$. The answer is $x = 4$ and $y = 2$.

We can check by substituting these values into the original equations to see that they are solutions to both equations.

Elimination

If none of the original coefficients of any of the terms is 1, it is usually better to use the elimination method. There are several ways to eliminate one of the variables, as seen in the following examples. Once we have eliminated one of the variables, we can solve for the other variable by using substitution.

Example 3:

$$2x + 3y = 12$$
$$5x - 3y = 9$$

Solution: If we add the equations, term by term, we can eliminate the y term. We get $7x = 21$, so $x = 3$; substituting $x = 3$ into either equation, we get $y = 2$. So the answer is $x = 3, y = 2$.

Example 4: Solve for x and y:

$$3x + 2y = 12$$
$$3x - 2y = 0$$

Solution: Again, just add the equations. The y term cancels out, and we get $6x = 12; x = 2$. We substitute this value for x into either equation to find a value for y: $3x + 2y = 12; 3(2) + 2y = 12; 2y = 6$; so $y = 3$. The answer is $x = 2$ and $y = 3$.

Example 5: Solve for x and y:

$$4x + y = 17$$
$$x + y = 2$$

Solution: If adding doesn't work to eliminate one variable, try subtracting. We get $3x = 15$, so $x = 5$, and $y = -3$, by substitution into the second equation, the easier one. Mathematicians always try to do things the easiest way possible!

Example 6:

$$5x + 4y = 14$$
$$5x - 2y = 8$$

Solution: Subtracting, we get $6y = 6$; so $y = 1$; substituting, we get $x = 2$.

If adding or subtracting doesn't work, we must find two numbers that when we multiply the first equation by one of them and the second equation by the other, and then add (or subtract) the resulting equations, one letter is eliminated, as shown in the following examples.

Example 7:

$$5x + 3y = 11 \qquad (1)$$
$$4x - 2y = 22 \qquad (2)$$

Solution: To eliminate x, multiply the first equation by 4 and the second by -5; then add.

$4(5x + 3y) = 4(11)$ or $20x + 12y = 44$

$-5(4x - 2y) = -5(22)$ or $-20x + 10y = -110$

Adding, we get $22y = -66$; so $y = -3$. We could substitute now, but we could also eliminate y by multiplying the original equation (1) by 2 and equation (2) by 3. Let's do that.

$2(5x + 3y) = 2(11)$ or $10x + 6y = 22$

$3(4x - 2y) = 3(22)$ or $12x - 6y = 66$

Adding, we get $22x = 88$; so $x = 4$. The answer is $x = 4, y = -3$.

Example 8: Solve for x and y:

$$5x + 4y = 11$$
$$2x - 3y = 9$$

Solution: Let's look at $5x$ and $2x$. If we multiply $5x$ by 2 and $2x$ by -5 and then add, the x terms will disappear.

$2(5x + 4y) = 2(11)$ or $10x + 8y = 22$

$-5(2x - 3y) = (-5)(9)$ or $-10x + 15y = -45$

Adding these two new equations, we get $23y = -23$; so $y = -1$. We can then get x by substitution into either original equation. Using the second equation (again, the easier one), we get $2x - 3(-1) = 9$, or $2x = 6$, so $x = 3$. The answer is $x = 3$ and $y = -1$.

Practice in Solving Simultaneous Equations

For those of you who are curious, the other three basic ways of solving simultaneous equations are by using graphs, matrices, or determinants.

Let's do some exercises.

Exercise 1: If $x + y = 12$ and $x - y = 18$, $y - 3 =$

A. -6
B. -3
C. 0
D. 12
E. 15

Exercise 2: $3x + 2y = 61$ and $4x + 5y = 16$; $x + y =$

A. 3
B. 5
C. 7
D. 11
E. Cannot be determined

Exercise 3: $6x - 7y = 42$ and $3x - 10y = 27$; $x + y =$

A. 3
B. 5
C. 7
D. 11
E. Cannot be determined

Note *Sometimes "cannot be determined" can occur as an answer; however, I've never found it could be the answer for two questions in a row.*

		Quantity A	Quantity B
Exercise 4:	$6x + 6y = 48$	The mean of x and y	4

Exercise 5: If $x = y + 3$ and $y = z + 7$, x (in terms of z) $=$

A. $z - 10$
B. $z - 4$
C. z
D. $z + 4$
E. $z + 10$

Exercise 6: Two apples and 3 pears cost 65 cents, and 5 apples and 4 pears cost \$1.10. Find the cost of one pear:

A. 10
B. 15
C. 20
D. 25
E. 30

Exercise 7: As in Exercise 6, 2 apples and 3 pears cost 65 cents, and 5 apples and 4 pears cost \$1.10. Find the cost in cents of one pear and one apple together:

A. 10
B. 15
C. 20
D. 25
E. 30

Exercise 8: Find $x + y$:

$$7x + 4y = 27$$
$$x - 2y = -3$$

A. 1
B. 3
C. 5
D. 7
E. 9

Exercise 9: For lunch, Ed buys 3 hamburgers and one soda for \$12.50, and Mei buys one hamburger and one soda for \$5.60. How much does Ed pay for his hamburgers?

A. \$2.15
B. \$3.45
C. \$6.90
D. \$10.35
E. \$18.10

A **Let's look at the answers.**

Answer 1: The answer is (A). Adding, we get $2x = 30$. So $x = 15$. By substitution, we get $y = -3$; so $-3 - 3 = -6$.

Answer 2: The answer is (D). This is a trick. We could solve for x and y, but it takes a long time. The problem asks for $x + y$. Eighty percent of the time, just add the equations. Here we get $7x + 7y = 77$; so $x + y = 11$.

Answer 3: The answer is (B). Another trick. We subtract the equations and get $3x + 3y = 15$; so $x + y = 5$.

Answer 4: The answer is (C). $x + y = 8$; the mean is defined as $\frac{x + y}{2}$, so the mean is 4.

Answer 5: The answer is (E). $x = y + 3 = (z + 7) + 3 = z + 10$.

Answer 6: The answer is (B). The equations are

$$2a + 3p = 65$$
$$5a + 4p = 110$$

In solving for p, eliminate a by multiplying the top equation by 5 and the bottom by -2.

$5(2a + 3p) = 5(65)$ or $10a + 15p = 325$

$-2(5a + 4p) = -2(110)$ or $-10a - 8p = -220$

Adding, we get $7p = 105$; $p = 15$.

Answer 7: The answer is (D). Much more often, we get a problem like this. The equations are the same as in Exercise 6, but rather than asking for the cost of one apple or the cost of one pear, this exercise asks for the cost of one apple plus one pear. The trick is simply to add the original equations to get $7a + 7p = 175$. Dividing both sides by 7, we get $a + p = 25$.

Answer 8: The answer is (C). Less frequently, when adding doesn't work, try subtracting. If we subtract here, the difference becomes $6x + 6y = 30$. So $x + y = 5$.

Answer 9: The answer is (D). The equations are

$$3h + s = 12.50$$
$$h + s = 5.60$$

Subtracting, we get $2h = 6.90$, so $h = 3.45$. Thus, Ed's three hamburgers cost $10.35.

NEW WORD PROBLEMS

Let's try some "new" word problems. The only true difference from what we saw in Chapter 7 involves tens and units digit problems.

Digit Problems

If we have a two-digit number, it is represented by t for the tens digit and u for the units digit. For example, for 68, $t = 6$ and $u = 8$. The value of the number is represented by $10t + u$. The number 68 would thus be $10(6) + 8$. The number with the digits reversed is $10u + t$, or $86 = 8(10) + 6$. The sum of the digits is $t + u$, or $6 + 8 = 14$, in this case.

Example 9: In a two-digit number, the sum of the digits is 8. If the digits are reversed, the new number is 36 more than the original number. What is the number?

Solution: There are two methods to answer this question:

Method A: $t + u = 8$ is the first equation. The new number, $10u + t$ is (=) 36 more than the original number, or $10t + u + 36$. So the equation is $10u + t = 10t + u + 36$, or $9u - 9t = 36$. In this type of problem only, we can divide the equation by 9 and get $u - t = 4$. Since $t + u = 8$, adding these two equations gives $2u = 12$, or $u = 6$, so $t = 2$, and the number is 26.

Method B: Since $t + u = 8$, the only possible answers could be 17, 26, or 35, since the number with the digits reversed is bigger. $71 - 17 \neq 38$, but $62 - 26 = 36$; so the number is 26.

Mixture Problems

Mixture problems with two unknowns are treated similarly to how we did mixture problems with one unknown in the last chapter. It often helps to construct a chart.

Example 10: How many pounds of peanuts at $3.00 a pound must be mixed with $7.00-per-pound cashews to give 20 pounds of a $6.00-per-pound mixture?

Solution: Construct a chart with the given information.

	Cost/Pound ×	Pounds =	Total Cost
Peanuts	3	x	$3x$
Cashews	7	y	$7y$
Mixture	6	20	120

Let x = pounds of peanuts and y = pounds of cashews. According to the chart,

$$x + y = 20$$
$$3x + 7y = 120$$

Since we want x, multiply the top equation by -7, and add the result to the second equation.

$$-7x + -7y = -140$$
$$3x + 7y = 120$$

Adding, we get $-4x = -20$, so $x = 5$ pounds of peanuts.

Age Problems

Age problems with two unknowns are treated similarly to how we did age problems with one unknown in the last chapter. It often helps to construct a chart.

Example 11: Joan is 4 times the age of Ben. In 4 years, Joan will be $2\frac{1}{2}$ times the age of Ben. Ben will be how many years old then?

Solution: Construct a chart with the given information.

	Age now	Age in 4 years
Joan	x	$x + 4$
Ben	y	$y + 4$

Let x = Joan's age and y = Ben's age. The first equation is $x = 4y$.

In 4 years, the equation is $x + 4 = (\frac{5}{2})(y + 4)$, or $2(x + 4) = 5(y + 4)$.

By the Distributive Law (Chapter 5), $2x + 8 = 5y + 20$, or $2x - 5y = 12$.

But we know $x = 4y$. So, by substitution, $2(4y) - 5y = 12$, or $3y = 12$, so $y = 4$ (Ben's present age). In 4 years, Ben will be $y + 4 = 8$ years old.

Fraction Problems

Sometimes, trial and error finds the answer for you. Simply substitute the answer choices into the problem to see what works. But you should also be able to set up simultaneous equations. You might ask, "What is the best method?" The answer is, "Whatever gives you the answer the fastest." Everyone is different.

Example 12: A fraction when reduced is $\frac{3}{4}$. If 1 is subtracted from the numerator and 2 is added to the denominator, the ratio becomes $\frac{2}{3}$. What is the original fraction?

Solution: We have $\frac{x}{y} = \frac{3}{4}$, or $3y = 4x$, which gives us $-4x + 3y = 0$. We also have $\frac{x-1}{y+2} = \frac{2}{3}$, or, by cross-multiplication, $3(x - 1) = 2(y + 2)$. This gives us $3x - 2y = 7$. Our simultaneous equations are

$$-4x + 3y = 0$$
$$3x - 2y = 7$$

If we eliminate x by multiplying the top equation by 3 and the bottom equation by 4 and adding the resulting equations, we get $y = 28$, and by substitution, $x = 21$. So the original fraction is $\frac{21}{28}$.

Q Let's do a few exercises.

Exercise 10: In a two-digit number, the tens digit is the square of the units digit. The difference between the number and the number reversed is 54. The original number is

A. 24
B. 39
C. 42
D. 71
E. 93

Exercise 11: How many ounces of 40% alcohol must be mixed with 10 ounces of 70% alcohol to give a solution that is 45% alcohol?

A. 20
B. 30
C. 40
D. 50
E. 60

Exercise 12: May's age is twice Fay's age. In 15 years, Fay will be $\frac{3}{5}$ as old as May. The sum of their original ages is

A. 66
B. 75
C. 90
D. 96
E. 105

Exercise 13: If 4 less than x is the same as 7 more than the product of 4 and y, which answer choice is true?

A. $x + 4y - 11 = 0$

B. $x + y + 15 = 0$

C. $x + y + 7 = 0$

D. $x + 4y - 11 = 0$

E. $4y - x + 11 = 0$

Exercise 14: The product of 4 and the sum of x and y is at least as large as the quotient of a divided by b. This can be written as

A. $4x + y - \frac{a}{b} \geq 0$

B. $4x + y - \frac{a}{b} > 0$

C. $4(x + y) - \frac{a}{b} \geq 0$

D. $4(x + y) + \frac{a}{b} > 0$

E. $\frac{a}{b} - 4x + 4y < 0$

Exercise 15: The sum of the digits of a two-digit number is 10. The number reversed is 18 more than the original number. The original number is

A. 19

B. 28

C. 37

D. 46

E. 55

Exercise 16: The equation of line 1 is $x - y = 6$ and the equation of line 2 is $ax - by = 20$, where a, b are integers. In exactly how many points may these lines intersect? Indicate *all* correct answers.

A. 0

B. 1

C. 2

D. 3

E. 5

F. Infinite number

Exercise 17: One hamburger costs \$2.00 and a bottle of soda costs \$1.25. John must buy twice as many hamburgers as bottles of soda. If he will spend less than \$20, how many hamburgers can he buy? Indicate *all* correct answers.

A. 2

B. 3

C. 4

D. 6

E. 8

F. 10

Exercise 18: If $y = x^2$ and $y = x + 6$ are graphed on the same coordinate axes, which of the following points lie on both curves? Indicate *all* correct answers.

A. $(-2, 9)$
B. $(-2, 4)$
C. $(1, 1)$
D. $(2, 4)$
E. $(3, 9)$
F. $(4, 16)$

Exercise 19: A principal sells \$600 worth of tickets to a school play. Children's tickets cost \$5 each and adult tickets cost \$8 each. Which of the following could be the number of children's tickets sold? Indicate *all* correct answers.

A. 20
B. 24
C. 40
D. 60
E. 80
F. 104

Exercise 20: What is the y-coordinate of the intersection point of the lines represented by $3x + 5y = 5$ and $2x - 5y = 55$? Be sure your answer is in fraction form.

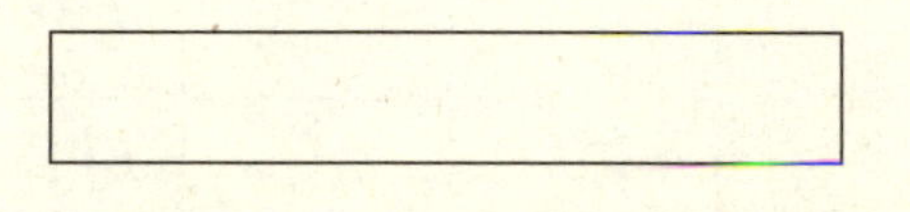

Exercise 21: Four pears and five apples cost \$7. Two pears and one apple cost \$5. What is the combined cost of one pear and one apple?

\$

Exercise 22: The sum of the digits of a two-digit number is 9. If the digits are reversed, the new number is 27 greater than the original number. What is the product of the digits?

Let's look at the answers.

Answer 10: The answer is (E). Trial and error is best for this problem. Of the answer choices, the only possible ones are 42 since $2^2 = 4$, and 93 since $3^2 = 9$. However, only for 93 is the second criterion true: $93 - 39 = 54$.

Answer 11: The answer is (D). This is a mixture problem. The principle is this: If we have 10 ounces of 70% alcohol, the amount of alcohol is $10(.70) =$ 7 ounces of alcohol. Now construct a chart for this problem; eliminate the decimal point since all items in this will have a decimal.

	Ounces	× % alcohol	= Amount of Alcohol in mixture
40% alcohol	x	40	$40x$
70% alcohol	10	70	700
45% alcohol mixture	y	45	$45y$

We let $x =$ the amount of 40% alcohol, and $y =$ the total ounces in the mixture. We get $x + 10 = y$ and $40(x) + 10(70) = 45(y)$, since we can eliminate all decimal points in this equation. Substitute the first equation for y because we want x: $40x + 700 = 45(x + 10)$, or $45x + 450 = 40x + 700$. Thus, $5x = 250$, and $x = 50$.

Answer 12: The answer is (C). Consruct a chart in which May's age is y and Fay's age is x.

	Age now	Age in 15 years
May	y	$y + 15$
Fay	x	$x + 15$

From the chart $y = 2x$ and $x + 15 = \left(\frac{3}{5}\right)(y + 15)$, or $5(x + 15) =$ $3(y + 15)$. Then $5x + 30 = 3y$. Substituting $y = 2x$, we get $5x + 30 = 3(2x)$, so $x = 30$ and $y = 60$. The sum of their ages is $x + y = 90$.

Answer 13: The answer is (E). $x - 4 = 4y + 7$. When we rearrange the terms, we see that only (E) is correct.

Answer 14: The answer is (C). $4(x + y) \geq \frac{a}{b}$. When we rearrange the terms, we see that only (C) is correct.

Answer 15: The answer is (D). $t + u = 10$ and $10u + t = 10t + u + 18$, or $9u - 9t = 18$. Dividing both sides of this equation by 9, we get $u - t = 2$. We thus have $t + u = 10$ and $u - t = 2$. Adding these equations, we get $2u = 12$, so $u = 6$ and $t = 4$. Thus, the number is 46. We could have used trial and error for this problem.

Answer 16: The correct answers are (A) and (B). In general, two lines may intersect in zero, one, or an infinite number of points. Choice (A) is correct if line 2 is parallel to line 1, which can occur if the slopes of their lines are equal. The slope of line 1 is 1, and the slope of line 2 is also 1 if $a = b$. If $a \neq b$, then choice (B) is correct because lines 1 and 2 will intersect in exactly one point. Choice (F) is wrong because two lines can share an infinite number of points only if they are the same line. This would require that one equation is a multiple of the other equation, but a and b are integers, and 20 is not a multiple of 6.

Answer 17: The correct answers are (A), (C), and (D). Let x represent the number of bottles of soda and $2x$ represent the number of hamburgers. Then $\$1.25x + (\$2.00)(2x) < \$20.00$. Dropping the dollar signs and simplifying the left side of the inequality, we get $5.25x < 20.00$. Then $x < 3.8$. Since x must be an integer, the only positive allowable values are 1, 2, and 3. Thus, the number of hamburgers John can buy, represented by $2x$, are 2, 4, and 6. (Note that choice (B) is impossible, because John would have to buy 1.5 bottles of soda.)

Answer 18: The correct answers are (B) and (E). The points of intersection can be found by the equation $x^2 = x + 6$, which can be written as $x^2 - x - 6 = 0$. Then $(x + 2)(x - 3) = 0$, so $x = -2$ or $x = 3$. We can use the equation $y = x + 6$ to determine the corresponding y values. If $x = -2$, then $y = 4$. If $x = 3$, then $y = 9$. Thus, the two intersection points are $(-2, 4)$ and $(3, 9)$. (Note that we could have used the equation $y = x^2$ to arrive at the same two points of intersection.)

Answer 19: The correct answers are (B), (C), (E), and (F). Each of the number of adult and student tickets must be a nonnegative integer. If x represents the number of student tickets and y represents the number of adult tickets, then $5x + 8y = 600$. For answer choice (B), when $x = 24$, $(5)(24) + 8y = 600$. This equation simplifies to $8y = 600 - (5)(24) = 480$, which means that $y = 60$. By substituting each of the given x values (number of student tickets) into $5x + 8y = 600$, the corresponding y value must be a nonnegative integer. For choices (C), (E), and (F), the y values are 50, 25, and 10, respectively. Choice A is wrong because $(5)(20) + 8y = 600$ leads to $8y = 500$, so y is not an integer (it is 62.5). Choice D is wrong because $(5)(60) + 8y = 600$ leads to $8y = 300$, so y isn't an integer (it is 37.5). You don't actually have to find y—you just have to realize it will have to be a positive integer.

Answer 20: The answer is $\frac{-31}{5}$. Adding the equations, we get $5x = 60$. Then $x = 12$. Substitute this value of x into either equation. Using the equation $3x + 5y = 5$, we get $(3)(12) + 5y = 5$. Then $5y = 5 - 36 = -31$. Therefore, $y = \frac{-31}{5}$.

Answer 21: The correct answer is 2. Let x represent the cost of one pear and let y represent the cost of one apple. Then $4x + 5y = 7$ and $2x + y = 5$. Adding these equations leads to $6x + 6y = 12$, which simplifies to $x + y = 2$. Thus, the combined cost of one pear and one apple is \$2. (Do *not* put the dollar sign inside the box.)

Answer 22: The correct answer is 18. Let t represent the tens digit and u represent the units digit of the original number. Then the original number is represented by $10t + u$, so the new number is represented by $10u + t$. Then $t + u = 9$ and $10u + t = 10t + u + 27$. The second of these two equations simplifies to $-9t + 9u = 27$, which can be further simplified to $-t + u = 3$. Add the equations $t + u = 9$ and $-t + u = 3$ to get $2u = 12$. Thus $u = 6$. Since the sum of the digits is 9, $t = 3$. Therefore, the product of the digits is $(6)(3) = 18$.

Let's take a break from algebra and word problems now, and look at some familiar lines and shapes.

CHAPTER 9: *Points and Lines*

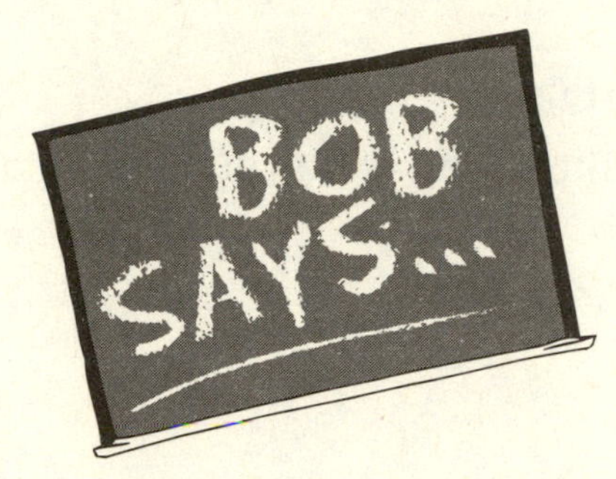

"Your journey began from a single point. You travel in a straight line; sometimes the slopes may be steep and the distance seems far, but you are now at the midpoint. The endpoint is in sight."

This topic used to be part of a course called analytic geometry (algebraic geometry), but it's important enough to have a chapter of its own.

POINTS IN THE PLANE

We start with a **plane**—a two-dimensional space, like a piece of paper. On this plane, we draw two perpendicular lines, or **axes**. The x-axis is horizontal; the y-axis is vertical. Positive x is to the right; negative x is to the left. Positive y is up; negative y is down. Points in the plane are indicated by **ordered pairs** (x, y). The x number, called the **first coordinate** or **abscissa**, is always given first; the y number, called the **second coordinate** or **ordinate**, is always given second. Here are some points on the plane.

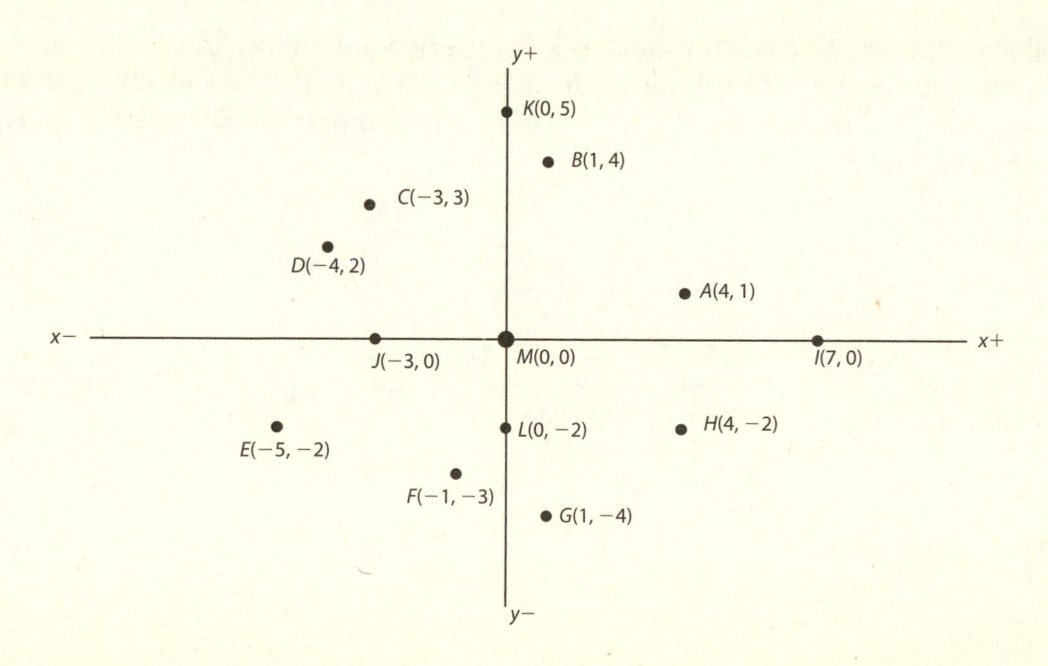

Note the following:

For any point on the x-axis, the y-coordinate always is 0.

For any point on the y-axis, the x-coordinate is 0.

The point where the two axes meet, (0,0), is called the **origin**.

The axes divide the plane into four quadrants, usually written with roman numerals, starting in the upper right quadrant and going counterclockwise.

In quadrant I, $x > 0$ and $y > 0$.

In quadrant II, $x < 0$ and $y > 0$.

In quadrant III, $x < 0$ and $y < 0$.

In quadrant IV, $x > 0$ and $y < 0$.

II	I
$x<0$, $y>0$	$x>0$, $y>0$
$x<0$, $y<0$	$x>0$, $y<0$
III	IV

In the following figure, we draw the line $y = x$. For every point on this line, the first coordinate has the same value as the second coordinate, or $y = x$. If we shade the area above this line, $y > x$ in the shaded portion. Similarly, $x > y$ in the unshaded portion. Sometimes, questions on the GRE ask about this.

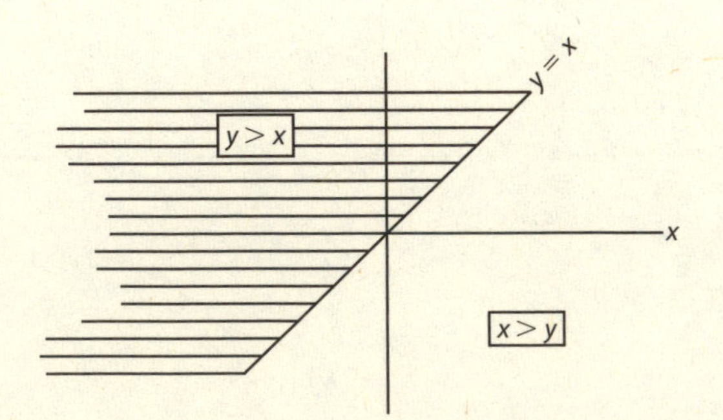

The following figure shows symmetry about the x-axis, y-axis, and the origin. Suppose (a, b) is in quadrant I. Then $(-a, b)$ would be in quadrant II, $(-a, -b)$ would be in quadrant III, and $(a, -b)$ would be in quadrant IV, as pictured.

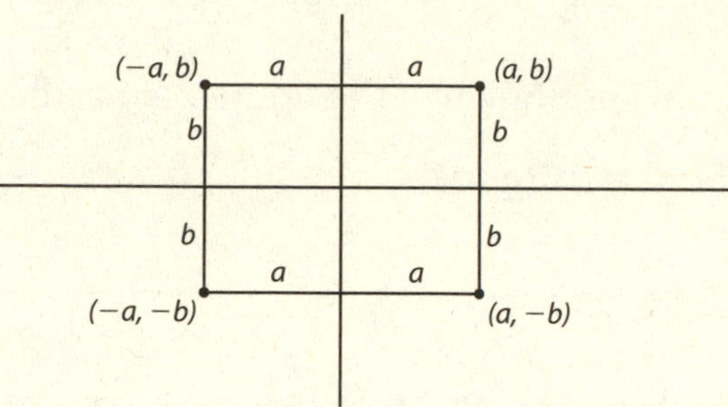

LINES

The formulas for distance and midpoint look a little complicated, but they are fairly easy to use. It just takes practice.

Distance

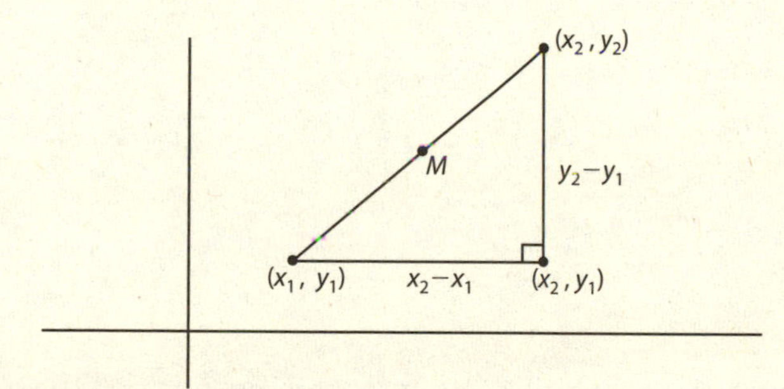

To find the **distance** between two points (x_1, y_1) and (x_2, y_2) on a plane, we must use the distance formula:

$$d = \sqrt{(x_2 - x_1)^2 + (y_2 - y_1)^2}$$

The distance formula is just the Pythagorean theorem (discussed in the next chapter).

Distances are always positive. You may be six feet tall, but you cannot be minus six feet tall.

Midpoint

The **midpoint** of a line between two points (x_1, y_1) and (x_2, y_2) on a plane is given by

$$M = \left(\frac{x_1 + x_2}{2}, \frac{y_1 + y_2}{2}\right)$$

If the line is horizontal, these formulas simplify to $d = x_2 - x_1$ and $M = \dfrac{x_1 + x_2}{2}$.

Similarly, if the line is vertical, these formulas simplify to $d = y_2 - y_1$ and $M = \dfrac{y_1 + y_2}{2}$.

For example, for the horizontal line shown in the figure below, the distance between the points is $d = x_2 - x_1 = 7 - (-3) = 10$, and the midpoint is $M = \dfrac{x_1 + x_2}{2} = \dfrac{-3 + 7}{2} = 2$.

−3 M 7

Similarly, for the vertical line shown in the figure below, the distance between the points is $d = y_2 - y_1 = -3 - (-7) = 4$, and the midpoint is $M = \dfrac{y_1 + y_2}{2} = \dfrac{(-7) + (-3)}{2} = -5$.

−3
M
−7

Slope

The **slope** of a line tells by how much the line is "tilted" compared to the x-axis. The formula for the slope of a line is

$$m = \frac{\text{rise}}{\text{run}} = \frac{\text{change in } y}{\text{change in } x} = \frac{y_2 - y_1}{x_2 - x_1},$$

where (x_1, y_1) and (x_2, y_2) are any two points on the line.

Note the following facts about the slope of a line, as shown in the figure below:

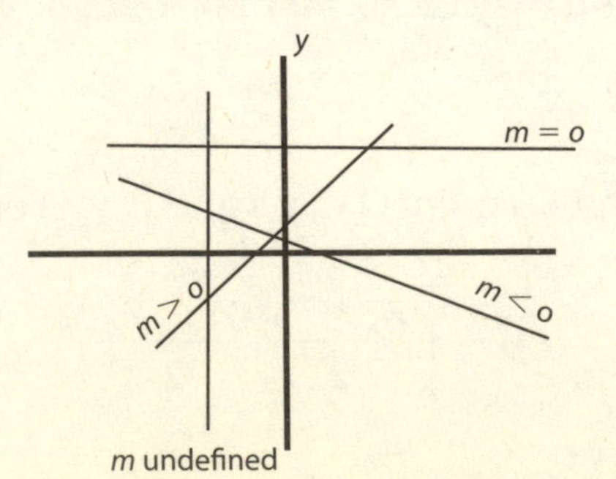

The slope is positive if the line goes from the lower left to the upper right.

The slope is negative if it goes from the upper left to the lower right.

Horizontal lines have zero slope.

Vertical lines have no slope or undefined slope or "infinite" slope.

Example 1: Find the distance, slope, and midpoint for the line segment joining these points:

a. (2, 3) and (6, 8)

b. (4, −3) and (−2, 0)

c. (7, 3) and (4, 3)

d. (2, 1) and (2, 5)

Solutions: **a.** We let $(x_1, y_1) = (2, 3) =$ and $(x_2, y_2) = (6, 8)$, although the other way around is also okay.

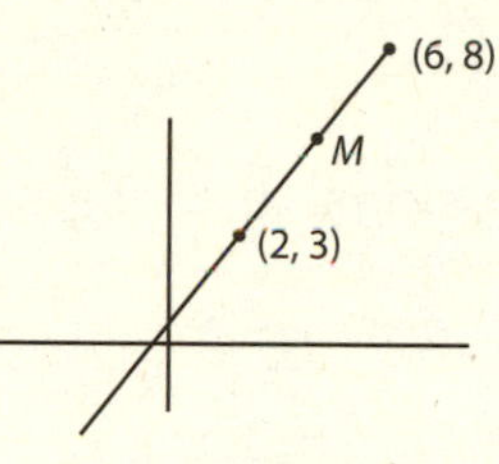

$$\text{Distance} = d = \sqrt{(x_2 - x_1)^2 + (y_2 - y_1)^2} = \sqrt{(6-2)^2 + (8-3)^2} = \sqrt{41}$$

$$\text{Slope} = m = \frac{y_2 - y_1}{x_2 - x_1} = \frac{8-3}{6-2} = \frac{5}{4}$$

$$\text{Midpoint} = M = \left(\frac{x_1 + x_2}{2}, \frac{y_1 + y_2}{2}\right) = \left(\frac{2+6}{2}, \frac{3+8}{2}\right) = (4,\ 5.5)$$

Notice that the slope is positive; the line segment goes from the lower left to the upper right.

b. We let $(x_1, y_1) = (4, -3) =$ and $(x_2, y_2) = (-2, 0)$.

$$\text{Distance} = d = \sqrt{(-2-4)^2 + (0-(-3))^2} = \sqrt{45} = \sqrt{3 \times 3 \times 5} = 3\sqrt{5}$$

$$\text{Slope} = m = \frac{0-(-3)}{-2-4} = \frac{-1}{2}$$

$$\text{Midpoint} = M = \left(\frac{4+(-2)}{2}, \frac{-3+0}{2}\right) = (1, -1.5)$$

Notice that the slope is negative; the line segment goes from the upper left to the lower right.

c. We let $(x_1, y_1) = (7, 3) =$ and $(x_2, y_2) = (4, 3)$.

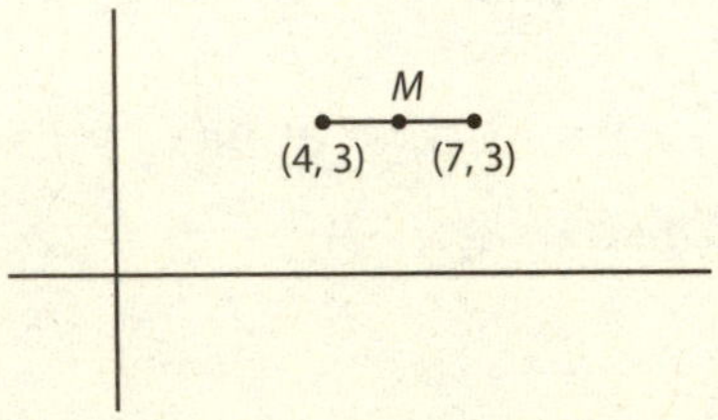

It is a one-dimensional distance, so

$$\text{Distance} = d = |4-7| = 3$$

$$\text{Slope} = m = \frac{3-3}{4-7} = \frac{0}{-3} = 0$$

$$\text{Midpoint} = M = \left(\frac{7+4}{2}, \frac{3+3}{2}\right) = (5.5,\ 3)$$

Notice that the horizontal line segment has slope $m = 0$.

d. We let $(x_1, y_1) = (2, 1) =$ and $(x_2, y_2) = (2, 5)$.

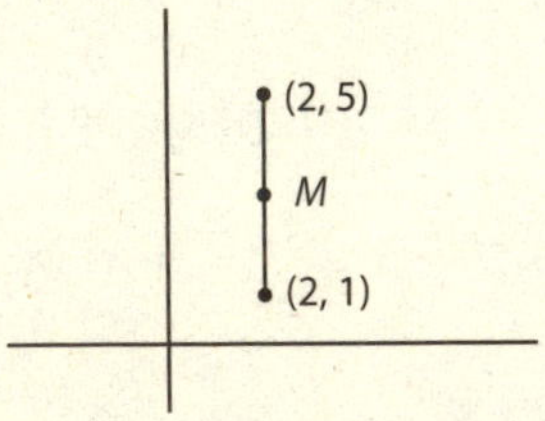

Again, this is a one-dimensional distance, so

$$\text{Distance} = d = |5-1| = 4$$

$$\text{Slope} = m = \frac{5-1}{2-2} = \frac{4}{0}, \text{ undefined}$$

$$\text{Midpoint} = M = \left(\frac{2+2}{2}, \frac{5+1}{2}\right) = (2,\ 3)$$

Notice that the slope of the vertical line segment is undefined.

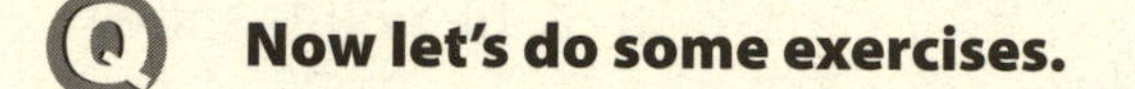

Now let's do some exercises.

Use the figure below for Exercises 1 and 2.

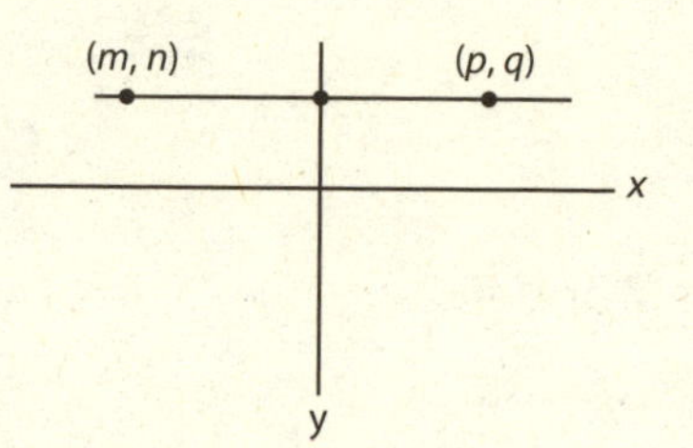

The line through (m, n) and (p, q) is parallel to the x-axis.

	Quantity A	**Quantity B**
Exercise 1:	m	p
Exercise 2:	n	q

Use the figure below for Exercises 3, 4, and 5.

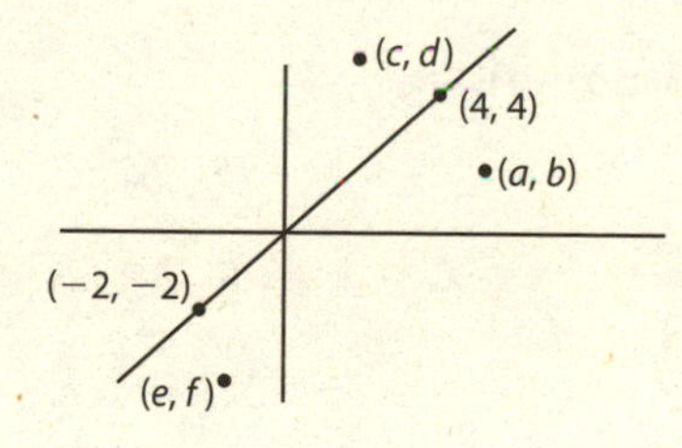

	Quantity A	**Quantity B**
Exercise 3:	c	d
Exercise 4:	e	f
Exercise 5:	$\frac{d}{c}$	$\frac{b}{a}$

Exercise 6: The coordinates of P are (j, k). If $s < k < j < r$, which of the points shown in the figure could have the coordinates (r, s)?

A. A

B. B

C. C

D. D

E. E

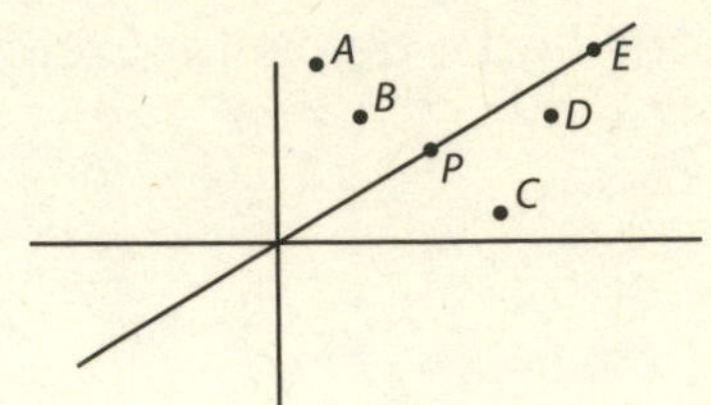

Use the figure below for Exercises 7 and 8.

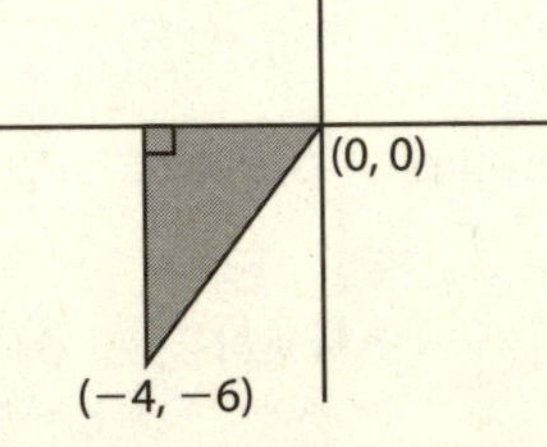

Exercise 7: Which of the following points is inside the triangle?

A. $(-3, 6)$

B. $(-5, -5)$

C. $(-2, -5)$

D. $(-3, -4)$

E. $(-1, -3)$

Exercise 8: The area of the triangle is

A. 6

B. 12

C. 18

D. 24

E. 48

Exercise 9: M is the midpoint of line segment AB. If the coordinates of A are $(m, -n)$, then the coordinates of B are

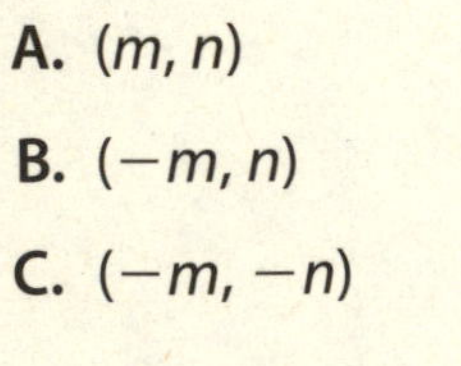

A. (m, n)

B. $(-m, n)$

C. $(-m, -n)$

D. (n, m)

E. $(-n, -m)$

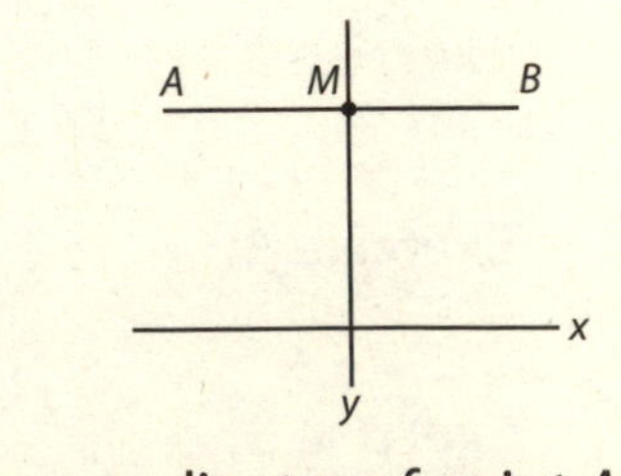

Exercise 10: In the given figure, $\overline{AB} \parallel x$-axis and $PQ = AB$. The coordinates of point A are

A. $(-1, 2)$

B. $(1, 2)$

C. $(9, -8)$

D. $(9, 0)$

E. $(-9, 2)$

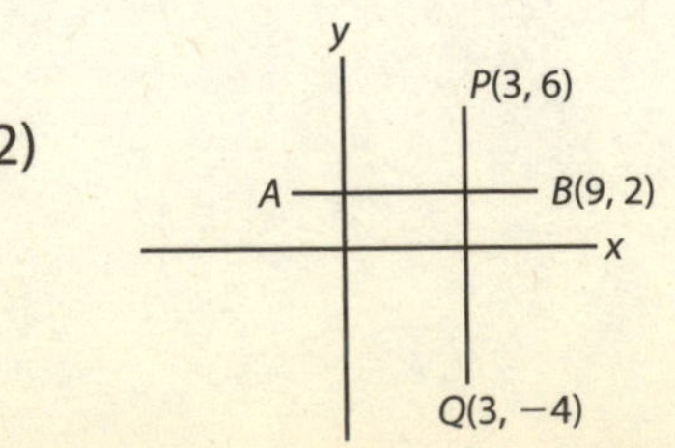

Let's look at the answers.

Answer 1: The answer is (B). $p > 0$ and $m < 0$.

Answer 2: The answer is (C). n and q are the same height.

Answer 3: The answer is (B). Point (c, d) is to the left and above point (4, 4), so $c < 4$, but $d > 4$.

Answer 4: The answer is (A). Point (e, f) is to the right and below $(-2, -2)$, so $e > -2$ and $f < -2$.

Answer 5: The answer is (A). Since d is bigger than c, $\frac{d}{c} > 1$; since a is bigger than b, $\frac{b}{a} < 1$.

Answer 6: The answer is (C). For points C, D, and E, the x value is bigger than the x value of P; only point C has a y value less than the y value of P.

Answer 7: The answer is (D).

Answer 8: The answer is (B). We really haven't gotten to this, but I asked it because we have the picture. The area of the triangle is half the area of the rectangle.

$$A = \frac{1}{2}bh = \frac{1}{2} \times 4 \times 6 = 12$$

Answer 9: The answer is (C). Slightly tricky. Point B has the same y value as A, but its x value is the negative of the x value for A.

Answer 10: The answer is (A). The length of $\overline{PQ} = 10$. For the length of $\overline{AB}$ to be 10, A must be $(-1, 2)$ since $9 - (-1) = 10$.

Standard Equation of a Line

Let's go over the facts we need.

Standard form of the line: $Ax + By = C$; A, B both $\neq 0$.

The ***x*-intercept**, the point at which the line hits the x-axis, occurs when $y = 0$

The ***y*-intercept**, the point at which the line hits the y-axis, occurs when $x = 0$.

Point-slope form of a line: Given slope m and point (x_1, y_1), the point-slope form of a line is $m = \frac{y - y_1}{x - x_1}$.

Slope-intercept form of a line: $y = mx + b$, where m is the slope and $(0, b)$ is the y-intercept.

Lines of the form:

$y =$ constant, such as $y = 2$, are lines parallel to the x-axis; the equation of the x-axis is $y = 0$.

$x =$ constant, such as $x = -3$, are lines parallel to the y-axis; the equation of the y-axis is $x = 0$.

$y = mx$ are lines that pass through the origin.

Example 2: For $Ax + By = C$, find the x- and y-intercepts.

Solution: The y-intercept means $x = 0$; so $y = \frac{C}{B}$, and the y-intercept is $(0, \frac{C}{B})$.

The x-intercept means $y = 0$; so $x = \frac{C}{A}$, and the x-intercept is $(\frac{C}{A}, 0)$.

Example 3: For $3x - 4y = 7$, find the x- and y-intercepts.

Solution: For the y-intercept, $x = 0$; so $y = \frac{7}{-4}$, and the y-intercept is $(0, -\frac{7}{4})$. For the x-intercept, $y = 0$; so $x = \frac{7}{3}$, and the x-intercept is $(\frac{7}{3}, 0)$.

Example 4: Given $m = \frac{3}{2}$ and point $(5, -7)$, write the equation of the line in standard form.

Solution: $m = \frac{y - y_1}{x - x_1}$, so $\frac{3}{2} = \frac{y - (-7)}{x - 5}$. Cross-multiplying, we get $3(x - 5) = 2(y + 7)$, or $3x - 2y = 29$.

Example 5: Given points (3, 6) and (7, 11), write the equation of the line in slope-intercept form.

Solution: $y = mx + b$. $m = \frac{11-6}{7-3} = \frac{5}{4}$, and we will use point (3,6), so $x = 3$ and $y = 6$. Therefore, $6 = \frac{5}{4}(3) + b$, and $b = \frac{9}{4}$. So the line is $y = \frac{5}{4}x + \frac{9}{4}$.

Example 6: Sketch lines $x = -3$, $y = 8$, and $y = \frac{2}{3}x$.

Solution:

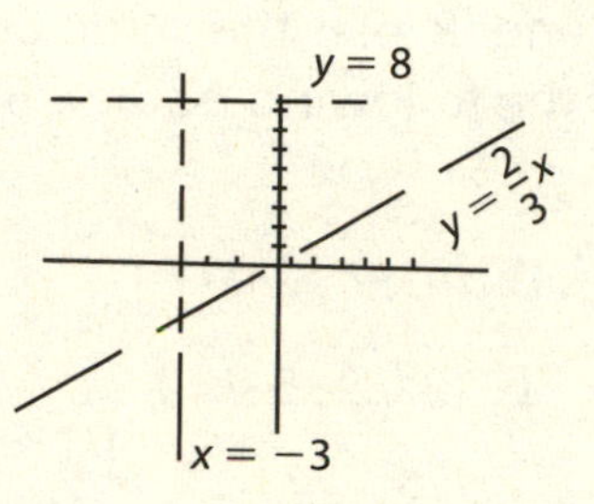

Let's do a few more exercises.

Exercise 11: A line with the same slope as the line $y = \frac{2}{3}x - 2$ is

A. $2x = 6 - 3y$
B. $2x + 3y = 6$
C. $2x - 3y = 6$
D. $-2x - 3y = 6$
E. $2y = 6 - 3x$

Exercise 12: Find the area of the triangle formed with the positive x-axis, positive y-axis, and the line through the point (3, 4) with slope -2. The area is

A. 5
B. 15
C. 25
D. 50
E. 10

Exercise 13: Which of the following equations represent lines parallel to the graph of $3x + 4y = 5$? Indicate all correct choices.

A. $y = -\frac{3}{4}x - 11$
B. $8y = -6x + 11$
C. $3x + 4y = 22$
D. $4y = 3x - 2$
E. $300x = -400y$
F. $4x + 3y = 7$

Exercise 14: Which of the following equations represent lines perpendicular to the graph of $3x + 4y = 5$? Indicate all correct choices.

A. $y = \frac{3}{4}x$

B. $y = -\frac{3}{4}x$

C. $y = \frac{4}{3}x$

D. $4x - 3y = 11$

E. $44x - 33y = 23$

Exercise 15: The distance between (0, 0) and (8, 6) is the same as the distance between (0, 0) and which of the following points? Indicate all correct choices.

A. $(-6, 8)$

B. $(5, 5\sqrt{3})$

C. $(9, 4)$

D. $(4\sqrt{2}, 2\sqrt{17})$

E. $(2\sqrt{5}, 5\sqrt{2})$

Exercise 16: Which of the following represent points on the line whose equation is $2x = 3y + 24$? Indicate all correct choices.

A. $(0, -8)$

B. $(6, -4)$

C. $(24, 8)$

D. $(30, 10)$

E. $(60, 32)$

For Exercises 17–20, point M has coordinates $(4, -2)$ and point N has coordinates $(8, 6)$.

Exercise 17: What is the y-coordinate of the midpoint of $\overline{MN}$?

Exercise 18: The length of $\overline{MN}$ can be expressed in reduced form as $c\sqrt{d}$. What is the value of d?

Exercise 19: What is the y-coordinate of the y-intercept of $\overleftrightarrow{MN}$?

Exercise 20: The equation of $\overleftrightarrow{MN}$ can be written in the form $Ax + By = C$, where A, B, and C are integers. In addition, there is no other common factor of A, B, and C other than 1. If A is positive, what is the value of B?

Let's look at the answers.

Answer 11: The answer is (C). You have to solve for y in each case. The only one that works is (C).

Answer 12: The answer is (C). You must draw the figure.

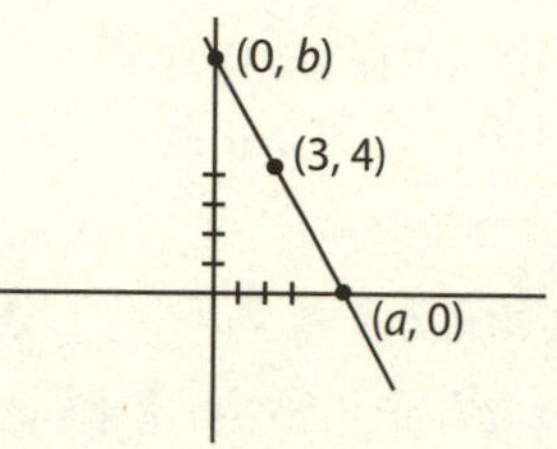

The area of the triangle is one-half the x-intercept times the y-intercept. The equation of the line is $-2 = \frac{y-4}{x-3}$. If we let $x = 0$, the y-intercept is 10. If we let $y = 0$, the x-intercept is 5. Area $= \frac{1}{2}ab = \frac{1}{2} \times 5 \times 10 = 25$.

Answer 13: The correct answers are (A), (B), (C), and (E). Parallel lines have the same slope. Rewrite $3x + 4y = 5$ as $y = -\frac{3}{4}x + \frac{5}{4}$. Thus, the slope is the coefficient of x, which is $-\frac{3}{4}$. Each of (A), (B), (C), and (E), when written in the form $y = mx + b$, has an m value of $-\frac{3}{4}$. The slope for choice (D) is $\frac{3}{4}$ and the slope for choice (F) is $-\frac{4}{3}$.

Answer 14: The correct answers are (C), (D), and (E). In Exercise 13, we determined that the slope of the corresponding line for $3x + 4y = 5$ is $-\frac{3}{4}$. Lines that are perpendicular to the given line must have a slope that is the negative reciprocal of $-\frac{3}{4}$, which is $\frac{4}{3}$. Each of (C), (D), and (E), when written in the form $y = mx + b$, has an m value of $\frac{4}{3}$. The slopes of choices (A) and (B) are $\frac{3}{4}$ and $-\frac{3}{4}$, respectively.

Answer 15: The correct answers are (A), (B), and (D). The distance between (0, 0) and (8, 6) can be found by the Pythagorean theorem. Its value is $\sqrt{(0-8)^2+(0-6)^2} = \sqrt{64+36} = \sqrt{100} = 10$, which matches the distance from each of (A), (B), and (D) to (0, 0). For choice (C), the distance is $\sqrt{97}$. For choice (E), the distance is $\sqrt{70}$.

Answer 16: The correct answers are (A), (B), (C), and (E). Each of these can be checked by direct substitution. For example, using answer choice (B), (2)(6) has the same value as $(3)(-4) + 24$, which is 12. For choice (D), $2(30) \neq (3)(10) + 24$.

Answer 17: The correct answer is 2. The midpoint of $\overline{MN}$ is $\left(\frac{4+8}{2}, \frac{-2+6}{2}\right) =$ (6, 2). Thus y-coordinate of the midpoint is 2.

Answer 18: The correct answer is 5. Using the Pythagorean theorem, the length of $\overline{MN}$ is $\sqrt{(8-4)^2+(6-(-2)^2} = \sqrt{16+64} = \sqrt{80} = \sqrt{16} \times \sqrt{5} = 4\sqrt{5}$. Thus, $d = 5$.

Answer 19: The correct answer is -10. First find the slope of $\overleftrightarrow{MN}$, which is $\frac{6-(-2)}{8-4} = 2$. Then $y = 2x + b$ represents the equation of the line and b represents the (y-coordinate of the) y-intercept. Substituting (8, 6), we get $6 = (2)(8) + b$, which means that $b = -10$.

Answer 20: The correct answer is -1. From the solution to Exercise 19, one form of the equation of $\overleftrightarrow{MN}$ is $y = 2x - 10$, which can be written as either $-2x + y = -10$ or $2x - y = 10$. Since A is positive, use the latter form, so that $B = -1$.

LINEAR INEQUALITIES IN TWO VARIABLES

Our last topic for this chapter deals with linear inequalities in two variables, usually x and y. Earlier in this book, we have discussed linear equations in two variables as well as linear inequalities in one variable.

Example 7: Graph the linear inequality $2x + 3y > 6$.

Solution: We can graph the equation $2x + 3y = 6$ by simply selecting the x- and y-intercepts. The x-coordinate of the x-intercept is found by substituting 0 for y, so that $2x + (3)(0) = 6$. We find that $x = 3$, so the x-intercept is (3, 0). In a similar fashion, we substitute zero for x to determine the y-intercept. Then $(2)(0) + 3y = 6$, so $y = 2$. The y-intercept is (0, 2). Below is the graph of $2x + 3y = 6$, indicated as L_1.

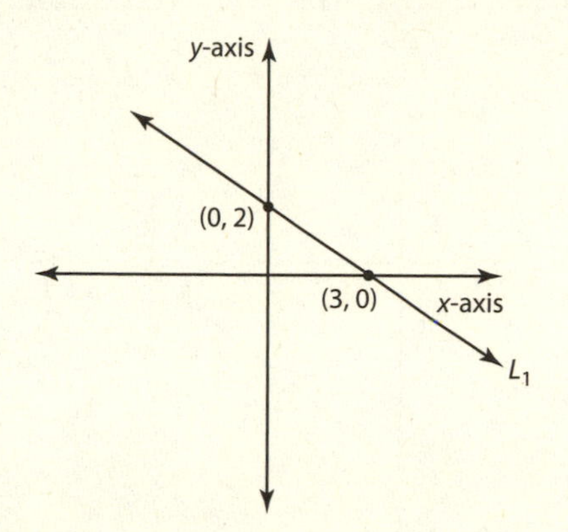

In order to graph $2x + 3y > 6$, we rewrite this inequality so that y is isolated. Subtract $2x$ from each side to get $3y > -2x + 6$. Dividing by 3, we get $y > \frac{-2}{3}x + 2$. This means that we are actually seeking y values that lie above the graph of the given line. We indicate this feature by using a dotted line and "shading" the section of the graph above this dotted line.

Another way to determine which side of the line to shade is quicker. Pick a point on one side of the line; the easiest one is (0, 0). If by substituting these values into the original inequality, the inequality is true, shade the side that includes that point. If the inequality is false, shade the other side. For the inequality $2x + 3y > 6$, (0, 0) gives $0 > 6$, which isn't true, so shade the side that doesn't include (0, 0).

Here is how the solution would appear.

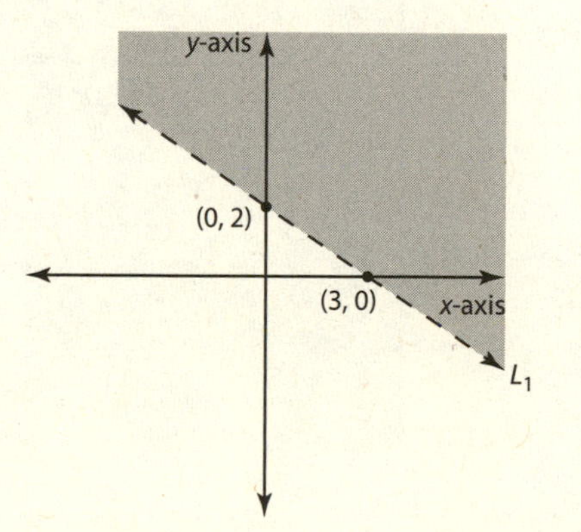

If the inequality had been $2x + 3y \geq 6$, we would have used a solid line in place of a dotted line to represent L_1, because the line would be included in the solution.

Example 8: Graph the linear inequality $3x - 4y > 24$.

Solution: Using the corresponding equation $3x - 4y = 24$, we first identify the x-intercept as (8, 0) and the y-intercept as (0, −6). Its graph appears below as L_2.

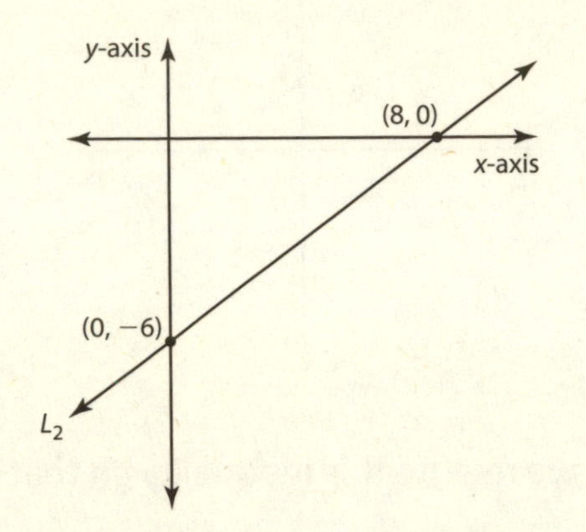

Now solve $3x - 4y > 24$ for y. Subtracting $3x$ from each side, we get $-4y > -3x + 24$. Finally, dividing by −4 and reversing the order of the inequality, we get $y < \frac{3}{4}x - 6$. This means that we are seeking y values below the graph of $3x - 4y = 24$. Or, alternatively, substituting (0, 0) in $3x - 4y > 24$ yields $0 > 24$, which is false, so shade the part of the graph on the other side of (0, 0).

The solution would appear as shown below. Note that L_2 is dotted.

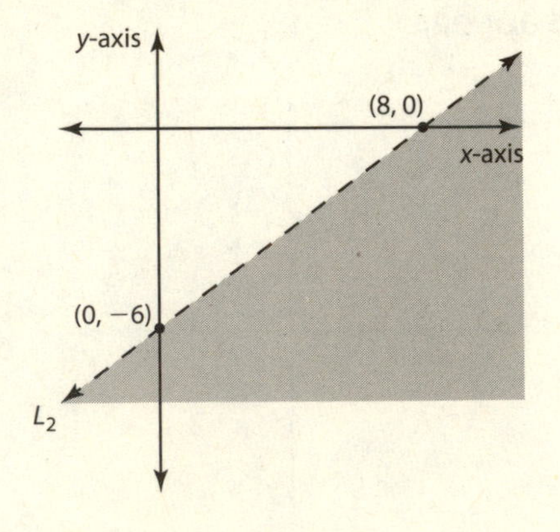

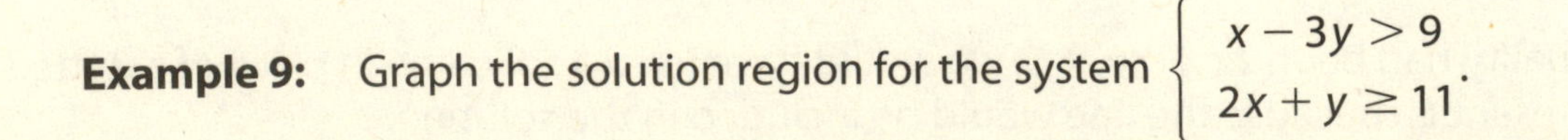

Example 9: Graph the solution region for the system $\begin{cases} x - 3y > 9 \\ 2x + y \geq 11 \end{cases}$.

Solution: Start with the equation $x - 3y = 9$ and find its intercepts to be (9, 0) and (0, −3). Now draw a dotted line and call it L_1. From the equation $2x + y = 11$, we can find its intercepts to be (5.5, 0) and (0, 11). Now draw a solid line and call it L_2. The graph of both lines appears below.

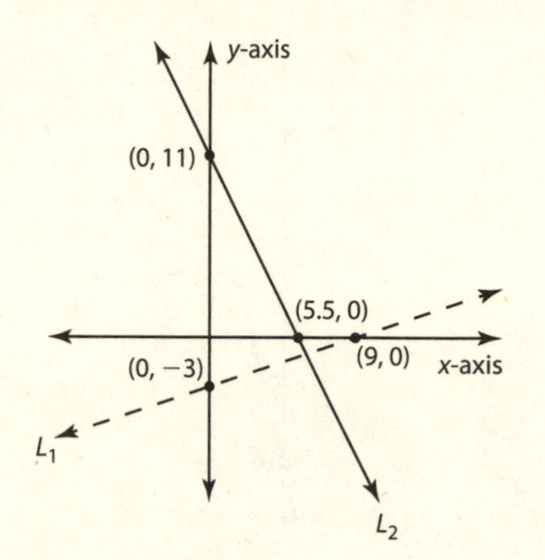

Note that L_1 is dotted and L_2 is solid. Next, solving $x - 3y > 9$ for y, we find that $y < \frac{1}{3}x - 3$. So, our solution region must lie below L_1. Similarly, solving $2x + y \geq 11$ for y, we find that $y \geq -2x + 11$. This means that our solution region must lie above L_2.

Alternatively, if we substitute (0, 0) into the first equation, we get $0 > 9$; and with the second equation, we get $0 \geq 11$. Both are false, so we shade the intersection of the areas that don't include (0, 0), which would be below L_1 and above L_2.

The shaded region shown below represents the solution to the original system of inequalities.

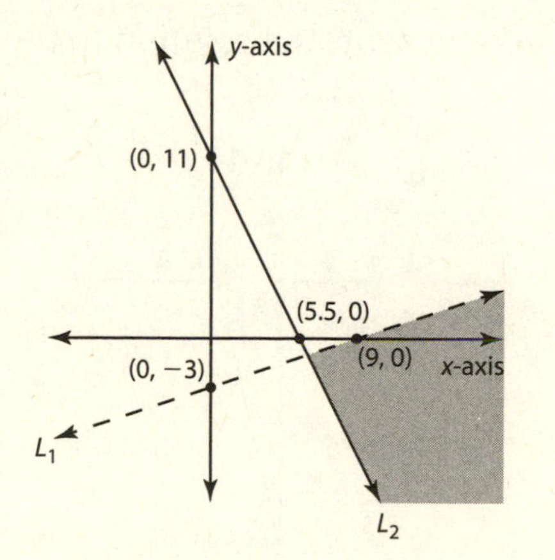

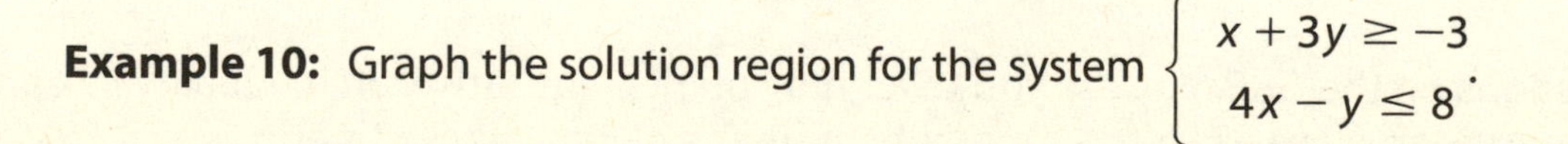

Example 10: Graph the solution region for the system $\begin{cases} x + 3y \geq -3 \\ 4x - y \leq 8 \end{cases}$.

Solution: For the line $x + 3y = -3$, the intercepts are $(-3, 0)$ and $(0, -1)$. Draw a solid line and call it L_1. For the line $4x - y = 8$, the intercepts are $(2, 0)$ and $(0, -8)$. Draw another solid line and call it L_2. The graph of both lines appears below.

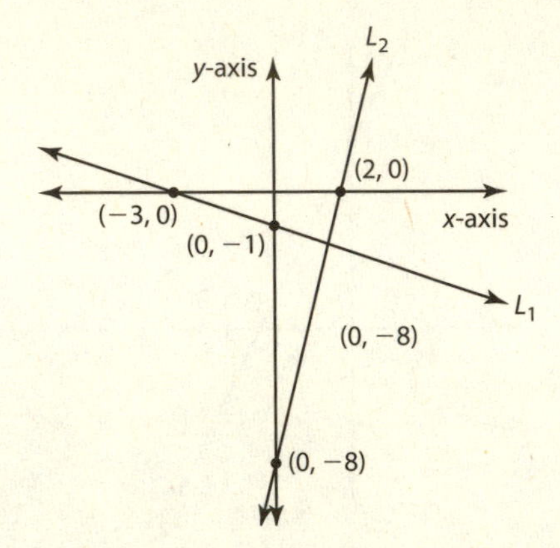

Now solve each inequality for y. For the inequality $x + 3y \geq -3$, subtract x from each side to get $3y \geq -x - 3$. Dividing each side by 3 leads to $y \geq -\frac{1}{3}x - 1$. This means that our solution region must lie above L_1. For the inequality $4x - y \leq 8$, subtract $4x$ from each side to get $-y \leq -4x + 8$. Dividing each side by -1 leads to $y \geq 4x - 8$. This means that our solution region must also lie above L_2.

Alternatively, if we substitute (0, 0) into the first equation, we get $0 \geq -3$; and with the second equation, we get $0 \leq 8$. Both are true, so we shade the area that includes (0, 0), which would be above L_1 and above L_2.

The shaded region shown below represents the solution to the given system of inequalities.

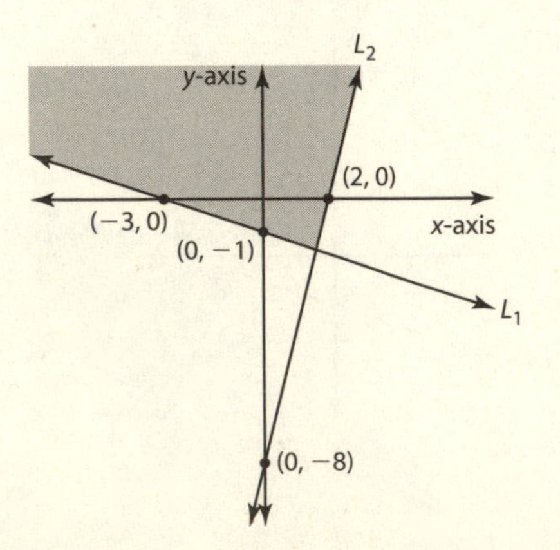

Some questions on the GRE may ask you to identify points that satisfy an inequality in x and y. For these questions, it is easiest to simply substitute the given values of x and y.

Example 11: Which of the following points satisfy the inequality $x - 7y < 12$. Indicate *all* correct answers.

A. $(1, -2)$
B. $(-1, 3)$
C. $(0, -2)$
D. $(3, 1)$
E. $(10, -1)$
F. $(26, 2)$

Solution: The correct answers are (B) and (D). For answer choice (B), $x - 7y = -1 - 21 = -22$, which is less than 12. For answer choice (D), $x - 7y = 3 - 7 = -4$, which is also less than 12. The value of $x - 7y$ for each of (A), (C), (E), and (F) are 15, 14, 17, and 12, respectively. None of these four numbers is less than 12.

Let's try a few exercises on linear inequalities in *x* and *y*.

Exercise 21: Look at the following graph with a solution region.

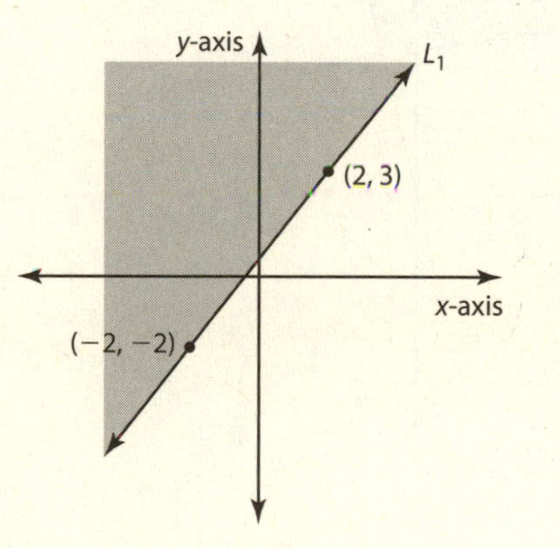

Which of the following inequalities corresponds to the shaded region that lies above line L_1?

A. $-5x + 4y \leq 2$
B. $5x - 4y > 2$
C. $-5x + 4y > 2$
D. $-5x + 4y \geq 2$
E. $5x + 4y > 2$

Exercise 22: Suppose line L_1 is represented by the equation $4x - y = 0$ and line L_2 is represented by the equation $x + 7y = 29$. Which of the following graphs represents the solution for $\begin{cases} 4x - y \leq 0 \\ x + 7y \leq 29 \end{cases}$?

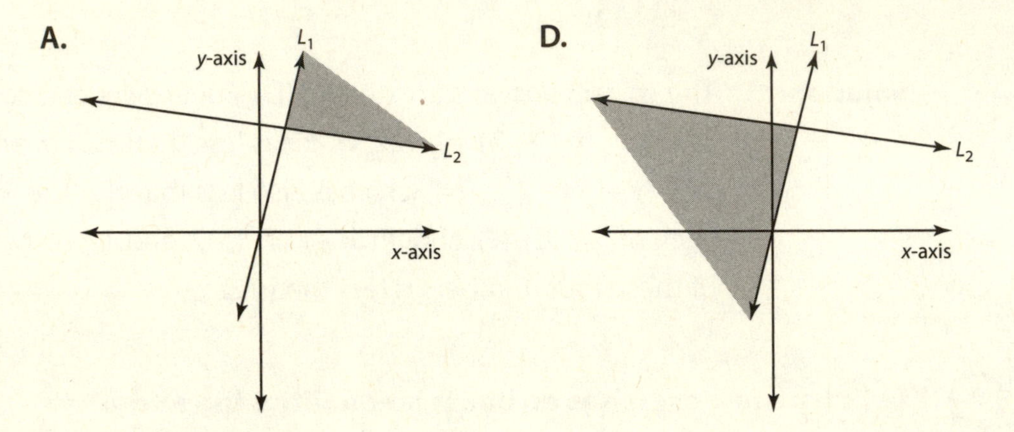

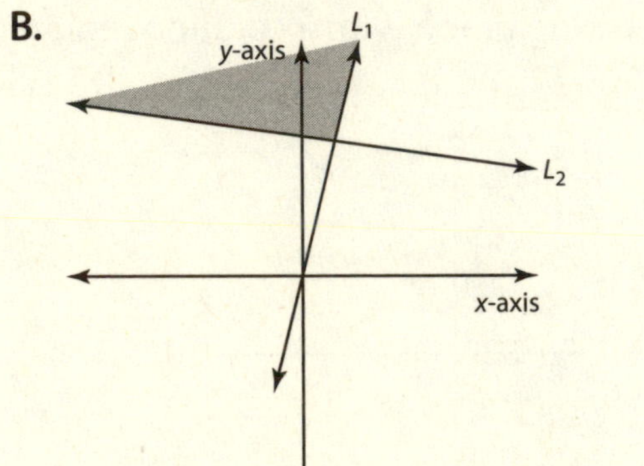

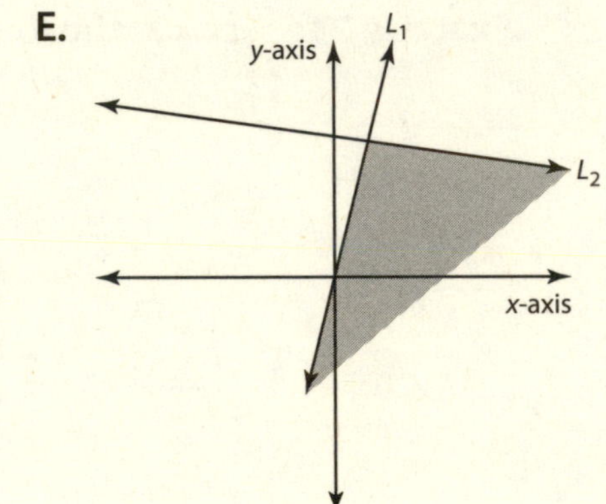

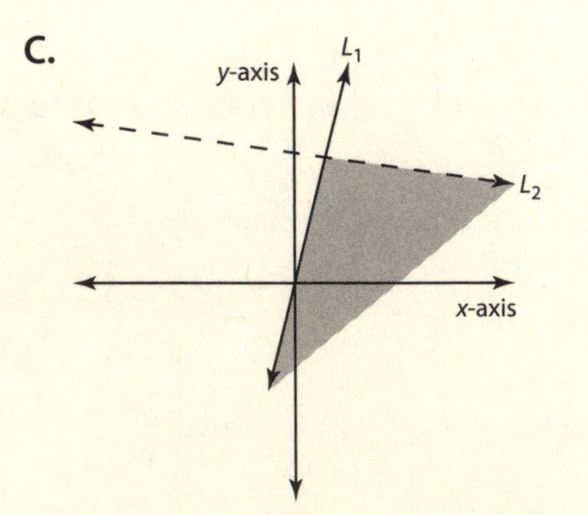

Exercise 23: Which of the following points satisfy the inequality $3x - 4y > 15$? Indicate *all* correct answers.

A. (7, 1)
B. (−1, −6)
C. (5, 0)
D. (9, 6)
E. (0, −3)
F. (2, −8)

Exercise 24: Which of the following points satisfy *both* $x + y < 8$ and $4x - 3y < 10$? Indicate all correct answers.

A. (2, 7)
B. (4, 1)
C. (6, −3)
D. (1, −1)
E. (−4, −2)
F. (−5, 9)

Let's look at the answers.

Answer 21: The correct answer is (C). Since the solution is above a *dotted* line, we can eliminate answer choices (A) and (D). For answer choice (B), solving the inequality for y leads to $y < \frac{5}{4}x - \frac{1}{2}$. The corresponding solution would lie below a given line, so this answer choice is wrong. The quickest method to determine which of (C) and (E) is correct is to substitute the point (2, 3) into their corresponding equations. Using the equation $-5x + 4y = 2$ for answer choice (C), we find that $(-5)(2) + (4)(3) = 2$ is a true statement. Answer choice (E) is wrong because $(5)(2) + (4)(3) = 2$ is a false statement.

Answer 22: The correct answer is (D). First rewrite $4x - y \leq 0$ as $y \geq 4x$. This inequality tells us that the solution region must lie above L_1. Now rewrite $x + 7y \leq 29$ as $y \leq -\frac{1}{7}x + \frac{29}{7}$. This inequality tells us that the solution region must lie below L_2. Only answer choice (D) satisfies both conditions. Note that answer choice (C) was automatically wrong because line L_2 was dotted.

Answer 23: The correct answers are (A), (B), and (F). For answer choice (A), $(3)(7) - (4)(1) = 17 > 15$ is true. For answer choice (B), $(3)(-1) - (4)(-6) = 21 > 15$ is true. For answer choice (F), $(3)(2) - 4(-8) = 38 > 15$ is true. The values of $3x - 4y$ for answer choices (C), (D), and (E) are 15, 3, and 12, respectively.

Answer 24: The correct answers are (D), (E), and (F). For answer choice (D), $1 - 1 < 8$ and $(4)(1) - (3)(-1) = 7 < 10$ are true. For answer choice (E), $-4 - 2 < 8$ and $(4)(-4) - (3)(-2) = -10 < 10$ are true. For answer choice (F), $-5 + 9 < 8$ and $(4)(-5) - (3)(9) = -47 < 10$ are true. Answer choice (A) is wrong because $2 + 7 = 9$, which is not less than 8. Answer choice (B) is wrong because $(4)(4) - (3)(1) = 13$, which is not less than 10. Answer choice (C) is wrong because $(4)(6) - (3)(-3) = 33$, which is not less than 10.

Let's finally get to angles and triangles.

CHAPTER 10: *About Angles and Triangles*

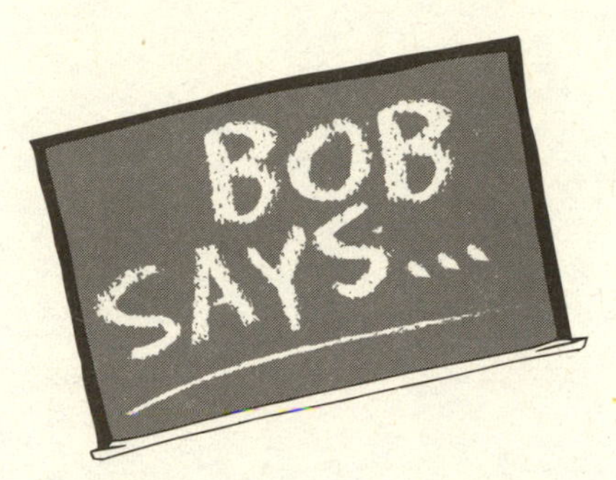

"Understanding the area and its perimeter will enhance your chances for success."

Before I wrote this chapter, I formulated in my head how the chapter would go. Too many of the questions on angles had to do with triangles. So I decided to write the chapters together. Let's start with some definitions.

TYPES OF ANGLES

There are several ways to classify angles, such as by angle measure, as shown here:

Acute angle: An angle of less than 90°.

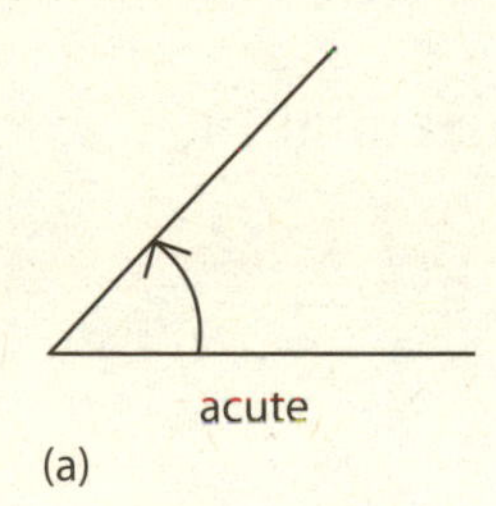

(a)

Right angle: A 90° angle. As we will see, some other words that indicate a right angle or angles are perpendicular (⊥), altitude, and height.

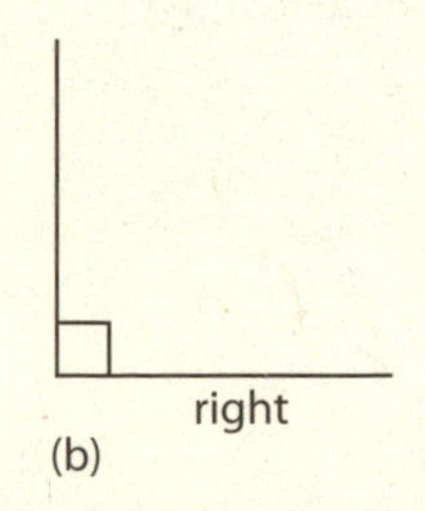

(b)

Obtuse angle: An angle of more than 90° but less than 180°.

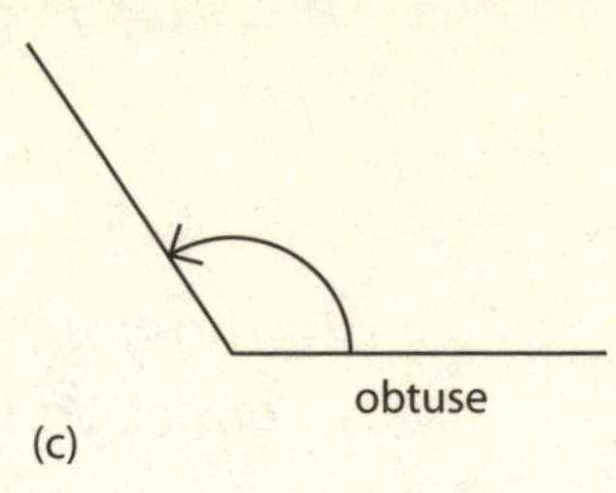

Straight angle: An angle of 180°.

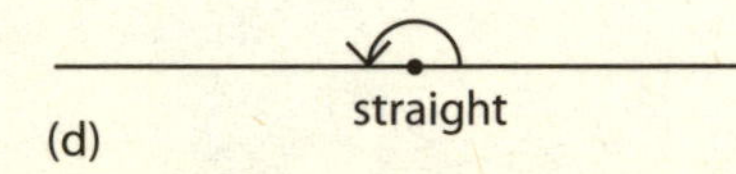

Reflex angle: An angle of more than 180° but less than 360°.

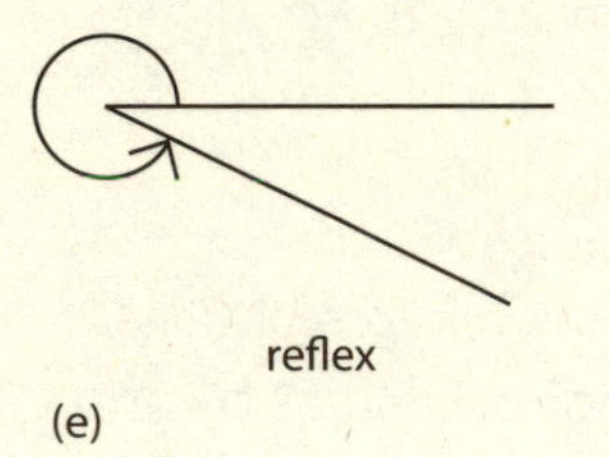

Angles are also named for their relation to other angles, such as:

Supplementary angles: Two angles that total 180°.

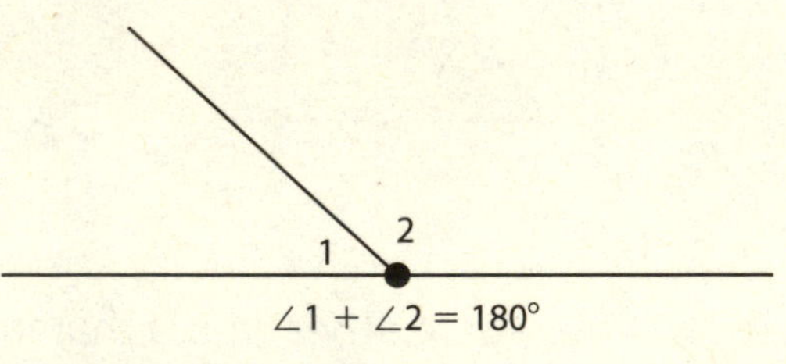

Complementary angles: Two angles that total 90°.

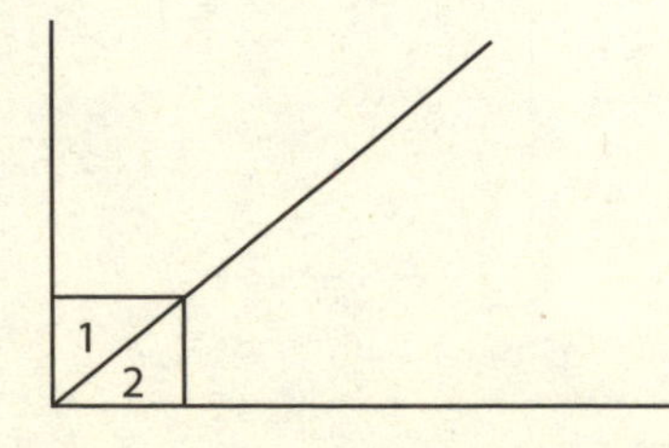

A note of interest: Once around a circle is 360°. The reason that it is 360° is that the ancient Babylonians, about 7,000 years ago, thought there were 360 days in a year. Three hundred sixty degrees is unique to the planet Earth.

You probably learned that angles are congruent and measures of angles are equal. I am using what I learned; it is simpler and makes understanding easier. So "angle 1 equals angle 2" (or $\angle 1 = \angle 2$) means the angles are both congruent and equal in degrees.

ANGLES FORMED BY PARALLEL LINES

Let's look at angles formed when a line crosses two parallel lines. In the figure below, $L_1 \parallel L_2$, and *t* is a transversal, a line that cuts two or more lines. It is not important that you know the names of these angles, although many of you will. It is important only to know that angles formed by a line crossing parallel lines that look equal are equal. The angles that are not equal add to 180°. In this figure, $\angle 1 = \angle 4 = \angle 5 = \angle 8$ and $\angle 2 = \angle 3 = \angle 6 = \angle 7$. Any angle from the first group added to any angle from the second group totals 180°.

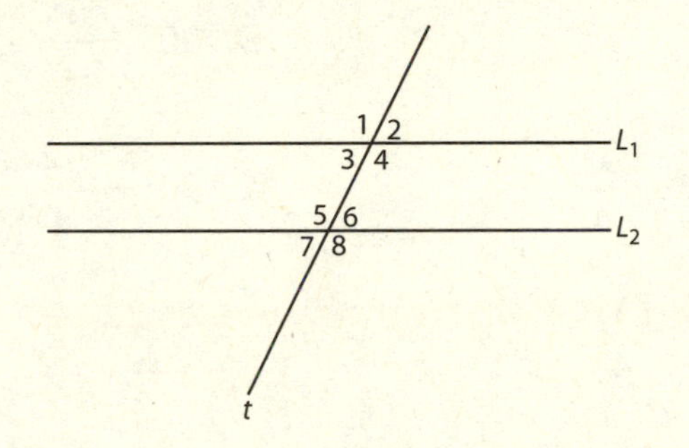

Vertical angles, which are the opposite angles formed when two lines cross, are equal. In the figure below, $\angle 1 = \angle 3$ and $\angle 2 = \angle 4$. Also, $\angle 1 + \angle 2 = \angle 2 + \angle 3 = \angle 3 + \angle 4 = \angle 4 + \angle 1 = 180°$.

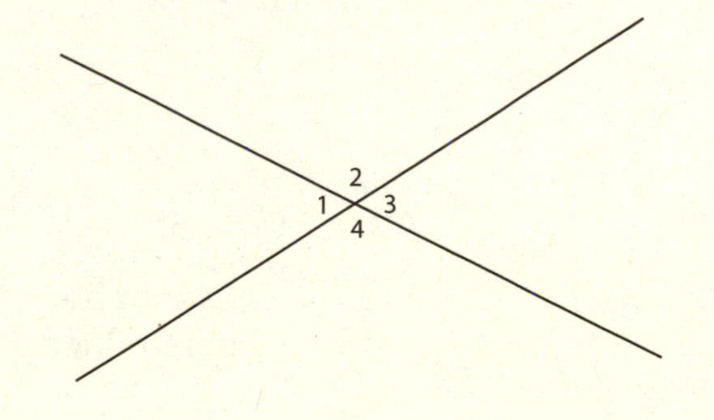

Let's do some exercises.

Exercise 1: $\angle b =$

A. 45°
B. 60°
C. 90°
D. 105°
E. 135°

Exercise 2: $L_1 \parallel L_2$. $m - n =$

A. 30°
B. 50°
C. 65°
D. 90°
E. 180°

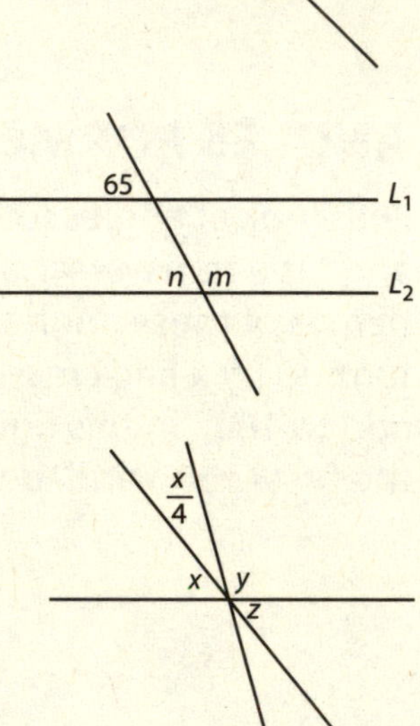

Exercise 3: $y + z =$

A. $180° - x$
B. $180° - \frac{x}{4}$
C. $45° - \frac{x}{4}$
D. $90° + \frac{5x}{4}$
E. $90° - \frac{5x}{4}$

Exercise 4: $180° - w =$

A. $x + w$
B. $x + y$
C. $y + z$
D. $y - z$
E. $z - w$

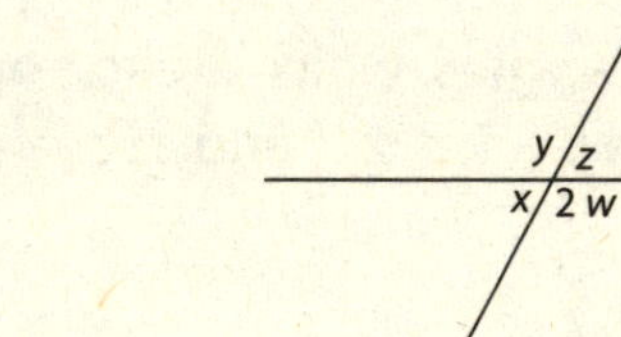

Exercise 5: $b =$

A. 5.5°
B. 7°
C. 10°
D. 12.5°
E. Cannot be determined

Exercise 6: y (in terms of x) =

A. x
B. $x + 40°$
C. $140° - x$
D. $140° + x$
E. $320° - x$

Exercise 7: $\angle x =$

A. 70°

B. 110°

C. 210°

D. 290°

E. 345°

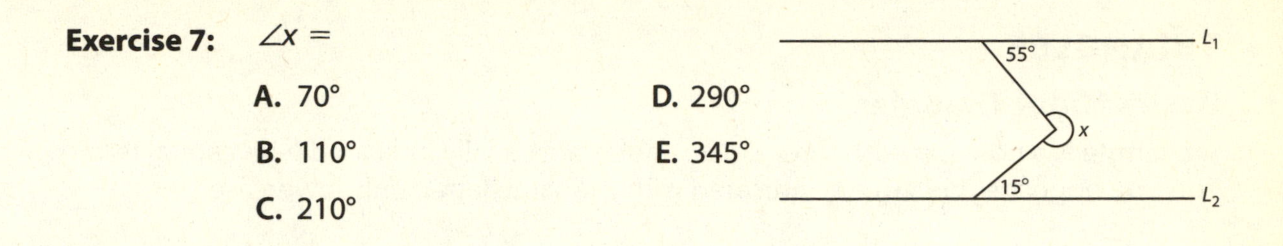

Now let's look at the answers.

Answer 1: The answer is (A). $3a + a = 180°$; $a = 45°$ and $b = a = 45°$.

Answer 2: The answer is (B). $n = 65°$ and $n + m = 180°$; so $m = 115°$, and $m - n = 50°$.

Answer 3: The answer is (B). $\frac{x}{4} + y + z = 180°$, so $y + z = 180° - \frac{x}{4}$.

Answer 4: The answer is (A). Below the line, $x + 2w = x + w + w = 180°$, so $x + w = 180° - w$.

Answer 5: The answer is (A). This is a toughie. Don't look at vertical angles, look at the supplementary angles. On the bottom, we have $5a + 2a + 5° = 180°$, so $7a = 175°$, and $a = 25°$. Then, on the left, $10b + 5a = 180°$. Substituting $a = 25°$, we get $10b = 180° - 125° = 55°$, or $b = 5.5°$.

We could also have looked at the vertical angles, once we determined that $a = 25°$. Then $10b = 2a + 5° = 2(25°) + 5° = 55°$, so $b = 5.5°$.

Answer 6: The answer is (C). $x + y + 40° = 180°$; so $y = 140° - x$.

Answer 7: The answer is (D). Draw $L_3 \parallel L_1$ and L_2.

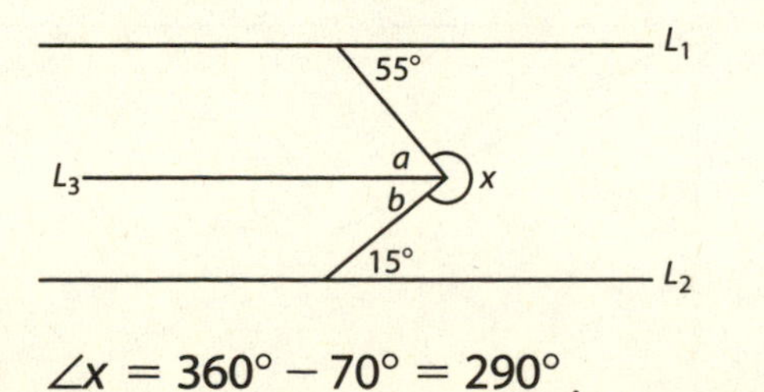

$\angle x = 360° - 70° = 290°$.

So many angle questions on the GRE involve triangles that we ought to look at triangles next.

TRIANGLES

Basics about Triangles

A **triangle** is a polygon with three sides. Angles are usually indicated with capital letters. The side opposite the angle is indicated with the same letter, only lowercase.

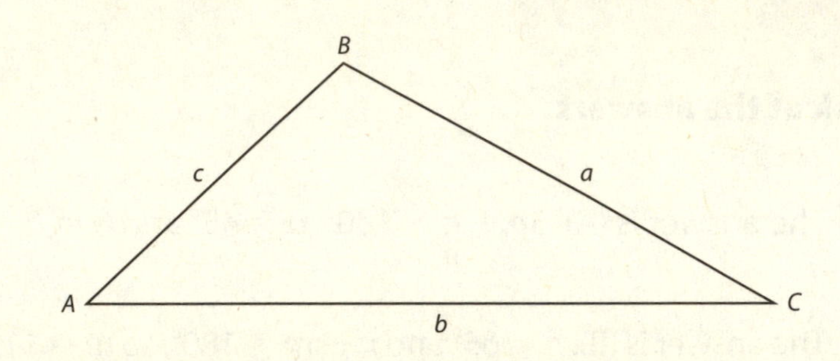

You should know the following general facts about triangles.

The **sum of the angles** of a triangle is 180°.

The **altitude**, or **height** (h), of ΔABC shown below is the line segment drawn from a vertex perpendicular to the base, extended if necessary. The **base** of the triangle is $AC = b$.

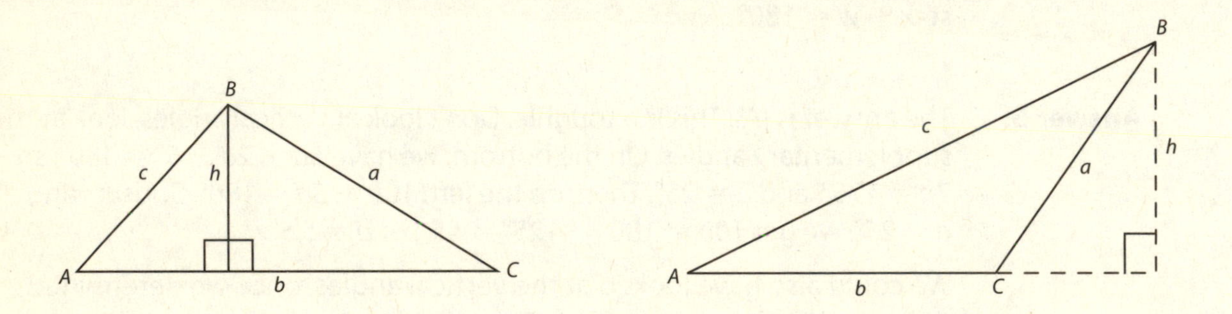

The **perimeter of a triangle** is the sum of the three sides: $p = a + b + c$.

The **area of a triangle** is $A = \frac{1}{2}bh$. The reason is that a triangle is half a rectangle. Since the area of a rectangle is base times height; a triangle is half a rectangle, as shown in the figure below.

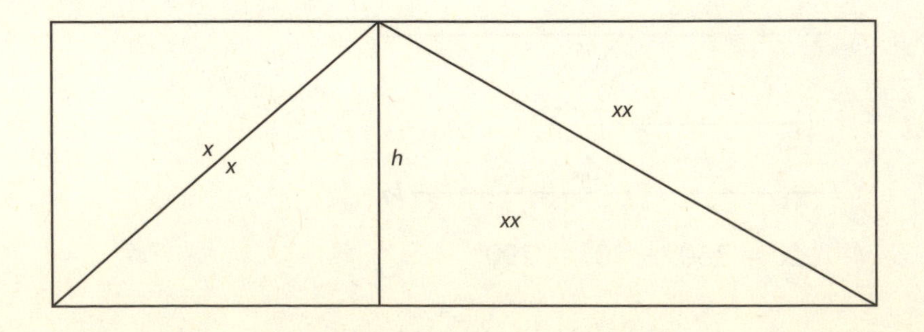

An **angle bisector** is a line that bisects an angle in a triangle. In the figure below, *BD* bisects $\angle ABC$ if $\angle 1 = \angle 2$.

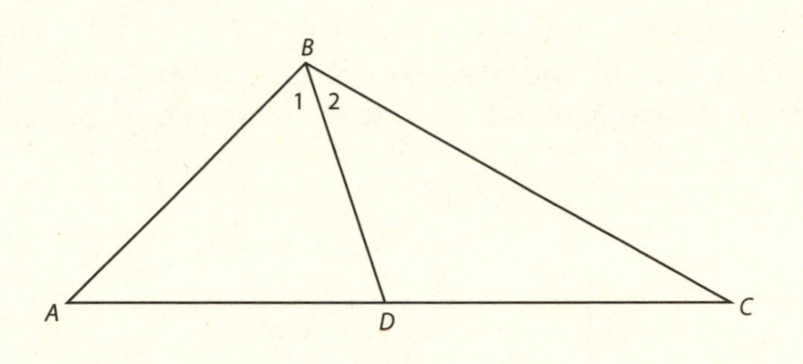

A **median** is a line drawn from any angle of a triangle to the midpoint of the opposite side. In the figure below, *BD* is a median to side *AC* if *D* is the midpoint of *AC*.

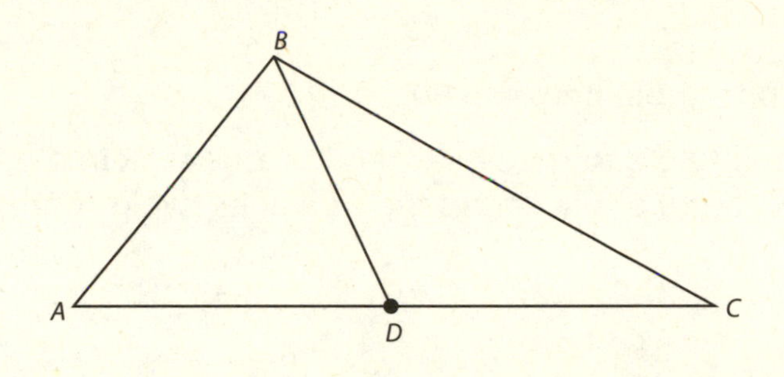

There are many kinds of triangles. One way to describe them is by their sides.

A **scalene** triangle has three unequal sides and three unequal angles.

An **isosceles** triangle has at least two equal sides. In the figure below, side *BC* (or *a*) is called the **base**; it may be equal to, greater than, or less than any other side. The **legs**, $AB = AC$ (or $b = c$) are equal. Angle *A* is the **vertex angle**; it may equal the others, or be greater than or less than the others. The **base angles** are equal: $\angle B = \angle C$.

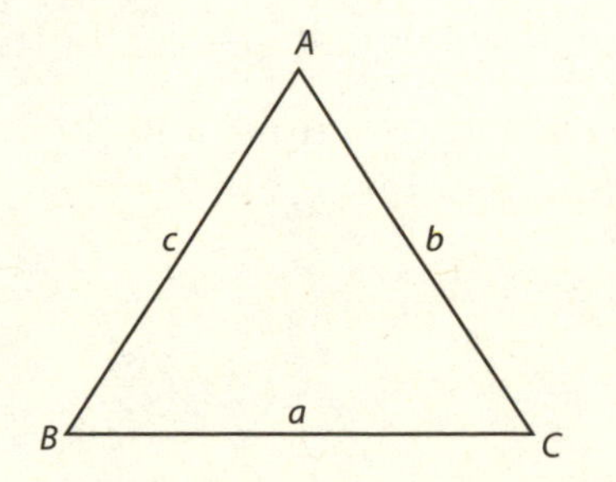

An **equilateral** triangle is a triangle with all equal sides. All angles equal 60°, so this triangle is sometimes called an **equiangular** triangle. For an equilateral triangle of side *s*, the perimeter $p = 3s$, and the area $A = \frac{s^2\sqrt{3}}{4}$. This formula seems to be very popular lately, and you may see it on the GRE.

Triangles can also be described by their angles.

An **acute** triangle has three angles that are less than 90°.

A **right** triangle has one right angle, as shown in the figure below. The **right angle** is usually denoted by the capital letter *C*. The **hypotenuse** *AB* is the side opposite the right angle. The **legs**, *AC* and *BC*, are not necessarily equal. $\angle A$ and $\angle B$ are always **acute** angles.

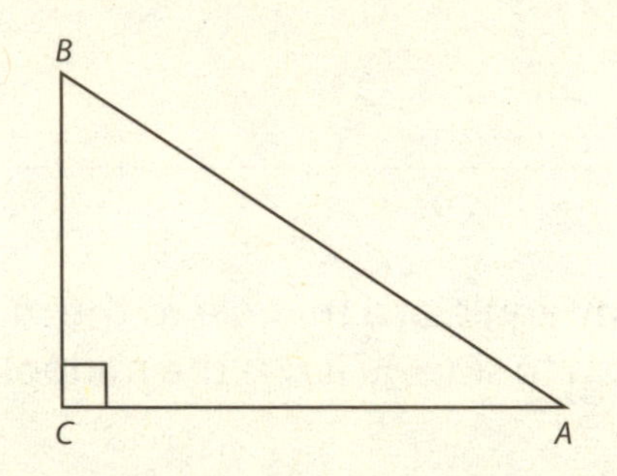

An **obtuse** triangle has one angle between 90° and 180°.

An **exterior angle** of a triangle is formed by extending one side. In the figure below, $\angle 1$ is an exterior angle. An exterior angle equals the sum of its two remote interior angles: $\angle 1 = \angle A + \angle B$.

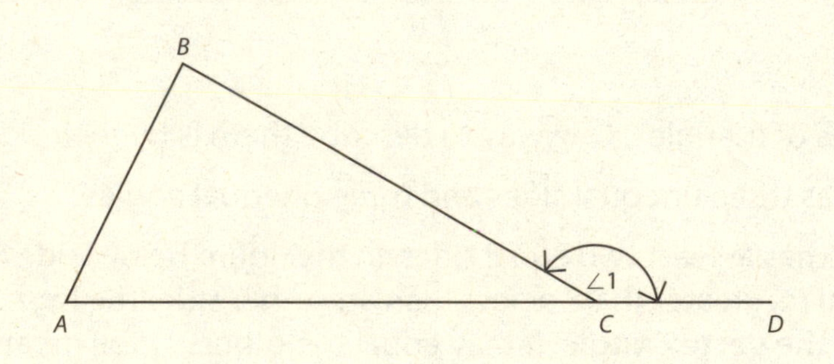

There are two other facts about triangles you should know:

1. The sum of any two sides of a triangle must be greater than the third side.
2. The largest side lies opposite the largest angle; and the largest angle lies opposite the largest side, as shown in the figure below.

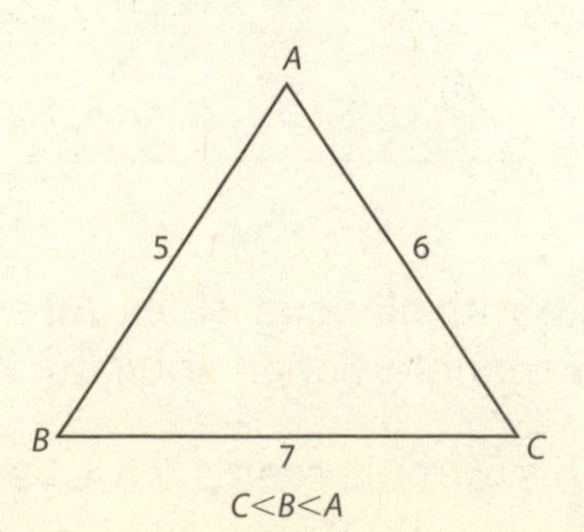

Example 1: Give one set of angles for a triangle that satisfies the following descriptions:

Description	Solution
a. Scalene, acute	50°, 60°, 70°
b. Scalene, right	30°, 60°, 90°: We will deal with this one soon.
c. Scalene, obtuse	30°, 50°, 100°
d. Isosceles, acute	20°, 80°, 80°
e. Isosceles, right	Only one: 45°, 45°, 90°: We will deal with this one soon also.
f. Isosceles, obtuse	20°, 20°, 140°
g. Equilateral	Only one: three 60° angles

Let's first do some exercises with angles. Then we'll turn to area and perimeter exercises. We'll then visit our old friend Pythagoras and his famous theorem.

Let's do some more exercises.

	Quantity A	Quantity B
Exercise 8:	a	b

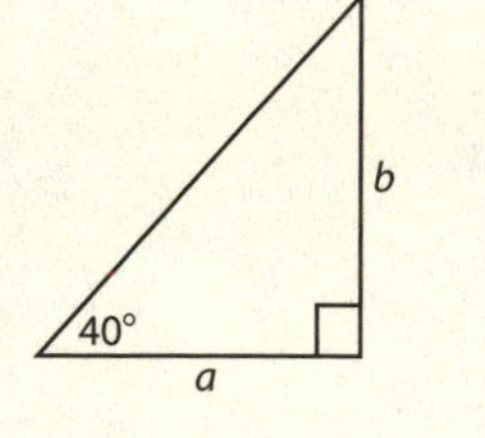

	Quantity A	Quantity B
Exercise 9:	$\angle 1$	$\angle 2$

Exercise 10: $L_1 \parallel L_2$ $x+y$ 180°

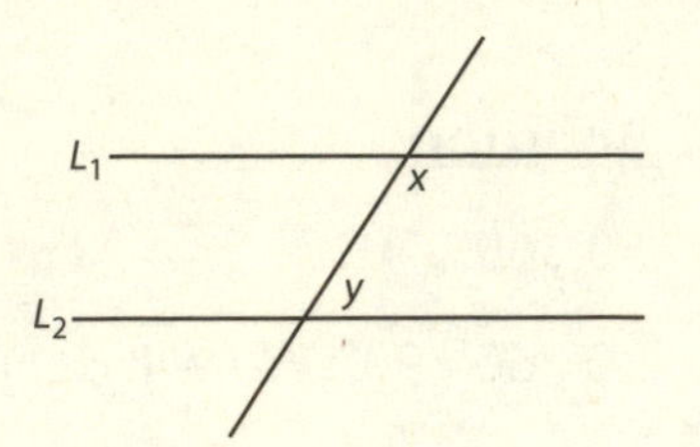

Exercise 11: If two sides of a triangle are 4 and 7, and if only integer measures are allowed for the sides, the third side must be taken from which set?

A. {5,6,7,8,9,10,11}
B. {4,5,6,7,8,9,10}
C. {3,4,5,6,7,8,9,10}
D. {3,4,5,6,7,8,9,10,11}
E. {1,2,3,4,5,6,7,8,9,10,11}

Exercise 12: Arrange the sides in order, largest to smallest, for the figure shown below.

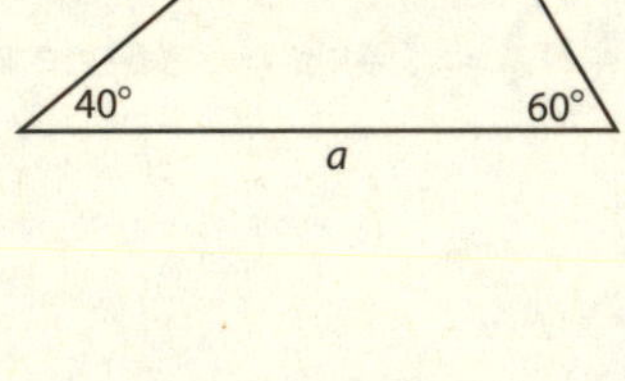

A. $a > b > c$
B. $a > c > b$
C. $b > a > c$
D. $b > c > a$
E. $c > a > b$

Exercise 13: $x = 2y; z =$

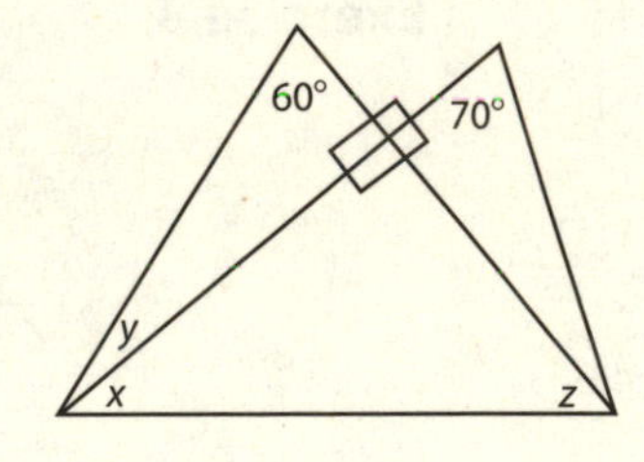

A. 30°
B. 40°
C. 50°
D. 60°
E. 90°

Exercise 14: WX bisects $\angle ZXY$; $\angle Z =$

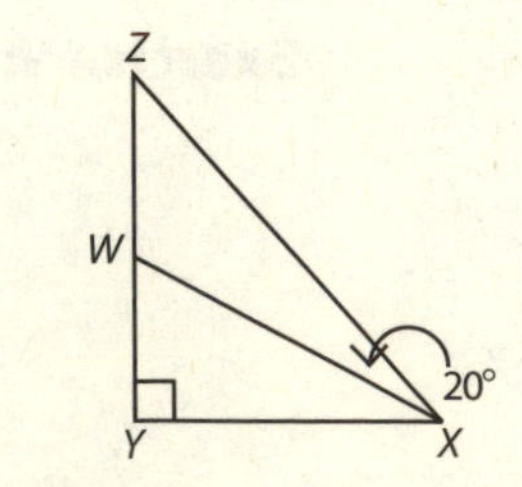

A. 20°
B. 40°
C. 50°
D. 60°
E. 70°

Exercise 15: $\angle TVW = 10x$; x could be

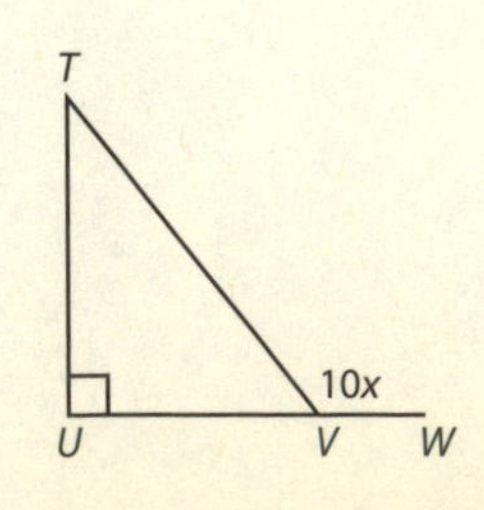

A. 3°
B. 6°
C. 9°
D. 16°
E. 20°

Exercise 16: Write b in terms of a:

A. $a + 90°$
B. $2a$
C. $2a + 90°$
D. $180° - a$
E. $180° - 2a$

Exercise 17: $a + b + c + d =$

A. 90°
B. 180°
C. 270°
D. 360°
E. 450°

Exercise 18: The largest angle is

A. 30°
B. 50°
C. 70°
D. 80°
E. 90°

Exercise 19: $L_1 \parallel AB$; $y =$

A. 40°
B. 60°
C. 70°
D. 80°
E. Cannot be determined

Exercise 20: $L_1 \parallel AB$; $y =$

A. 40°
B. 60°
C. 70°
D. 80°
E. Cannot be determined

Use ΔABC for Exercises 21 and 22.

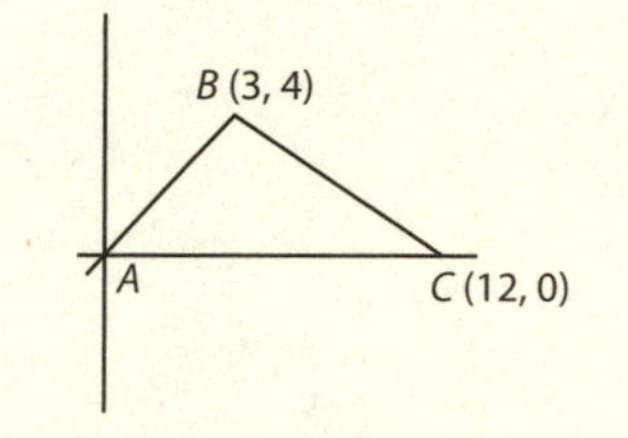

Exercise 21: The area of ΔABC is

A. 18
B. 24
C. 36
D. 48
E. 60

Exercise 22: The perimeter of ΔABC is

A. $17 + \sqrt{97}$
B. 27
C. 32
D. $\sqrt{266}$
E. $10\sqrt{10}$

For Exercises 23 and 24, use this figure of a square with an equilateral triangle on top of it, $AE = 20$.

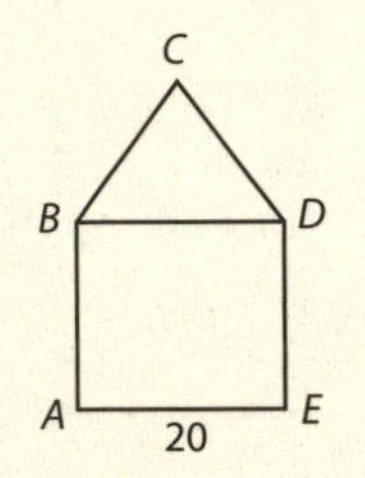

Exercise 23: The perimeter of *ABCDE* is

A. 50
B. 100
C. 120
D. 160
E. 200

Exercise 24: The area of *ABCDE* is

A. 600
B. $100(4 + \sqrt{2})$
C. $100(4 + \sqrt{3})$
D. 800
E. 1,000

For Exercises 25 and 26, use ΔABC with midpoints *X*, *Y*, and *Z*.

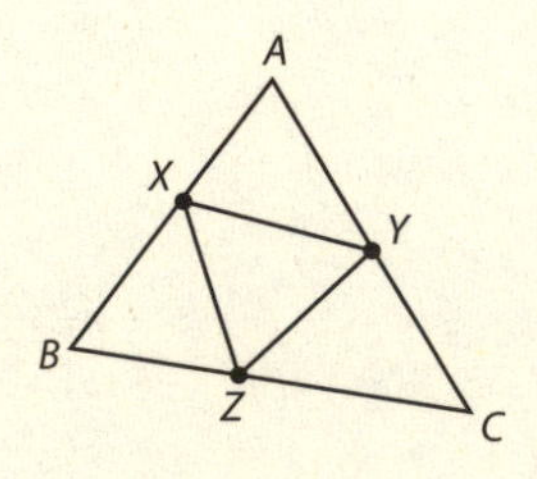

Exercise 25: If the perimeter of ΔABC is 1, the perimeter of ΔXYZ is

A. $\frac{1}{16}$

B. $\frac{1}{8}$

C. $\frac{1}{4}$

D. $\frac{1}{2}$

E. 1

Exercise 26: If the area of ΔABC is 1, the area of ΔXYZ is

A. $\frac{1}{16}$

B. $\frac{1}{8}$

C. $\frac{1}{4}$

D. $\frac{1}{2}$

E. 1

Exercise 27: In the figure shown, $BC = \frac{1}{3}BD$. If the area of $\Delta ABC = 10$, the area of rectangle $ABDE$ is

A. 30

B. 40

C. 60

D. 120

E. Cannot be determined

Let's look at the answers.

Answer 8: The answer is (A). Since a is opposite the 50° angle, it is larger than b, which is opposite the 40° angle. Beware! The figure is not drawn to scale.

Answer 9: The answer is (B). Since $\angle 2$ is an exterior angle, it is equal to the sum of the two remote interior angles, so it is bigger than either of them.

Answer 10: The answer is (C). Any two unequal angles formed in this figure total 180°.

Answer 11: The answer is (B). The third side s must be greater than the difference and less than the sum of the other two sides, or $> 7 - 4$ and $< 7 + 4$. Thus the third side must be between 3 and 11.

Answer 12: The answer is (B). Judge the relative lengths of the sides by the sizes of the angles opposite them. Then $a > c > b$.

Watch out for the words "Not drawn to scale." If it is a simple figure, "not drawn to scale" usually means it is not drawn to scale, and you cannot assume relative sizes without being given actual measurements. However, if it is a semi-complicated or complicated figure, the figure probably *is* drawn to scale.

Answer 13: The answer is (A). $y = 30°$; $x = 60°$; and $z = 30°$.

Answer 14: The answer is (C). $\angle ZXY = 40°$, so $\angle Z$ must be 50°.

Answer 15: Only answer (D) is correct. $\angle TVW$ must be between 90° and 180°, so $9° < x < 18°$.

Answer 16: The answer is (A). This is really tricky. UX is drawn to confuse you. In ΔTVW, b is the exterior angle, so $b = a + 90°$.

Answer 17: The answer is (C). The sum of 4 triangles is $4 \times 180° = 720°$. The sum of 5 right angles (don't forget the one in the lower left of the figure, which is the sum of four acute angles of the triangles) is 450°; so $a + b + c + d = 720° - 450° = 270°$.

Answer 18: The answer is (D). $x + 2x + 20 + 3x - 20 = 180$, or $6x = 180$, so $x = 30$. $2x + 20 = 80$ and $3x - 20 = 70$. The largest angle is 80°.

Answer 19: The answer is (A). $2x + x + 60 = 180$; $x = 40°$. But $y = x = 40°$ (because $L_1 \parallel AB$).

Answer 20: The answer is (E). y cannot be determined.

The GRE occasionally asks a question for which there is no answer. However, I've never seen two in a row and I've seen thousands of similar questions.

Answer 21: The answer is (B). $A = \frac{1}{2}bh = \frac{1}{2} \times 12 \times 4 = 24$.

Answer 22: The answer is (A). Use the distance formula to find sides *AB* and *BC*.

$$\begin{aligned} p &= AC + AB + BC \\ &= 12 + \sqrt{4^2 + 3^2} + \sqrt{(3-12)^2 + (4-0)^2} \\ &= 12 + \sqrt{25} + \sqrt{97} = 17 + \sqrt{97}. \end{aligned}$$

Answer 23: The answer is (B). Do not include *BD*; $p = 5 \times 20 = 100$.

Answer 24: The answer is (C).

$$\text{Area} = s^2 + \frac{s^2\sqrt{3}}{4} = 20^2 + \frac{20^2\sqrt{3}}{4} = 400 + 100\sqrt{3} = 100\left(4 + \sqrt{3}\right).$$

Answer 25: The answer is (D). If the perimeter of ΔABC is 1, and all the sides of ΔXYZ are half of those of ΔABC, so is the perimeter.

Answer 26: The answer is (C). If the sides of ΔXYZ are half of those of ΔABC, the area of ΔXYZ is $\frac{1}{4}A = \frac{1}{4}$.

Answer 27: The answer is (C). If we draw lines parallel to *DE* to divide the original rectangle into three congruent rectangles, and then divide each rectangle into two triangles, we see that each triangle is one-sixth of the rectangle. So the area of the rectangle is $6(10) = 60$.

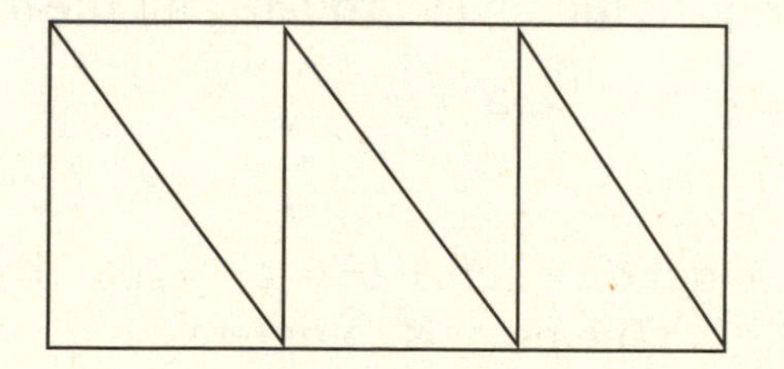

We'll have more of these type of exercises as part of Chapter 12, Circles.

Let's go on to good old Pythagoras.

PYTHAGOREAN THEOREM

This is perhaps the most famous math theorem of all. Most theorems have one proof. A small fraction of these have two. This theorem, however, has more than a hundred, including three by past presidents of the United States. We've had some smart presidents who actually knew some math.

The Pythagorean theorem simply states:

In a right triangle, the hypotenuse squared is equal to the sum of the squares of the legs.

In symbols, $c^2 = a^2 + b^2$.

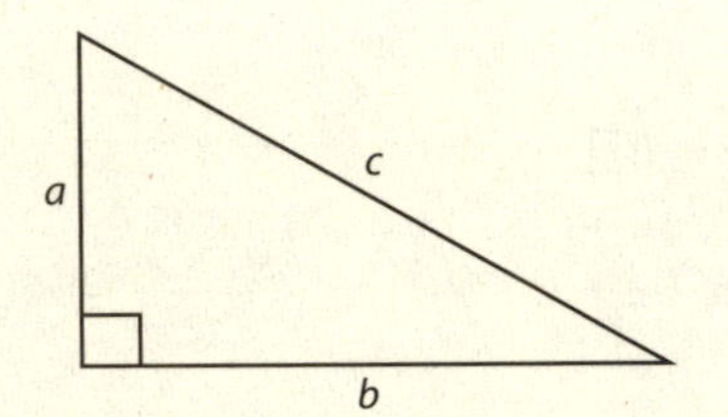

As a teacher, I must show you one proof.

Proof:

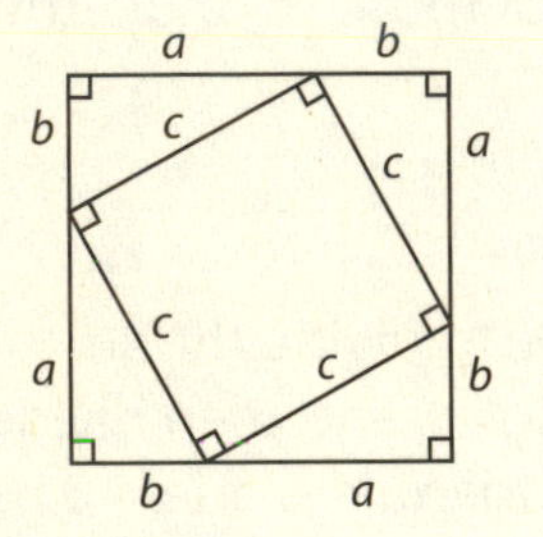

In this figure, the larger square equals the smaller square plus the four congruent triangles. In symbols, $(a + b)^2 = c^2 + 4\left(\frac{1}{2}ab\right)$.

Multiplying this equation out, we get $a^2 + 2ab + b^2 = c^2 + 2ab$. Then, canceling $2ab$ from both sides, we get $c^2 = a^2 + b^2$. The proof is complete.

There are two basic problems for the Pythagorean theorem that you need to know how to do: finding the hypotenuse and finding one of the legs of the right triangle.

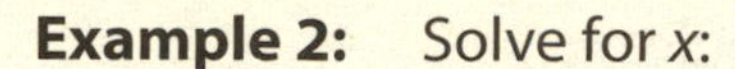

Example 2: Solve for *x*:

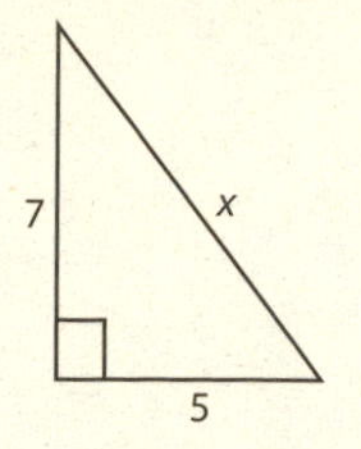

Solution: $x^2 = 7^2 + 5^2$; $x = \sqrt{74}$.

Example 3: Solve for *x*:

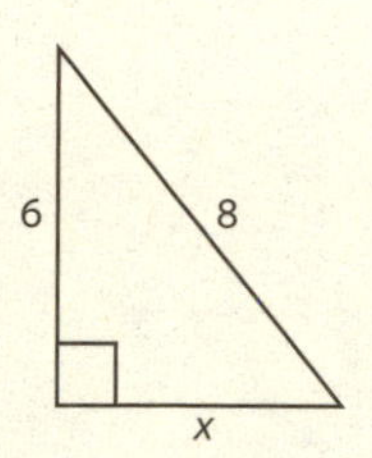

Solution: $8^2 = 6^2 + x^2$, or $x^2 = 64 - 36 = 28$. So $x = \sqrt{28} = \sqrt{2 \times 2 \times 7} = 2\sqrt{7}$.

Notice that the hypotenuse squared is always by itself, whether it is a number or a letter.

Pythagorean Triples

It is a good idea to memorize some Pythagorean triples. These are the measures of sides of triangles that are *always* right triangles. The hypotenuse is always listed third in the group.

The 3-4-5 group: 3-4-5, 6-8-10, 9-12-15, 12-16-20, 15-20-25

The 5-12-13 group: 5-12-13, 10-24-26

The rest: 8-15-17, 7-24-25, 20-21-29, 9-40-41, 11-60-61

Special Right Triangles

You ought to know two other special right triangles, the isosceles right triangle (with angles 45°-45°-90°) and the 30°-60°-90° right triangle. The facts about these triangles can all be found by using the Pythagorean theorem.

1. The 45°-45°-90° isosceles right triangle:
   - The legs are equal.
   - To find a leg given the hypotenuse, divide by $\sqrt{2}$ (or multiply by $\frac{\sqrt{2}}{2}$).
   - To find the hypotenuse given a leg, multiply by $\sqrt{2}$.

Example 4: Find x and y for this isosceles right triangle.

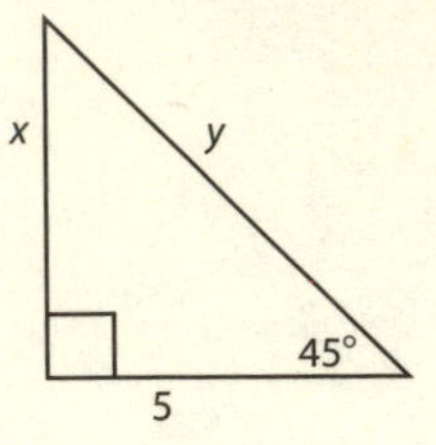

Solution: $x = 5$ (the legs are equal); $y = 5\sqrt{2}$.

Example 5: Find x and y for this isosceles right triangle.

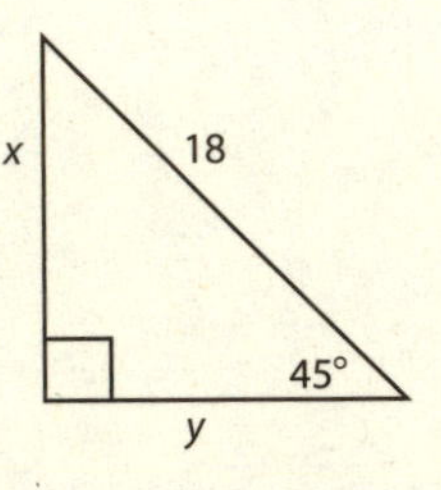

Solution: $x = y = \dfrac{18}{\sqrt{2}} = 18 \times \dfrac{\sqrt{2}}{2} = 9\sqrt{2}$.

2. The 30°-60°-90° right triangle.
   - If the shorter leg (opposite the 30° angle) is not given, get it first. It is always half the hypotenuse.
   - To find the short leg given the hypotenuse: divide by 2.
   - To find the hypotenuse given the short leg: multiply by 2.
   - To find the short leg given the long leg: divide by $\sqrt{3}$ (or multiply by $\dfrac{\sqrt{3}}{3}$).
   - To find the long leg given the short leg: multiply by $\sqrt{3}$.

Example 6: Find x and y for this right triangle.

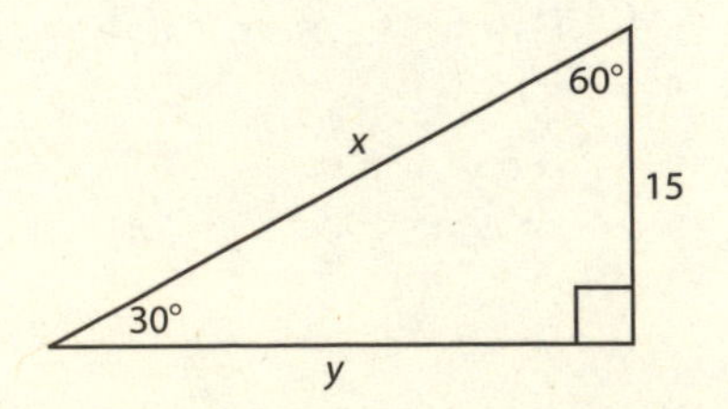

Solution: The short leg is given (15); $x = 2(15) = 30$; $y = 15\sqrt{3}$.

Example 7: Find x and y for this right triangle.

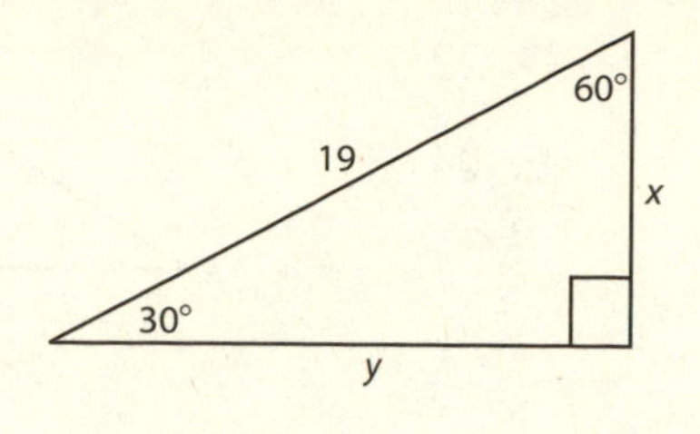

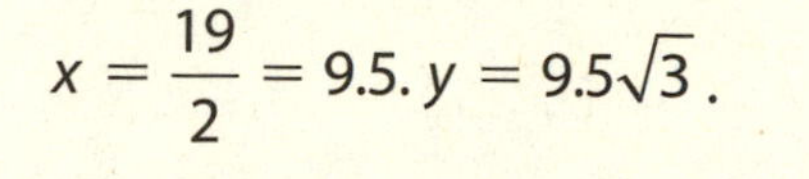

Solution: $x = \dfrac{19}{2} = 9.5.\ y = 9.5\sqrt{3}$.

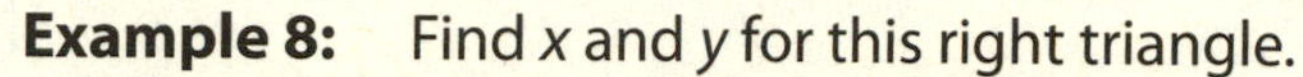

Example 8: Find x and y for this right triangle.

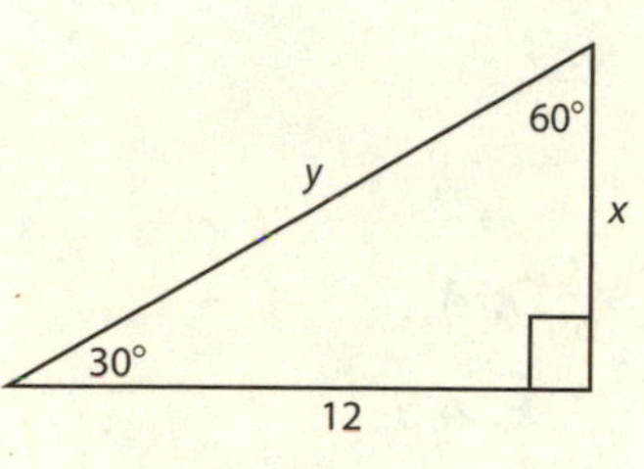

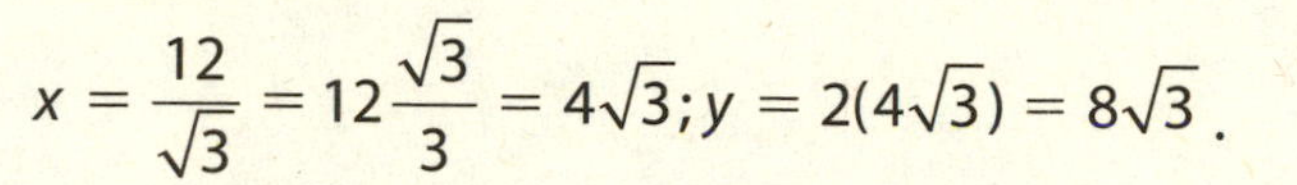

Solution: $x = \dfrac{12}{\sqrt{3}} = 12\dfrac{\sqrt{3}}{3} = 4\sqrt{3}; y = 2(4\sqrt{3}) = 8\sqrt{3}$.

Let's do a few exercises.

Exercise 28: Two sides of a right triangle are 3 and $\sqrt{5}$.

I. The third side is 2.

II. The third side is 4.

III. The third side is $\sqrt{14}$.

Which of the following choices is correct?

A. Statement II is true
B. Statement III is true
C. Statements I and II are true
D. Statements I and III are true
E. Statements I, II, and III are true

Exercise 29: The area of square $ABCD =$

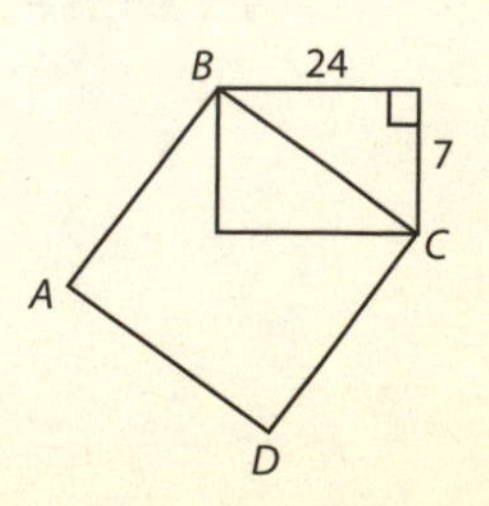

A. 50
B. 100
C. 225
D. 576
E. 625

Exercise 30: $x =$

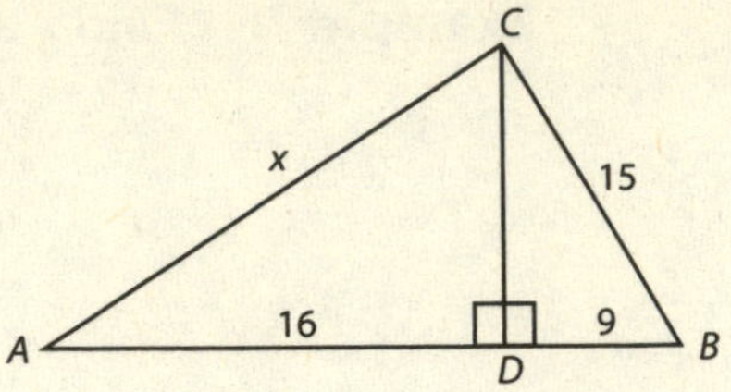

A. 16

B. 18

C. 20

D. 22

E. 24

Exercise 31: $c^2 - b^2 =$

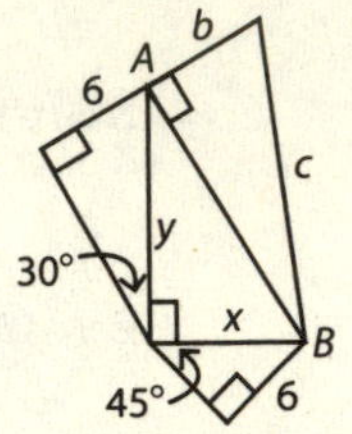

A. 72

B. 144

C. 216

D. 252

E. 288

Exercise 32: $x =$

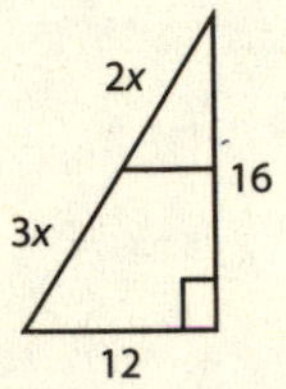

A. 1

B. 2

C. 3

D. 4

E. 4.5

Exercise 33: A 25-foot ladder is leaning on the floor. Its base is 15 feet from the wall. If the ladder is pushed until it is only 7 feet from the wall, how much farther up the wall is the ladder pushed?

A. 4 feet

B. 8 feet

C. 12 feet

D. 20 feet

E. 24 feet

Exercise 34: A triangle has a base of 4 units and a height of 2 units. Which of the following could be its perimeter, in units? Indicate *all* correct choices.

A. 12

B. 16

C. 24

D. 48

E. 400,000

F. 6.023×10^{23}

Exercise 35: Which of the following represents the lengths of the sides of a right triangle? Indicate *all* correct choices.

A. 8, 9, 10

B. 5, 12, 13

C. 8, 15, 17

D. 7, 24, 25

E. 10, 40, 41

F. 11, 22, 33

Exercise 36: For which of the following figures and dimensions will the area be 32? Indicate *all* correct choices.

A. Rectangle with a base of 8 and a height of 4

B. Triangle with a base of 8 and a height of 4

C. Parallelogram with a base of 4 and a height of 8 to that base

D. Rhombus with a base of 4 and a height of 8

E. Trapezoid with a median of 8 and a height of 4

Exercise 37: Which of the following could represent the measures of two of the angles of an isosceles triangle? Indicate *all* correct choices.

A. 40° and 60°

B. 50° and 80°

C. 59° and 62°

D. 45° and 90°

E. 20° and 120°

Exercise 38: The lengths of two sides of a triangle are 7 and 11. Which of the following could be the length of the third side? Indicate *all* correct choices.

A. 3

B. 5

C. 11

D. 16

E. 18

F. 20

Exercise 39: If two parallel lines are cut by a transversal, which of the following always illustrate congruent angles? Indicate *all* correct choices.

A. Corresponding angles

B. Alternate exterior angles

C. Alternate interior angles

D. Interior angles on the same side of the transversal

E. Exterior angles on the same side of the transversal

Exercise 40: Two sides of a right triangle are 3 and 4. Which of the following could be the length of the third side? Indicate *all* correct choices.

A. 2

B. $\sqrt{5}$

C. $\sqrt{7}$

D. 4

E. 5

F. 7

Exercise 41: The median to the base of an isosceles triangle is 10. If the base is 6, what is the area?

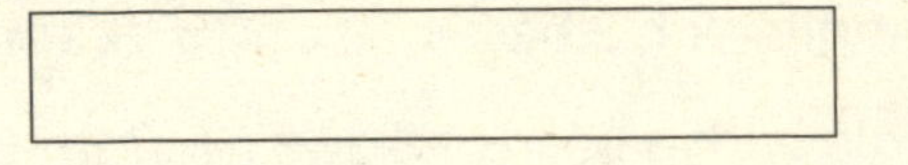

Exercise 42: The area of an equilateral triangle with side of 100 is expressed in simplest form as $a\sqrt{b}$. What is the value of a?

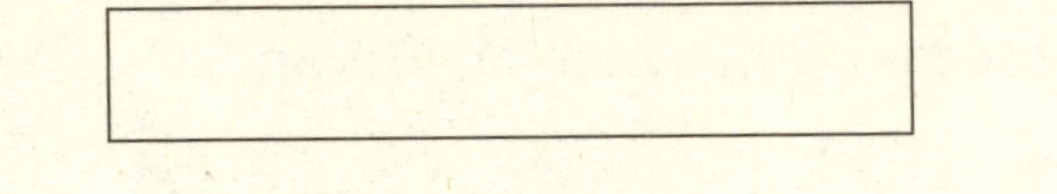

Exercise 43: Two of the angles of a triangle measure 30° and 40°. In degrees, what is the sum of the exterior angles?

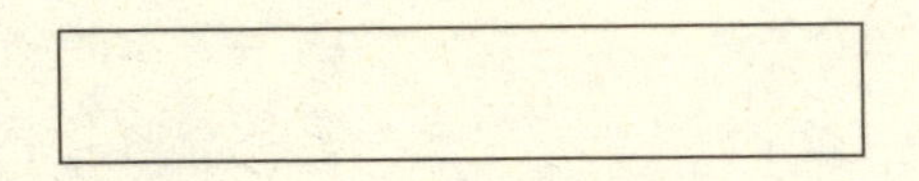

Let's look at the answers.

Answer 28: The answer is (D). Try the Pythagorean theorem with various combinations of 3, $\sqrt{5}$, and x (the third side). The only ones that work are Statement I: $2^2 + \left(\sqrt{5}\right)^2 = 3^2$, and Statement III: $3^2 + \left(\sqrt{5}\right)^2 = \left(\sqrt{14}\right)^2$.

Answer 29: The answer is (E). We recognize the right triangle as a 7-24-25 triple, so side $BC = 25$. The area of the square is $(25)^2 = 625$.

Answer 30: The answer is (C). This is a 15-20-25 triple, so $x = 20$.

Answer 31: The answer is (C). We see that AB is the side of two triangles. By the Pythagorean theorem, we get $c^2 - b^2 = x^2 + y^2 = \left(6\sqrt{2}\right)^2 + 12^2 = 72 + 144 = 216$.

Answer 32: The answer is (D). This triangle is a 12-16-20 triple, so $3x + 2x = 5x = 20$, and $x = 4$.

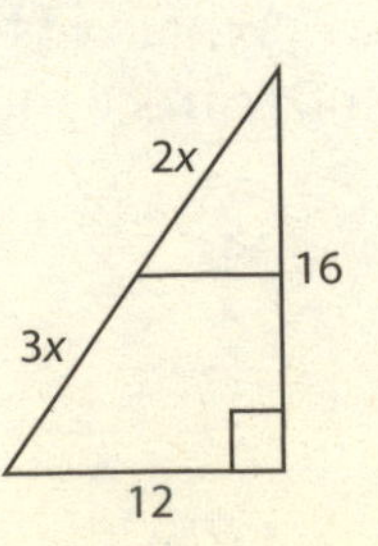

Answer 33: The answer is (A). The first figure shows a 15-20-25 right triangle with the ladder 20 feet up the wall. The second figure is a 7-24-25 triple with the ladder 24 feet up the wall. The ladder is pushed another $24 - 20 = 4$ feet up the wall.

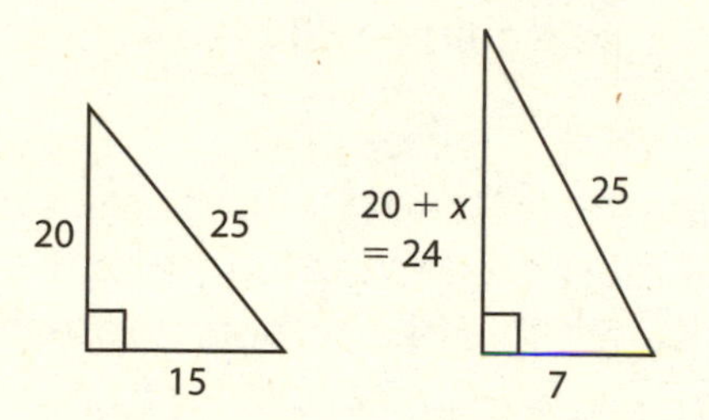

Answer 34: The correct answers are (A), (B), (C), (D), (E), and (F). Remarkably, there is no maximum perimeter! As one of the base angles approaches 180°, the lengths of the other two sides increase without bound. (There is a minimum perimeter of $4 + 4\sqrt{2}$ if the triangle is isosceles.)

Answer 35: The correct answers are (B), (C), and (D). The sum of the squares of the two shortest sides must equal the square of the longest side. For choice (B), $5^2 + 12^2 = 25 + 144 = 169 = 13^2$. For choice (C), $8^2 + 15^2 = 64 + 225 = 289 = 17^2$. For choice (D), $7^2 + 24^2 = 49 + 576 = 625 = 25^2$. However, choice (A), $8^2 + 9^2 = 145 \neq 10^2$, and choice (E), $10^2 + 40^2 = 1{,}700 \neq 41^2$, are wrong. Choice (F) is wrong not only because $11^2 + 22^2 \neq 33^2$, but also because the sum of 11 and 22 is not greater than 33. In any triangle, the sum of the lengths of any two sides must exceed the length of the third side.

Answer 36: The correct answers are (A), (C), (D), and (E). In each of choices (A), (C), and (D), the area is the product of the base and height. For choice E, the area of a trapezoid is $\frac{1}{2}h(b_1 + b_2)$, where h is the height and each of b_1 and b_2 is a base. Note that $\frac{1}{2}h(b_1 + b_2)$ can also be written as $\left(\frac{1}{2}\right)(b_1 + b_2)(h)$, and the expression $\left(\frac{1}{2}\right)(b_1 + b_2)$ is the value of the median. Choice (B) is wrong because the area of a triangle is one-half the product of a base and its associated height.

Answer 37: The correct answers are (B), (C), and (D). For an isosceles triangle, at least two angles must have the same measure. In choice (B), the measure of the third angle is $180° - 50° - 80° = 50°$. In choice (C), the measure of the third angle is $180° - 59° - 62° = 59°$. In choice (D), the measure of the third angle is $180° - 45° - 90° = 45°$. For choices (A) and (E), the measure of the third angle would be 80° and 40°, respectively.

Answer 38: The correct answers are (B), (C), and (D). The sum of the lengths of any two sides of a triangle must exceed the length of the third side. The simplest way to check any triple of numbers is to add the two smallest lengths. For choice (B), $7 + 5 > 11$. For choice (C), $7 + 11 > 11$. For choice (D), $7 + 11 > 16$. Choice (A) is wrong because $3 + 7 < 11$. Choice (E) is wrong because $7 + 11 = 18$. Choice (F) is wrong because $7 + 11 < 20$.

Answer 39: The correct answers are (A), (B), and (C). Interior (or exterior) angles on the same side of the transversal are supplementary, so they are equal only when the transversal is perpendicular to the two parallel lines. Therefore, choices (D) and (E) are not correct choices.

Answer 40: The correct answers are (C) and (E). In a right triangle, the sum of the squares of the two shortest sides must equal the square of the hypotenuse. If the two shortest sides are 3 and 4, then the hypotenuse must be $\sqrt{3^2 + 4^2} = \sqrt{9+16} = \sqrt{25} = 5$. However, if the hypotenuse is 4, then the third side must be $\sqrt{4^2 - 3^2} = \sqrt{16-9} = \sqrt{7}$.

Answer 41: The correct answer is 30. The median to the base of an isosceles triangle is identical to the altitude to the base. Thus, the area is $\left(\frac{1}{2}\right)(6)(10) = 30$.

Answer 42: The correct answer is 2,500. The area of an equilateral triangle is $\frac{s^2}{4}\sqrt{3} = \frac{100^2\sqrt{3}}{4} = \frac{10{,}000\sqrt{3}}{4} = 2{,}500\sqrt{3} = a\sqrt{b}$, so a is 2,500.

Answer 43: The answer is 360. The sum of the exterior angles of any polygon, regardless of any individual measures of interior angles, is always 360°.

Congruent Triangles

The GRE will contain questions concerning the congruence and similarity (see next section) of triangles, but (thankfully) there will be no proofs.

Two triangles are **congruent** if each of the three sides and angles of one triangle are equal to each of the three sides and angles of a second triangle. The symbol for congruence is $\cong$. The order in which the letters of each triangle are listed is important. By stating that $\Delta ABC \cong \Delta DEF$, we are declaring that the following six congruencies are true: $\overline{AB} \cong \overline{DE}$, $\overline{AC} \cong \overline{DF}$, $\overline{BC} \cong \overline{EF}$, $\angle A \cong \angle D$, $\angle B \cong \angle E$, and $\angle C \cong \angle F$.

Two triangles can be proved to be congruent with just a minimum of three sets of congruencies. Let's discuss each of these situations. In each example, we can state that $\Delta ABC \cong \Delta DEF$.

Side-Side-Side (SSS): Three sides of one triangle are congruent, respectively, to the three sides of a second triangle. A diagram is shown below.

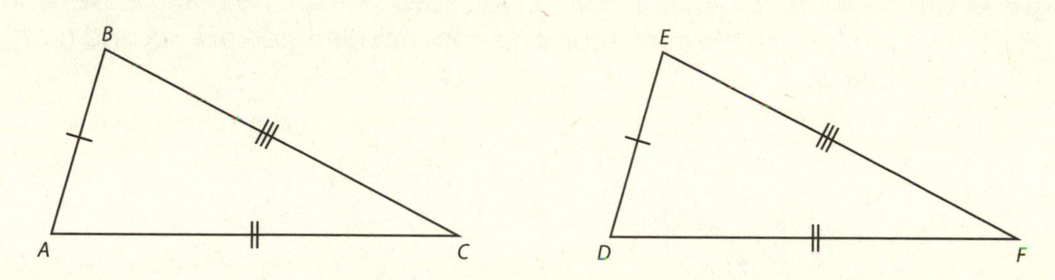

The indicated markings show that $\overline{AB} \cong \overline{DE}$, $\overline{AC} \cong \overline{DF}$, and $\overline{BC} \cong \overline{EF}$.

Side-Angle-Side (SAS): Two sides and the included angle of one triangle are congruent, respectively, to two sides and the included angle of a second triangle. A diagram is shown below.

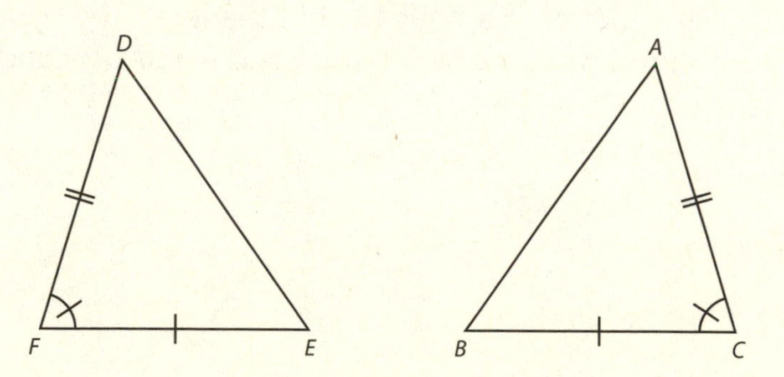

The indicated markings show that $\overline{AC} \cong \overline{DF}$, $\overline{BC} \cong \overline{EF}$, and $\angle C \cong \angle F$.

Angle-Side-Angle (ASA): Two angles and the included side of one triangle are congruent, respectively, to two angles and the included side of a second triangle. A diagram is shown below. Note that vertices C and F are the same point.

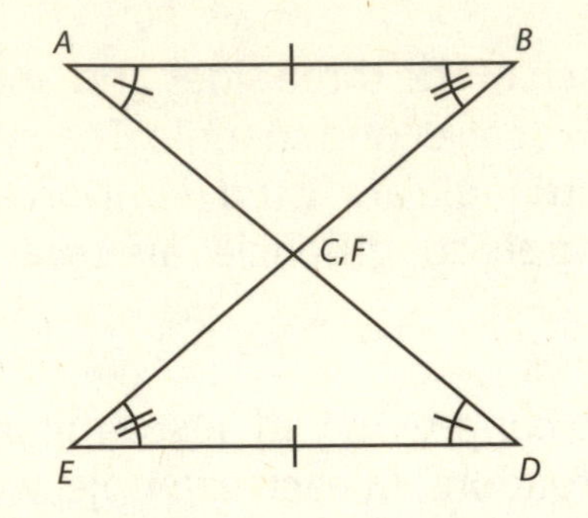

The indicated markings show that $\overline{AB} \cong \overline{DE}$, $\angle A \cong \angle D$, and $\angle B \cong \angle E$.

Side-Angle-Angle (SAA): Two angles and a non-included side of one triangle are congruent, respectively, to two angles and the corresponding non-included side of a second triangle. A diagram is shown below.

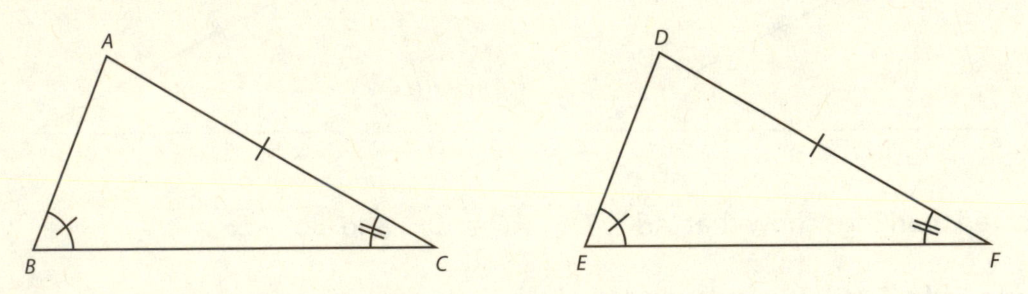

The indicated markings show that $\overline{AC} \cong \overline{DF}$, $\angle B \cong \angle E$, and $\angle C \cong \angle F$.

Hypotenuse-Leg (HL): This situation is unique to right triangles. The hypotenuse and leg of one right triangle are congruent to the hypotenuse and leg of a second right triangle. A diagram is shown below.

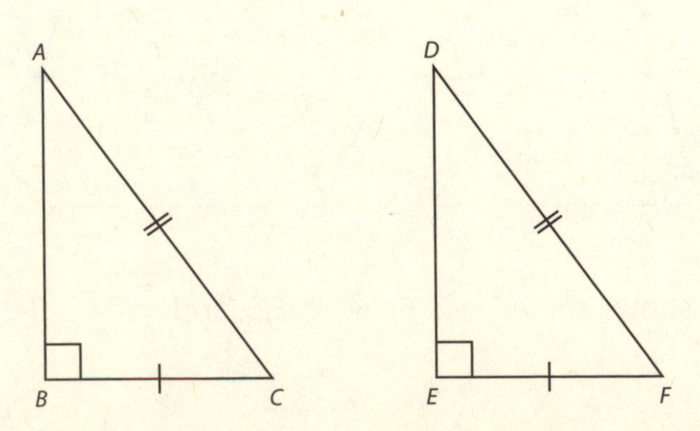

The indicated markings show that there is a right angle at vertices B and E. Also, $\overline{BC} \cong \overline{EF}$ and $\overline{AC} \cong \overline{DF}$.

It is important to recognize when certain combinations of congruencies between some of the parts of two triangles do *not* imply that the triangles are congruent. These are known as fallacies. Here are the two most popular fallacies.

Side-Side-Angle (SSA): Two sides of one triangle are congruent to two sides of a second triangle. In addition, a pair of non-included angles are congruent. The following diagram shows that the two triangles need *not* be congruent.

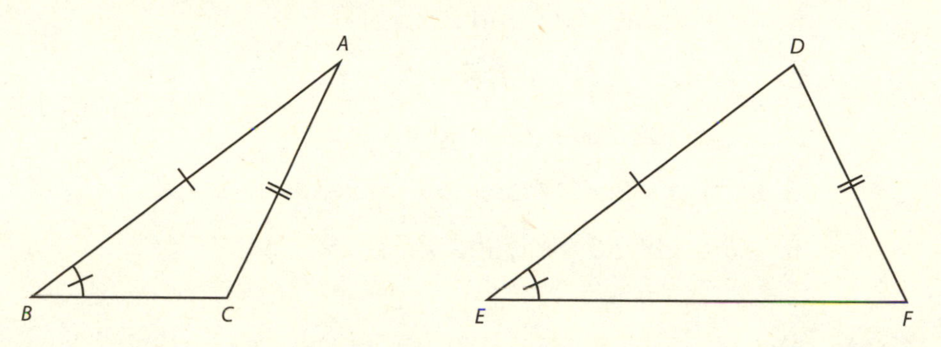

The indicated markings show that $\overline{AB} \cong \overline{DE}$, $\overline{AC} \cong \overline{DF}$, and $\angle B \cong \angle E$. Note that $\overline{BC}$ is not congruent to $\overline{EF}$, and that $\angle A$, $\angle C$, $\angle D$, and $\angle F$ are different in their measures.

Angle-Angle-Angle (AAA): Each of three angles of one triangle is congruent to three corresponding angles in a second triangle. The following diagram shows that the two triangles need *not* be congruent.

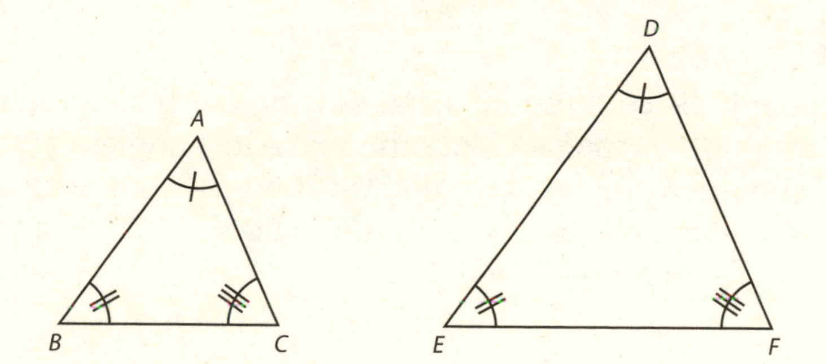

The indicated markings show that $\angle A \cong \angle D$, $\angle B \cong \angle E$, and $\angle C \cong \angle F$. Note that the second triangle is larger than the first triangle. Although these triangles are not congruent, there does exist a relationship between them. This relationship, similarity, is discussed in the next section.

Note that in any ΔABC, $\angle A$ is opposite $\overline{BC}$, $\angle B$ is opposite $\overline{AC}$, and $\angle C$ is opposite $\overline{AB}$. This assignment of letters is consistent for any triangle; so, if we are given ΔXYZ, $\angle X$ must lie opposite $\overline{YZ}$.

Be aware that a GRE test question may mention that two sides are either "equal" or "congruent." In taking the GRE, you need not make any distinction between these two words, although in most geometry books, congruence refers to the actual sides, whereas equality refers to distances.

Let's try this exercise on congruent triangles.

Exercise 44: Which of the following would be sufficient to conclude that $\Delta ABC \cong \Delta XYZ$? Indicate *all* correct answers.

A. $AB = XY$, $AC = YZ$, and $BC = XZ$.

B. $AB = XY$, $AC = XZ$, and $\angle A \cong \angle X$.

C. $\angle A \cong \angle X$, $\angle C \cong \angle Z$, and $BC = YZ$

D. $\angle C \cong \angle Z$, $\angle B \cong \angle Y$, and $\angle A \cong \angle X$.

E. Each of $\angle B \cong \angle Y$ are right angles and $AC = XZ$.

F. $\angle B \cong \angle Y$, $BC = YZ$, and $\angle C \cong \angle Z$.

Answer 44: The correct answers are (B), (C), and (F). Choice (B) is correct by Side-Angle-Side (SAS). Choice (C) is correct by Side-Angle-Angle (SAA). Choice (F) is correct by Angle-Side-Angle (ASA). Answer choice (A) is wrong because the letters of the vertices are not matched correctly. Answer choice (D) is wrong because there is no pair of congruent sides. Answer choice (E) is wrong because there are only two given matched congruencies.

Similar Triangles

Two triangles are **similar** if the corresponding pairs of angles are congruent. Technically, we only need two pairs of congruent angles. Since the sum of the angles of any triangle must be 180°, two pairs of congruent angles imply that the third pair must also be congruent. The symbol for similarity is ~. In the diagram below, $\Delta ABC \sim \Delta DEF$, with $\overline{AG}$ and $\overline{DH}$ representing the corresponding altitudes of these triangles.

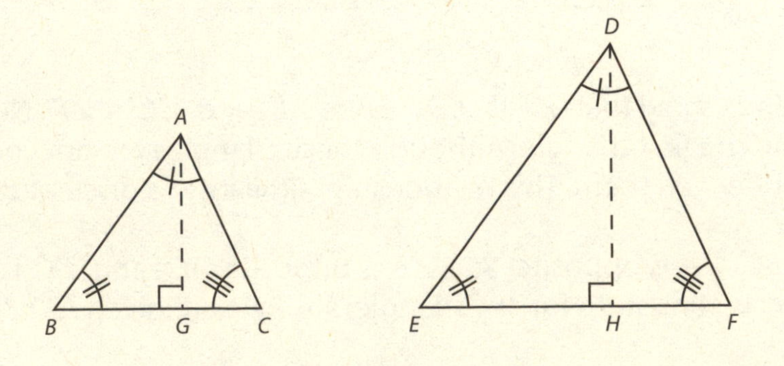

Although the corresponding sides are not congruent, the ratio of any two corresponding sides must be constant. This means that $\frac{AB}{DE} = \frac{AC}{DF} = \frac{BC}{EF}$. There are three additional key ratios.

1. The ratio of the perimeters of these two triangles must equal the ratio of any two corresponding sides. For example, $\frac{\text{Perimeter of } \Delta ABC}{\text{Perimeter of } \Delta DEF} = \frac{AB}{DE}$.
2. The ratio of any two corresponding linear measures, such as altitudes, is in the same ratio as a pair of corresponding sides. In the diagram above, $\frac{AG}{DH} = \frac{AB}{DE}$.
3. The ratio of the areas of these two triangles must equal the square of the ratio of any two corresponding sides. For example, $\frac{\text{Area of } \Delta ABC}{\text{Area of } \Delta DEF} = \left(\frac{AB}{DE}\right)^2$.

Note that this also means if we are given the areas of two similar triangles, we may conclude that the ratio of any two corresponding sides is the square root of the corresponding ratio of the areas. For example, we could express this relationship mathematically as $\frac{AB}{DE} = \sqrt{\frac{\text{Area of } \Delta ABC}{\text{Area of } \Delta DEF}}$.

Just as we had established congruency between triangles with a minimum set of equalities, we can also prove that two triangles are similar with a minimum amount of information. In each of the following examples, we can state that $\Delta ABC \sim \Delta DEF$.

Side-Side-Side (SSS): The ratios of the three pairs of corresponding sides are in proportion. This means that $\frac{AB}{DE} = \frac{AC}{DF} = \frac{BC}{EF}$. A diagram, with numerical values, is shown below.

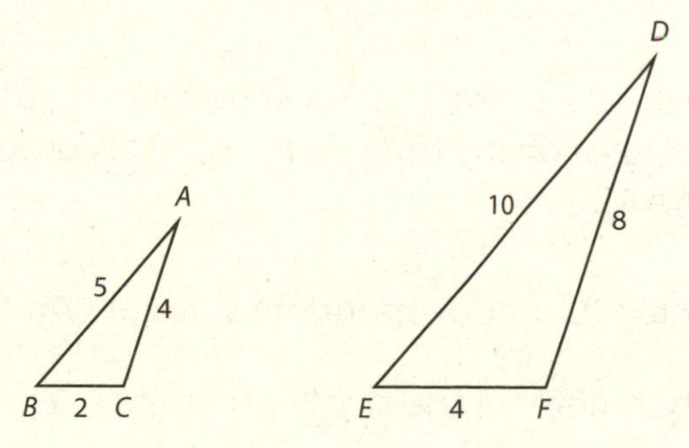

Notice that each side of the second triangle is double the size of the corresponding side of the first triangle. The inverse of these ratios would also be equal; that is $\frac{DE}{AB} = \frac{DF}{AC} = \frac{EF}{BC} = \frac{2}{1}$.

Side-Angle-Side (SAS): The ratio of two pairs of corresponding sides forms a proportion and the corresponding included angles are congruent. A diagram, with numerical values, is shown below.

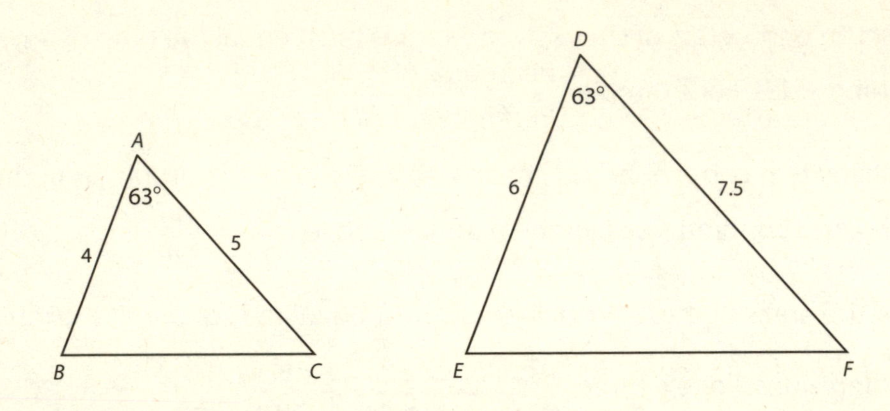

Note that $\frac{AB}{DE} = \frac{AC}{DF} = \frac{2}{3}$ and that $\angle A \cong \angle D$.

Angle-Angle (AA): Each of two angles of one triangle is congruent to each of two corresponding angles of a second triangle. A diagram, with numerical values, is shown below.

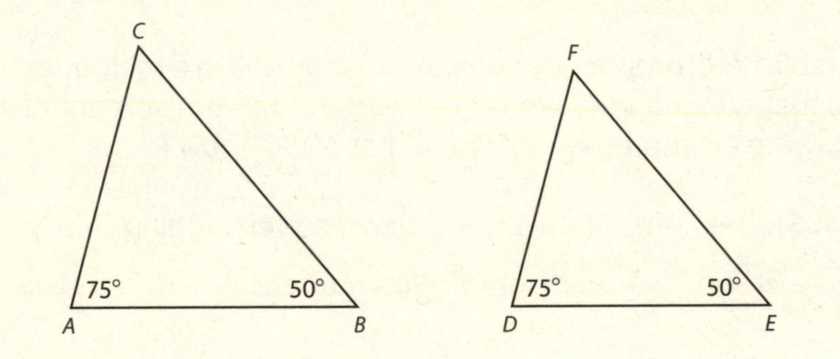

Note that the measure of each of $\angle C$ and $\angle F$ must be $180° - 50° - 75° = 55°$ because the sum of the measures of the angles of any triangle is 180°. This property is sometimes referred to as **Angle-Angle-Angle (AAA).**

Example 9: The ratio of the corresponding sides of two similar triangles is $\frac{7}{10}$.

If the perimeter of the smaller triangle is 21, what is the perimeter of the larger triangle?

Solution: The ratio of the perimeters is the same as the ratio of the corresponding sides. Let x represent the perimeter of the larger triangle. Then $\frac{7}{10} = \frac{21}{x}$. Cross-multiply to get $7x = 210$. Therefore, $x = 30$.

Example 10: The ratio of the areas of two similar triangles is $\frac{81}{16}$. One side of the smaller triangle is 10. What is the length of the corresponding side of the larger triangle?

Solution: The ratio of any two corresponding sides equals the square root of the ratio of the areas, which becomes $\sqrt{\frac{81}{16}} = \frac{9}{4}$. Let x represent the length of the side of the larger triangle. Then $\frac{9}{4} = \frac{x}{10}$. Cross-multiply to get $4x = 90$. Thus, $x = 22.5$.

Let's try a few exercises on similar triangles.

Exercise 45: Which of the following would be sufficient to conclude that $\Delta CDE \sim \Delta RST$? Indicate *all* correct answers.

A. Each of $\angle D$ and $\angle S$ is a right angle, $\frac{CD}{RS} = \frac{DE}{ST}$.

B. $\frac{CD}{RS} = \frac{CE}{RT}$ and $\angle D \cong \angle S$.

C. $\angle E \cong \angle T$ and $\frac{DE}{ST} = \frac{1}{2}$.

D. $\angle C \cong \angle R$ and $\angle E \cong \angle T$.

E. $\frac{CD}{RS} = \frac{CE}{RT} = \frac{DE}{ST}$.

F. $\frac{CD}{RT} = \frac{CE}{RS}$ and each of $\angle C$ and $\angle R$ is a right angle.

Exercise 46: The ratio of the corresponding sides of two similar triangles is $\frac{7}{9}$. If one side of the smaller triangle is 35, how much larger is the corresponding side of the larger triangle?

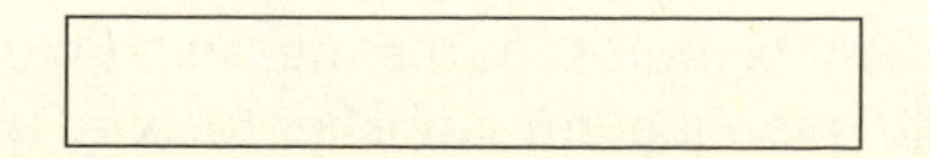

Exercise 47: $\angle GHJ$ is similar to $\angle KLM$. If the measure of $\angle G$ is 60° and $\angle J$ is twice as large as $\angle H$, what is the measure (in degrees) of $\angle M$?

Exercise 48: The ratio of the areas of two similar triangles is $\frac{25}{36}$. What is the ratio of their perimeters? Write your answer as a ratio of integers.

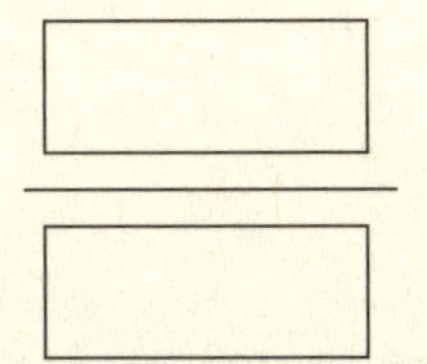

Exercise 49: The ratio of a pair of corresponding sides of two similar triangles is $\frac{3}{8}$. The area of the smaller triangle is 36. What is the area of the larger triangle?

Let's look at the answers.

Answer 45: The correct answers are (A), (D), and (E). Choice (A) is correct by Side-Angle-Side (SAS). Choice (D) is correct by Angle-Angle (AA). Choice (E) is correct by Side-Side-Side (SSS). Answer choice (B) is wrong because it illustrates two pairs of corresponding sides and a corresponding pair of nonincluded angles. Answer choice (C) is wrong because it illustrates only one pair of corresponding sides and one pair of corresponding angles. Answer choice (F) is wrong because the letters that represent the vertices are not matched in the correct order.

Answer 46: The correct answer is 10. Let x represent the corresponding side of the larger triangle. Then $\frac{7}{9} = \frac{35}{x}$. Cross-multiply to get $7x = 315$, from which $x = 45$. Therefore, the larger side is $45 - 35 = 10$ more than the smaller side.

Answer 47: The correct answer is 80. Let x represent the measure (in degrees) of $\angle H$ and let $2x$ represent the measure (in degrees) of $\angle J$. Then $60 + x + 2x = 180$. This equation simplifies to $3x = 180 - 60 = 120$. This means that $x = 40$, so the measure of $\angle J$, in degrees, must be 80. Since the triangles are similar, the number of degrees in the corresponding $\angle M$ is also 80.

Answer 48: The correct answer is $\frac{5}{6}$. The ratio of the perimeters equals the square root of the ratio of the areas, which is $\sqrt{\frac{25}{36}} = \frac{5}{6}$.

Answer 49: The correct answer is 256. The ratio of the areas equals the square of the ratio of any pair of corresponding sides, which is $\left(\frac{3}{8}\right)^2 = \frac{9}{64}$. Let x represent the area of the larger triangle. Then $\frac{9}{64} = \frac{36}{x}$. Cross-multiply to get $9x = 2{,}304$. Therefore $x = 256$.

That's all for angles and triangles for now. We will see more when circles are discussed in Chapter 12. For now, though, let's look at rectangles and other polygons.

CHAPTER 11: *Quadrilaterals and Other Polygons*

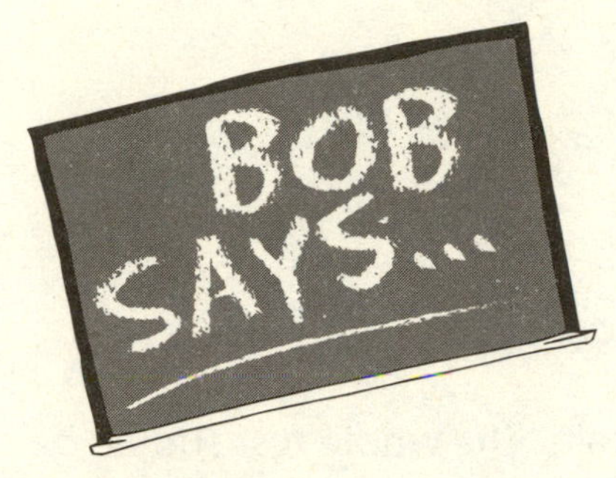

"Mastering all shapes and sizes will enhance your journey. We now deal with the rest of the polygons (closed figures with line-segment sides)."

QUADRILATERALS

Parallelograms

A parallelogram is a quadrilateral (four-sided polygon) with parallel opposite sides.

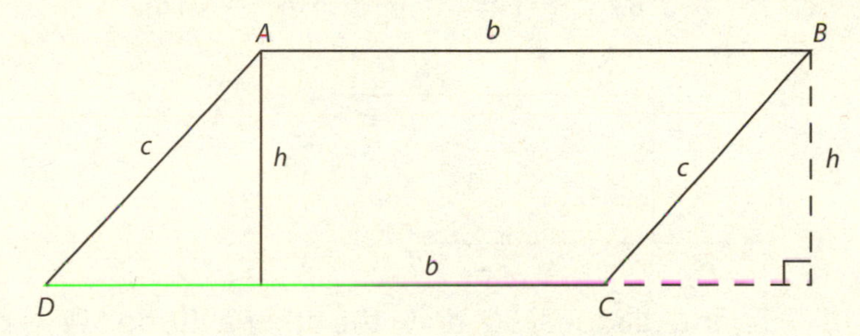

You should know the following properties about parallelograms:

- The opposite angles are equal. $\angle DAB = \angle BCD$ and $\angle ADC = \angle ABC$.
- The consecutive angles are supplementary. $\angle DAB + \angle ABC = \angle ABC + \angle BCD = \angle BCD + \angle CDA = \angle CDA + \angle DAB = 180^\circ$.
- The opposite sides are equal. $AB = CD$ and $AD = BC$.
- The diagonals bisect each other. $AE = EC$ and $DE = EB$.

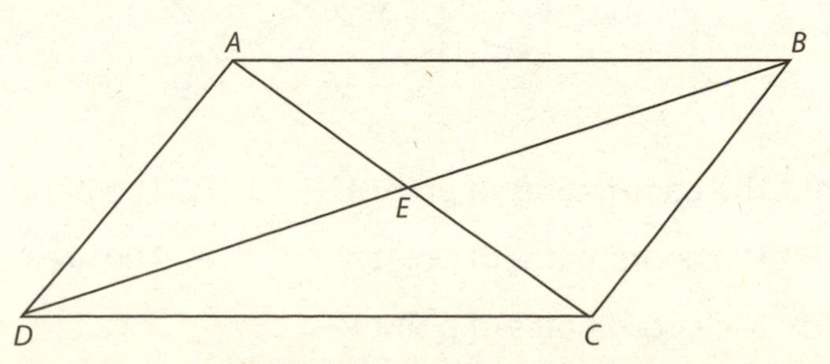

- Area $= A = bh$. This is a postulate (law taken to be true without proof) from which we get the area of all other figures with sides that are line segments.
- Perimeter $= p = 2b + 2c$.

Example 1: For parallelogram *RSTU*, find the following if $RU = 10$:

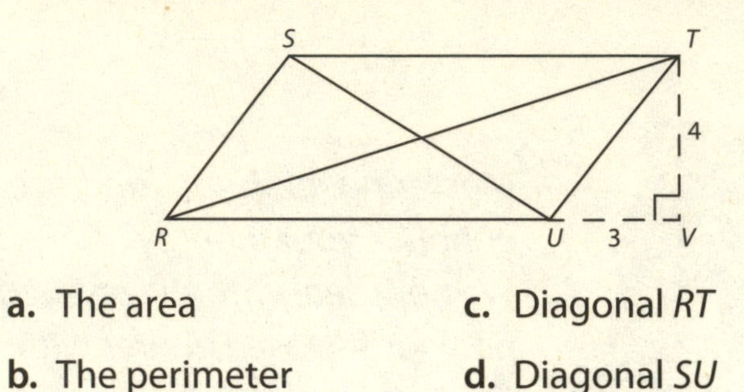

a. The area

b. The perimeter

c. Diagonal *RT*

d. Diagonal *SU*

Solutions:

a. $A = bh = (10)(4) = 40$ square units. The whole test should be this easy!

b. We have to find the length of $RS = TU$. $TU = 5$ because it is the hypotenuse of a 3-4-5 right triangle. So the perimeter is $p = 2(10) + 2(5) = 30$ units.

c. $RT = \sqrt{(RV)^2 + (TV)^2} = \sqrt{13^2 + 4^2} = \sqrt{185}$

d.

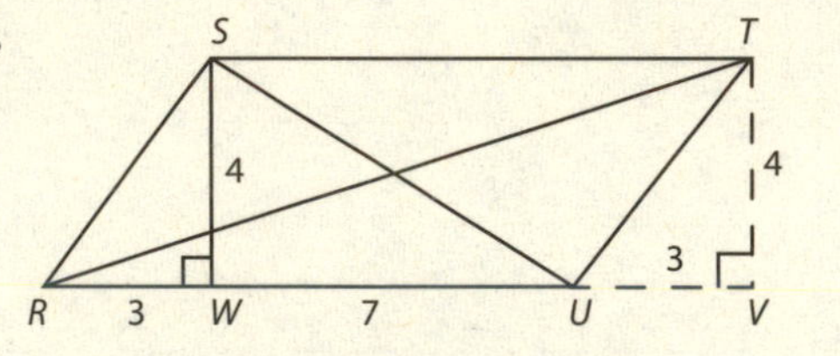

To find diagonal *SU*, draw the other altitude *SW* as pictured.

$SU = \sqrt{WU^2 + SW^2} = \sqrt{7^2 + 4^2} = \sqrt{65}$

Example 2: For parallelogram *WXYZ* with altitudes *XM* and *YN*, find the following in terms of *a*, *b*, and *c*:

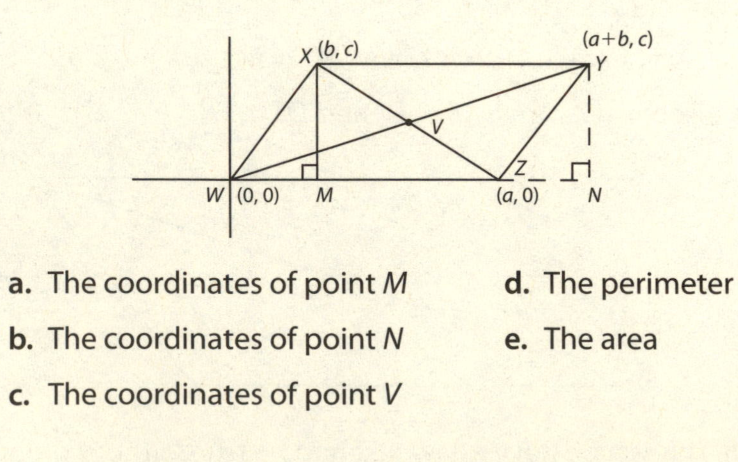

a. The coordinates of point *M*

b. The coordinates of point *N*

c. The coordinates of point *V*

d. The perimeter

e. The area

Solutions:

a. M has the same x-coordinate as point X and the same y-coordinate as point W, so the coordinates of M are $(b, 0)$.

b. N has the same x-coordinate as point Y and the same y-coordinate as point W, so the coordinates of N are $(a + b, 0)$.

c. V is halfway between W and Y, so use the formula for the midpoint between $Y(a + b, c)$ and $W(0,0)$: Midpoint $V = \left(\frac{a+b+0}{2}, \frac{c+0}{2}\right) = \left(\frac{a+b}{2}, \frac{c}{2}\right)$.

d. $WZ = XY$ is length a. By the distance formula, $WX = ZY = \sqrt{(b-0)^2 + (c-0)^2} = \sqrt{b^2 + c^2}$. Therefore, the perimeter is $P = 2a + 2\sqrt{b^2 + c^2}$.

e. Area $= A =$ base $\times$ height $= ac$.

Example 3: For parallelogram $EFGH$, find the angle.

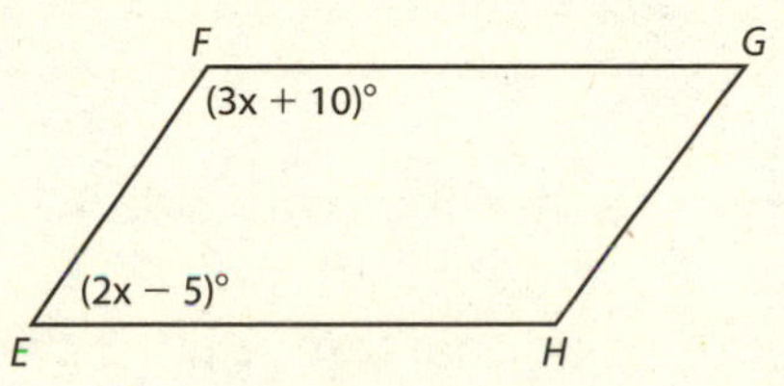

Solution: Consecutive angles of a parallelogram are supplementary. Therefore, $(3x+10)° + (2x - 5)° = 180°$; $x = 35°$; so the smaller angle is $2(35°) - 5° = 65°$. Be careful to give the answer the GRE wants. Two of the other choices would be 35° and 115°, for those who do not read carefully!!!

Rhombus

A **rhombus** is an equilateral parallelogram.

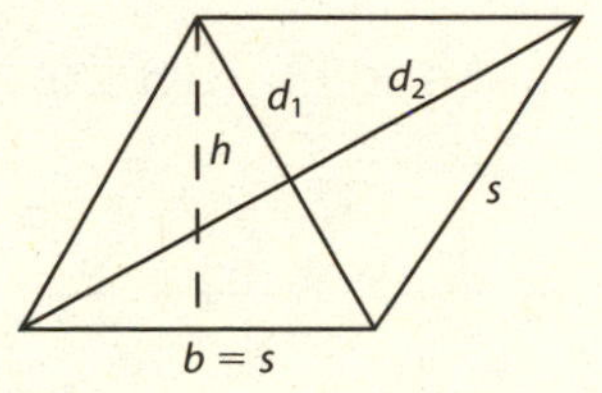

Thus, a rhombus has all of the properties of a parallelogram plus the following:

- The opposite angles are equal.
- All sides are equal.
- The diagonals are perpendicular to each other.

- Perimeter = $p = 4s$.
- $A = bh = \frac{1}{2} \times d_1 \times d_2$, or, the area equals half the product of its diagonals.

Example 4: For the given rhombus with side $s = 13$ and larger diagonal $BD = 24$, find the other diagonal and the area.

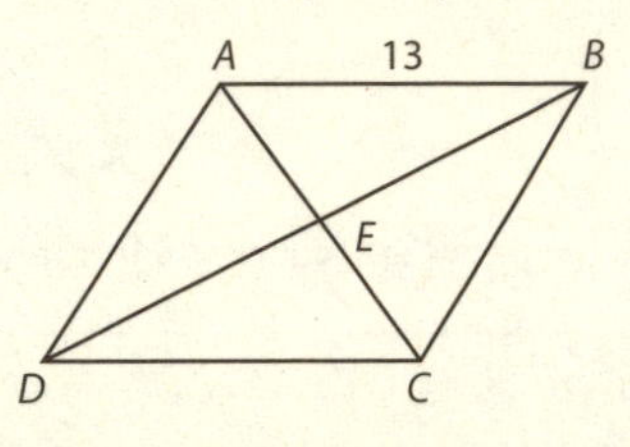

Solutions: $AB = 13$ and $BD = 24$. Since the diagonals bisect each other, $BE = 12$. The diagonals are perpendicular to each other, so ΔABE is a 5-12-13 right triangle, and $AE = 5$. Therefore, the other diagonal $AC = 10$. The area $= A = \frac{1}{2} \times d_1 \times d_2 = \frac{1}{2}(24)(10) = 120$ square units.

Example 5: Find the area of a rhombus with side 10 and smaller interior angle of 60°.

Solution: If you draw the diagonal through the two larger angles, you will have two congruent equilateral triangles. The area of this rhombus is twice the area of each triangle, or $2 \times \frac{s^2\sqrt{3}}{4}$. Since $s = 10$, the area is $A = 2 \times \frac{10^2\sqrt{3}}{4} = 50\sqrt{3}$ square units.

Now let's go on to more familiar territory.

Rectangle

A **rectangle** is a parallelogram with right angles. Therefore, it has all of the properties of a parallelogram plus the following:

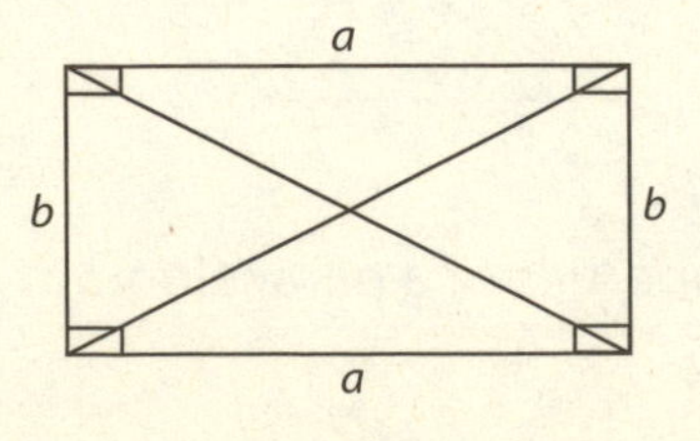

- All angles are 90°.
- Diagonals are equal (but *not* perpendicular).

- Perimeter = $p = 2b + 2a$
- Area = $A = ab$

The easier the shape, the more likely the GRE will have a problem or problems about it.

Example 6: One base is 8; one diagonal is 9. Find all the sides and the other diagonal. Find the perimeter and area.

Solution: The top base and bottom base are both 8. Both diagonals are 9. The other two sides are each $\sqrt{9^2 - 8^2} = \sqrt{17}$. So the perimeter is $p = 16 + 2\sqrt{17}$ units; and the area is $A = 8\sqrt{17}$ square units.

Example 7: $AB = 10$, $BC = 8$, $EF = 6$, and $FG = 3$. Find the area of the shaded region of the figure.

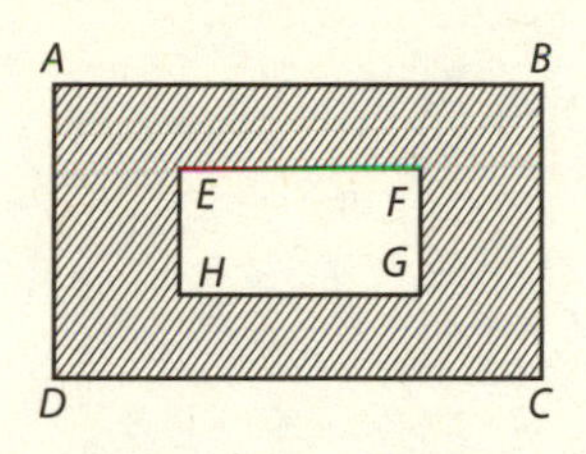

Solution: The area of the shaded region is the area of the outside rectangle minus the area of the inside one. $A = (10)(8) - (6)(3) = 62$ square units.

Example 8: In polygon $ABCDEF$, $BC = 30$, $AF = 18$, $AB = 20$, and $CD = 11$. Find the perimeter and area of the polygon.

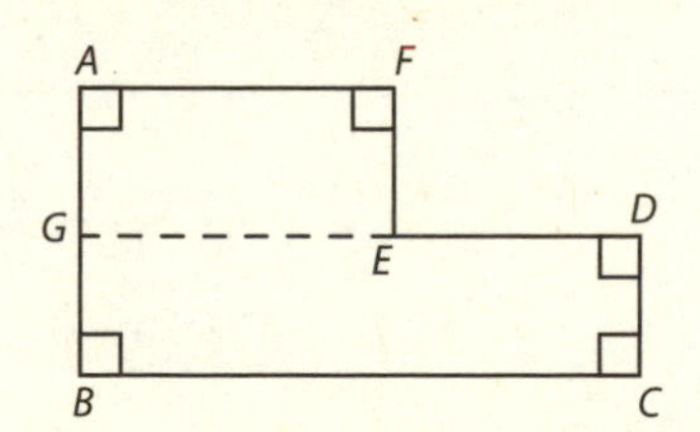

Solution: Draw a line through DE, hitting AB at point G. Then $AF = GE$ and $BC = GD$. Since $DG = 30$ and $GE = 18$, $DE = 12$. $AB = CD + EF$. $AB = 20$ and $CD = 11$, so $EF = 9$. This gives the lengths of all the sides. The perimeter thus is $p = AB + BC + CD + DE + EF + AF = 30 + 20 + 11 + 12 + 9 + 18 = 100$ units.

The area of rectangle $BCDG$ is $BC \times CD = (30)(11) = 330$. The area of rectangle $AFEG$ is $AF \times FE = (18)(9) = 162$. Therefore, the total area is $330 + 162 = 492$ square units. There are other ways to find this area, as you might be able to see.

Square

A **square** is a rectangle with equal sides, or it can be thought of as a rhombus with four equal 90° angles. Therefore, it has all of the properties of a rectangle and a rhombus:

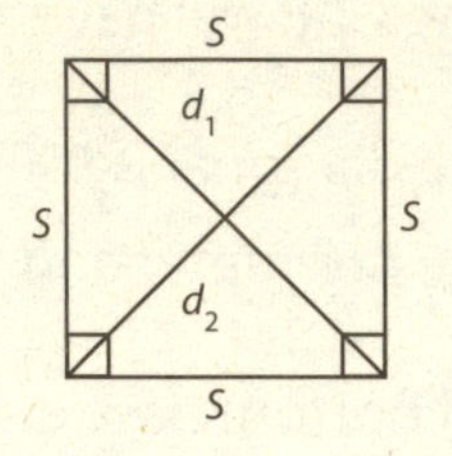

- All sides are equal.
- All angles are 90°.
- Both diagonals bisect each other, are perpendicular to each other, and are equal.
- Each diagonal $d = d_1 = d_2 = s\sqrt{2}$, where s = a side.
- Perimeter = $p = 4s$.
- Area = $A = \frac{d^2}{2} = s^2$.

Let's do some exercises.

Exercise 1: The areas of the rectangle and triangle are the same. If $\frac{LW}{4} = 20$, then $bh =$

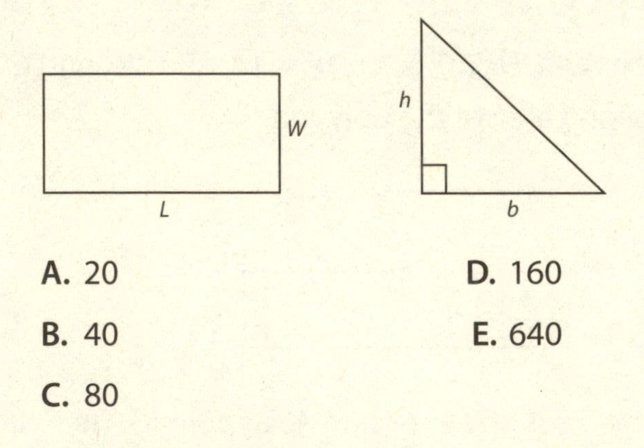

A. 20
B. 40
C. 80
D. 160
E. 640

Exercise 2: The area of this square is

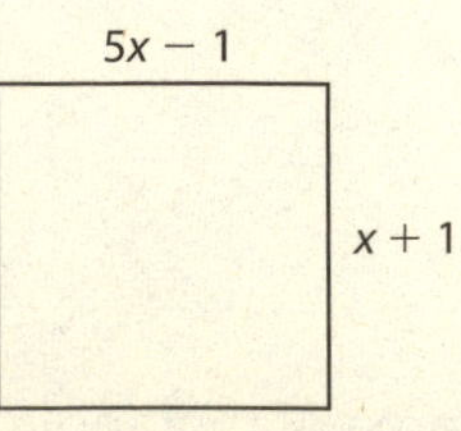

A. $\frac{1}{4}$
B. $\frac{1}{2}$
C. $1\frac{1}{2}$
D. $2\frac{1}{4}$
E. 3

Exercise 3: The area of square C is 36; the area of square B is 25. The area of square A is

A. 61
B. 121
C. 900
D. 100
E. 61^2

This figure is a square surmounted by an equilateral triangle. (I've always wanted to write that word.) $CE = 10$. Use this figure for Exercises 4 and 5.

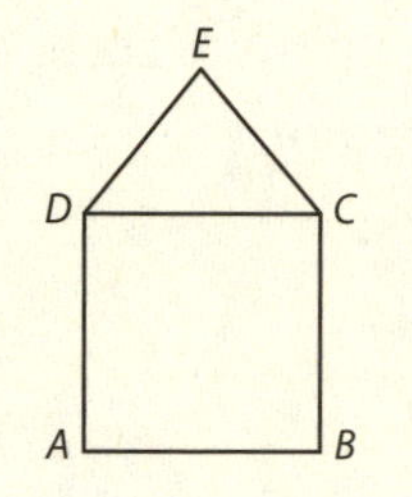

Exercise 4: The perimeter of the figure is

A. 50
B. 60
C. 600
D. 1,200
E. 2,400

Exercise 5: The area of the figure is

A. 150
B. $25(4 + \sqrt{3})$
C. $125\sqrt{3}$
D. $2{,}500\sqrt{3}$
E. 7,500

Let's look at the answers.

Answer 1: The answer is (D). $\frac{LW}{4} = 20$; so the area of the rectangle is $LW = 80$. So the area of the triangle is $\frac{1}{2}bh = 80$, and $bh = 160$.

Answer 2: The answer is (D). Since it is a square, $5x - 1 = x + 1$, so $x = \frac{1}{2}$. By substitution, one side of the square is $\frac{1}{2} + 1 = 1\frac{1}{2}$. Then $A = \left(1\frac{1}{2}\right)^2 = 2\frac{1}{4}$.

Answer 3: The answer is (B). The side of square *C* must be 6, and the side of square *B* must be 5. Therefore, the side of square *A* is 11, and the area of square *A* is $11^2 = 121$.

Answer 4: The answer is (A). The perimeter is 5(10) = 50. Note that *CD* is not part of the perimeter.

Answer 5: The answer is (B). $A = s^2 + \frac{s^2\sqrt{3}}{4} = 10^2 + \frac{10^2\sqrt{3}}{4} = 100 + 25\sqrt{3} = 25(4 + \sqrt{3})$. Note that we factor out this problem since the answer choices are factored out.

TRAPEZOID

A **trapezoid** is a quadrilateral with exactly one pair of parallel sides.

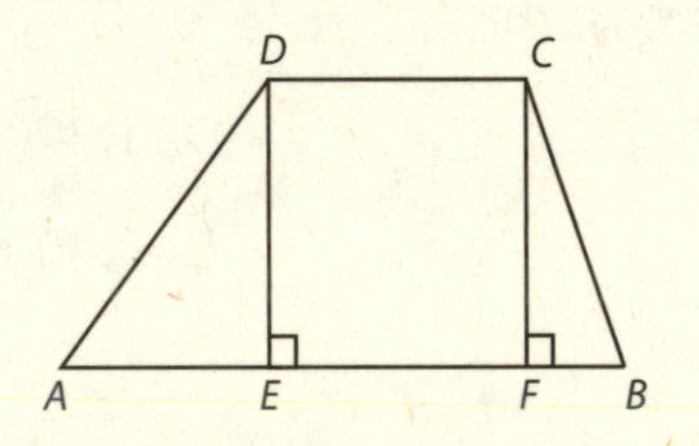

Because a trapezoid is *not* a type of parallelogram, it has its own unique set of properties, as follows:

- The parallel sides, *AB* and *CD*, are called **bases**.
- The heights, *DE* and *CF*, are equal.
- The legs, *AD* and *BC*, may or may not be equal.
- The diagonals, *AC* and *BD*, may or may not be equal.
- Perimeter $= p = AB + BC + CD + AD$.
- Area $= A = \frac{1}{2}h(b_1 + b_2)$, where b_1 and b_2 are the bases.

Note *If we draw one of the diagonals, we see that a trapezoid is the sum of two triangles. Factoring out* $\frac{1}{2}h$, *we get the formula for the area of the trapezoid.*

If the legs are equal, the trapezoid is called an **isosceles trapezoid**, shown below.

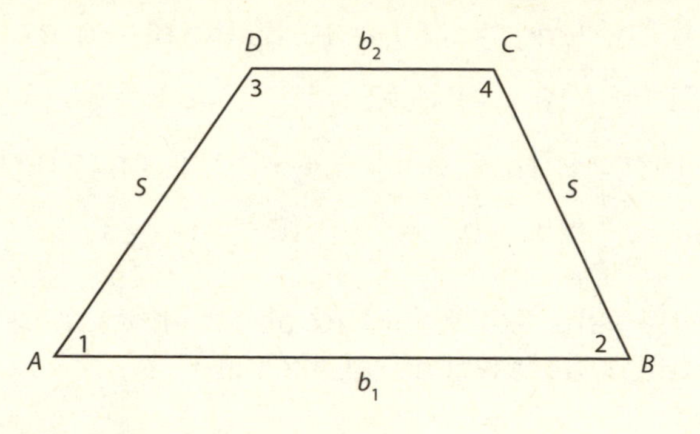

An isosceles trapezoid has the additional properties:

- Perimeter $= p = b_1 + b_2 + 2s$
- The diagonals are equal, $AC = BD$
- The base angles are equal, $\angle 1 = \angle 2$ and $\angle 3 = \angle 4$

Example 9: Find the area and the perimeter of Figure *ABCD*.

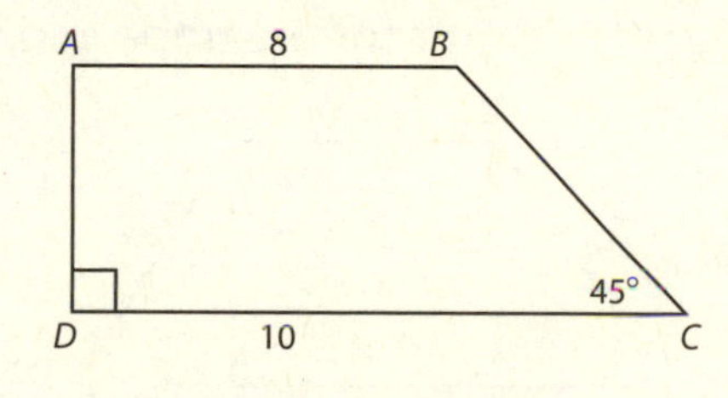

Solution: Draw the other height, *BG*, as shown.

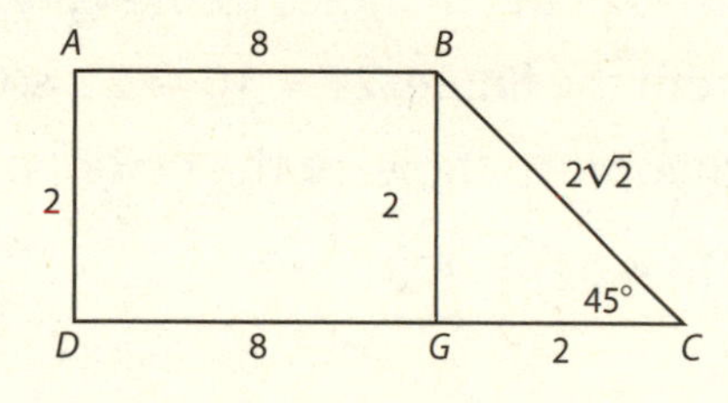

$DG = 8$; $CG = 2$; since ΔBGC is an isosceles right triangle, the height *BG* (and *AD*) $= 2$. *BC*, the hypotenuse of the isosceles right triangle, is therefore $2\sqrt{2}$. Therefore, the perimeter is $p = 10 + 2 + 8 + 2\sqrt{2} = 20 + 2\sqrt{2}$, and the area is $A = \frac{1}{2}h(b_1 + b_2) = \frac{1}{2}(2)(8 + 10) = 18$.

Example 10: Given trapezoid *ORST*, with $RS \parallel OT$, find the coordinates of point *S*. Find the perimeter and the area of trapezoid *ORST*.

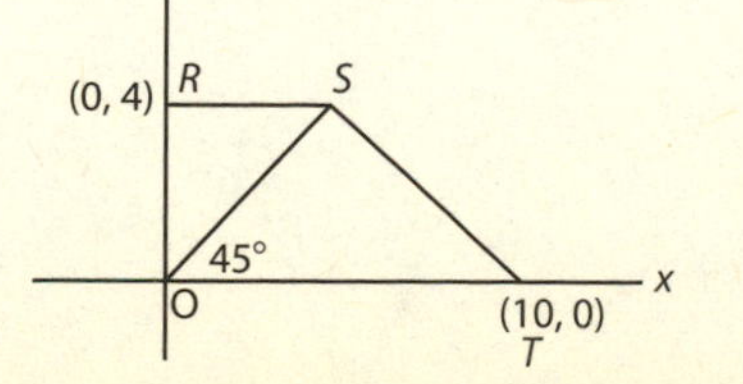

Solution: Since ΔORS is a 45°-45°-90° triangle, $OR = RS = 4$, so S is the point (4, 4). The length of $OT = 10$. By the distance formula, the length of $ST = \sqrt{(10-4)^2 + (0-4)^2} = \sqrt{52} = 2\sqrt{13}$. Therefore, the perimeter is $p = 10 + 4 + 4 + 2\sqrt{13}$, or, to be fancy, $2\left(9 + \sqrt{13}\right)$.
Area $= \frac{1}{2}h(b_1 + b_2) = \frac{1}{2}(4)(10 + 4) = 28$.

As a multiple-choice question, the GRE would ask about either the area or perimeter, but not both. But sometimes the GRE is a bit whimsical, like here.

Example 11: Find the area of isosceles trapezoid $EFGH$.

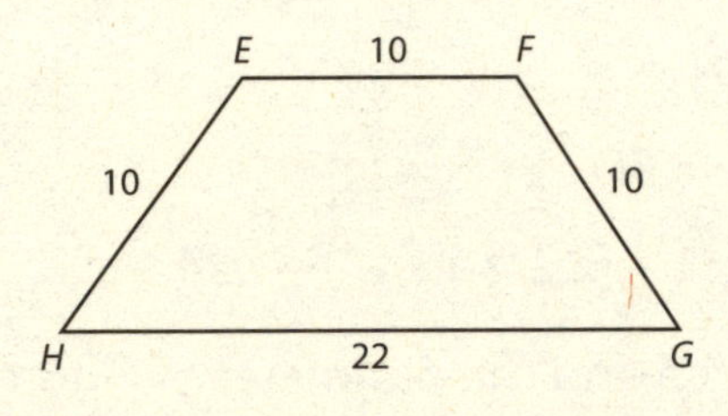

Solution: Draw in the two heights for the trapezoid.

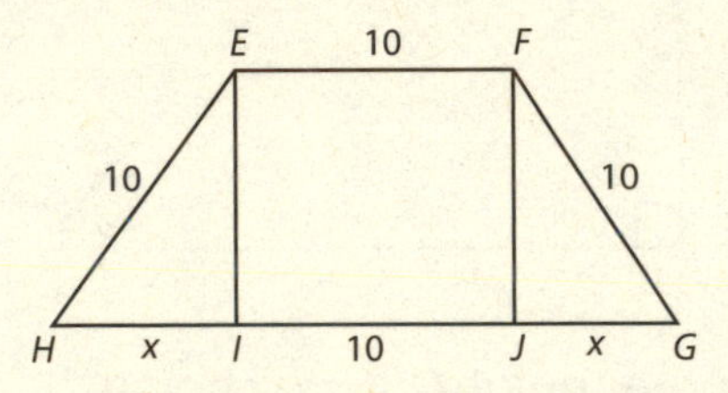

The two bases of the triangles formed are equal since it is an isosceles triangle. From the figure, $2x + 10 = 22$, so $x = 6$. Each of the triangles is a 6-8-10 Pythagorean triple, so the height of the trapezoid is 8. Therefore, $A = \frac{1}{2}(8)(10 + 22) = 128$.

KITE

The last type of quadrilateral for discussion is called a **kite**, which has two pairs of adjacent congruent sides, as shown in the diagram below.

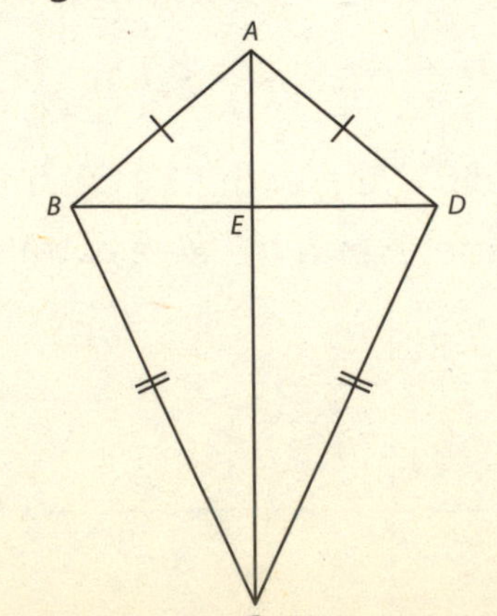

ABCD is a kite, and its two diagonals $\overline{AC}$ and $\overline{BD}$ are also shown intersecting at *E*. There are some additional properties regarding the kite that you should memorize.

1. The diagonals are perpendicular to each other. Thus, there are four right angles at point *E*, the intersection of the diagonals.
2. The longer diagonal bisects the shorter diagonal, but not vice versa. Thus, $BE = ED$, but $AE \neq CE$.
3. The longer diagonal bisects the two angles whose vertices are its endpoints. Thus, $\angle BAE \cong \angle DAE$ and $\angle BCE \cong \angle DCE$. But $\angle ABE$ is *not* congruent to $\angle CBE$, and $\angle ADE$ is *not* congruent to $\angle CDE$.

Example 12: Using the kite shown above, given that $AB = 10$, $BD = 16$, and $BC = 17$, what is the length of $\overline{AC}$?

Solution: Each of triangles *ABE*, *ADE*, *CBE*, and *CDE* has a right angle at *E*. Since $\overline{AC}$ bisects $\overline{BD}$, $BE = DE = 8$. Using the Pythagorean theorem in ΔABE, $8^2 + (AE)^2 = 10^2$. This equation simplifies to $(AE)^2 = 10^2 - 8^2 = 100 - 64 = 36$.

Then $AE = \sqrt{36} = 6$. Now use the Pythagorean theorem in ΔBEC to get $8^2 + (CE)^2 = 17^2$. This equation simplifies to $(CE)^2 = 17^2 - 8^2 = 289 - 64 = 225$. Then $CE = \sqrt{225} = 15$. Therefore, $AC = AE + CE = 21$.

Example 13: Look at the following kite:

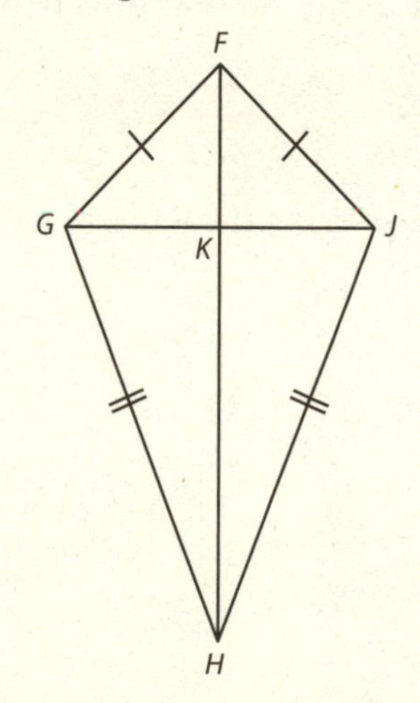

$FH = 20$, *HK* is three times as large as *KF*, and $GJ = 8$. What is the perimeter of the kite, to the nearest tenth?

Solution: $GK = \frac{1}{2} \times GJ = 4$. Let *x* represent *KF*, so that 3*x* represents *HK*. Then $x + 3x = 20$, which simplifies to $4x = 20$. This means that $x = KF = 5$, and that $HK = 15$.

Using the Pythagorean theorem in ΔFGK, we have $(FG)^2 = 4^2 + 5^2 = 16 + 25 = 41$.

Then $FG = FJ = \sqrt{41} \approx 6.4$. Using the Pythagorean theorem in ΔGHK, we have $(GH)^2 = 4^2 + 15^2 = 16 + 225 = 241$. Then $GH = HJ = \sqrt{241} \approx 15.5$. Thus, the perimeter of the kite is approximately $(2)(6.4) + (2)(15.5) = 43.8$.

POLYGONS

Let's talk about polygons in general. Most of the time we deal with **regular** polygons. A regular polygon has all sides equal and all angles equal. A square and an equilateral triangle are examples of regular polygons we have already discussed.

Any n-sided polygon has the following properties:

- The sum of all the interior angles is $(n - 2)180°$.
- The sum of all exterior angles always equals 360°.
- The number of diagonals is $\frac{n(n-3)}{2}$, where $n \geq 3$.

In addition, if the polygon is regular, it has the following additional properties:

- One exterior angle $= \frac{360°}{n}$.
- An interior angle plus its exterior angle always add to 180°.
- One interior angle $= \frac{(n-2)180°}{n}$.

Polygons are named for the number of sides they have.

A **pentagon** is a 5-sided polygon.

A **hexagon** is a 6-sided polygon.

A **heptagon** is a 7-sided polygon.

An **octagon** is an 8-sided polygon.

A **nonagon** is a 9-sided polygon.

A **decagon** is a 10-sided polygon.

A **dodecagon** is a 12-sided polygon.

An **n-gon** is an n-sided polygon.

Example 14: An octagon has a perimeter of 27. If 5 is added to each side, what is the perimeter of the new octagon?

Solution: It doesn't matter how long each side is! If 5 is added to each of 8 sides, 40 is added to the perimeter. The new perimeter is $27 + 40 = 67$.

Example 15: The side of a hexagon is 4. Find its area.

Solution: A regular hexagon is made up of six equilateral triangles. The side of each triangle is 4, and the area is $A = 6\frac{s^2\sqrt{3}}{4} = 6\frac{4^2\sqrt{3}}{4} = 24\sqrt{3}$.

Example 16: The sum of the interior angles of a regular polygon is 720°. Find the number of sides, the number of degrees in one exterior angle, and the number of degrees in one interior angle.

Solution: $(n - 2)(180) = 720$. Divide each side by 180 to simplify: $n - 2 = 4$, so $n = 6$ sides.

One exterior angle $= \frac{360°}{6} = 60°$. An interior angle is supplemental to its external angle, by definition, so $180° - 60° = 120°$ for each interior angle.

Let's try some exercises on the properties of various polygons.

Exercise 6: The areas of which of the following figures can be determined by knowing the lengths of all the sides? Indicate *all* correct choices.

A. Triangle
B. Square
C. Rectangle
D. Parallelogram
E. Rhombus
F. Trapezoid
G. Kite

Exercise 7: For which of the following figures must the diagonals bisect each other? Indicate *all* correct choices.

A. Triangle
B. Square
C. Rectangle
D. Parallelogram
E. Rhombus
F. Trapezoid
G. Kite

Exercise 8: For which of the following figures must the diagonals be equal? Indicate *all* correct choices.

A. Triangle

B. Square

C. Rectangle

D. Parallelogram

E. Rhombus

F. Trapezoid

G. Kite

Exercise 9: For which of the following figures must the diagonals be perpendicular to each other? Indicate *all* correct choices.

A. Triangle

B. Square

C. Rectangle

D. Parallelogram

E. Rhombus

F. Trapezoid

G. Kite

Exercise 10: For which of the following figures must the base angles be congruent? Indicate *all* correct choices.

A. An isosceles triangle

B. A square with a side of 1,000 meters

C. A rectangle whose length is twice its width

D. A parallelogram with a base angle of 60°

E. A rhombus with a base angle of 60°

F. An isosceles trapezoid

Exercise 11: The height and one of the bases of a trapezoid is 10. If the area is 1,000, what is the length of the other base?

Exercise 12: What is the area of a square whose diagonal is 20?

Exercise 13: If the measure of each interior angle of a regular polygon is 140°, how many sides does the polygon have?

Exercise 14: If a polygon has five diagonals, how many sides are there?

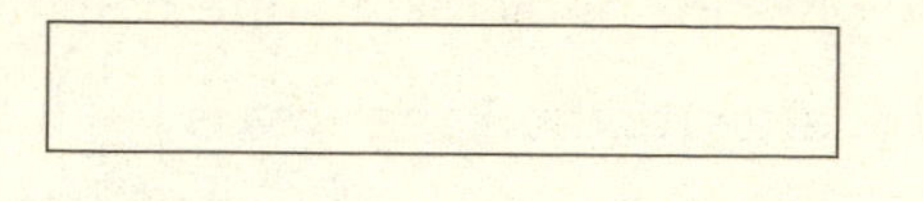

Exercise 15: For kite $WXYZ$, diagonals $\overline{WY}$ and $\overline{XZ}$ intersect at P. $\overline{WY}$ is the longer diagonal. The perimeter of $WXYZ$ is 90, $WZ = 20$, and $ZX = 14$. What is the length of $\overline{PY}$?

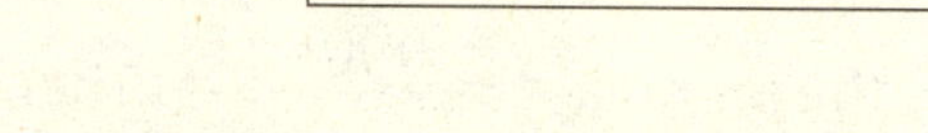

Let's look at the answers.

Answer 6: The correct answers are (A), (B), and (C). For choice (A), the area is $\sqrt{s(s-a)(s-b)(s-c)}$, where s is the semi-perimeter, and a, b, and c, are the sides. For choice (B), the area is s^2, where s is the length of each side. For choice (C), the area is $l \times w$, where l is the length and w is the width. Each of choices (D), (E), (F), and (G) is wrong because the height would need to be known in order to find the area. Knowing only the lengths of the sides would be insufficient.

Answer 7: The correct answers are (B), (C), (D), and (E). Choice (A) is wrong because a triangle has no diagonals. For choice (G), the longer diagonal bisects the shorter diagonal, but not vice versa.

Answer 8: The correct answers are (B) and (C). Choice (A) is wrong because there are no diagonals in a triangle.

Answer 9: The correct answers are (B), (E), and (G). Choice (A) is wrong because there are no diagonals in a triangle.

Answer 10: The correct answers are (A), (B), (C), and (F). Choices (A) and (F) are correct by definition. For choices (B) and (C), all angles measure 90°. Choices (D) and (E) are wrong because the other base angle must be 120°.

Answer 11: The correct answer is 190. The area of a trapezoid is $\frac{1}{2}h(b_1 + b_2)$, where h is the height and the bases are represented by b_1 and b_2. Then $1{,}000 = \left(\frac{1}{2}\right)(10)(10 + b_2)$, where b_2 is the unknown base. This equation simplifies to $1{,}000 = 5(10 + b_2)$. Dividing both sides by 5 leads to $200 = 10 + b_2$, so $b_2 = 190$.

Answer 12: The correct answer is 200. The area of a square can be found by either squaring one side or by taking one-half the product of the diagonals. Using the latter method, the area is $\left(\frac{1}{2}\right)(20)(20) = 200$.

Answer 13: The correct answer is 9. The measure of each exterior angle is $180° - 140° = 40°$. Since the sum of the measures of all exterior angles is 360°, the number of sides is $\frac{360°}{40°} = 9$.

Answer 14: The correct answer is 5. The number of diagonals (d) for a polygon of n sides is given by the formula $d = \frac{(n)(n-3)}{2}$. Then $5 = \frac{(n)(n-3)}{2}$. Multiplying both sides by 2 and removing the parentheses leads to $10 = n^2 - 3n$, which can be written as $n^2 - 3n - 10 = 0$. Then $(n - 5)(n + 2) = 0$, which means that $n = 5$ or $n = -2$. Since n must be positive, we reject the answer of -2.

Answer 15: The correct answer is 24. Here is a diagram to assist you in the solution.

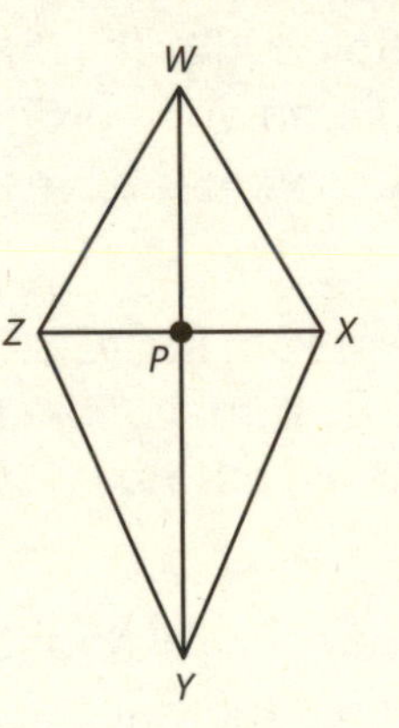

$WZ = WX = 20$, so $ZY + YX = 90 - 40 = 50$. Since $ZY = YX$, $ZY = \frac{1}{2} \times 50 = 25$. We know that $\overline{WY}$ bisects $\overline{ZX}$, so $ZP = \frac{1}{2} \times 14 = 7$. Using the Pythagorean theorem for ΔPYZ, we have $(PY)^2 + 7^2 = 25^2$. Then $(PY)^2 = 25^2 - 7^2 = 625 - 49 = 576$. Thus, $PY = \sqrt{576} = 24$.

CONGRUENT AND SIMILAR QUADRILATERALS

The concepts of congruence and similarity that we have explored for triangles resemble the ones needed for quadrilaterals. Two quadrilaterals are **congruent** if each pair of angles and each pair of sides can be matched. Two quadrilaterals are **similar** if each pair of angles can be matched and each pair of corresponding sides are in the same ratio. As with triangles, the symbols for congruence and similarity are $\cong$ and $\sim$, respectively.

Two other important aspects concerning similar quadrilaterals are the following:

1. The ratio of corresponding sides is identical to the ratio of perimeters, corresponding altitudes, and corresponding diagonals.
2. The ratio of the areas is the square of the ratio of corresponding sides.

Note that any two squares of different size are automatically similar; however, this information would be insufficient to declare similarity for other quadrilaterals.

Look at the diagram shown below, in which *ABCD* is similar to *RSTU*.

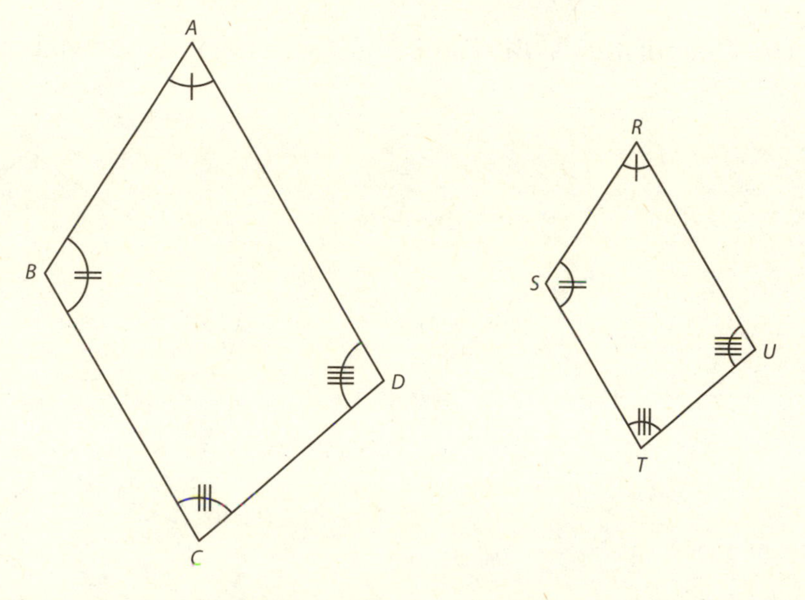

As with triangles, the order in which the vertices are listed is critical. Thus, $\angle A \cong \angle R$, $\angle B \cong \angle S$, $\angle C \cong \angle T$, $\angle D \cong \angle U$, and $\frac{AB}{RS} = \frac{BC}{ST} = \frac{CD}{TU} = \frac{DA}{UR}$.

Example 17: The ratio of two corresponding sides of two similar quadrilaterals is $\frac{7}{2}$. If one of the sides of the larger quadrilateral is 42 inches, how many inches is the corresponding side of the smaller quadrilateral?

Solution: The answer is 12. Let x represent the side of the smaller quadrilateral. Then $\frac{7}{2} = \frac{42}{x}$. Cross-multiply to get $7x = 84$. Thus, $x = 12$.

Example 18: Rectangles *TVAB* and *UXCD*, shown below, are similar.

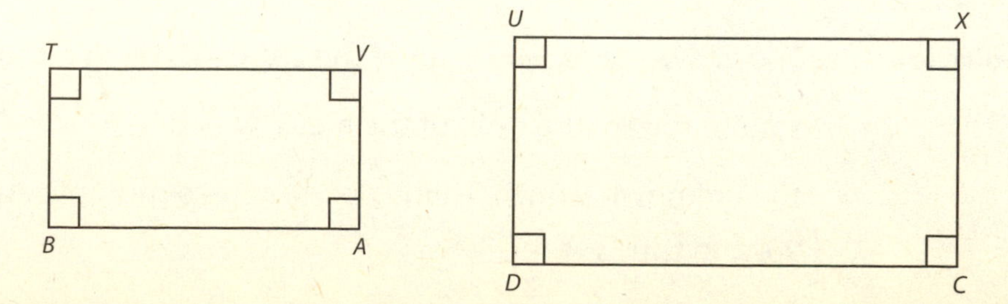

The ratio of the perimeter of *TVAB* to that of *UXCD* is $\frac{7}{10}$. If *CD* is nine units larger than *AB*, what is the length of $\overline{CD}$?

Solution: The answer is 30. Let x and $x + 9$ represent *AB* and *CD*, respectively. Then $\frac{7}{10} = \frac{x}{x+9}$. Cross-multiply to get $7x + 63 = 10x$. By subtracting $7x$ from each side, the equation simplifies to $63 = 3x$. So, $x = 21$. Thus, *CD* is nine units longer than *AB*, or 30.

Example 19: Quadrilaterals *UWYZ* and *VABD* are similar, as shown below.

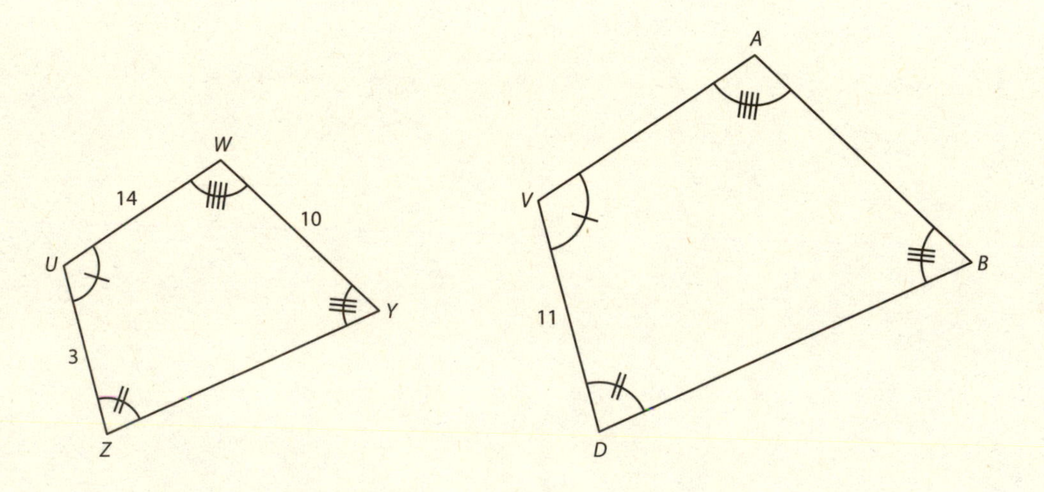

If the perimeter of *UWYZ* is 51, what is the value of *DB*?

Solution: The answer is 88. $ZY = 51 - 3 - 14 - 10 = 24$. Let x represent *DB*. Then we can use the proportion $\frac{UZ}{VD} = \frac{ZY}{DB}$. By substitution of numerical values, we get $\frac{3}{11} = \frac{24}{x}$. Cross-multiply to get $3x = 264$. Thus, $x = 88$.

Example 20: The ratio of the areas of two similar parallelograms is $\frac{4}{81}$. One altitude of the smaller parallelogram is 10. What is the length of the corresponding altitude of the larger parallelogram?

Solution: The answer is 45. The ratio of the corresponding altitudes equals the square root of the ratio of the areas, which is $\sqrt{\frac{4}{81}} = \frac{2}{9}$. Let x represent the unknown length. Then $\frac{2}{9} = \frac{10}{x}$. Cross-multiplication leads to $2x = 90$, and thus $x = 45$.

Let's try a few exercises on similar quadrilaterals.

For Exercises 16–19, trapezoids *ABCD* and *EFGH* are similar. Each trapezoid contains two pairs of right angles. The trapezoid on the left represents a scale model of the actual dimensions of a parking lot shown on the right.

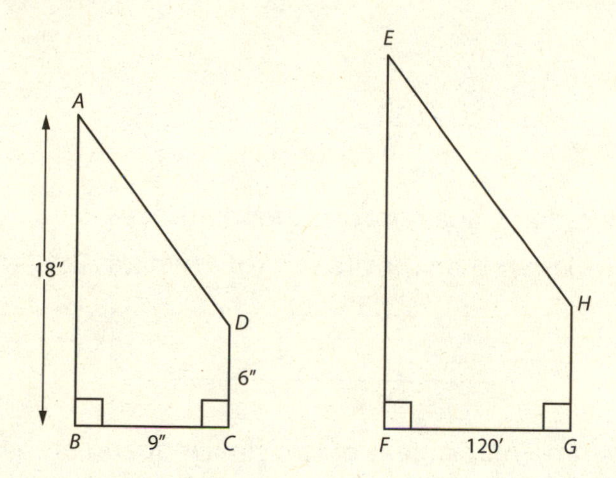

Exercise 16: What is the length, in inches, of $\overline{AD}$? (Hint: Draw a horizontal line segment from *D* to $\overline{AB}$.)

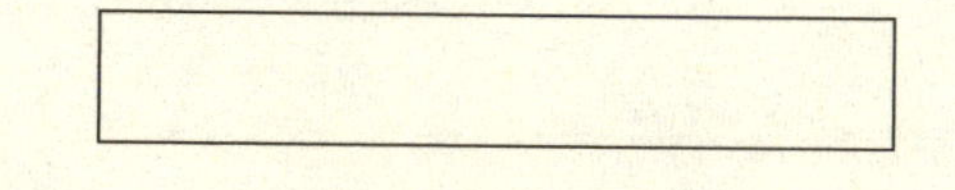

Exercise 17: What is the length, in feet, of $\overline{GH}$?

Exercise 18: What is the perimeter, in feet, of the actual parking lot?

Exercise 19: What is the ratio of the area of *ABCD* to *EFGH*? (Be sure to change to a common unit for both trapezoids.) Write your answer as a ratio of integers.

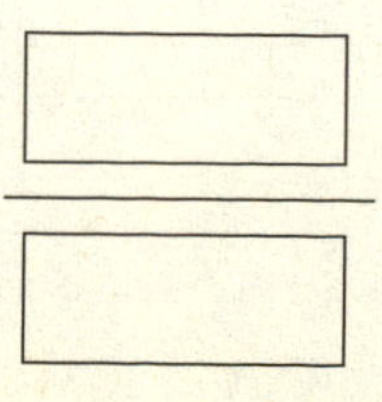

Exercise 20: Two rhombi are similar, as shown below.

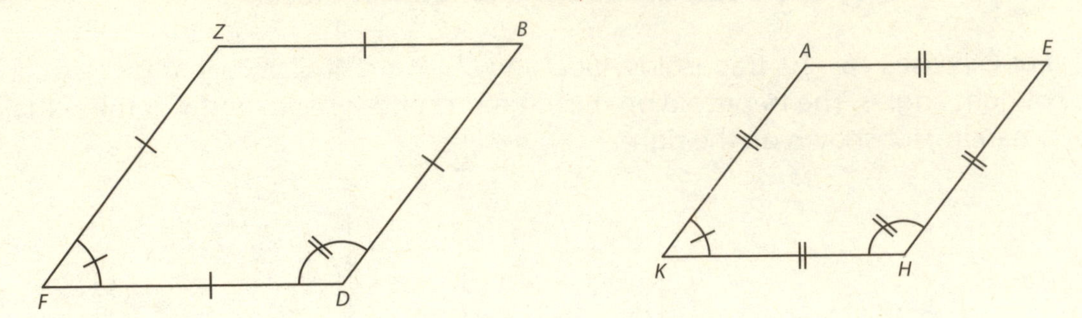

The ratio of a pair of corresponding sides is $\frac{4}{3}$. If the area of *FDBZ* is 28 units larger than the area of *KHEA*, what is the area of *KHEA*?

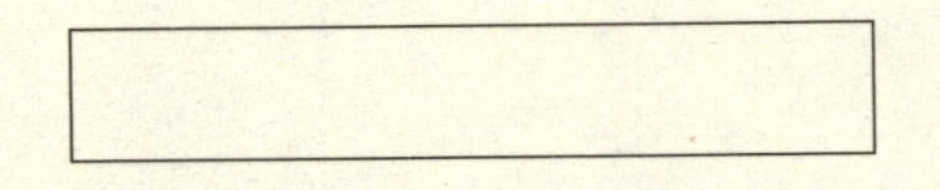

Exercise 21: The ratio of the areas of two similar quadrilaterals is $\frac{9}{100}$. Side $\overline{JK}$ of the smaller quadrilateral corresponds to side $\overline{PQ}$ of the other quadrilateral. If $JK = 27$, what is the value of PQ?

Let's look at the answers.

Answer 16: The correct answer is 15. Draw a horizontal segment from D to $\overline{AB}$, as shown below. Call the point of intersection *Z*.

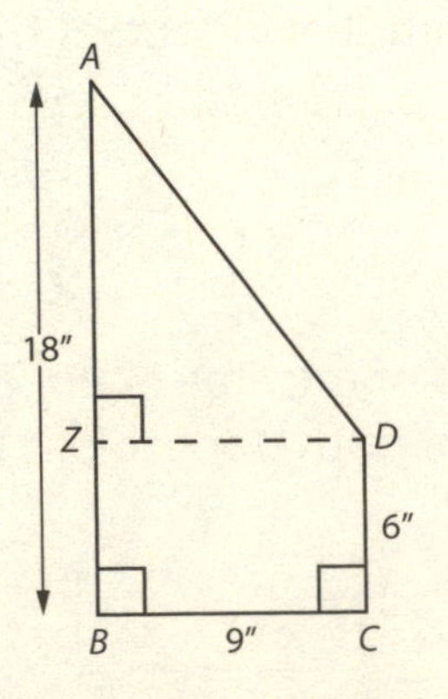

Then $BZ = DC = 6$, so $AZ = 18 - 6 = 12$. Also, $ZD = BC = 6$. Triangle *AZD* has a right angle at *Z*, so we can use the Pythagorean theorem to find the value of *AD*. In fact, $(AD)^2 = 9^2 + 12^2 = 81 + 144 = 225$. Thus, $AD = \sqrt{225} = 15$.

Answer 17: The correct answer is 80. Let x represent the length (in feet) of $\overline{GH}$. Then $\frac{6}{x} = \frac{9}{120}$. Cross-multiply to get $9x = 720$. Thus, $x = 80$. Note that we need not convert all units to inches.

Answer 18: The correct answer is 640. The perimeter of the scale model, in inches, is $18 + 9 + 6 + 15 = 48$. Let x represent the perimeter of the actual parking lot, in feet. Then, $\frac{9}{120} = \frac{48}{x}$. This means that $9x = 5{,}760$, so $x = 640$.

Answer 19: The correct answer is $\frac{1}{25{,}600}$. In order to determine the actual ratio of the perimeters, change 120 feet to $(120)(12) = 1{,}440$ inches. Then the ratio of the perimeters is $\frac{9}{1{,}440} = \frac{1}{160}$. Thus, the ratio of the areas is $\left(\frac{1}{160}\right)^2 = \frac{1}{25{,}600}$.

Answer 20: The correct answer is 36. The ratio of the areas is $\left(\frac{4}{3}\right)^2 = \frac{16}{9}$. Let $x + 28$ and x represent the areas of *FDBZ* and *KHEA*, respectively. Then $\frac{16}{9} = \frac{x+28}{x}$. Cross-multiply to get $16x = 9x + 252$. This equation simplifies to $7x = 252$. Thus, $x = 36$.

Answer 21: The correct answer is 90. The ratio of corresponding sides is $\sqrt{\frac{9}{100}} = \frac{3}{10}$. Let x represent the length of $\overline{PQ}$. Then $\frac{3}{10} = \frac{27}{x}$, which means that $3x = 270$. Thus, $x = 90$.

We'll get more GRE-looking questions at the end of the chapter on circles, which is next.

CHAPTER 12: *Circles*

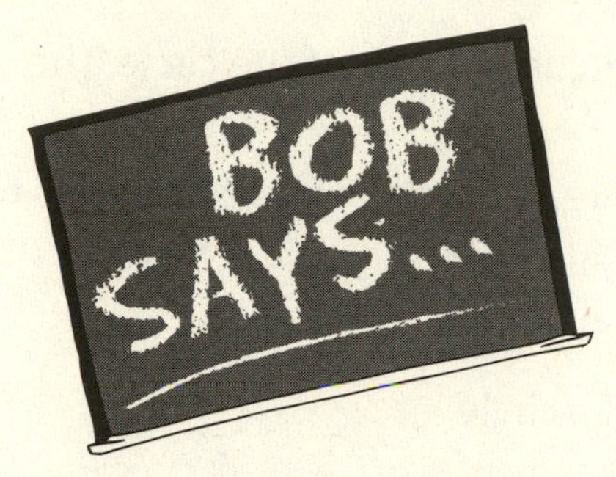

"Although sometimes it seems you are going in circles, you are really heading toward your goal."

Circles are a favorite topic of the GRE. Circles allow many short questions that can be combined with the other geometric chapters. Let's get started.

PARTS OF A CIRCLE

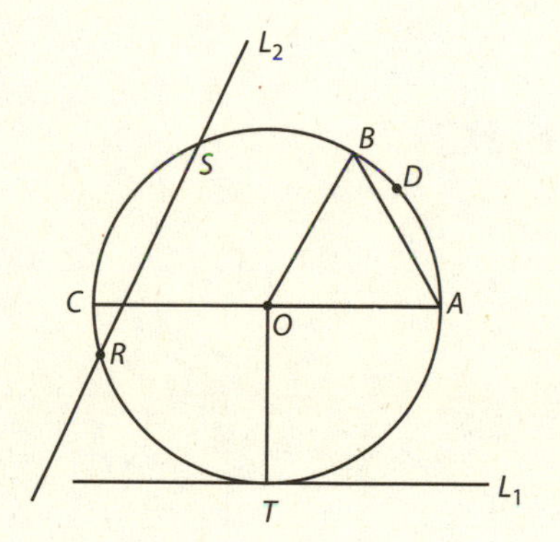

We all know what a circle looks like, but maybe we're not familiar with its "parts."

O is the **center** of the circle. A circle is often named by its center, so this is circle *O*.

OA, *OT*, *OC*, and *OB* are **radii** (singular: radius); a radius is a line segment from the center to the **circumference**, or edge, of the circle.

All radii (r) of a circle are equal. This is a postulate or axiom, a law taken to be true without proof. It is probably a good idea to tell you there are no proofs on the GRE, as there were when you took geometry.

AC is the **diameter**, *d*, the distance from one side of the circle through the center to the other side; $d = 2r$ and $r = \frac{d}{2}$.

L_1 is a **tangent**, a line that touches a circle in one and only one point.

T is a **point of tangency**, the point where a tangent touches the circle. The radius to the point of tangency (*OT*) is always perpendicular to the tangent, so $OT \perp L_1$.

L_2 is a **secant**, a line that passes through a circle in two places.

RS is a **chord**, a line segment that has each end on the circumference of the circle. The diameter is the longest chord in a circle.

OADBO is a **sector** (a pie-shaped part of a circle). There are a number of sectors in this figure; others include *BOCSB* and *OATRCSBO*. We will see these again soon.

An **arc** is any distance along the circumference of a circle.

Arc *ADB* is a **minor arc** because it is less than half a circle.

Arc *BDATRC* is a **major arc** because it is more than half a circle.

Arc *ATRC* is a **semicircle** because it is exactly half a circle

Whew! Enough! However, we do need some more facts about circles.

The following are mostly theorems, proven laws. Again, there are no proofs on the GRE, but you need to be aware of these facts.

AREA AND CIRCUMFERENCE

Area of a circle:

$$A = \pi r^2$$

Circumference (perimeter of a circle):

$$C = 2\pi r \text{ or } \pi d.$$

SECTORS

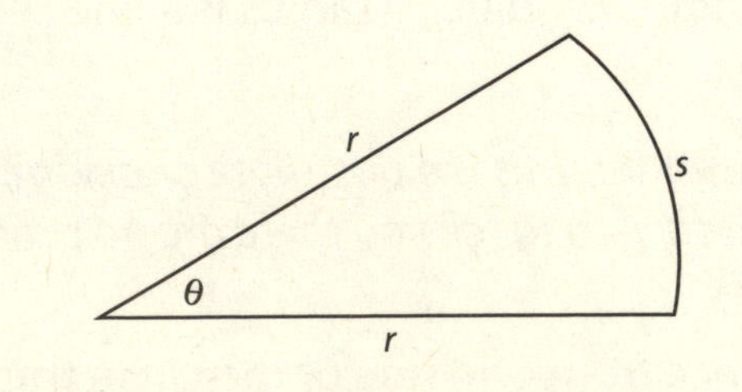

Area of a sector:

$$A = \frac{\theta}{360^\circ}\pi r^2,$$

where θ (theta) is the angle of the sector in degrees.

Arc length of a sector:

$$s = \frac{\theta}{360°} \times 2\pi r$$

Perimeter of a sector:

$$p = s + 2r,$$

where s is the arc length

Example 1: Find the area and perimeter of a 60° sector of a circle of diameter 12.

Solution:

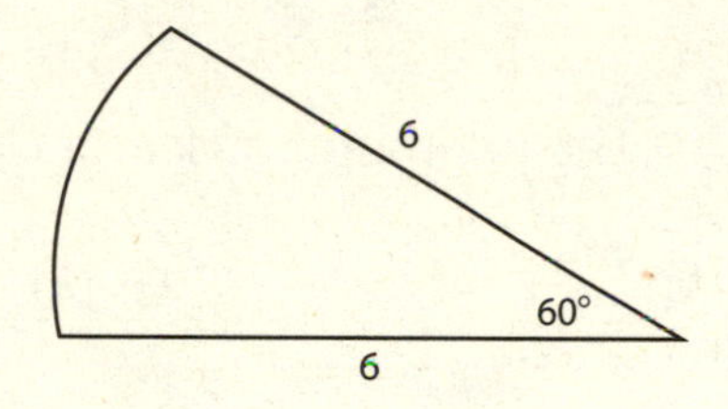

If the diameter is 12, the radius is 6. The sector is pictured here. Its area is $A = \frac{60°}{360°} \times \pi 6^2 = 6\pi$ square units. Although you should know that pi (π) is about 3.14, I've never seen a problem for which you had to multiply 6 times 3.14. The answer is left in terms of π. The perimeter of the sector is $s = 2(6) + \frac{60°}{360°} \times 2\pi(6) = 12 + 2\pi$ units.

Let's do some exercises.

For Exercises 1 through 5, refer to the following circle. O is the center of the circle.

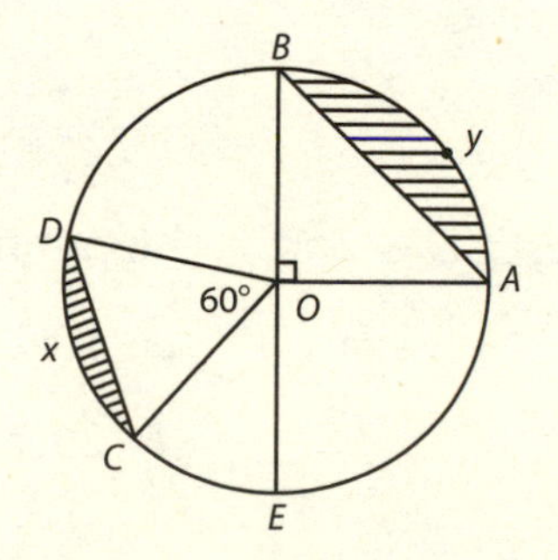

Exercise 1: If the area of ΔAOB is 25, the area of circle O is

A. 12.5π

B. 25π

C. 50π

D. 100π

E. 200π

Exercise 2: If $OA = 8$, the area of the shaded region $BAYB$ is

A. $16(\pi - 2)$

B. $16(\pi - 1)$

C. $8(2\pi - 1)$

D. $64(\pi - 1)$

E. $32(\pi - 2)$

Exercise 3: If $CD = 10$, the perimeter of sector $DOCXD$ is

A. $30 + 10\frac{\pi}{3}$

B. $30 + 20\frac{\pi}{3}$

C. $20 + 10\frac{\pi}{3}$

D. $20 + 20\frac{\pi}{3}$

E. $30 + 30\pi$

Exercise 4: If $OC = 2$, the area of the shaded portion $DCXD$ is

A. $\pi - \sqrt{3}$

B. $2\pi - \sqrt{3}$

C. $4\pi - \sqrt{3}$

D. $\dfrac{2\pi - 3\sqrt{3}}{3}$

E. $\dfrac{8\pi - 3\sqrt{3}}{3}$

Exercise 5: If the area of ΔCOD is $25\sqrt{3}$, the perimeter of semicircle $EOBDXCE$ is

A. 10π

B. $10(\pi + 1)$

C. $10(\pi + 2)$

D. $10(2\pi + 1)$

E. $20(\pi + 1)$

I bet you get the idea.

Let's look at the answers.

Answer 1: The answer is (C). $A = \frac{1}{2}(r)(r) = \frac{1}{2}r^2$, so $r^2 = 50$. The area of the circle is thus $\pi r^2 = 50\pi$. Notice that once you have a value for r^2, you don't have to find r to do this problem.

Answer 2: The answer is (A). The area of region *BAYB* is the area of one-fourth of a circle minus the area of ΔAOB. So the area is $A = \frac{1}{4}\pi 8^2 - \frac{1}{2}(8)(8) = 16\pi - 32 = 16(\pi - 2)$.

Answer 3: The answer is (C). The perimeter of sector *DOCXD* $= 2r + s$, where s is the length of arc *CXD*. ΔCOD is equilateral, so $CD = CO = DO = r = 10$. $s = \frac{60°}{360°}2\pi(10) = \frac{10\pi}{3}$. So the perimeter of sector *DOCXD* is $p = 20 + \frac{10\pi}{3}$.

Answer 4: The answer is (D). The area of region *DCXD* is the area of sector *ODXCO* minus the area of ΔDOC, when $OC = 2$. So the area is $A = \frac{60°}{360°}\pi 2^2 - \frac{2^2\sqrt{3}}{4} = \frac{2\pi}{3} - \sqrt{3} = \frac{2\pi - 3\sqrt{3}}{3}$.

Answer 5: The answer is (C). We must first find the radius. The area of equilateral $\Delta COD = \frac{s^2\sqrt{3}}{4} = 25\sqrt{3}$. So $s^2 = 100$, and $s = r = 10$. The perimeter of the semicircle is $\frac{1}{2}(2\pi r) + 2r = \pi r + 2r = 10\pi + 20 = 10(\pi + 2)$.

There are a few more things we need to know. When we talked about two intersecting lines earlier, we saw that *CE* might equal *ED*; however, if the description of the figure doesn't say so, you cannot assume it. Also, *ED* might be perpendicular to *CE*, but if it doesn't say so, you cannot assume it, either. In fact, we can say *CD* **bisects** *AB* at *E* only if we know that $AE = EB$ or *E* is the midpoint of *AB*.

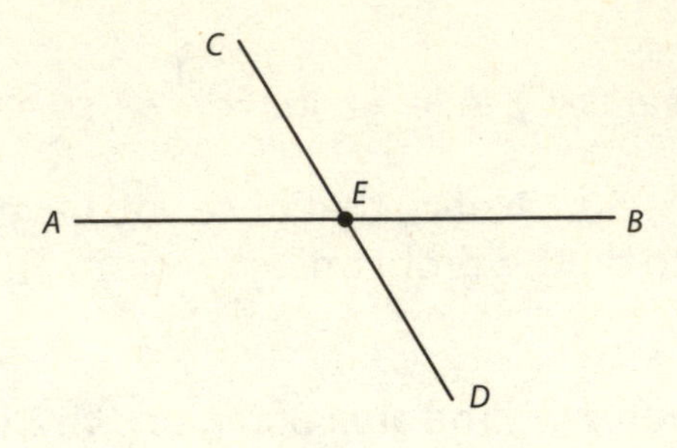

Now we consider two intersecting lines in a circle, such as chord *AB* and radius *CO* in circle *O*.

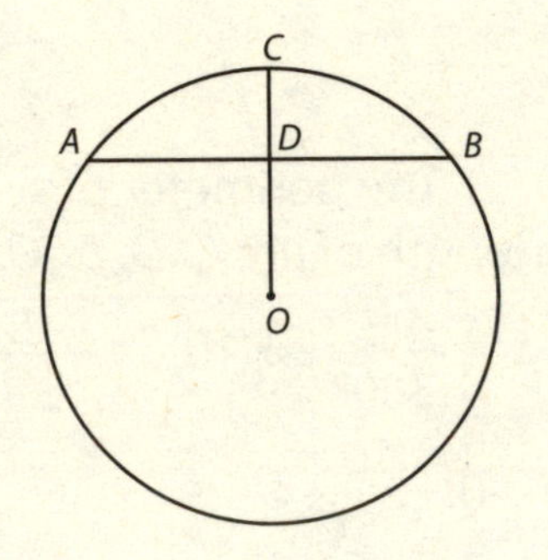

If one of the following facts is true, all are true:

1. $OD \perp AB$
2. *CO* bisects *AB*
3. *CO* bisects $\overparen{ACB}$ (read "arc ACB")

 **Let's do some more exercises.**

For Exercises 6 and 7, use this figure, which is a triangle-semicircle shape.

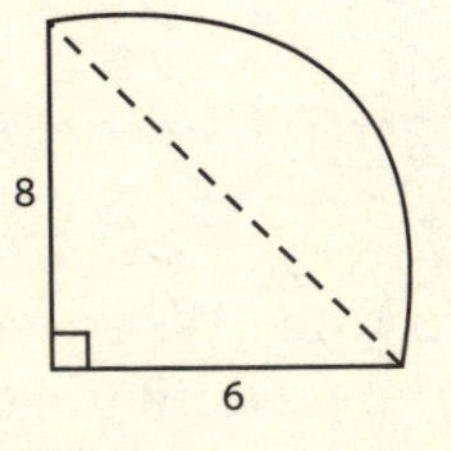

Exercise 6: The perimeter of this figure is

A. $14 + 5\pi$

B. $14 + 10\pi$

C. $24 + 5\pi$

D. $24 + 10\pi$

E. $12 + 10\pi$

Exercise 7: The area of the figure is

A. $24 + \frac{25\pi}{2}$

B. $24 + 25\pi$

C. $24 + 50\pi$

D. $48 + 25\pi$

E. $48 + 50\pi$

Exercise 8: A circle is **inscribed** in (inside and touching) figure *MNPQ*, which has all right angles. Diameter $AB = 10$. The area of the shaded portion is

A. $100 - 12.5\pi$

B. $100 - 25\pi$

C. $40 - 10\pi$

D. $40 - 5\pi$

E. $100 - 100\pi$

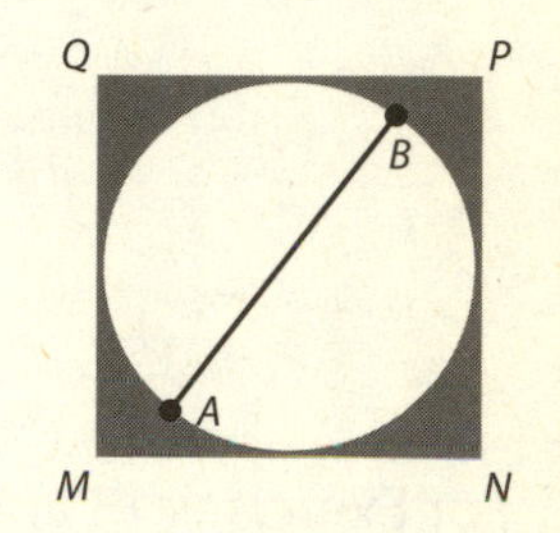

Exercise 9: If $AB = 10$, the area of the shaded portion in the figure is

A. $100 - 12.5\pi$

B. $100 - 25\pi$

C. $40 - 10\pi$

D. $40 - 5\pi$

E. $100 - 100\pi$

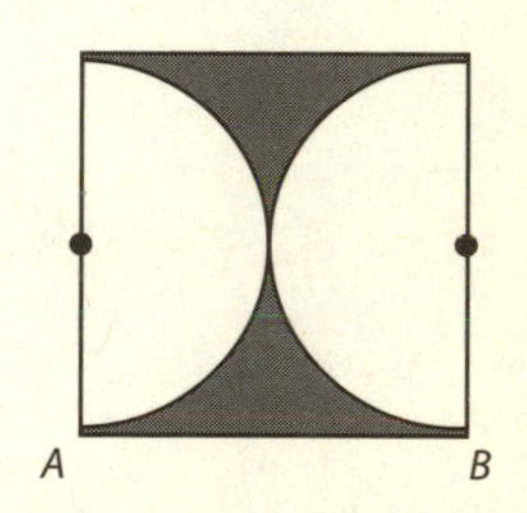

For Exercises 10 and 11, use this figure. The perimeter of the 16 semicircles is 32π.

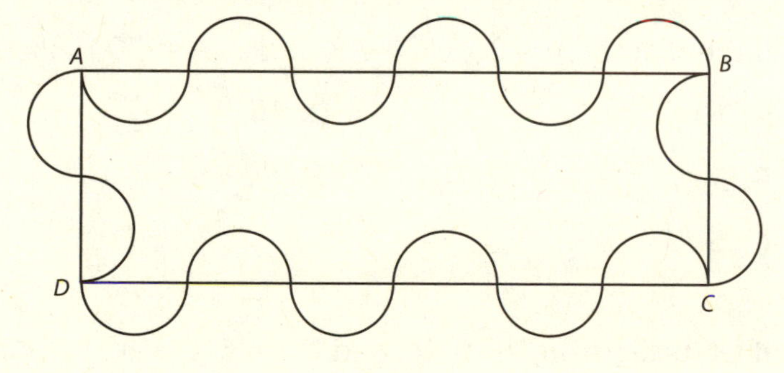

Exercise 10: The area of rectangle *ABCD* is

A. 64

B. 128

C. 192

D. 16π

E. Cannot be determined

Exercise 11: The area inside the region formed by the semicircular curves from A to B to C to D and back to A is

A. 64
B. 128
C. 192
D. 16π
E. Are you for real??!!

Exercise 12: In the figure, $EF = CD = 12$, B is the midpoint of OD, and A is the midpoint of CO. The area of the shaded portion is

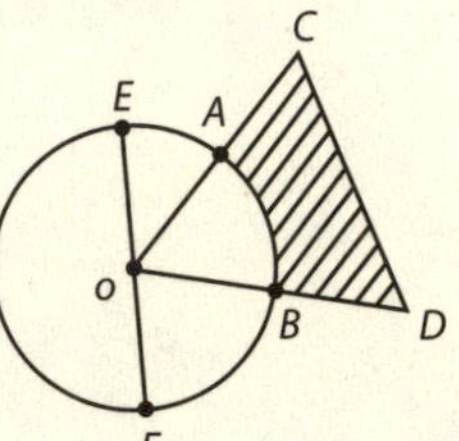

A. $36(4\sqrt{3} - \pi)$
B. $6(6\sqrt{3} - \pi)$
C. $144(\pi - 3)$
D. $72(3\sqrt{3} - \pi)$
E. $36(6\sqrt{3} - \pi)$

For Exercises 13 and 14, use this figure.

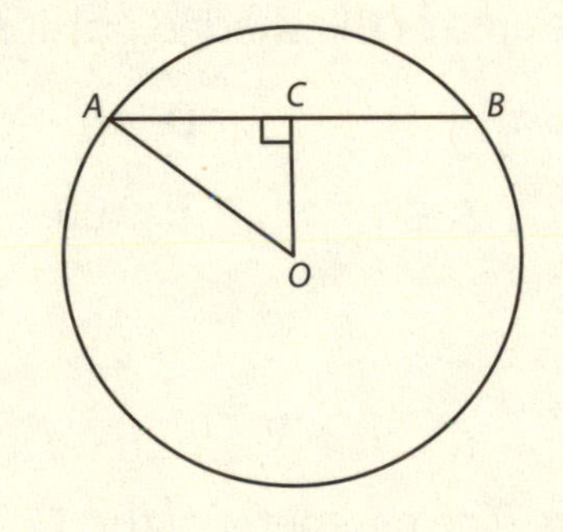

Exercise 13: If the diameter $= 20$, $OC \perp AB$, and $\angle A = 30°$, $AB =$

A. 10
B. 5
C. $5\sqrt{3}$
D. $10\sqrt{3}$
E. $5\sqrt{2}$

Exercise 14: If OC bisects AB, $AB = 16$, and $OC = 6$, the area of circle O is

A. 10π
B. 20π
C. 40π
D. 100π
E. 400π

Exercise 15: In a circle with center *O*, diameter $\overline{EC}$ is perpendicular to chord $\overline{AB}$ at point *D*. Which of the following statements are true? Indicate *all* correct choices.

A. $\overline{EC}$ bisects minor arc *AB*.

B. $\overline{AE} \cong \overline{BE}$.

C. $\overline{EC}$ bisects $\overline{AB}$.

D. OA = OB.

E. *OD* is the distance between $\overline{AB}$ and point *O*.

Exercise 16: Which of the following lengths is sufficient information to find the area of a circle? Indicate *all* correct choices.

A. Radius

B. Diameter

C. Circumference

D. Any chord

E. Each of two intersecting chords

F. A chord that is perpendicular to a tangent of the circle

Exercise 17: A circle with a diameter of 12 has the same area as a square. To the nearest tenth, what is the side of the square?

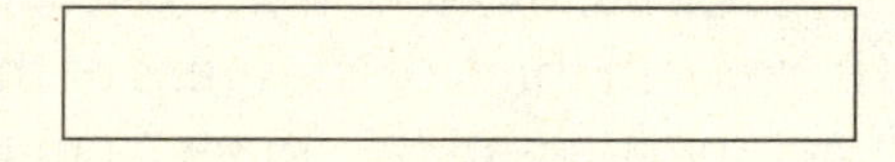

Exercise 18: A sector of a circle has a central angle of 90°. If the radius of the circle is 10, the perimeter of this sector can be represented as $a + b\pi$. What is the sum of *a* and *b*?

Exercise 19: The radius of a circle is 4. To the nearest tenth, what is the area of a sector whose central angle is 60°?

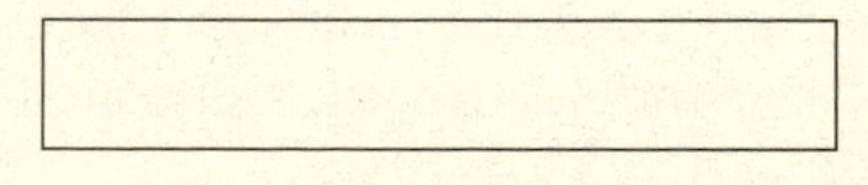

Let's look at the answers.

Answer 6: The answer is (A). The figure is a 6-8-10 Pythagorean triple, but 10 is not part of the perimeter. $p = 6 + 8 + \frac{1}{2}2\pi(5) = 14 + 5\pi$.

Answer 7: The answer is (A). $A = \frac{1}{2}bh + \frac{1}{2}\pi r^2 = \frac{1}{2}6 \times 8 + \frac{1}{2}\pi 5^2 = 24 + \frac{25\pi}{2}$.

Answer 8: The answer is (B). The area is the area of the square minus the area of the circle. $A = s^2 - \pi r^2 = 10^2 - \pi 5^2 = 100 - 25\pi$.

Answer 9: The answer is (B). Exercise 8 and Exercise 9 are exactly the same problems. In Exercise 8, we could also say the square **circumscribes** the circle.

Answer 10: The answer is (C). Each semicircle has arc length $\frac{180°}{360°}\pi d$, and there are 16 semicircles, so $16\left(\frac{1}{2}\pi d\right) = 32\pi$, or $8\pi d = 32\pi$, so $d = 4$. The rectangle's dimensions are thus 8 and 24. The area is $A = b \times h = 8(24) = 192$.

Answer 11: The answer is (C). Believe it or not, Exercise 11 is exactly the same as Exercise 10! You can think of the areas of the "outer" semicircles as canceling out the areas of the "inner" semicircles, and you are left with only the area of rectangle *ABCD*.

Answer 12: The answer is (B). The information is enough to tell us the triangle is equilateral and $\angle AOB = 60°$. The shaded area is the area of ΔCOD minus the area of sector *OABO*. Thus,

$$A = \frac{s^2\sqrt{3}}{4} - \frac{1}{6}\pi r^2 = \frac{12^2\sqrt{3}}{4} - \frac{1}{6}\pi 6^2 = 36\sqrt{3} - 6\pi = 6(6\sqrt{3} - \pi).$$

Answer 13: The answer is (D). *AO*, the radius, is 10; *CO*, the side opposite the 30° angle, is 5; and *AC*, the side opposite the 60° angle, is $5\sqrt{3}$. $AB = 2(AC) = 2(5\sqrt{3}) = 10\sqrt{3}$.

Answer 14: The answer is (D). To find the area of the circle, we need to find the radius OA. We know AC is 8 and OC is 6. We have a 6-8-10 right triangle, so $AO = r = 10$. The area is $\pi(10)^2 = 100\pi$.

Answer 15: The correct answers are (A), (B), (C), (D), and (E). Choices (A), (B), and (C) can be proven formally. Choice (D) is true because any two radii of the same circle must be congruent. Choice (E) is true because of the definition of the distance between a line segment and a point.

Answer 16: The correct answers are (A), (B), (C), and (F). Choice (A) is correct because the area of a circle is πr^2, where r is the radius. Choice (B) is correct because, given the diameter, we can determine the radius by dividing by 2, and then apply the area formula. Choice (C) is correct because, given the circumference, the radius can be found by dividing by 2π, and then applying the area formula. For choice (F), this chord must be the diameter, and thus the radius and area can be determined.

Answer 17: The correct answer is 10.6. The radius of the circle is 6, so its area is $(\pi)(6^2) = 36\pi$. Thus, the side of the square must be $\sqrt{36\pi} \approx \sqrt{113.097} \approx 10.6$.

Answer 18: The correct answer is 25. The circumference of the circle is $(2)(\pi)(10) = 20\pi$. The arc of this sector represents $\frac{90°}{360°} = \frac{1}{4}$ of the circumference, which is 5π. The perimeter of the sector consists of two radii and the corresponding arc length. Then the perimeter of the sector is $20 + 5\pi = a + b\pi$. Therefore, the sum of a and b is 25.

Answer 19: The correct answer is 8.4. The area of the circle is $(\pi)(4^2) = 16\pi$. Then the area of the sector must be $\frac{60°}{360°} = \frac{1}{6}$ of the area of the circle. Thus, the area of the sector is $\frac{16\pi}{6} \approx 8.4$.

EQUATION OF A CIRCLE

Another property of circles that is required for the GRE test is its equation in the xy-coordinate plane. The definition of a circle is the set of all points at a fixed distance from a given point. The fixed distance is called the radius and the given point is called the center. Let the center be represented by the coordinates (h, k) and let r represent the radius. Then the equation of this circle is $(x - h)^2 + (y - k)^2 = r^2$. If a point (a, b) lies inside the circle, then $(a - h)^2 + (b - k)^2 < r^2$. Likewise, if a point (c, d) lies outside the circle, then $(c - h)^2 + (d - k)^2 > r^2$.

The following diagram shows the graph of $(x - 1)^2 + (y + 2)^2 = 9$.

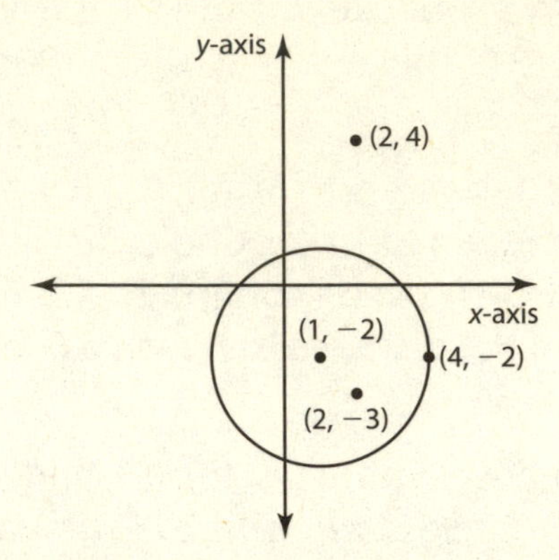

The equation can be written in the form $(x - 1)^2 + (y - (-2))^2 = 9$. This means that $h = 1$ and $k = -2$, so the center is located at $(1, -2)$. The point $(4, -2)$ is on the circle because $(4 - 1)^2 + (-2 + 2)^2 = 3^2 + 0^2 = 9$. The point $(2, -3)$ is inside the circle because $(2 - 1)^2 + (-3 + 2)^2 = 1^2 + (-1)^2 = 2 < 9$. Also, note that the point $(2, 4)$ is outside the circle because $(2 - 1)^2 + (4 + 2)^2 = 1^2 + (6)^2 = 1 + 36 = 37 > 9$.

Caution *Never write the equation of a circle as $(x - h) + (y - k) = r$.*

Q **Let's do some more exercises.**

Exercise 20: What is the sum of the coordinates of the center of a circle whose equation is $(x - 4)^2 + (y + 7)^2 = 100$?

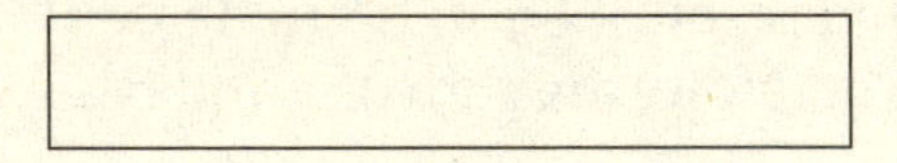

Exercise 21: To the nearest hundredth, what is the radius of a circle whose equation is $(x + 5)^2 + (y - 3)^2 = 20$?

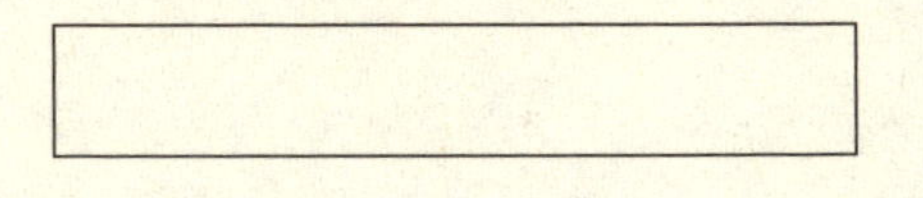

Exercise 22: Which of the following points lie outside the circle whose equation is $(x + 2)^2 + (y + 4)^2 = 25$? Indicate *all* correct answers.

A. $(1, -2)$
B. $(3, -4)$
C. $(-3, -1)$
D. $(2, -2)$
E. $(4, -5)$
F. $(0, 1)$

Exercise 23: The point (6, 2) lies inside the circles associated with which of the following equations? Indicate *all* correct answers.

A. $(x - 3)^2 + (y - 2)^2 = 16$

B. $(x - 1)^2 + (y + 4)^2 = 65$

C. $(x + 1)^2 + (y + 6)^2 = 113$

D. $(x + 2)^2 + (y + 1)^2 = 70$

E. $(x + 7)^2 + (y + 3)^2 = 200$

F. $(x - 4)^2 + (y + 5)^2 = 60$

Exercise 24: Which one of the following equations represents a circle with its center at (−1, −6) and with a radius of 16?

A. $(x + 1)^2 + (y + 6)^2 = 256$

B. $(x - 1)^2 + (y - 6)^2 = 256$

C. $(x - 6)^2 + (y - 1)^2 = 256$

D. $(x + 6)^2 + (y + 1)^2 = 16$

E. $(x + 1)^2 + (y + 6)^2 = 16$

A Let's look at the answers.

Answer 20: The correct answer is −3. Rewrite the equation as $(x - 4)^2 + (y - (-7))^2 = 100$ to identify $h = 4$ and $k = -7$. Therefore, the center is located at (4, −7), and the sum of its coordinates is −3. Note that the fact that $r^2 = 100$ isn't needed to find the center.

Answer 21: The correct answer is 4.47. Since $r^2 = 20$, the radius is $\sqrt{20} \approx 4.47$.

Answer 22: The correct answers are (E) and (F). By substitution, choice (E) becomes $(4 + 2)^2 + (-5 + 4)^2 = 6^2 + (-1)^2 = 37 > 25$, and choice (F) becomes $(0 + 2)^2 + (1 + 4)^2 = 2^2 + 5^2 = 29 > 25$. Each of choices (A), (B), (C), and (D) are wrong because substitution of their values into the left side of the equation $(x + 2)^2 + (y + 4)^2 = 25$ does not produce a number greater than 25. The left sides of the equation for choices (A), (B), (C), and (D) become 5, 25, 10, and 20, respectively.

Answer 23: The correct answers are (A), (B), (E), and (F). The easiest way to determine the correct responses is to substitute 6 for x and 2 for y in each equation and compare the two sides of the equation. If the two sides are equal, (6, 2) lies on the circle; if the left side is smaller, (6, 2) lies inside the circle; if the left side is larger, (6, 2) lies outside the circle. The results for each answer choice are

A. $(6 - 3)^2 + (2 - 2)^2 = 3^2 + 0^2 = 9 < 16$, which means inside the circle.

B. $(6 - 1)^2 + (2 + 4)^2 = 5^2 + 6^2 = 25 + 36 = 61 < 65$, which means inside the circle.

C. $(6 + 1)^2 + (2 + 6)^2 = 7^2 + 8^2 = 49 + 64 = 113$, which means on the circle.

D. $(6 + 2)^2 + (2 + 1)^2 = 8^2 + 3^2 = 64 + 9 = 73 > 70$, which means outside the circle.

E. $(6 + 7)^2 + (2 + 3)^2 = 13^2 + 5^2 = 169 + 25 = 194 < 200$, which means inside the circle.

F. $(6 - 4)^2 + (2 + 5)^2 = 2^2 + 7^2 = 4 + 49 = 53 < 60$, which means inside the circle.

Answer 24: The correct answer is (A). The equation $(x + 1)^2 + (y + 6)^2 = 256$ can be rewritten as $(x - (-1))^2 + (y - (-6))^2 = 16^2$. In this form, $h = -1$, $k = -6$, and $r = 16$. Note that choice (E) is wrong because we need r^2, not r.

Okay. Now let's go from two dimensions to three dimensions.

CHAPTER 13: *Three-Dimensional Figures*

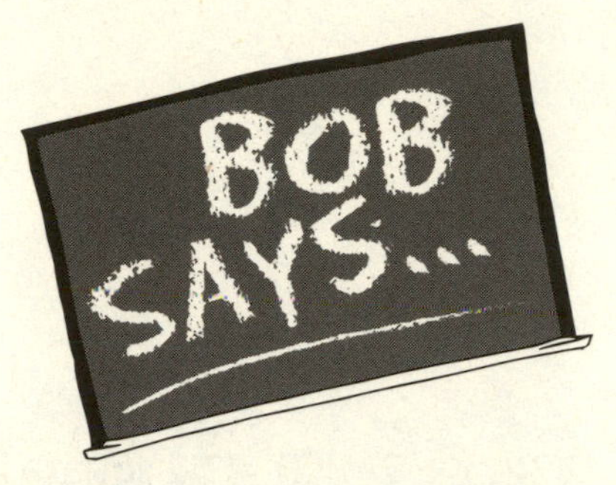

"Your ultimate success will depend on your ability to see in different dimensions."

This chapter is relatively short. There are only a few figures we need to know. Since these are three-dimensional figures, we discuss their volumes and surface areas (areas of all of the sides). The diagonal is the distance from one corner internally to an opposite corner.

BOX

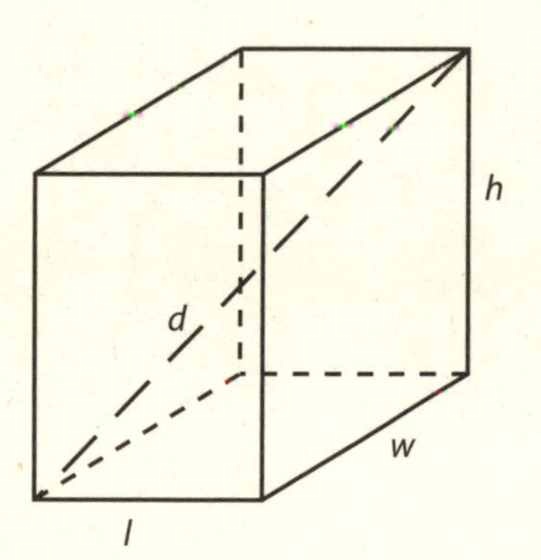

This figure is also known as a **rectangular solid**, and if that isn't a mouthful enough, its correct name is a **rectangular parallelepiped**. But essentially, it's a **box**.

- Volume = $V = lwh$
- Surface area = $SA = 2lw + 2lh + 2wh$
- Diagonal = $d = \sqrt{l^2 + w^2 + h^2}$, known as the 3-D Pythagorean theorem

Example 1: For the given figure, find V, SA, and d.

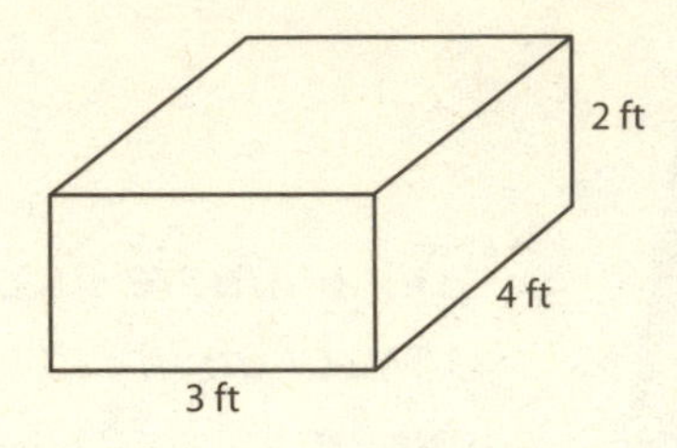

Solution: $V = lwh = (3)(4)(2) = 24$ cubic feet;

$SA = 2lw + 2lh + 2wh = 2(3)(4) + 2(3)(2) + 2(4)(2) = 52$ square feet;

$d = \sqrt{l^2 + w^2 + h^2} = \sqrt{3^2 + 4^2 + 2^2} = \sqrt{29} \approx 5.4$ feet

CUBE

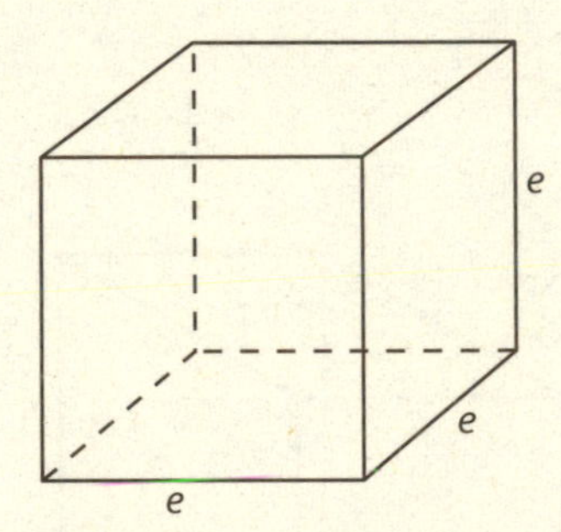

A **cube** is a box for which all of the faces, or sides, are equal squares.

- $V = e^3$ (say "e cubed"). Cubing comes from a cube!
- $SA = 6e^2$
- $d = e\sqrt{3}$
- A cube has 6 faces, 8 vertices, and 12 edges.

Example 2: For a cube with an edge of 10 meters, find V, SA, and d.

Solution: $V = 10^3 = 1{,}000$ cubic meters; $SA = 6e^2 = 6(10)^2 = 600$ square meters;

$d = e\sqrt{3} = 10\sqrt{3} \approx 17.32$ meters

CYLINDER

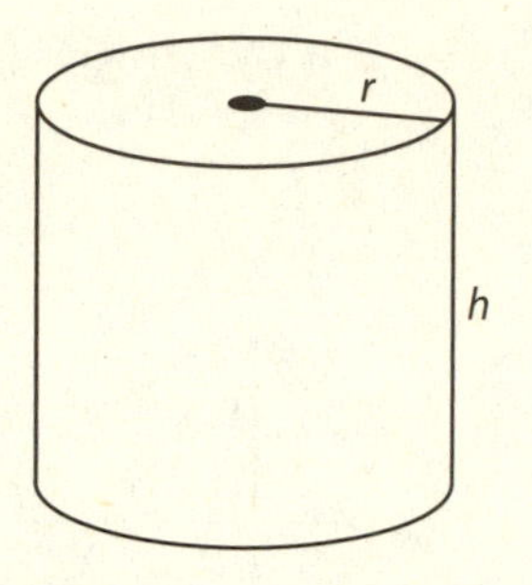

A cylinder is shaped like a can. The curved surface is considered as a side, and the top and bottom are equal circles.

- $V = \pi r^2 h$
- SA = top + bottom + curved surface = $2\pi r^2 + 2\pi rh$

Once a neighbor of mine wanted to find the area of the curved part of a cylinder. He wasn't interested in why, just the answer. Of course, being a teacher I had to explain it to him. I told him that if you cut a label off a soup can and unwrap it, the figure is a rectangle; neglecting the rim, the height is the height of the can and the width is the circumference of the circle. Multiply this height and width, and the answer is $2\pi r \times h$. He waited patiently and then soon moved out of the neighborhood. Just kidding!

In general, the volume of any figure for which the top is the same as the bottom is $V = Bh$, where B is the area of the base. If the figure comes to a point, the volume is $\left(\frac{1}{3}\right)Bh$. The surface area is found by adding up all the sides.

Example 3: Find V and SA for a cylinder of height 10 yards and diameter of 8 yards.

8 yd
10 yd

Solution: We see that since $d = 8$, $r = 4$. Then $V = \pi r^2 h = \pi(4^2 \times 10) = 160\pi$ cubic yards; $SA = 2\pi r^2 + 2\pi rh = 2\pi 4^2 + 2\pi(4)(10) = 112\pi$ square yards.

Let's do some exercises.

Use this figure for Exercises 1 through 3. It is a pyramid with a square base. $WX = 8$, $BV = 3$, and B is in the middle of the base.

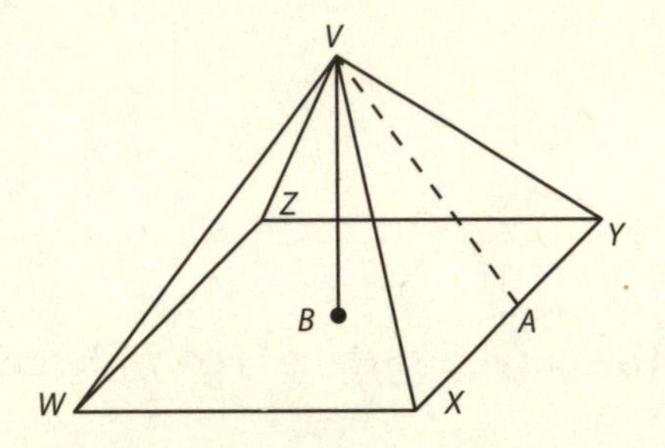

Exercise 1: The volume of the pyramid is

A. 192
B. 96
C. 64
D. 32
E. 16

Exercise 2: The surface area of the pyramid is

A. 72
B. 112
C. 144
D. 224
E. 448

Exercise 3: $VY =$

A. 6
B. $\sqrt{41}$
C. 7
D. 9
E. $\sqrt{89}$

Exercise 4: In the given rectangular solid, the perimeter of $\Delta ABC =$

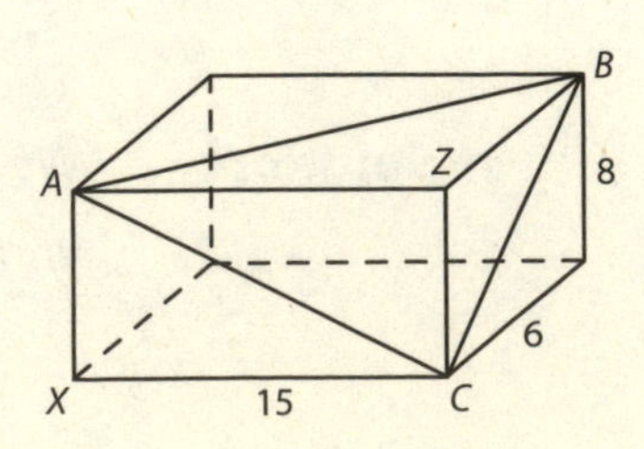

A. $\sqrt{325}$
B. 30
C. $27 + \sqrt{261}$
D. 37
E. 41

Exercise 5: The volume of the cylinder shown is:

A. 640π

B. 320π

C. 288π

D. 144π

E. 72π

Exercise 6: *ABKL* is the face of a cube with $AB = 10$, and box *BCFG* has a square front with $BC = 6$.

The surface area that can be viewed in this configuration is

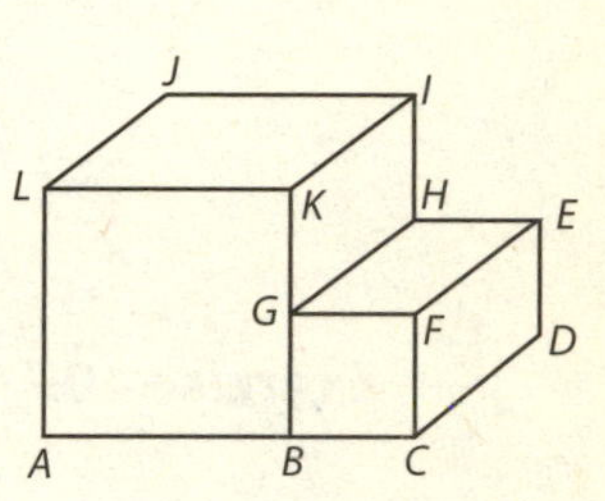

A. 300

B. 356

C. 396

D. 400

E. 1360

Exercise 7: A cylinder has volume *V*. If we triple its radius, by what factor should we multiply the height in order that the volume stays the same?

A. $\frac{1}{9}$

B. $\frac{1}{3}$

C. 1

D. 3

E. 9

Exercise 8: The numerical value of which of the following is sufficient to determine the volume of a cube? Indicate *all* correct choices.

A. Edge

B. Total surface area

C. Surface area of one face

D. Diagonal of one face

E. Diagonal of the cube

F. Distance between the middle of one face and the middle of the opposite face

Exercise 9: The numerical value of which of the following is sufficient to determine the volume of a cone? Indicate *all* correct choices.

A. Radius of the base

B. The vertical height

C. The diameter of the base and the vertical height

D. The diameter of the base and the slant height

E. The value of r^2h

F. The volume of a cylinder whose radius and height match those of the cone

Exercise 10: The area of the base of a pyramid is 20 and its vertical height is 6. What is the volume?

Exercise 11: The volume of a cube with edge 6 is the same as the volume of a rectangular box with a height of 4 and a width of 3. What is the length of the box?

Let's look at the answers.

Answer 1: The answer is (C). $V = \left(\frac{1}{3}\right)Bh = \frac{1}{3}s^2h = \frac{1}{3}(8^2)(3) = 64$.

Answer 2: The answer is (C). $SA = s^2 + 4\left(\frac{1}{2}bh\right)$. $AB = \left(\frac{1}{2}\right)WX = 4$; ΔABV is a 3-4-5 right triangle with $AB = 4$ and $BV = 3$, so $AV = 5$. AV is the height of each triangular side, h, and $b = XY = 8$. So $SA = 8^2 + 2(8)(5) = 144$.

Answer 3: The answer is (B). ΔAVY is a right triangle with right angle at A. $AY = 4$ and $AV = 5$, so $VY = \sqrt{4^2 + 5^2} = \sqrt{41}$.

Answer 4: The answer is (C). In the given figure, we have to use the 2-D Pythagorean theorem three times to find the sides of ΔABC. ΔBCY is a 6-8-10 triple, so $BC = 10$, and ΔACX is a 8-15-17 triple, so $AC = 17$.

For ΔABZ, we actually have to calculate the missing side $AB = \sqrt{6^2 + 15^2} = \sqrt{261}$. So the perimeter is $10 + 17 + \sqrt{261}$.

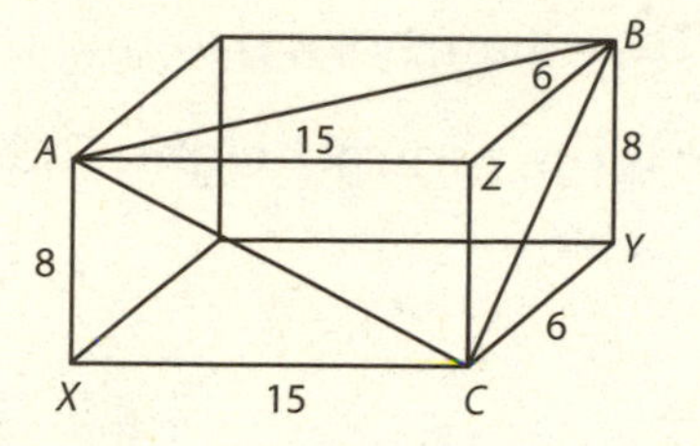

Answer 5: The answer is (E). The diameter of the base is 6, and again we have a Pythagorean triple; so $h = 8$. The volume is $\pi(3^2)(8) = 72\pi$.

Answer 6: The answer is (C). The areas are: $ABKL = 100$; $IJLK = 100$; $BCFG = 36$; $CDEF = 60$; $EFGH = 60$; $GHIK = 40$. The total is 396.

Answer 7: The answer is (A). The volume $V = \pi r^2 h$. For simplicity, let $r = 1$ and $h = 1$. So $V = \pi$. If we triple the radius, $V = \pi(3)^2 h$. For the original volume to still be π, $9h = 1$ or $h = \frac{1}{9}$.

Answer 8: The correct answers are (A), (B), (C), (D), (E), and (F). Since the volume of a cube is e^3, where e is the length of one edge, any information that yields the length of one edge will be sufficient for finding the volume. Choice (A) becomes obviously correct. Choices (B) and (C) are correct because the total surface area is given by $6e^2$, and the surface area of one face is e^2. Choices (D) and (E) are correct because the diagonal of one face equals an edge multiplied by $\sqrt{2}$ and the diagonal of the cube equals an edge multiplied by $\sqrt{3}$. Choice (F) describes a length equivalent to an edge, so it must be correct.

Answer 9: The correct answers are (C), (D), (E), and (F). The volume of a cone is $\frac{1}{3}\pi r^2 h$, where r is the radius of the base and h is the vertical height, so we need to be able to find *both* r and h. Choice (C) is correct because the radius is just one-half the diameter. Choice (D) is correct because the vertical height can be determined from the slant height and the radius by using the Pythagorean theorem ((radius)^2 + (vertical height)^2 = (slant height)^2). Choice (E) is correct because of the known variables. Choice (F) is correct because the volume of a cylinder is $\pi r^2 h$, so the volume of a cone is simply one-third this value. Choices (A) and (B) give one value (r or h) but not the other.

Answer 10: The correct answer is 40. The volume of a pyramid is $\frac{1}{3}Bh$, where B is the area of the base and h is the vertical height. Thus, the volume is $\left(\frac{1}{3}\right)(20)(6) = 40$.

Answer 11: The correct answer is 18. The volume of the cube is $6^3 = 216$. The volume of a rectangular solid is given by the formula $V = lwh$, where l = length, w = width, and h = height. Then $216 = (l)(3)(4) = 12l$. Thus, $l = \frac{216}{12} = 18$.

Let's go to the last review chapter of the book.

CHAPTER 14: *Working with Data*

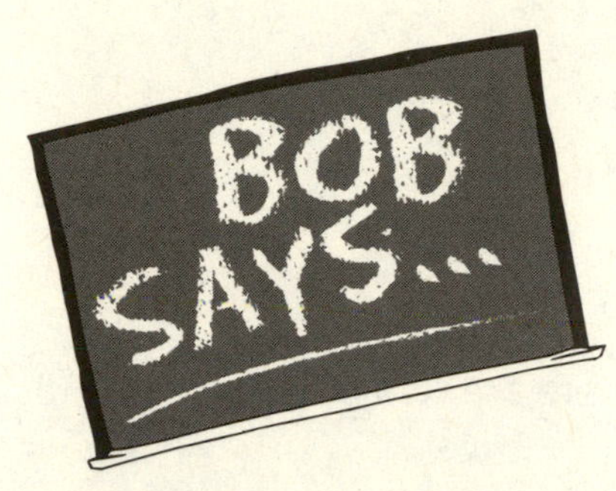

"At this point, your probability of success has greatly increased. This chapter is a combination of related topics. Let's start with measures of central tendency."

CENTRAL TENDENCY

People say you can prove anything with statistics. You need to know what you are taking statistics of, how many in the group, and many other variables. Even then, depending on the "spin" you want, you can choose among three measures to describe the data and prove your point. These measures of central tendency are ways to find a "typical" value. The measures of central tendency, introduced in Chapter 1 are:

Mean: Add up the number of terms and divide the sum by the number of terms; that's the way your grades are usually determined in school.

Median: The middle term when the numbers are put in order from smallest to largest (or the other way around); for an odd number of terms, it is the middle term; for an even number, it's the mean of the middle two numbers.

Mode: The most common term; there can be one mode, two modes (bimodal), or any number of modes.

Example 1: For the data consisting of the numbers 5, 6, 8, 9, 12, 12, 18,

The mean is $\frac{5+6+8+9+12+12+18}{7} = \frac{70}{7} = 10$.

The median is 9. There are three numbers above it and three numbers below it.

The mode is 12. It is the most common number, appearing twice.

Now can you see how you can prove anything with statistics?

Let's do some exercises.

For Exercises 1–3, use the following numbers:

8, 10, 10, 16, 16, 18

Exercise 1: The mean is

A. 8
B. 10
C. 13
D. 16
E. There are two of them

Exercise 2: The median is

A. 8
B. 10
C. 13
D. 16
E. There are two of them

Exercise 3: The mode is

A. 8
B. 10
C. 13
D. 16
E. There are two of them

Let's look at the answers.

Answer 1: The answer is (C). $\frac{8+10+10+16+16+18}{6}=13$.

Answer 2: The answer is (C). There are an even number of numbers, so we have to take the average of the middle two: $\frac{10+16}{2}=13$.

Answer 3: The answer is (E). It's bimodal; the modes are 10 and 16, each appearing twice.

Sometimes statistics are given in frequency distribution tables, such as this one showing the grades Sandy received on 10 English quizzes.

Example 2: Find the measures of central tendency of Sandy's quiz scores.

	Grade	Number
	100	4
	98	3
	95	2
	86	1
Total		10

Solution: The mean is the longest measure to compute:

$$\frac{4 \times 100 + 3 \times 98 + 2 \times 95 + 86}{10} = 97.$$

The median is determined by putting all of the numbers in order, so we have 100, 100, 100, 100, 98, 98, 98, 95, 95, 86. The middle terms are 98 and 98, so the median is 98.

The mode is 100 since that is the most common score; there are four of them.

STANDARD DEVIATION

Look at these two sets of numbers:

Set A: {16, 18, 18, 19, 22, 23, 24}

Set B: {2, 18, 18, 19, 25, 28, 30}

If we find the median for each set, it is 19; if we find the mean for each set, it is 20; if we find the mode for each set, it is 18. The measures of central tendency are the same for both sets. However, there is something different about each set. In set A, all the numbers are relatively close to the mean. In set B, that is not true. We can measure the spread of the data by finding the **standard deviation**. Here are the steps to calculate it:

1. Find the mean of the set.
2. For each number, subtract the mean and square the result.
3. Add these squares together and divide by the number of elements in the set.
4. Take the square root of this result. That is the standard deviation.

The standard deviation of set *A* is:

$$\sqrt{\frac{(16-20)^2+(18-20)^2+(18-20)^2+(19-20)^2+(22-20)^2+(23-20)^2+(24-20)^2}{7}}=2.78$$

The standard deviation of set *B* is:

$$\sqrt{\frac{(2-20)^2+(18-20)^2+(18-20)^2+(19-20)^2+(25-20)^2+(28-20)^2+(30-20)^2}{7}}=8.64$$

By comparing these two results, we have proof that the numbers in set *B* are more spread out, or dispersed, than those in set *A*. The standard deviation is a useful measure, especially in relation to the normal or bell-shaped curve. For example, by using multiples of the standard deviation (there are published tables for this), a manufacturer can determine how many items to produce. Suppose the manufacturer wanted to produce 100,000 pairs of a particular shoe. The standard deviation will tell how many of each size to produce. It also says that if you are a man wearing size 15 or a woman wearing size 12, you must go to a specialty store. If you are a man wearing size 5 or a woman wearing size 3, most of your shoes are children's shoes. The statistics tell you that it doesn't pay to make many shoes, if any, in those sizes.

This topic will be on the GRE exam. You should be familiar with the vocabulary presented here.

Let's try some exercises.

Exercise 4: Group 1 has five data, a median of 10, and a lowest value of 0. Group 2 has five data, a median of 10, and a lowest value of 8.

Quantity A	Quantity B
The standard deviation of group 1	The standard deviation of group 2

For Exercises 5, 6, and 7, you are given the following list of data:

1, 1, 1, 2, 2, 3, 3, 3, 4, 5, 5, 5, 6, 7, 12

Exercise 5: Which of the following individual numbers could be inserted in this list and *not* change the median? Indicate *all* correct choices.

A. 2

B. 3

C. 4

D. 6

E. 8

F. 13

Exercise 6: Which additional pairs of numbers would change the mode(s)? Indicate *all* correct choices.

A. 0, 1
B. −2, 4
C. 2, 9
D. 0, 7
E. 6, 12
F. 3, 5

Exercise 7: Which additional pairs of numbers would *not* change the mean? Indicate all correct choices.

A. 4, 7
B. 2, 6
C. 3, 4
D. 1, 7
E. −1, 9
F. −2, 12

Exercise 8: For which of the following groups of numbers is the range equal to 8? Indicate *all* correct choices.

A. 2, 4, 5, 6, 6, 7, 8, 9
B. 3, 3, 3, 3, 4, 4, 7, 14
C. 4, 5, 8, 8, 10, 10, 10, 12
D. 5, 7, 9, 10, 12, 14, 17
E. 6, 6, 6, 9, 9, 13, 13, 19
F. 7, 7, 9, 9, 11, 11, 15, 15

Exercise 9: The formula for the standard deviation of a sample of data is $\sqrt{\dfrac{\sum_i (x_i - \overline{x})^2}{n-1}}$, where x_i represents each datum, $\overline{x}$ represents the mean, and n is the number of data. The notation $\sum_i$ means "sum of." For which of the following groups of data is the standard deviation less than 2? Indicate *all* correct choices.

A. 0, 3, 6, 11, 15
B. 0, 2, 3, 5, 10
C. 4, 5, 6, 7, 8
D. 8, 9, 9, 9, 10
E. 7, 7, 7, 7, 7
F. 6, 9, 12, 12, 16

A Let's look at the answers.

Answer 4: The correct answer is (D). It is impossible to determine which group has the larger standard deviation. For example, suppose the data in Quantity A were 0, 5, 10, 15, and 20. The standard deviation for Quantity A would be $\sqrt{62.5} \approx 7.91$. If the data in Quantity B were 8, 9, 10, 11, and 12, then the corresponding standard deviation would be $\sqrt{2.5} \approx 1.58$. But if the data in Quantity B were 8, 10, 10, 32, and 100, then the corresponding standard deviation would be approximately 39.42.

Answer 5: The correct answers are (A) and (B). The original list has 15 numbers arranged in ascending order. The median is the 8th number, which is 3. Choice (A) is correct because by inserting the number 2, there would be 16 numbers for which the median would be in position 8.5. This would appear between the second and third 3's, so the median would still be 3. Choice (B) is correct for the same reason. Each of choices (C), (D), (E), and (F) would be wrong because there would still be 16 numbers, but the 8.5th position would land between the numbers 3 and 4. Thus, the median would change to 3.5.

Answer 6: The correct answers are (A), (C), and (F). The original list has the three modes, 1, 3, and 5. For choice (A), there would be four 1's, so the only mode would be 1. For choice (C), there would be three 2's, so there would be four modes, namely 1, 2, 3, and 5. For choice (F), there would be four 3's and four 5's. So the two modes would be 3 and 5. The addition of any of the pairs from choices (B), (D), or (E) would not affect the modes of the original list.

Answer 7: The correct answers are (B), (D), and (E). The sum of the 15 numbers of the original list is 60, so its mean is $\frac{60}{15} = 4$. If the new list of 17 numbers had the same mean, its total would be $(17)(4) = 68$. This implies that if we add two numbers whose sum is $68 - 60 = 8$, the mean will remain unchanged. The sum of each of the pairs of numbers in choices (B), (D), and (E) is 8.

Answer 8: The correct answers are (C) and (F). For any group of data, the range is defined as the difference between the highest and lowest values. For choices (C) and (F), this difference is 8. The range for choices (A), (B), (D), and (E) are 7, 11, 12, and 13, respectively.

Answer 9: The correct answers are (C), (D), and (E). You need only to check whether the standard deviation is < 2, or whether the value under the radical is < 4.

For choice (C), the standard deviation is $\sqrt{\frac{(4-6)^2+(5-6)^2+(6-6)^2+(7-6)^2+(8-6)^2}{4}} = \sqrt{\frac{4+1+0+1+4}{4}} = \sqrt{2.5}$.

For choice (D), the standard deviation is $\sqrt{\frac{(8-9)^2+(9-9)^2+(9-9)^2+(9-9)^2+(10-9)^2}{4}} = \sqrt{\frac{1+0+0+0+1}{4}} = \sqrt{0.5}$.

For choice (E), the standard deviation is $\sqrt{\frac{(7-7)^2+(7-7)^2+(7-7)^2+(7-7)^2+(7-7)^2}{4}} = \sqrt{\frac{0+0+0+0+0}{4}} = \sqrt{0}$.

The standard deviations for each of choices (A), (B), and (F) are greater than 2. Their standard deviations are $\sqrt{\frac{146}{4}}$, $\sqrt{\frac{58}{4}}$, $\sqrt{\frac{56}{4}}$, respectively.

COUNTING

The **basic law of counting** says: "If you can do something in p ways, and a second thing in q ways, and a third thing in r ways, and so on, the total number of ways you can do the first thing, then the second thing, then the third thing, etc., is $p \times q \times r \times \ldots$

Example 3: If you have a lunch choice of 5 sandwiches, 4 desserts, and 3 drinks, and you can have one of each, how many different meals could you choose?

Solution: You can choose from $(5)(4)(3) = 60$ different meals.

Arrangements

Let $n(A)$ be the number of elements in set A. In how many ways can these elements be arranged? The answer is that the first has n choices, the second has $(n - 1)$ choices (since one is already used), the third has $(n - 2)$ choices, all the way down to the last element, which has only one choice. In general, if there are n choices, the number of ways to choose is $n!$ (n **factorial**) = $n(n - 1)(n - 2) \times \ldots (3)(2)(1)$.

The factorial symbol is used only with nonnegative integers, so that, for example, $(-2)!$ and $(\frac{1}{3})!$ have no meaning. It is easy to see that $1! = 1$ and $2! = (2)(1) = 2$, but what about $0!$? Most books will simply state that $0! = 1$, which may seem confusing. However, there is a rational reason for this. Consider that $4! = (4)(3)(2)(1) = 24$. If we divide 24 by 4, we get 6, which is equivalent to 3! Now divide 6 by 3, we get 2, which is the value of 2! Dividing 2 by 2 leads to 1, which is 1!. Continuing this pattern, if we divide 1 by 1, we should get 0!. But 1 divided by 1 = 1. This line of reasoning helps us to equate 0! with 1.

Example 4: How many ways can five people line up?

Solution: This is just $5 \times 4 \times 3 \times 2 \times 1 = 120$.

Example 5: How many ways can 5 people sit in a circle?

Solution: It would appear to be the same question as Example 4, but it's not. If you draw the picture, each of 5 positions would be the same. The answer is $(5)(4)(3)(2)(1) \div 5 = (4)(3)(2)(1) = 24$. So n people can sit in a circle in $(n - 1)!$ ways.

Permutations

Permutations are essentially the law of counting without repeating, but order counts.

Example 6: How many ways can 7 people occupy 3 seats on a bench?

Solution: Any one of 7 people can be in the first seat, then any one of 6 people can be in the second seat, and any one of 5 people can be in the third seat. The total number would be $(7)(6)(5) = 210$ ways. There are many notations for permutations. One notation for this example would be $P(7, 3)$.

If we were to determine the number of ways in which seven people can occupy seven seats on a bench, the answer would be $7 \times 6 \times 5 \times 4 \times 3 \times 2 \times 1 = 7! = 5{,}040$.

Combinations

Combinations are essentially the law of counting, with no repetition, and order doesn't count.

Example 7: How many sets of three different letters can be made from eight different letters?

Solution: Since order doesn't count, unlike with permutations, *AB* is the same as *BA*. So we can take the number of permutations, but we have to divide by the number of duplicates. It turns out that the duplicates for 3 letters is $3 \times 2 \times 1 = 6$. So we would have $\frac{8 \times 7 \times 6}{3 \times 2 \times 1} = 56$. Again, there are many notations for combinations. One notation for this example is $C(8,3)$. Another notation is $\binom{8}{3}$. In general, $\binom{n}{r} = \frac{n!}{r!(n-r)!}$.

Avoiding Duplicates

When we count how many ways to do *A or B*, we should be careful not to count any item twice. We must subtract out any items that include both *A* and *B*:

$$N(A \text{ or } B) = N(A) + N(B) - N(A \text{ and } B)$$

Example 8: Thirty students take French or German. If 20 took French and 18 took German, and if each student took at least one language, how many took both French and German?

Solution: $N(A \text{ or } B) = N(A) + N(B) - N(A \text{ and } B)$, or $30 = 20 + 18 - x$, so $x = 8$ took both languages.

Example 9: Forty students take Chinese or Japanese. If 9 take both and 20 take Japanese, how many students take only Chinese?

Solution: $N(C \text{ or } J) = N(C) + N(J) - N(\text{both})$, or $40 = x + 20 - 9$, so $x = 29$ take only Chinese.

Let's do some exercises.

For Exercises 10–15, use the set {*e*, *f*, *g*, *h*, *i*}. A word is considered to be any group of letters together; for example, *hhg* is a three-letter word.

Exercise 10: From this set, the number of three-letter words is:

A. 6
B. 27
C. 30
D. 60
E. 125

Exercise 11: How many three-letter permutations are there in this set?

A. 6
B. 27
C. 30
D. 60
E. 125

Exercise 12: How many three-letter words starting with a vowel and ending in a consonant can be made from this set?

A. 6
B. 27
C. 30
D. 60
E. 125

Exercise 13: How many three-letter words with the second and third numbers the same can be made from this set?

A. 5
B. 20
C. 25
D. 60
E. 125

Exercise 14: How many three-letter permutations with the first and last letters *not* vowels can be made from this set?

A. 18
B. 27
C. 30
D. 45
E. 125

Exercise 15: Fifty students take Spanish or Portuguese. If 20 take both and 40 take Spanish, the number of students taking *only* Portuguese is

A. 0
B. 5
C. 10
D. 20
E. 30

Let's look at the answers.

Answer 10: The answer is (E). $(5)(5)(5) = 125$.

Answer 11: The answer is (D). $(5)(4)(3) = 60$.

Answer 12: The answer is (C). The first letter has 2 choices, the second can be any 5, and the third has 3 choices, so $(2)(5)(3) = 30$.

Answer 13: The answer is (C). There are 5 choices for the first two letters, but there is only 1 choice for the third letter since it must be the same as the second, so $(5)(5)(1) = 25$.

Answer 14: The answer is (A). There are 3 choices for the first letter, but only 2 choices for the last letter since it can't be a vowel and must be different than the first letter. There are 3 choices for the middle letter since two letters have already been used; so the answer is $(3)(3)(2) = 18$. These questions must be read very carefully!

Answer 15: The answer is (C). This is not quite the same. $N(S \text{ or } P) = N(S) + N(P) - N(\text{both})$; $50 = 40 + x - 20$; $x = 30$, but that is not the answer. If 30 take Portuguese and 20 take both, then 10 take only Portuguese.

VENN DIAGRAMS

Venn diagrams are graphical illustrations that show the relationship between two sets or among several sets. Our discussion will be limited to two sets, so our Venn diagram consists of a rectangle with two overlapping circles inside it. Let's revisit Examples 8 and 9.

In Example 8, we found out that eight students took both languages. Here is a partial picture of a Venn diagram with this information.

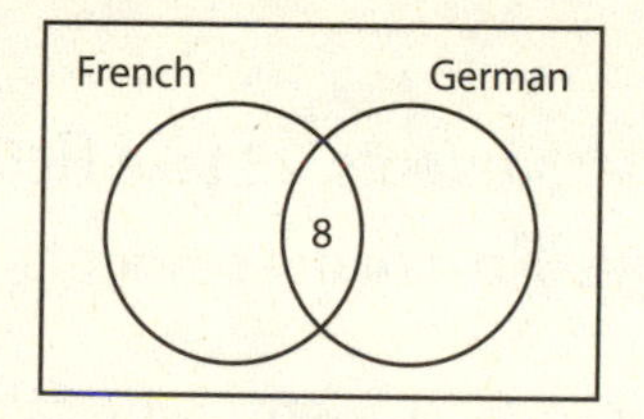

The 20 students who take French include the 8 students who take both languages, so there must be $20 - 8 = 12$ students who take French but not German. Similarly, the 18 students who take German also include the 8 students who take both languages. This means that $18 - 8 = 10$ students who take German but not French. Here is the completed Venn diagram.

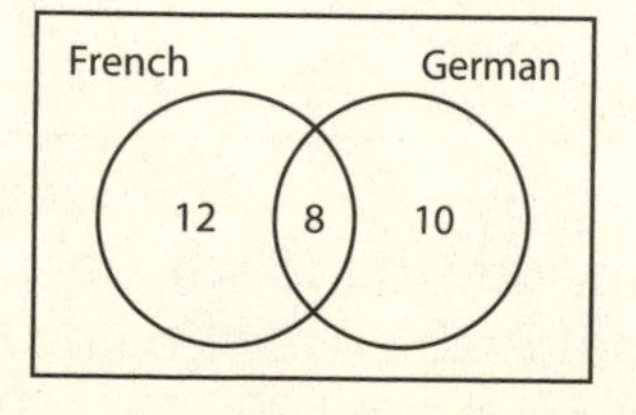

In Example 9, we start with the nine students who take both Chinese and Japanese. Here is a partial Venn diagram with this information.

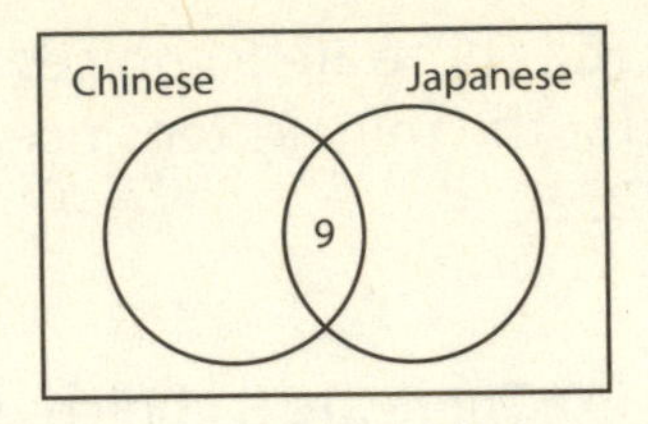

We know that a total of 20 students take Japanese. Since this total includes the 9 students who take both languages, there must be $20 - 9 = 11$ students who take Japanese but not Chinese. Now, of the 40 students, we know the number of students who take Japanese but not Chinese (11) and the number of students who take both languages (9). This means that the number of students who take Chinese but not Japanese must be $40 - 11 - 9 = 20$. Here is the completed Venn diagram.

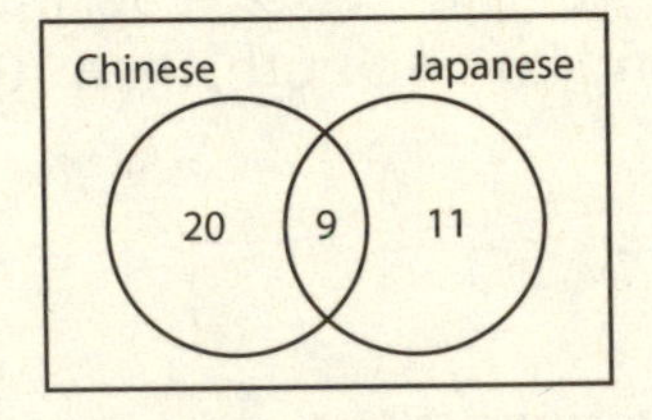

In some instances, we may have a numerical value that lies outside the two circles but within the rectangle. In the diagram above, that would indicate the students who do not take Chinese or Japanese.

Note *If there were no students who take both Chinese and Japanese, the two circles would not overlap.*

Example 10: In a group of 50 students, 25 take Hebrew, 22 take Arabic, and 15 take both languages. How many students take neither of these languages?

Solution: We start with the 15 students who take both Hebrew and Arabic. Put this number in the overlapping region of the two circles, as shown below.

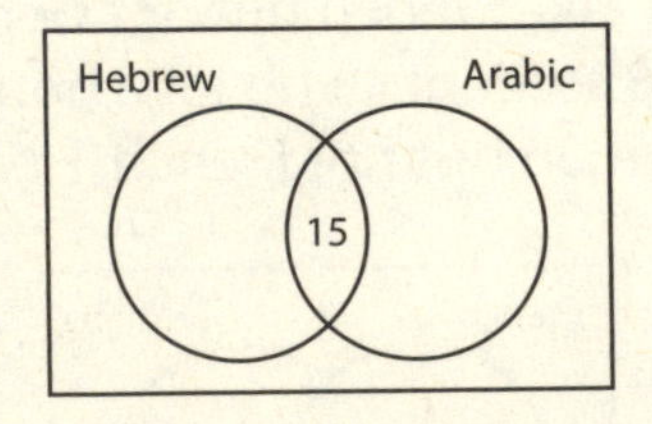

The 25 students who take Hebrew include the 15 who take both languages. So, $25 - 15 = 10$ students who take Hebrew but not Arabic. We also know that the 22 students who take Arabic include the 15 who take both languages. So, $22 - 15 = 7$ students who take Arabic but not Hebrew. Here is the Venn diagram thus far.

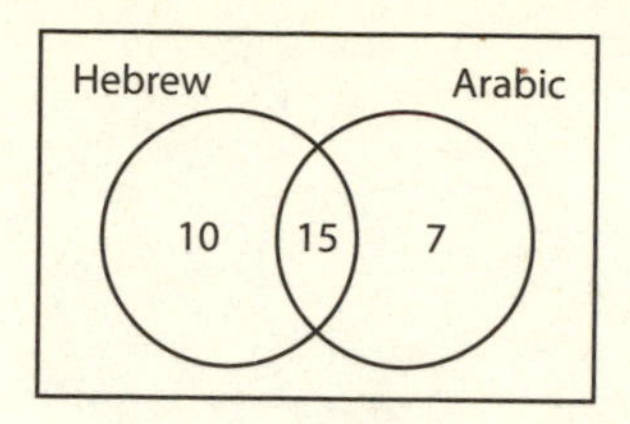

But notice that the number of students that we have accounted for is $10 + 15 + 7 = 32$. This means that $50 - 32 = 18$ students are taking neither Hebrew nor Arabic. The number 18 is traditionally placed in the lower right-hand corner of the rectangle. The completed Venn diagram appears below.

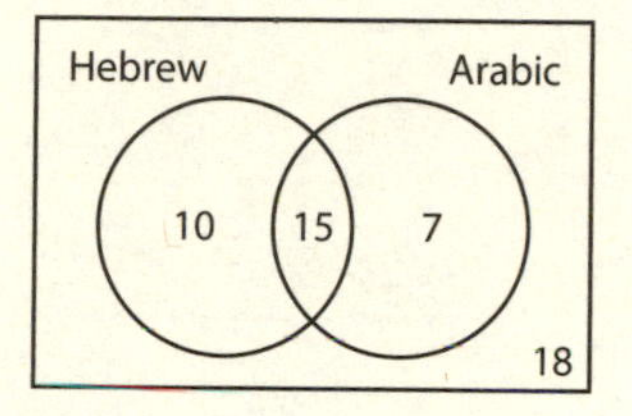

Let's try two exercises on Venn diagrams.

Exercise 16: In a certain group of 60 people, 30 enjoy rock music, 21 enjoy country music, and 4 people enjoy both rock and country music. How many people enjoy neither rock nor country music?

Exercise 17: In a group of 100 people, a survey was taken to determine how many people like vanilla ice cream and how many people like chocolate ice cream. The results showed that 53 people like vanilla ice cream, including 9 people who also like chocolate ice cream. If 22 people like neither of these two flavors of ice cream, how many people like chocolate ice cream?

Let's look at the answers.

Answer 16: The correct answer is 13. We start with the 4 people who enjoy both types of music. Since the 30 people who enjoy rock music includes the 4 people who enjoy both types of music, there must be $30 - 4 = 26$ people who enjoy rock but not country music. Likewise, there are $21 - 4 = 17$ people who enjoy country music but not rock. Here is how the Venn diagram looks thus far.

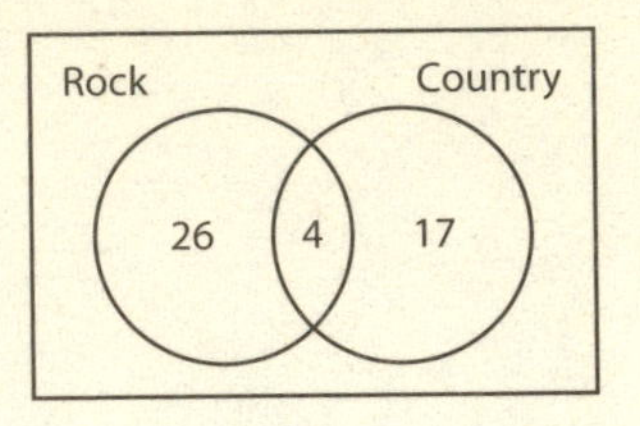

However, we have only accounted for $26 + 4 + 17 = 47$ people. Therefore, the number of people who do not enjoy either type of music is $60 - 47 = 13$. The completed Venn diagram appears below.

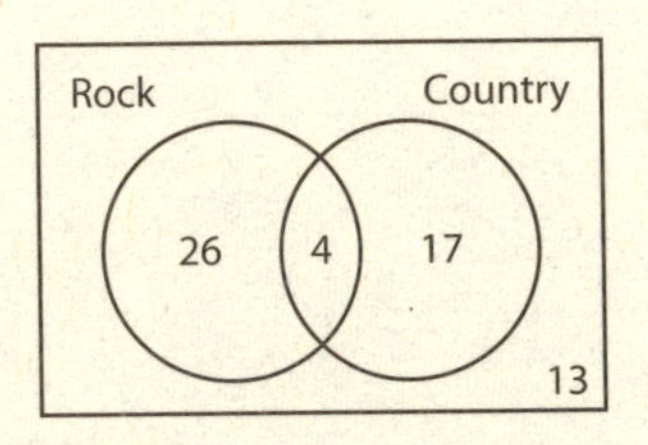

Answer 17: The correct answer is 34. We start with the 9 people who like both flavors. The number of people who like vanilla but not chocolate ice cream must be $53 - 9 = 44$. The number of people who like neither flavor (22) should be placed in the lower right-hand corner of the rectangle. Here is how the Venn diagram looks thus far.

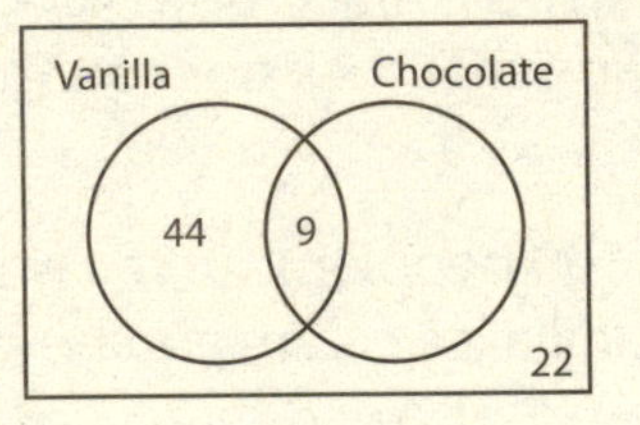

Now we can determine the number of people who like chocolate but not vanilla ice cream to be $100 - 44 - 9 - 22 = 25$. The completed Venn diagram is shown below.

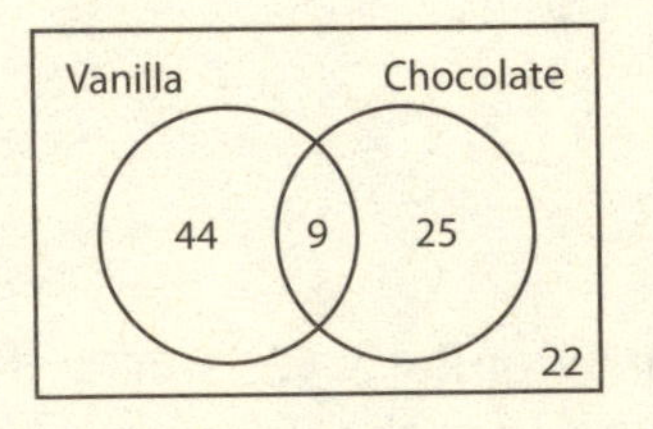

Therefore, the number of people who like chocolate ice cream is $9 + 25 = 34$.

PROBABILITY

The probability of an event is the number of "good" outcomes divided by the total number of outcomes possible, or $Pr(\text{success}) = \dfrac{\text{good outcomes}}{\text{total outcomes}}$.

Example 11: Consider the following sets: {26 letter English alphabet}; vowels = {*a*, *e*, *i*, *o*, *u*}; consonants = {the rest of the letters}. What are the probabilities of choosing a vowel? a consonant? any letter? π?

Solution: $Pr(\text{vowel}) = \dfrac{5}{26}$; $Pr(\text{consonant}) = \dfrac{21}{26}$; $Pr(\text{letter}) = \dfrac{26}{26} = 1$; $Pr(\pi) = \dfrac{0}{26} = 0$.

Probability follows the same rule about avoiding duplicates, as discussed in the previous section.

$$\text{Pr(A or B)} = \text{Pr(A)} + \text{Pr(B)} - \text{Pr(A and B)}$$

Example 12: What is the probability that a spade or an ace is pulled from a 52-card deck?

Solution: $Pr(\text{Spade or ace}) = Pr(\text{Spade}) + Pr(\text{Ace}) - Pr(\text{Spade ace}) =$
$\dfrac{13}{52} + \dfrac{4}{52} - \dfrac{1}{52} = \dfrac{16}{52} = \dfrac{4}{13}$.

As weird as it sounds, whenever I taught this in a class, I never failed to have at least two students who didn't know what a deck of cards was, and I taught in New York City!

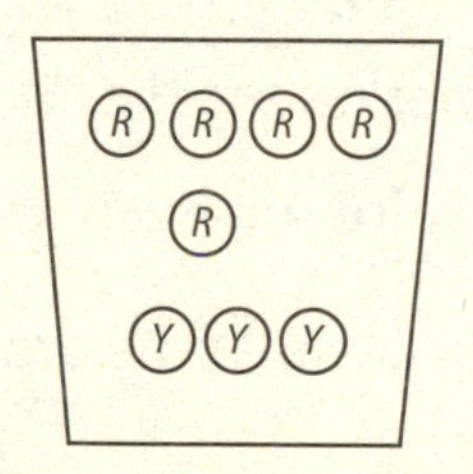

Use this figure for Examples 13 and 14. In the jar are 5 red balls and 3 yellow balls.

Example 13: What is the probability that two yellow balls are picked, with replacement?

Solution: $Pr(\text{2 yellow balls, with replacement}) = \left(\dfrac{3}{8}\right)\left(\dfrac{3}{8}\right) = \dfrac{9}{64}$

Example 14: What is the probability of picking two yellow balls, without replacement?

Solution: $Pr(\text{2 yellow balls, no replacement}) = \left(\frac{3}{8}\right)\left(\frac{2}{7}\right) = \frac{3}{28}$

Independent Events

Two events are **independent** if the occurrence of one of them has no effect on the probability of the other event to occur. The probability that both events occur is the product of the individual probabilities of each event to occur. Thus, if A and B are independent events, then $Pr(A \text{ and } B) = Pr(A) \times Pr(B)$.

Example 15: A coin is flipped once and a die is rolled. What is the probability that the coin will show heads and the die will show a number greater than 1?

Solution: There are only two outcomes for the coin, so the probability that it will show heads is $\frac{1}{2}$. There are six outcomes for the die, so the probability that it will show a number greater than 1 (that is, 2, 3, 4, 5, or 6) is $\frac{5}{6}$. Therefore, the probability that both events will occur is $\frac{1}{2} \times \frac{5}{6} = \frac{5}{12}$.

Example 16: A die is rolled once and a card is randomly drawn from an ordinary deck. What is the probability that the die will show a number less than 3 and the selected card is an ace?

Solution: Of the six outcomes on the die, the only numbers less than 3 are 1 and 2. So, the probability for this event is $\frac{2}{6} = \frac{1}{3}$. Of the 52 cards in the deck, 4 are aces. This means that the probability of drawing an ace is $\frac{4}{52} = \frac{1}{13}$. Therefore, the probability that both events occur is $\frac{1}{3} \times \frac{1}{13} = \frac{1}{39}$.

Example 17: Events E and F are independent. The probability is 0.8 that at least one of these events will occur. If the probability is 0.6 that event E will occur, what is the probability that event F will occur?

Solution: We need to use the formula $Pr(E \text{ or } F) = Pr(E) + Pr(F) - Pr(E \text{ and } F)$. Let x represent $Pr(F)$. Then $0.8 = 0.6 + x - (0.6)(x)$, which simplifies to $0.8 = 0.6 + 0.4x$. Subtract 0.6 from each side to get $0.2 = 0.4x$. Thus, $x = \frac{0.2}{0.4} = 0.5$.

Conditional Probability

Conditional probability is used when the probability of an event is dependent upon whether or not another event occurs. Usually, conditional probability problems contain the word "given."

Example 18: A person randomly selects a letter of the alphabet. What is the probability that the selected letter is the letter *e* given that we know he has selected one of the five vowels?

Solution: Rather than look at the entire alphabet, we need consider only the five vowels. Since the person has chosen a vowel, the probability that the letter *e* was selected is $\frac{1}{5}$.

Example 19: A person selects one card from an ordinary deck of 52 cards. Given that the selected card is black, what is the probability that the card is the ace of clubs?

Solution: There are 26 black cards in the deck. Since there is only one ace of clubs, the probability is $\frac{1}{26}$.

Example 20: There are two boxes of radios. The first box has nine radios, of which three are defective. The second box has ten radios, of which only one is defective. All the radios are placed in a large container. A person randomly selects one radio and finds that it is defective. What is the probability that this defective radio came from the first box?

Solution: Although there are a total of 19 radios, we need only note that there are just four defective radios. Since three out of the four defective radios belonged to the first box, the probability is $\frac{3}{4}$.

Note *In Example 20, the sentence, "A person randomly selects one radio and finds that it is defective," could have said, "Given that a radio selected at random is defective," indicating that this is a conditional probability problem.*

EXPECTED VALUE

An important application of probability deals with expected value. **Expected value** is the sum of the products of individual probabilities and their associated values. As applied to game theory, there are usually dollar amounts that can be won or lost, as well as associated probabilities.

Example 21: A wheel contains ten evenly divided sections, numbered 1 through 10, with a spinner. The game involves spinning the wheel once, for a cost of \$10 to the player. If the spinner lands on a number from 1 to 7, the player loses his or her \$10. If the spinner lands on either 8 or on 9, the player gets back \$30. If the spinner lands on the number 10, the player gets back \$60. What is the expected value?

Solution: The expected value is the sum of the product of individual prohabilities and their associated values. Be aware that when a player gets back a certain dollar amount, it includes the original investment. Thus, if a player gets back \$30 with a \$10 investment, the amount won is actually $\$30 - \$10 = \$20$. Also, a loss of any dollar amount can be recorded as a negative number. Thus, for this particular game, the expected value is $(0.7)(-\$10) + (0.2)(\$20) + (0.1)(\$50) = -\$7 + \$4 + \$5 = \$2$. This is the average amount that a player can expect to win per game.

Note *There is a very logical way to check this computation. Suppose a player plays this game ten times, and the spinner lands on each of the ten numbers once. Then the total amount played would be (10)(\$10) = \$100. The player would receive no money for each of the times that the spinner lands on the numbers 1 through 7. But the player would receive (2)(\$30) = \$60 for the times that the spinner lands on 8 or 9. In addition, the player would receive \$60 for the time that the spinner lands on the number 10. So, for the ten spins, the player would receive \$60 + \$60 = \$120. The net gain for the ten games is \$120 − \$100 = \$20. This means that the average gain per game is* $\frac{\$20}{10} = \$2$. *Be aware, however, that games of chance at a casino are designed so that a player can expect to lose money, on average.*

Q Let's do a few exercises on probability and expected value.

Exercise 18: A coin is flipped once and a card is randomly drawn from an ordinary deck. What is the probability that the coin will show tails and a diamond picture card is drawn? Write your answer as a ratio of integers.

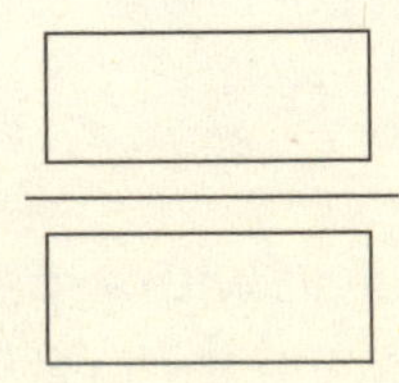

Exercise 19: Two dice are rolled and a card is randomly drawn from an ordinary deck. What is the probability that the sum of the dice is 3 and a black ace is drawn? Write your answer as a ratio of integers.

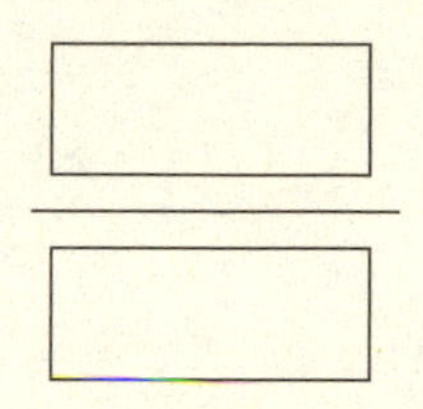

Exercise 20: Events *A* and *B* are independent. The probability is 0.5 that event *A* occurs and the probability is 0.4 that event *B* occurs. What is the probability that at least one of these events occurs?

Exercise 21: At a carnival, a wheel with a spinner contains five evenly divided sections, labeled as A, B, C, D, and E. The game involves spinning the wheel once, for a cost of $6 to the player. If the spinner lands on A or B, the player loses his or her money. If the spinner lands on either C or D, the player gets back $8. If the spinner lands on E, the player gets back $12. What is the expected value of this game?

A. −$1.20
B. −$0.80
C. −$0.60
D. −$0.40
E. −$0.20

For Exercises 22−24, use the following chart regarding the ages and gender of 100 people attending a concert. One person will be randomly selected.

	Age 18−29	Age 30−49	Age 50−69	Over age 69
Male	32	10	16	2
Female	22	11	4	3

Exercise 22: What is the probability that the given person is male, given that a person under 30 years old has been selected? Write your answer as a ratio of integers.

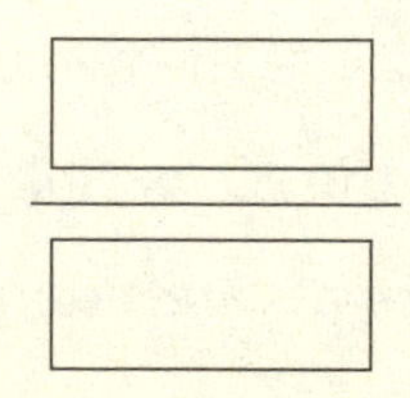

Exercise 23: What is the probability that the given person is over 69 years old, given that a female has been selected?

A. $\frac{37}{40}$

B. $\frac{3}{5}$

C. $\frac{37}{100}$

D. $\frac{3}{40}$

E. $\frac{3}{100}$

Exercise 24: What is the probability that the given person is between ages 30 and 69, given that a male has been selected? Write your answer as a ratio of integers.

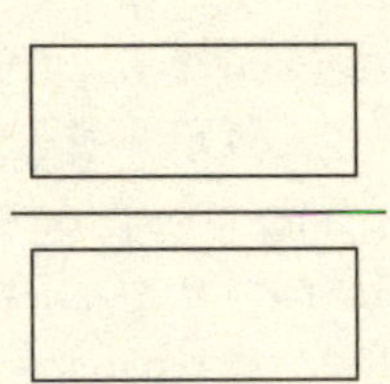

Let's look at the answers.

Answer 18: The correct answer is $\frac{3}{104}$. The probability that the coin will land on tails is $\frac{1}{2}$. There are three picture diamonds in a deck of cards, namely the jack, queen, and king. So the probability of drawing a picture diamond is $\frac{3}{52}$. Since these events are independent, the probability that both occur is $\frac{1}{2} \times \frac{3}{52} = \frac{3}{104}$.

Answer 19: The correct answer is $\frac{1}{468}$. There are (6)(6) = 36 different possible outcomes when two dice are rolled. Of these, the only two outcomes in which the sum is 3 are: (a) 1 on the first die and 2 on the second die or (b) 2 on the first die and 1 on the second die. Its associated probability is $\frac{2}{36} = \frac{1}{18}$. The two black aces in a deck of cards are the ace of spades and the ace of clubs, so its associated probability is $\frac{2}{52} = \frac{1}{26}$. These events are independent, so the required probability is $\frac{1}{18} \times \frac{1}{26} = \frac{1}{468}$.

Answer 20: The correct answer is 0.7. The probability that at least one of these events occurred is denoted as $Pr(A \text{ or } B)$, which equals $Pr(A) + Pr(B) - Pr(A \text{ and } B)$. Note that $Pr(A \text{ and } B) = Pr(A) \times Pr(B)$ because the events are independent. Thus, by substitution, $Pr(A \text{ or } B) = 0.5 + 0.4 - (0.5)(0.4) = 0.5 + 0.4 - 0.2 = 0.7$.

Answer 21: The correct answer is (D). The probability that the spinner lands on *A* or *B* and the player loses \$6 is $\frac{2}{5}$. If the spinner lands on *C* or *D*, the person will win \$2 (\$8 − \$6). So the probability that a player wins \$2, is also $\frac{2}{5}$. There is a probability of $\frac{1}{5}$ that the player will win \$6 (\$12 − \$6). Therefore, the expected value is $\left(\frac{2}{5}\right)(-\$6) + \left(\frac{2}{5}\right)(\$2) + \left(\frac{1}{5}\right)(\$6) = -\$2.40 + \$0.80 + \$1.20 = -\$0.40$.

Answer 22: The correct answer is $\frac{16}{27}$. There are $32 + 22 = 54$ people under the age of 30. Of these, 32 are male. Thus, the required probability is $\frac{32}{54}$, which reduces to $\frac{16}{27}$.

Answer 23: The correct answer is (D). There are a total of $22 + 11 + 4 + 3 = 40$ females. Of these, three of them are over the age of 69. Thus, the required probability is $\frac{3}{40}$.

Answer 24: The correct answer is $\frac{13}{30}$. There are a total of $32 + 10 + 16 + 2 = 60$ males. Of these, there are $10 + 16 = 26$ between the ages of 30 and 69. Thus, the required probability is $\frac{26}{60}$, which reduces to $\frac{13}{30}$.

CHARTS AND GRAPHS

A significant part of the GRE consists of charts and graphs. In all likelihood, out of 60 questions, there will be 10 such questions: two graphs and chart problems, with five questions each. Here is one problem having one pie chart and one bar graph. There will be more such exercises in the practice tests.

Circle Graph

One popular way to present data in a pictorial form is the **circle graph**. Other names for this type of data display are *pie graph* and *pie chart*. This type of graph is most useful when comparing the component categories of one heading. Each component part becomes a sector of the circle that represents the entire heading.

Example 22: A survey was sent to the residents of the town of Peopleville, in which residents were asked to rank the town mayor. The five categories from which a resident could enter a response were (a) excellent, (b) very good, (c) average, (d) below average, and (e) poor. Use the following circle graph, with a fraction assigned to each category, to determine the central angles for the "excellent" and "very good" categories.

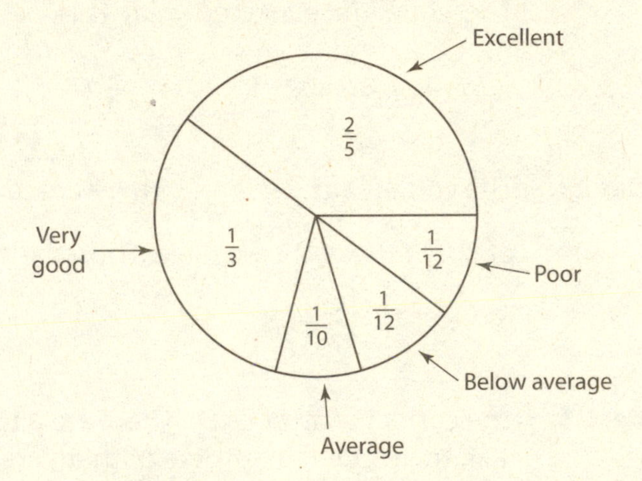

Solution: The answers are 144° and 120°, respectively. Note that the fractions must add up to 1, which is equivalent to 100%. Each category represents a sector, which is a portion of a circle that is bounded by two radii and an included arc. The central angles of each sector are calculated by multiplying the associated fraction by 360°. For instance, the fraction $\frac{2}{5}$ corresponds to a central angle of $\left(\frac{2}{5}\right)(360°) = 144°$. Likewise, a fraction of $\frac{1}{3}$ corresponds to a central angle of $\left(\frac{1}{3}\right)(360°) = 120°$.

For Examples 23 and 24, assume that 1,080 residents responded to the survey mentioned in Example 22.

Example 23: How many residents ranked the mayor as either "excellent" or "very good"?

Solution: The answer is 792. The fraction of residents who ranked the mayor in either of those categories was $\frac{2}{5}+\frac{1}{3}=\frac{6}{15}+\frac{5}{15}=\frac{11}{15}$. Thus, the answer is $\left(\frac{11}{15}\right)(1,080)=792$.

Example 24: How many residents did *not* rank the mayor as "poor."

Solution: The answer is 990. The quickest way to solve this question is to determine the number of residents who did rank the mayor as "poor." That number is $\left(\frac{1}{12}\right)(1,080)=90$. Therefore, the required number is $1,080-90=990$.

Line Graph

A second popular way to illustrate data is the **line graph**. This type of graph is most advantageous when we are showing a trend of a quantity over a period of time. A line graph typically is a plot of individual data points. For example, consider the following graph, which shows data for the number of projects for each of the first six months of the year.

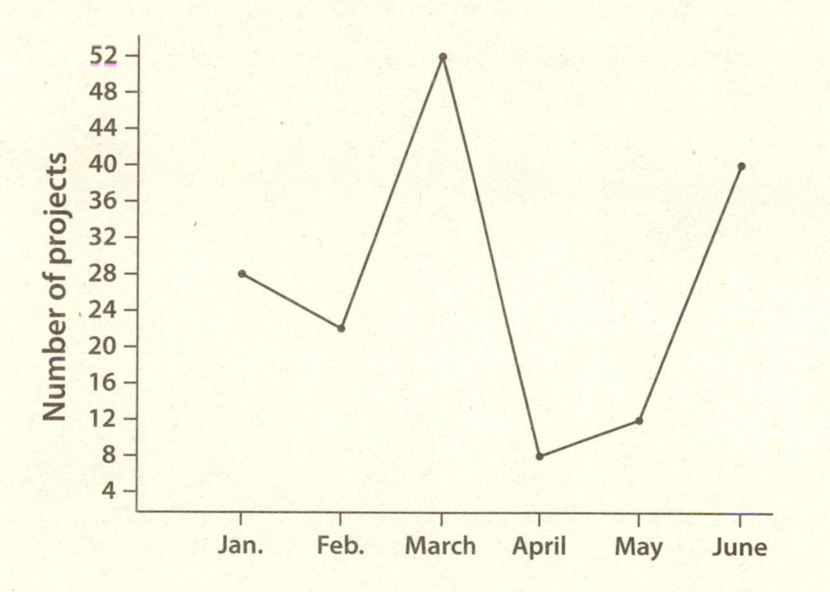

Note that the months are evenly spaced along the horizontal axis. The vertical scale represents a list of numbers that encompasses the number of projects. The lowest number of projects was 8 and the highest number was 52. Since many of the number of projects are divisible by 4, the scale was developed by using multiples of 4. In reality, other patterns of numbers on the vertical axis could have been used, such as multiples of 6.

Examples 25 and 26 refer to the line graph shown above.

Example 25: The number of projects assigned in February was what percent lower than the number of projects assigned in June?

Solution: The answer is 45. There were $40 - 22 = 18$ fewer projects in February than in June. Thus, the percent decrease was $\left(\frac{18}{40}\right)(100\%) = 45\%$.

Example 26: What was the average (mean) number of projects assigned for the six-month period January through June?

Solution: The mean number of projects was $\frac{28 + 22 + 52 + 8 + 12 + 40}{6} = 27$.

Bar Graph

A third way to display data is a **bar graph**. This special type graph simply shows a set of categories (usually non-numerical along the horizontal axis). Their associated frequencies are displayed on the vertical axis. The bars are shown as rectangles with the same width.

Example 27: In Mrs. Triple's math class, each of the 20 students is taking a foreign language. Each student is taking exactly one foreign language. Here is the bar graph showing how many students take each language. Note that the vertical scale has a maximum value of 7.

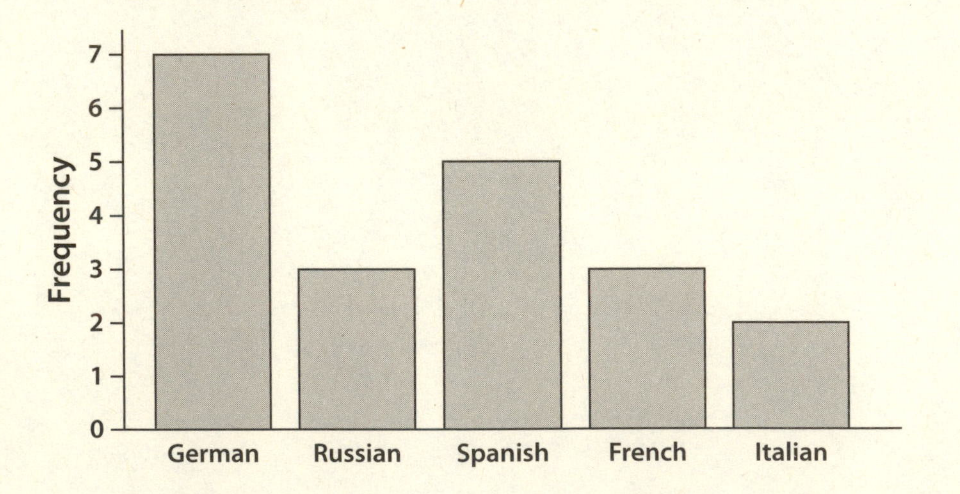

Example 28: What percent of the students in Mrs. Triple's class are studying either Spanish or French?

Solution: There are $5 + 3 = 8$ students who are studying one of these two languages. Thus, the answer is $\frac{8}{20} = 40\%$.

Histogram

A fourth way to graphically display data is a **histogram**, which bears some resemblance to a bar graph. Just as the case for a bar graph, a histogram is a series of connected bars that have the same width, but different heights, and the heights represent the frequency of the data for each bar. The difference is that the horizontal data are not non-numerical categories, but rather groupings of the data. So for a histogram, the data are first summarized into groups, called classes. The upper and lower limits on these groups, or class intervals, depend on how the data are distributed. The bars touch but they do not overlap. Example 29 shows how data are grouped for a histogram.

Example 29: Members of the Weightless Gym Club were asked to record their initial weight when they first joined the club. The weights in pounds, and in ascending order for all 40 members are 97, 97, 113, 116, 117, 121, 125, 130, 132, 135, 136, 138, 139, 148, 149, 159, 161, 162, 163, 166, 166, 189, 191, 192, 192, 195, 196, 197, 198, 208, 212, 219, 222, 225, 233, 233, 236, 239, 250, and 254. Construct a histogram of the data and determine what percent of the Weightless Gym members weigh more than 194 pounds.

Solution: Group the weights into the following seven classes with lower and upper limits: 95 − 119, 120 − 144, 145 − 169, 170 − 194, 195 − 219, 220 − 244, and 245 − 269. Notice that all these classes are of equal width. For example $119 - 95 = 24$, which is the same as $144 - 120$.

The next step is create "boundaries" for these seven classes so that the corresponding bars will touch. Do this by subtracting 0.5 units from each lower limit and adding 0.5 units to each upper limit. (While the rationale for this procedure is beyond the scope of the GRE, the exercise is bound to help you cope with the material on the test.) Then the seven classes appear as follows: 94.5 − 119.5, 119.5 − 144.5, 144.5 − 169.5, 169.5 − 194.5, 194.5 − 219.5, 219.5 − 244.5, and 244.5 − 269.5.

Now count the frequencies for each class, where the frequency is the number of data points in that class:

Class	Frequency
94.5 − 119.5	5
119.5 − 144.5	8
144.5 − 169.5	8
169.5 − 194.5	4
194.5 − 219.5	7
219.5 − 244.5	6
244.5 − 269.5	2

It is critical that each of the 40 weights be assigned to exactly one class and that the classes do not overlap. The completed histogram is shown below.

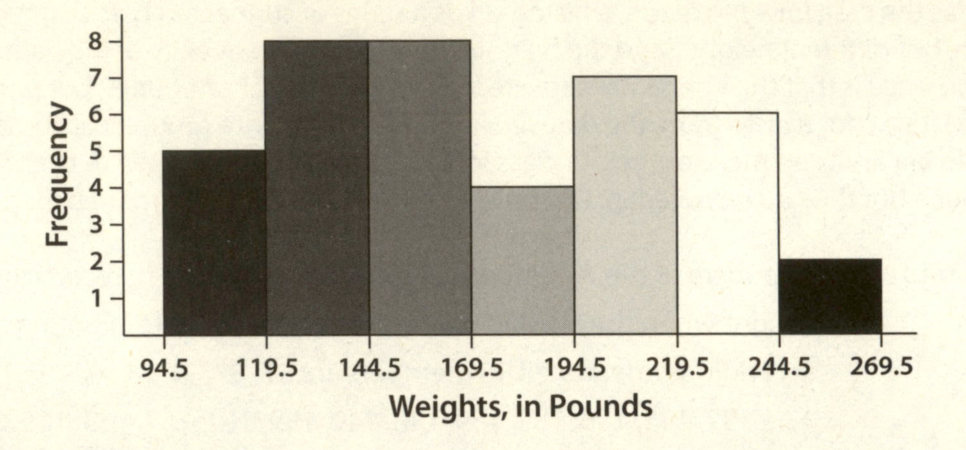

There are seven members in the weight class 194.5−219.5, six members in the weight class 219.5−244.5, and two members in the weight class 244.5−269.5. Thus, there are a total of 15 members whose weights exceed 194 pounds. Therefore, the answer is $\frac{15}{40} = 37.5\%$.

You could have obtained this answer from the original given data, but the idea of this example is to show how a histogram is constructed. On the GRE, you will be given a histogram but not the raw data.

Let's try some exercises on the various types of graphs.

Use the following circle graph for Exercises 25 and 26. There are a total of 1,500 employees.

Growing Strong Hospital Employees

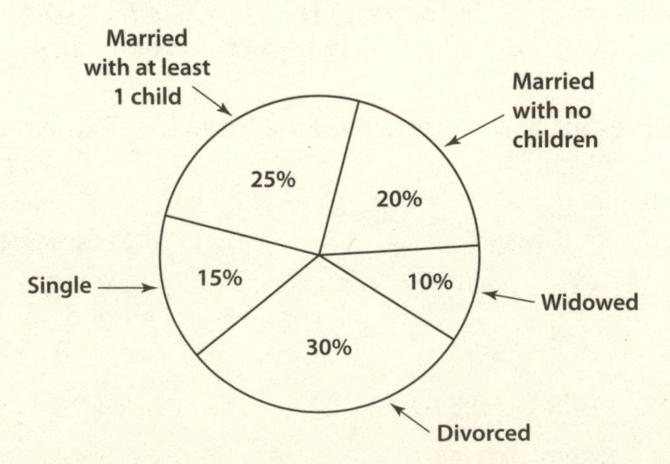

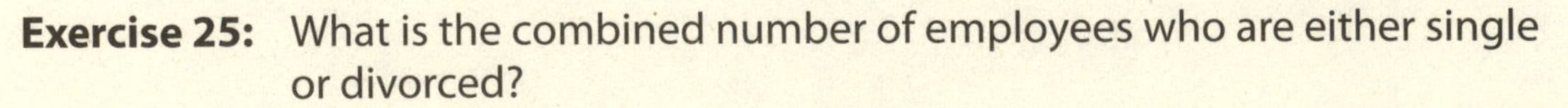

Exercise 25: What is the combined number of employees who are either single or divorced?

Exercise 26: If the hospital administration hires 250 additional widowed individuals, what will be the new percent for that category? Write your answer to the nearest whole number percent. Assume that there are no other changes.

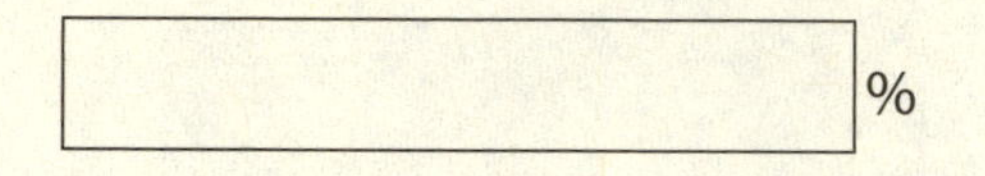
%

Use the following line graph for Exercises 27 and 28. The graph represents the number of books sold by the Reading Aloud Book Company.

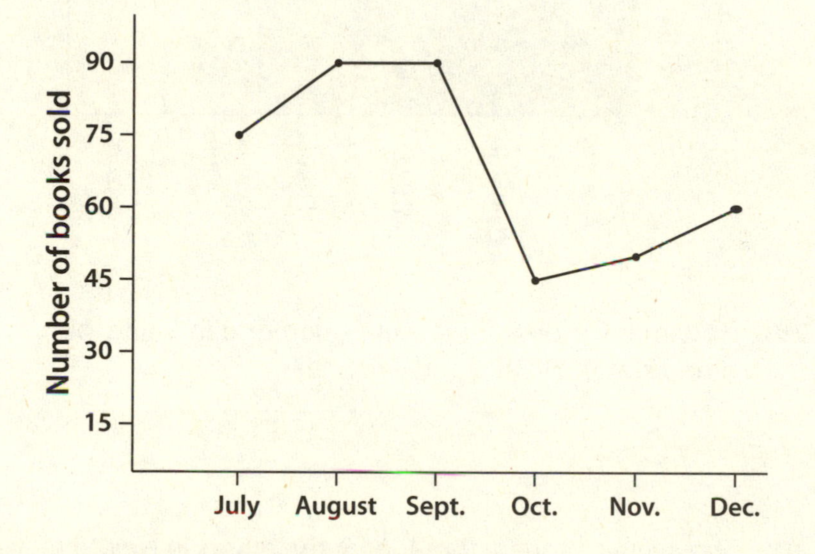

Exercise 27: The number of books sold in December was what percent lower than the number of books sold in July?

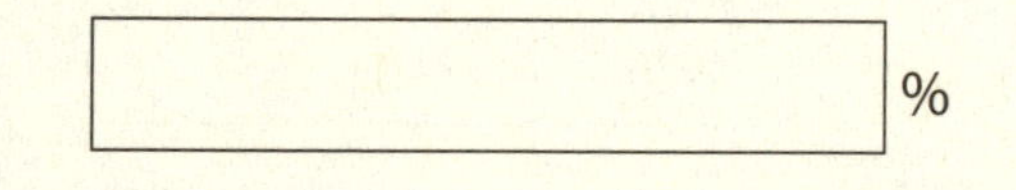
%

Exercise 28: The average (mean) price of a book sold in October was $20. If the total sales for the books sold in September was $612 more than the total sales for the books sold in October, what was the average price of a book sold in September?

$
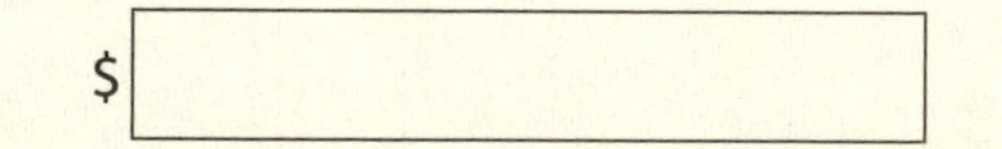

Use the following bar graph for Exercises 29 and 30. The graph shows the number of old-style diners in a select group of six states that were still operating as of 2011.

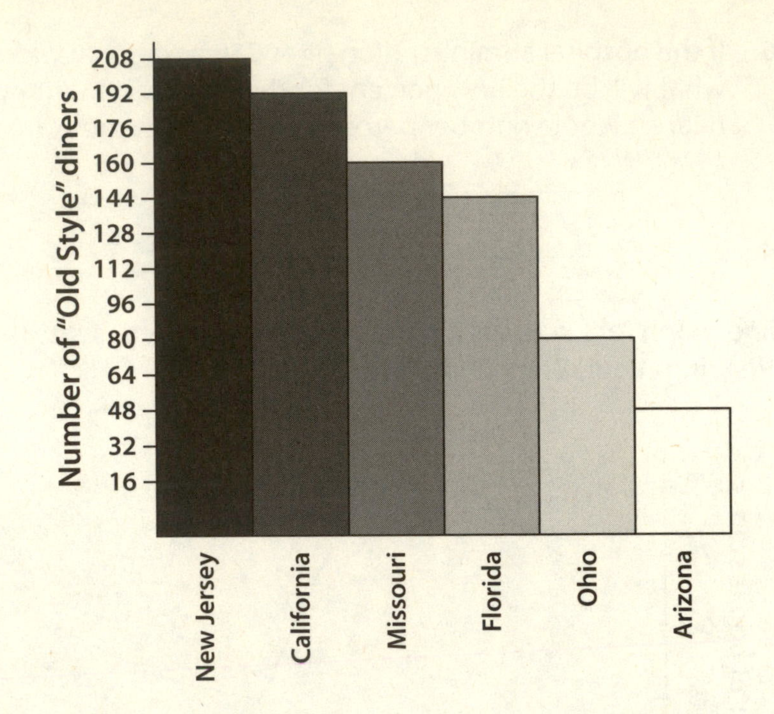

Exercise 29: How many more diners were operating in California than in the combined states of Ohio and Arizona?

Exercise 30: The average square footage for the diners in New Jersey is 3,600 square feet. If the total square footage for all the diners in Florida is 288,000 square feet less than the total square footage for all the diners in New Jersey, what is the average square footage for the diners in Florida?

Use the following histogram for Exercises 31 and 32. The graph refers to the number of minutes that each of 48 students in a specific math class devotes to homework each night.

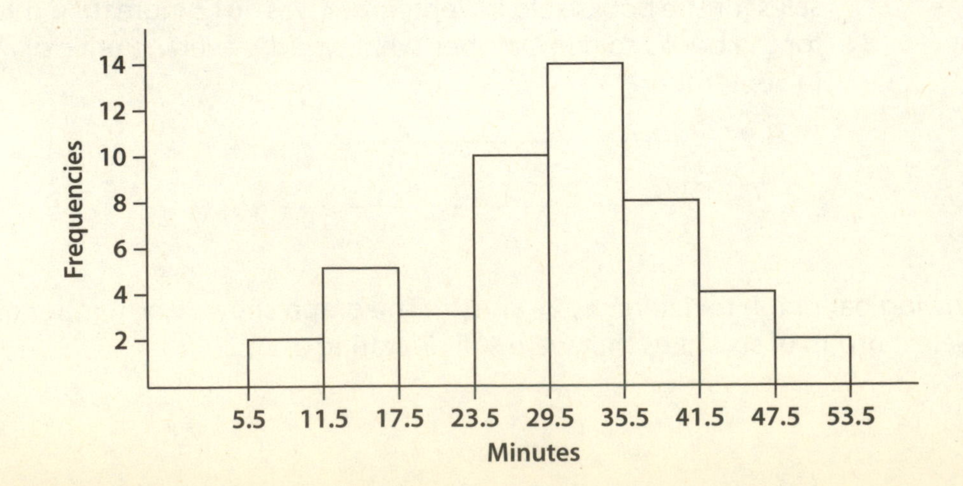

Exercise 31: What is the combined number of students who studied fewer than 24 minutes or more than 47 minutes each night?

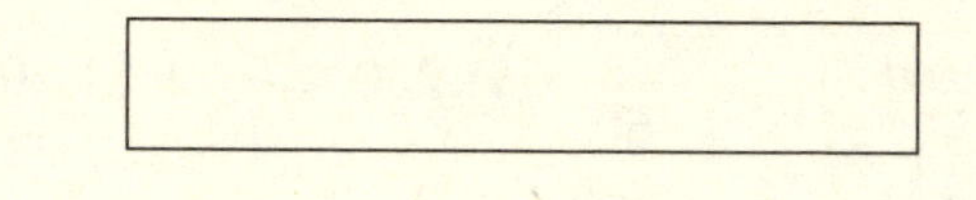

Exercise 32: What percent of the students studied more than 29 minutes per night? Write your answer to the nearest one-tenth of one percent.

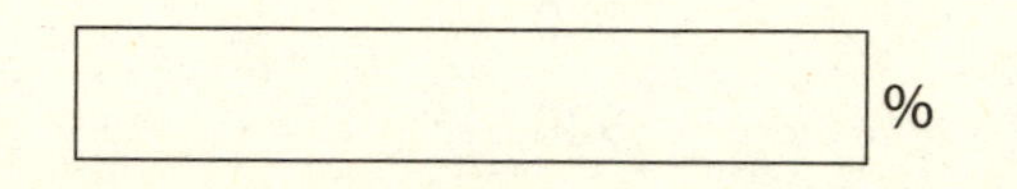 %

The arithmetic on the actual GRE could be less or more, nicer or messier, than the following exercises. It depends on the test form you actually take.

Use the following graphs for Exercises 33–37. Some of the major expenses of the apartment of Mr. and Mrs. Smith in Smallville, USA, are shown in this pie chart and bar graph. The pie chart is for year *M* with a $1,200 budget, and the bar graph is for year *N*, some years later, with an $1,800 budget.

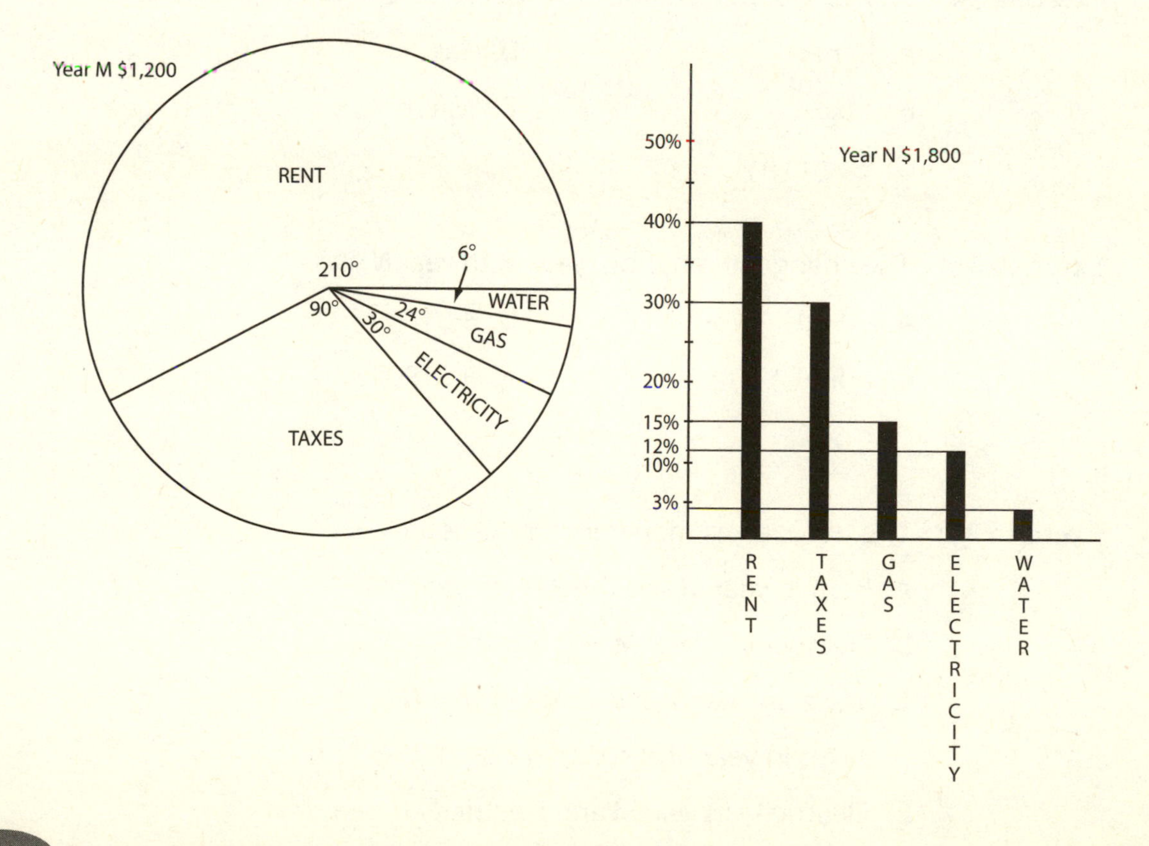

Note *Exercises 33–37 are easier to answer if we exactly calculate all of the money answers and put the items next to each other in a table:*

	Year M	Year N
Rent (sample calculations)	$\frac{210}{360} \times \$1{,}200 = \frac{7}{12} \times \$1{,}200 =$	$.40 \times \$1{,}800 =$
Rent	\$700	\$720
Taxes	\$300	\$540
Electricity	\$100	\$216
Gas	\$80	\$270
Water	\$20	\$54

Exercise 33: The smallest percentage increase from year M to year N is for

A. Rent
B. Taxes
C. Electricity
D. Gas
E. Water

Exercise 34: The largest percentage increase from year M to year N is for

A. Rent
B. Taxes
C. Electricity
D. Gas
E. Water

Exercise 35: The change in rent from year M to year N was

A. $-\$80$
B. none
C. $+\$20$
D. $+\$100$
E. $+\$190$

Exercise 36: The two closest monetary amounts are

A. Rent in year M and the Rent in year N
B. Electricity in year M and Gas in year N
C. Water in year M and Water in year N
D. Taxes in year M and Gas in year N
E. Electricity in year M and Electricity in year N

Exercise 37: Which expenses exceeded the percentage increase in the total budget?

A. All the expenses

B. All except Rent

C. All except Water

D. All except Water and Rent

E. All except Rent and Taxes

For Exercises 38–47, use the following information concerning the percentage change of gross revenue from year X to year Y, and from year Y to year Z for stores identified as *Q*, *R*, *S*, *T*, *U*, *V*, and *W*.

Store	% Change from X to Y	% Change from Y to Z
Q	+10	−10
R	+25	−20
S	−20	+25
T	+40	−30
U	+15	+15
V	+10	+20
W	+20	+10

Exercise 38: Which stores had a loss from year X to year Z? Indicate *all* correct choices.

A. *Q*

B. *R*

C. *S*

D. *T*

E. *U*

F. *V*

G. *W*

Exercise 39: Which stores showed no gain or loss from year X to year Z? Indicate *all* correct choices.

A. *Q*

B. *R*

C. *S*

D. *T*

E. *U*

F. *V*

G. *W*

Exercise 40: Besides stores *R* and *S*, which two of the following stores had exactly the same dollar change from year X to year Z? Indicate *exactly two* choices.

A. *Q*

B. *T*

C. *U*

D. *V*

E. *W*

Exercise 41: Which stores experienced both a percentage gain from year X to year Y and a percentage loss from year Y to year Z. Indicate *all* correct choices.

A. *Q*

B. *R*

C. *S*

D. *T*

E. *U*

F. *V*

G. *W*

Exercise 42: What is the highest percentage gain of any of these seven stores from year X to year Z?

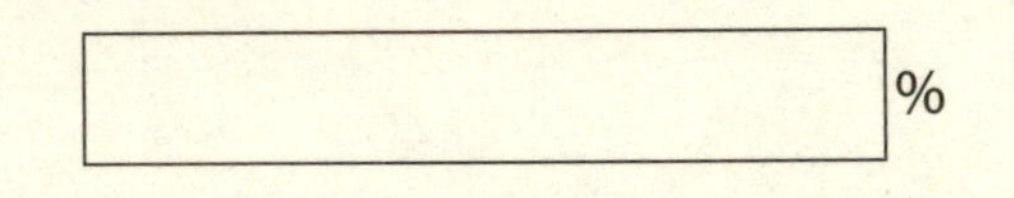
%

Exercise 43: For store *T*, the gross revenue in year Y was $840,234. To the nearest thousand dollars, what was the gross revenue for store *T* in the year X?

$
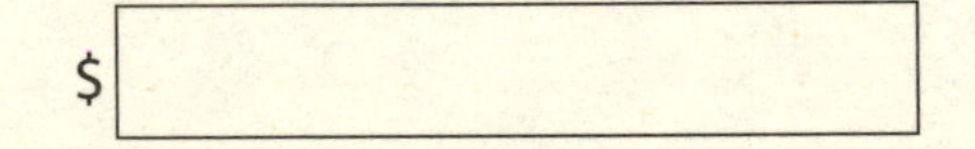

Exercise 44: Store *R* had gross revenue of $949,357 in year Z. To the nearest dollar, what was this store's gross revenue in year Y?

$
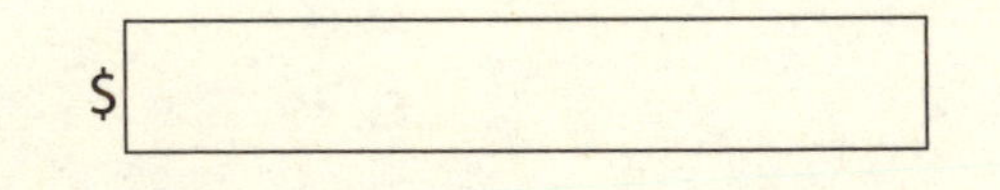

Exercise 45: Store *W* had gross revenue of $821,698 in year X, which was 15% greater than the gross revenue of store *V* in year X. What was the gross revenue of store *V* in year Y?

$
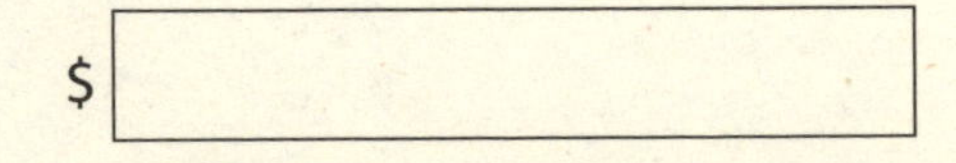

Exercise 46: Store *S* had gross revenue of $554,722 for year Z, which was 30% less than the gross revenue of store *U* in year Z. To the nearest dollar, what was the gross revenue of store *U* in year Y?

$
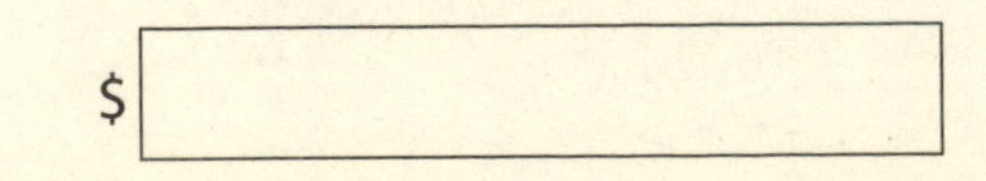

Exercise 47: Each of stores *Q* and *W* had gross revenues of $821,698 in year X. In year Z, store *W*'s gross revenue was what percent higher than store *Q*'s gross revenue? Round your answer to the nearest whole number percent.

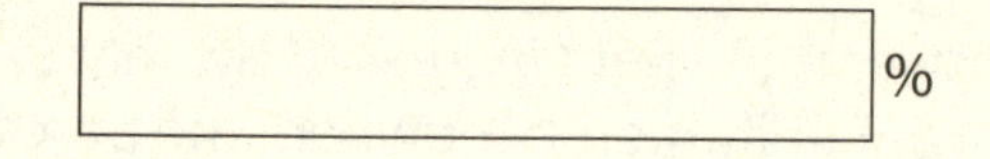 %

Let's look at the answers.

Answer 25: The correct answer is 675. There are a total of 15% + 30% = 45% of the employees who are single or divorced. Thus, the actual number of employees in either of these categories is (1,500)(0.45) = 675.

Answer 26: The correct answer is 23. Currently, there are (1,500)(0.10) = 150 widowed employees. With the addition of 250 widowed individuals, there will be a total of 400 widowed employees and a new grand total of 1,500 + 250 = 1,750 employees. Thus, $\frac{400}{1,750} \approx 23\%$.

Answer 27: The correct answer is 20. There were 75 − 60 = 15 fewer books sold in December than in July. Then $\frac{15}{75} = 20\%$.

Answer 28: The correct answer is 16.80. The total book sales for October was (45)($20) = $900. Then the total book sales for September was $900 + $612 = $1,512. Thus, the average price of a book sold in September was $\frac{\$1,512}{90} = \$16.80$.

Answer 29: The correct answer is 64. The combined number of diners in Ohio and Arizona was 80 + 48 = 128. Thus, there were 192 − 128 = 64 more diners in California than there were in Ohio and Arizona combined.

Answer 30: The correct answer is 3,200. The total square footage for all New Jersey diners is (208)(3,600) = 748,800 square feet. Then the square footage for all Florida diners is 748,800 − 288,000 = 460,800 square feet. Therefore, the average square footage is $\frac{460,800}{144} = 3,200$.

Answer 31: The correct answer is 12. There were 2 + 5 + 3 = 10 students who studied fewer than 24 minutes per night. In addition, there were 2 students who studied more than 47 minutes per night.

Answer 32: The correct answer is 58.3. There were $14 + 8 + 4 + 2 = 28$ students who studied more than 29 minutes per night. Then $\frac{28}{48} \approx 58.3\%$.

Answer 33: The answer is (A). Rent increased by only \$20 (due perhaps to rent control or family member owner); the percentage increase is the smallest increase $(= \frac{20}{700} \times 100)$. You don't actually have to calculate the exact percentage. You only have to note the percentage increase is obviously much smaller than the percentage increase of any other item.

Answer 34: The answer is (D). The percentage increase for gas is $\frac{190}{80} \times 100\%$, or more than a 200% increase.

Answer 35: The answer is (C). $\$720 - \$700 = \$20$.

Answer 36: The answer is (A). The rents in year *M* and year *N* are only \$20 apart. No other choices are this close.

Answer 37: The answer is (B). The total increase from year *M* to year *N* is 50%; taxes almost doubled; electricity more than doubled; gas more than tripled, and water almost tripled.

For the answers to Exercises 38–40, the easiest way to do problems of this nature is to use dollar amounts. Assume that each store had a gross revenue of \$100 in Year X. For store Q, its gross revenue in Year Y would be $(\$100)(1.10) = \$110$. Its gross revenue in Year Z would be $(\$110)(0.90) = \$99$. Note that a 10% increase is equivalent to multiplying by 1.10 and a 10% loss is equivalent to multiplying by 0.90 $(1.00 - 0.10 = 0.90)$. Here is how the chart would now appear with revenue in place of percents:

Store	Year X Revenue	Year Y Revenue	Year Z Revenue
Q	\$100	\$110	\$99
R	\$100	\$125	\$100
S	\$100	\$80	\$100
T	\$100	\$140	\$98
U	\$100	\$115	\$132.25
V	\$100	\$110	\$132
W	\$100	\$120	\$132

Answer 38: The correct answers are (A) and (D). From the table above, store *Q* had a loss of \$1 and store *T* had a loss of \$2 from year X to year Z.

Answer 39: The correct answers are (B) and (C). Each of stores *R* and *S* had a gross revenue of \$100 in year X and year Z.

Answer 40: The correct answers are (D) and (E). Each of stores *V* and *W* gained \$32 from year X to year Z.

Answer 41: The correct answers are (A), (B), and (D). Each of stores *Q*, *R*, and *T* showed a percentage gain from year X to year Y and a percentage loss from year Y to year Z.

Answer 42: The correct answer is 32.25. Using the base amount of \$100 for year X, Store *U* increased to \$132.25 in year Z, for a $132.25 - 100 = 32.25\%$ increase. (Do *not* put the percent sign in the box.) Note that this percent increase would not change even if we knew the exact gross revenues for the stores.

Answer 43: The correct answer is 600,000. Since store *T* had a 40% increase from year X to year Y, the gross revenue in year Y was 140% (or equivalently 1.40) of the gross revenue in year X. Thus, the gross revenue in year X equals $\frac{\$840,234}{1.40} \approx \$600,167$. To the nearest thousand, this figure becomes \$600,000. (Do *not* put the dollar sign in the box.)

Answer 44: The correct answer is 1,186,696. Since store *R* had a 20% decrease from year Y to year Z, the gross revenue in year Z was 80% (or equivalently 0.80) of the gross revenue for year Y. Thus, the gross revenue in year Y equals $\frac{\$949,357}{0.80} \approx \$1,186,696$, rounded to the nearest dollar. (Do *not* put the dollar sign in the box.)

Answer 45: The correct answer is 785,972. The gross revenue of store *W* in year X was 115% of the gross revenue of store *V* in that year. So, the gross revenue of store *V* in year X was $\frac{\$821,698}{1.15} = \$714,520$. Thus, the gross revenue of store *V* in year Y was $(\$714,520)(1.10) = \$785,972$. (Do *not* put the dollar sign in the box.)

Answer 46: The correct answer is 689,096. The gross revenue of store S in year Z was 70% (100% − 30%) of the gross revenue of store *U* in year Z. So the gross revenue of store *U* in year Z was $\frac{\$554,722}{0.70} = \$792,460$. Thus, the gross revenue of store *U* in year Y was $\frac{\$792,460}{1.15} = \$689,095.65$. To the nearest dollar, this figure becomes $689,096. (Do *not* put the dollar sign in the box.)

Answer 47: The correct answer is 33. The gross revenue of store *Q* in year Y was ($821,698)(1.10) ≈ $903,868, and its gross revenue in year Z was ($903,868)(0.90) ≈ $813,481. The gross revenue of store *W* in year Y was ($821,698)(1.20) ≈ $986,038, and its gross revenue in year Z was ($986,038)(1.10) ≈ $1,084,642. Then the difference of the gross revenues of these two stores in year Z was approximately $1,084,642 − $813,481 = $271,161. Thus, store W's gross revenue was $\frac{\$271,161}{\$813,481} \approx 33\%$ higher than that of store Q. (Do *not* put the percent sign in the box.)

PERCENTILES

Percentiles are assigned to each data in a group in order to indicate their relative position to the other data. It is understood that the data must be arranged in ascending order, and that all occurrences of an individual value are represented. In general, if a score of *p* is assigned the *n*th percentile, it means that approximately *n*% of all scores were equal to or lower than *p*. For example, if your score on a test was assigned to the 97th percentile, then approximately 97% of all students who took this test had the same score or a lower score than you achieved. If your score was assigned to the 50th percentile, then approximately half of all students who took this test had a score equal to or lower than your score.

It is extremely important to realize that the same score on different tests could easily have a different percentile. Suppose there are two classes of 100 students each. If Jimmy got a score of 90 in the first class and only three students scored higher than him, his score would be the 97th percentile. If Nancy got a score of 90 in the second class and 50 students scored higher than her, her score would only be the 50th percentile.

Quartiles

Certain percentiles are much more commonly used than others. One such measure is that of quartiles. The **first quartile**, denoted as Q_1, represents the 25th percentile. It is equivalent to the median of the lower half of the data. Approximately 25% of all the data are either equal to or lower than Q_1. It is also called the *lower quartile*.

The **second quartile**, denoted as Q_2, represents the 50th percentile. It is equivalent to the median of the group of data. Approximately 50% of all the data are either equal to or lower than Q_2.

The **third quartile**, denoted as Q_3, represents the 75th percentile. It is equivalent to the median of the upper half of the data. Approximately 75% of all the data are either equal to or lower than Q_3. It is also called the upper quartile.

The **interquartile range**, commonly abbreviated as IQR, is equal to $Q_3 - Q_1$.
Some rules exist for the location of these quartiles. Let n represent the number of data in a group. If n is an odd number, the location of Q_1 is given by $\frac{n+1}{4}$, the location of Q_2 is given by $\frac{n+1}{2}$, and the location for Q_3 is given by $\frac{3(n+1)}{4}$ or equivalently $\frac{3n+3}{4}$.

Example 30: A group consists of 17 data points. What are the locations of the first, second, and third quartiles?

Solution: The location of Q_1 is $\frac{17+1}{4} = 4.5$, so its value is the mean of the 4th and 5th data points. The location of Q_2 is $\frac{17+1}{2} = 9$, so its value is the 9th data point. The location of Q_2 is $\frac{3(17+1)}{4} = 13.5$, so its value is the mean of the 13th and 14th data points.

Example 31: Consider the following group of data: 4, 7, 8, 10, 13, 14, 20, 21, 25, 25, 29. What are the values of the three quartiles?

Solution: There are a total of 11 data points. Don't forget to count each of the 25s. The location of Q_1 is $\frac{11+1}{4} = 3$, so its value is the third number, which is 8. The location of Q_2 is $\frac{11+1}{2} = 6$, so its value is the sixth number, which is 14. The location of Q_3 is $\frac{3(11+1)}{4} = 9$, so its value is the ninth number, which is 25. In summary, $Q_1 = 8$, $Q_2 = 14$, and $Q_3 = 25$.

The expressions for the locations of Q_1 and Q_3 change if the number of data, n, is even. The location of Q_2 remains as $\frac{n+1}{2}$. For Q_1, its location is given by $\frac{n+2}{4}$. For Q_3, its location is given by $\frac{3n+2}{4}$.

Example 32: A group consists of 26 data points. What are the locations of the first, second, and third quartiles?

Solution: The location of Q_1 is $\frac{26+2}{4} = 7$, so its value is the 7th data point. The location of Q_2 is $\frac{26+1}{2} = 13.5$, so its value is the mean of the 13th and 14th data points. The location of Q_3 is $\frac{3(26)+2}{4} = 20$, so its value is the 20th data point.

Example 33: Consider the following group of data: 5, 8, 13, 15, 15, 19, 24, 30, 36, 40, 42, 42. What are the values of the three quartiles and what is the value of the interquartile range?

Solution: There are a total of 12 data points. Don't forget to count the duplicates. The location of Q_1 is $\frac{12+2}{4} = 3.5$, so its value is the mean of the 3rd and 4th data points, which is 14. The location of Q_2 is $\frac{12+1}{2} = 6.5$, so its value is the mean of the 6th and 7th data points, which is 21.5. The location of Q_3 is $\frac{3(12)+2}{4} = 9.5$, so its value is the mean of the 9th and 10th data points, which is 38. In summary, $Q_1 = 14$, $Q_2 = 21.5$. and $Q_3 = 38$. Also, the interquartile range (IQR) is $38 - 14 = 24$.

Sometimes a quartile can refer to a group of data, not just the location of one particular data. Consider Example 33. We found that $Q_1 = 14$. A GRE test question might refer to the data in the first quartile. In this context, your answer would be the numbers 5, 8, and 13. Each of these numbers has a value less than or equal to Q_1.

Likewise, the data that are found in the second quartile would be 15 and 19, since each of these numbers has a value greater than Q_1 but less than or equal to Q_2. (Repetition of 15 would not be necessary if we are just naming the data within a quartile.)

Continuing in this fashion, the data that are found in the third quartile would be 24, 30, and 36. Each of these numbers has a value greater than Q_2 but less than or equal to Q_3.

The numbers 40 and 42 are considered to be in the fourth quartile because their values are greater than Q_3. Note that there is no assigned number for Q_4, even though data will exist in the fourth quartile.

Here is a trick in remembering the locations of the first and third quartiles for any group of data. The sum of the locations of Q_1 and Q_3 is always 1 more than the number of data points.

Referring to Example 33, the locations of Q_1 and Q_3 is 3.5 and 9.5, respectively. Notice that $3.5 + 9.5 = 13$, which is one more than the number of data points (12).

Boxplots

A useful graphical way to summarize key elements of a group of data is a **boxplot**, also known as a **box-and-whisker plot**. In particular, a boxplot shows the following values of a group of data, namely, (a) the lowest value, (b) the first quartile, (c) the median, (d) the third quartile, and (e) the highest value. Let's look at a completed boxplot, as shown below.

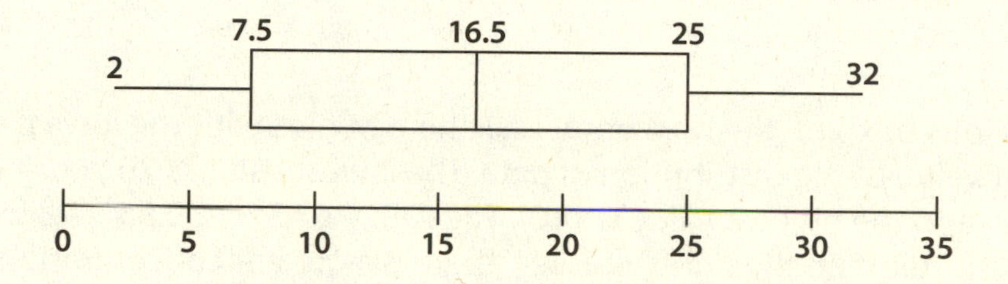

Note that there is a horizontal scale with numbers evenly spaced. The numbers on this scale are chosen such that the lowest and highest numbers in the given group of data are included. A horizontal segment is shown to the left of the box. This segment connects the lowest value of the group of data (2) with the first quartile (7.5). The box is actually split vertically so that the first vertical segment identifies the first quartile (7.5), the second vertical segment identifies the median (16.5), and the third vertical segment identifies the third quartile (25). The horizontal segment to the right of the box connects the third quartile with the highest value (32). The IQR $= Q_3 - Q_1 = 25 - 7.5 = 17.5$. Notice that the scale extends beyond both the lowest and the highest values of the given data. Also, notice that the mean of this data group is *not* shown.

In the previous boxplot, the box appears to be evenly split by the median. It looks as if the median lies midway between the lower quartile (Q_1) and the upper quartile (Q_3). However, this appearance of symmetry is not required. Consider, as an example, the following boxplot.

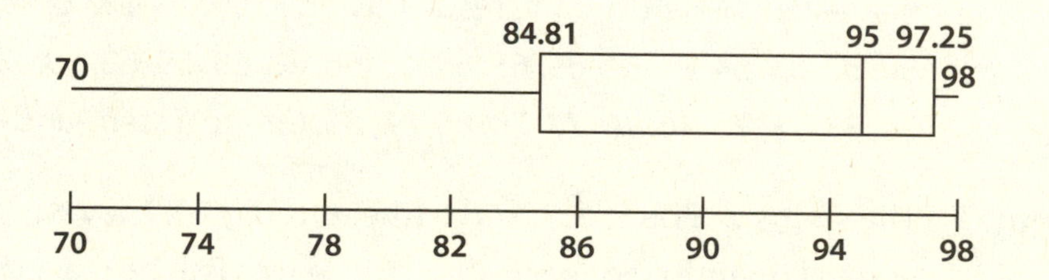

Here the horizontal scale begins and ends with the lowest and highest values, respectively, of the group of data. For this group of data, we observe that the lowest value is 70, $Q_1 = 84.81$, $Q_2 = 95$, $Q_3 = 97.25$, and the highest value is 98. The IQR $= 97.25 - 84.81 = 12.44$.

Since the left "whisker" (which extends from the lowest value to Q_1) is longer than the right "whisker" (which extends from Q_3 to the highest value), we can deduce that there would be a greater concentration of higher values than lower values. Remember that each quartile contains the same number of values. For example, in this boxplot, there are as many values between 95 and 97.25 as there are between 70 and 84.81.

The following boxplot has a longer "whisker" to the right of the box.

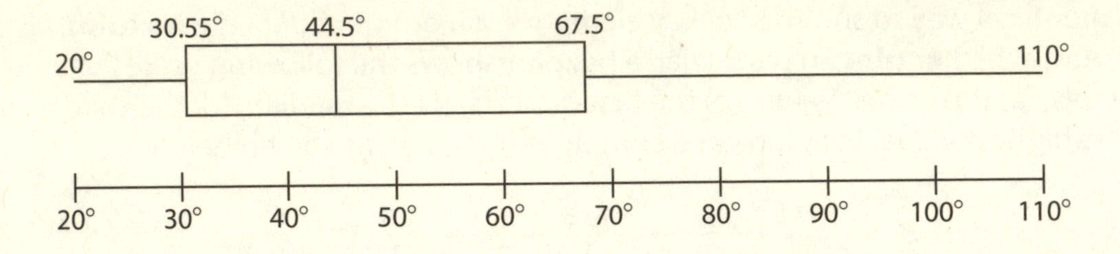

As with the previous boxplot, the horizontal scale here begins with the lowest value and ends with the highest value of the distribution of data. The lowest value is 20°, $Q_1 = 30.55°$, $Q_2 = 44.5°$, $Q_3 = 67.5°$, and the highest value is 110°. The IQR = 67.5° − 30.55° = 36.95°. Since the left "whisker" is shorter than the right "whisker," there is a greater concentration of smaller values than of larger values. Notice that there are as many values between 20° and 30.55° as there are between 67.5° and 110°.

Stem-and-Leaf Plot

A useful way to tabulate data is a method called **stem-and-leaf plot**. This method is best used when (a) the range of data is relatively small, (b) there are some repetitions of data values, and (c) each data value has the same number of digits. The data must first be arranged in ascending order (including all repeating values). The stem consists of all digits, except the units digit. The leaf consists of only the units digit. So if each of the data points is between 100 and 999, the stems would consist of the hundreds digit and the tens digit. But if each of the data lies between 10 and 99, the stem would consist of only the tens digit. The data are arranged in ascending order in a vertical manner, with the lowest number appearing at the top.

Example 34: The 36 employees at the XYZ watch company listed their heights, to the nearest inch. Here are the results, listed in ascending order: 58, 59, 59, 59, 60, 62, 63, 64, 64, 64, 65, 65, 65, 66, 66, 68, 68, 68, 68, 69, 70, 71, 71, 71, 71, 72, 73, 73, 75, 76, 76, 77, 79, 80, 82, 86. Create a stem-and-leaf plot.

Solution: The stems will be 5, 6, 7, and 8 (the tens digits). They will be placed in a vertical quantity. For each stem, the leaves will be placed in ascending order, from left to right. The actual plot is shown below.

5 | 8 9 9 9
6 | 0 2 3 4 4 4 5 5 5 6 6 8 8 8 8 9
7 | 0 1 1 1 1 2 3 3 5 6 6 7 9
8 | 0 2 6

Example 35: Referring to the stem-and-leaf plot of Example 34, what is the interquartile range?

Solution: For 36 data, the location of Q_1 is 9.5 and the location for Q_3 is 27.5. Since the 9th and 10th numbers are 64, $Q_1 = 64$. Since the 27th and 28th numbers are both 73, $Q_3 = 73$. Thus, the interquartile range is 9.

Let's try a few exercises on quartiles, boxplots, and stem-and-leaf plots.

For Exercises 48–51, use the following group of data: 76, 77, 82, 82, 85, 92, 95, 96, 98.

Exercise 48: What position number is the location of Q_3?

A. 2.5th
B. 4th
C. 5th
D. 6.5th
E. 7.5th

Exercise 49: What is the interquartile range?

Exercise 50: Which of the following numbers are in the second quartile? Indicate *all* correct answers.

A. 77
B. 82
C. 85
D. 92
E. 95
F. 96

Exercise 51: Which of the following numbers are in the fourth quartile? Indicate *all* correct answers.

A. 82
B. 85
C. 92
D. 95
E. 96
F. 98

For Exercises 52–54, refer to the following boxplot.

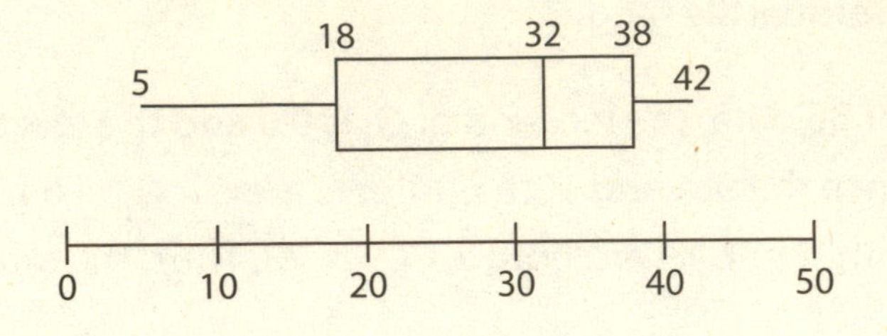

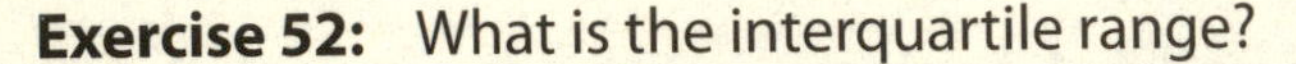

Exercise 52: What is the interquartile range?

Exercise 53: What is the sum of the lowest value and the median?

Exercise 54: Suppose that there are 25 data in the first quartile. Which of the following represent a range of numbers for which there would be 25 data? Indicate *all* correct answers.

A. Greater than 18 but less than or equal to 32

B. Greater than 18 but less than or equal to 38

C. Greater than 5 but less than or equal to 42

D. Greater than 32 but less than or equal to 38

E. Greater than 32 but less than or equal to 42

F. Greater than 38 but less than or equal to 42

Exercise 55: Consider the following stem-and-leaf plot

16 | 0 1 2 3 8 9
17 | 5 6 8
18 | 2 4 8 9 9
19 | 2 2 5 5 6 7 8
20 | 2 9
21 | 0 0 0 2 3 8 9

Which of the following numbers are found in the second quartile? Indicate *all* correct answers.

A. 176

B. 178

C. 184

D. 189

E. 192

F. 196

G. 202

Let's look at the answers.

Answer 48: The correct answer is (E). For an odd number of data, the location of Q_3 is $\frac{3(n+1)}{4} = \frac{3(9+1)}{4} = 7.5$.

Answer 49: The correct answer is 16. The location of Q_1 is $\frac{(9+1)}{4} = 2.5$, so $Q_1 = \frac{77+82}{2} = 79.5$. Also, the location of Q_3 is 7.5, so $Q_3 = \frac{95+96}{2} = 95.5$. Therefore, the IQR $= 95.5 - 79.5 = 16$.

Answer 50: The correct answers are (B) and (C). $Q_1 = 79.5$ and $Q_2 = 85$. Each of 82 and 85 are greater than 79.5 and less than or equal to 85.

Answer 51: The correct answers are (E) and (F). The fourth quartile consists of numbers that are greater than Q_3. Since $Q_3 = 95.5$, only 96 and 98 are greater than Q_3.

Answer 52: The correct answer is 20. The interquartile range equals $Q_3 - Q_1 = 38 - 18 = 20$.

Answer 53: The correct answer is 37. The lowest value is 5 and the median is the middle vertical bar, which is 32.

Answer 54: The correct answers are (A), (D), and (F). Each quartile must have 25 data points. The first quartile is represented by 5 through 18, the second quartile is represented by 18 through 32, the third quartile is represented by 32 through 38, and the fourth quartile is represented by 38 through 42.

Answer 55: The correct answers are (B), (C), (D), and (E). We determine that the location of Q_1 is the $\left(\frac{30+2}{4} = \right)$ 8th number and the location of Q_2 is the $\left(\frac{30+1}{2} = \right)$ 15.5th number. The 8th number is 176 and the average (mean) of the 15th and 16th numbers is 192. Therefore, each number in the second quartile must be greater than 176 and less than or equal to 192. The numbers 178, 184, 189, and 192 satisfy this requirement.

Scatterplots

A **scatterplot** is a method of displaying the relationship between two numerical quantities on the *xy*-coordinate plane. It is simply a plot of all the data points, with one variable on the horizontal axis and the other on the vertical axis. The points are not connected so they look like scattered points, thus the name scatterplot; however, if there is a relationship between the variables, it usually shows up as a trend on the scatterplot. Exercise 36 shows such a trend.

Example 36: In a small class of nine students, the teacher was interested in comparing the number of absences during the school year with each student's final numerical grade. Here are the results in tabular form:

Number of Absences:	0	5	3	9	1	7	3	2	6
Final Grade:	98	80	90	60	93	55	85	90	75

Draw a scatterplot of these results.

Solution: The positive *x*-axis will be labeled "Number of Absences" and the positive *y*-axis will be labeled "Final Grade." The scatterplot is shown below.

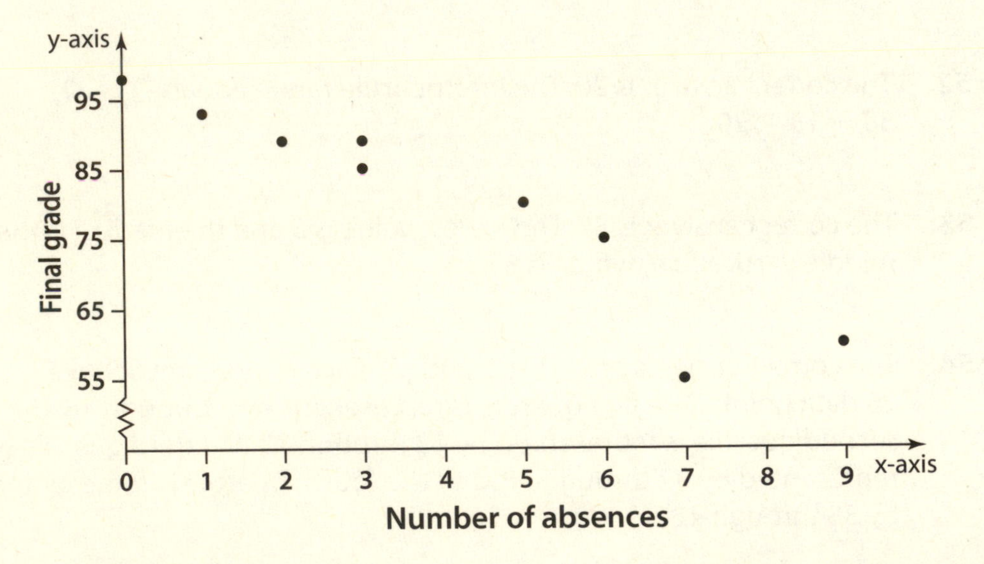

Note that since the grades range from 55 to 98, a squiggle line is shown between 0 and 55 on the vertical axis. This indicates that there are no values between 0 and 55. Looking at the trend of the data points, the teacher could conclude that absences negatively affect a student's final grade.

Line of Best Fit

In some cases, the data points appear to lie in a straight line. The GRE will present examples for which a **line of best fit** will be given for a set of data points. This is the line for which the distances between the data points and the line are minimized. The GRE will not require the derivation of the equation for this line. Be aware that although some of the data points may lie on this line, it is *not* a requirement. Often, the line of best fit contains very few, if any, of the data points.

For Examples 37–41, use the following information.

Suppose that a college instructor asked eight of his students to indicate how many hours they studied for the exams he gave each week. The instructor then calculated each of these eight students' average exam grades. Here are the results, with x representing the number of hours of study and y representing the average exam grade.

x	1	1.25	1.5	2	2.5	3	4	5
y	70	76	78	75	83	81	86	85

The instructor then calculated the equation of the line of best fit to be $y = 2.95x + 70.79$. Below are the scatterplot and the line of best fit.

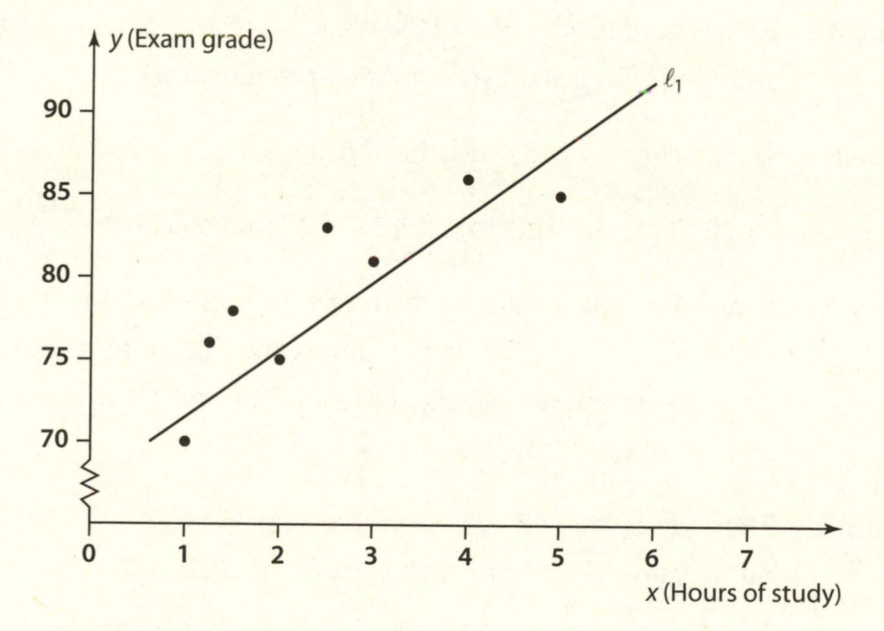

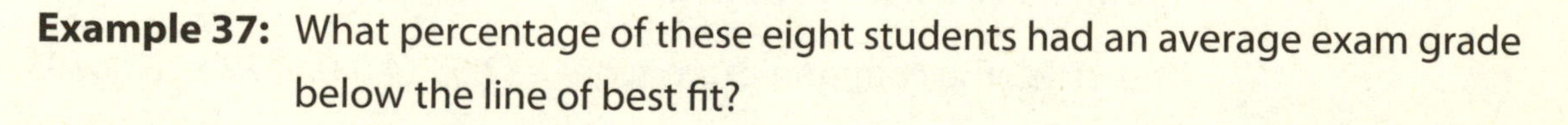

Example 37: What percentage of these eight students had an average exam grade below the line of best fit?

Solution: The answer is 37.5. The data points (1, 70), (2, 75), and (5, 85) lie below the line of best fit. This represents $\frac{3}{8}$ of the points, so the answer is 37.5%.

Example 38: For the data point that lies farthest from the line of best fit, by what amount does the actual score differ from the projected score? (Note that the projected score is the value of y that is computed from the line of best fit equation.)

Solution: The answer is 4.835. The point (2.5, 83) lies farthest from the line of best fit. This can be observed by noting the vertical distance at $x = 2.5$ from the point to the line. The line of best fit represents the projected score of $(2.95)(2.5) + 70.79 = 78.165$. Thus, the answer is $83 - 78.165 = 4.835$.

Example 39: Suppose this line of best fit applies to all 40 students in the class. What would be the projected exam score, rounded off to the nearest hundredth, of a student who studied for 3.5 hours?

Solution: The answer is 81.12. By substitution, $y = (2.95)(3.5) + 70.79 = 81.115 \approx 81.12$.

Example 40: A projected exam score of 79 would correspond to how many hours of studying? (Round off your answer to the nearest tenth.)

Solution: The answer is 2.8. By substitution, $79 = 2.95x + 70.79$. Then subtract 70.79 from each side to get $8.21 = 2.95x$. Thus, $x = \frac{8.21}{2.95} \approx 2.8$.

Example 41: In another class similar to the one in Examples 37–40, the line of best fit was $y = 2.65x + 72$. Which common exam score for these two classes would yield the same projected score? Round off your answer to the nearest hundredth.

Solution: The answer is 82.68. We start with $2.95x + 70.79 = 2.65x + 72$. Subtracting $2.65x$ from each side, we get $0.3x + 70.79 = 72$. Now subtract 70.79 from each side to get $0.3x = 1.21$. Then, $x = \frac{1.21}{0.3} \approx 4.03$. Therefore, the common exam score is $(2.65)(4.03) + 72 = 82.6795 \approx 82.68$.

(Note that we could have also substituted 4.03 for x in the equation $y = 2.95x + 70.79$.)

Let's try a few exercises on scatterplots and lines of best fit.

For Exercises 56–60, use the following information.

A 64-ounce block of substance Y is undergoing a procedure to melt it. The independent variable (x) represents number of minutes and the dependent variable (y) represents the number of ounces the block contains. Its corresponding line of best fit is $y = -0.7x + 63.3$.

A second substance Z is also undergoing a procedure to melt it. The corresponding line of best fit is $y = -0.5x + 48$. *No data points are given for substance Z.* Here is the graph of the line of best fit for substance Y with the following data points: (5, 60), (10, 56.5), (15, 51), (20, 48.5), (25, 44.5), and (30, 42).

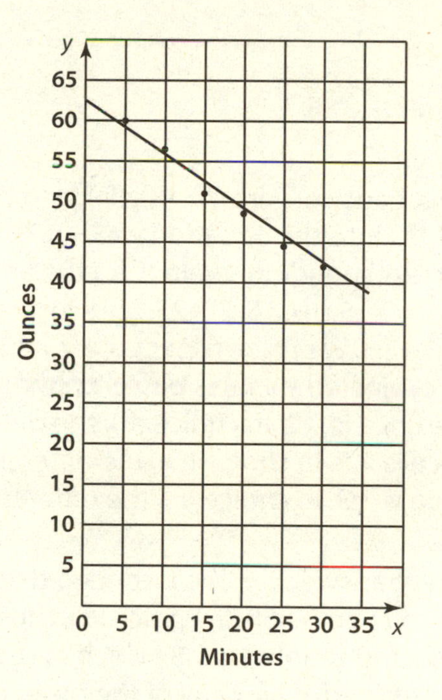

Exercise 56: For which data points does the projected weight (given by the equation of the line of best fit) for substance Y differ from the actual weight by less than one ounce? Indicate *all* correct answers.

A. (5, 60)

B. (10, 56.5)

C. (15, 51)

D. (20, 48.5)

E. (25, 44.5)

F. (30, 42)

Exercise 57: For how many data points does the difference between the actual weight and the projected weight exceed 1.5 ounces for substance Y?

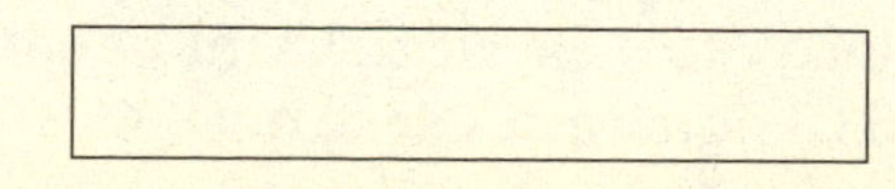

Exercise 58: In how many minutes will the two substances weigh the same?

Exercise 59: What will be the weight, in ounces, of each when the two substances are of equal weight?

Exercise 60: How many more minutes, to the nearest tenth of a minute, will it take for substance Z to melt completely than for substance Y to melt completely?

Let's look at the answers.

Answer 56: The correct answers are (A), (B), (D), and (F). By substituting each of the x values into the equation $y = -0.7x + 63.3$ (line of best fit), we get the corresponding y values on the actual line. The corresponding values for $x = 5, 10, 15, 20, 25$, and 30, are $y = 59.8, 56.3, 52.8, 49.3, 45.8$, and 42.3. We then inspect the y values of the given data points and the projected y values based on the line of best fit. In choice (A), the difference is 0.2. In choice (B), the difference is 0.2. In choice (C), the difference is 1.8. In choice (D), the difference is 0.8. In choice (E), the difference is 1.3. In choice (F), the difference is 0.3.

Answer 57: The correct answer is 1. We just need to look at the computations in the solution to Exercise 56. In choice (C), the difference between the actual and projected weights is 1.8, which exceeds 1.5. This weight difference does not exceed 1.5 for any of the other choices.

Answer 58: The correct answer is 76.5. We need to solve the equation $-0.7x + 63.3 = -0.5x + 48$. Adding $0.5x$ to each side, we get $-0.2x + 63.3 = 48$. Next, subtract 63.3 from each side. This leads to $-0.2x = -15.3$. Thus,

$$x = \frac{-15.3}{-0.2} = 76.5\cdot$$

Answer 59: The correct answer is 9.75. From answer 58, we need only substitute 76.5 into either equation $y = -0.7x + 63.3$ or $y = -0.5x + 48$. Choosing the first equation, we get $y = (-0.7)(76.5) + 63.3 = 9.75$.

Answer 60: The correct answer is 5.6. In order to determine the number of minutes for substance Y to melt, we solve the equation $0 = -0.7x + 63.3$. Subtract 63.3 from each side to get $-63.3 = -0.7x$. Then

$x = \frac{-63.3}{-0.7} \approx 90.4$. In order to determine the number of minutes for substance Z to melt, we solve the equation $0 = -0.5x + 48$. Subtracting 48 from each side yields $-48 = -0.5x$, so $x = \frac{-48}{-0.5} = 96$. Thus, the required number of minutes is $96 - 90.4 = 5.6$.

NORMAL CURVE

Earlier in this chapter, we studied a type of graphical display of data called a histogram. For this type of graph, each bar represented a specific (numerical) class of data for which there was a corresponding frequency. None of the classes contained overlapping data on the *x*-axis.

There are instances where the histogram resembles a bell-shaped curve, as shown below.

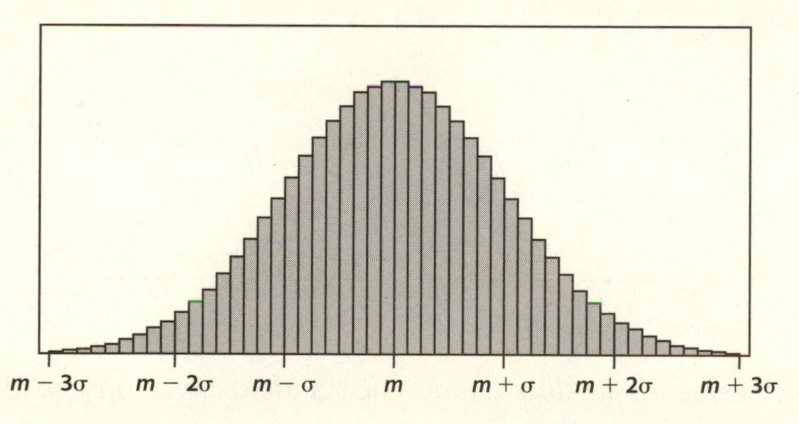

For this curve, *m* represents the mean of the data and *σ* represents the standard deviation, which is a measure of the spread of the data about the mean.

Note *On the GRE exam, sometimes the letter d is used for standard deviation.*

Examples of data that would resemble this bell-shaped distribution include (a) heights of all adult women, (b) weights of all adult men, (c) highest daily temperatures in a given city over a period of years, and (d) amount of ounces of coffee dispensed in a cup by a vending machine.

This type of distribution is called a **normal curve**. The two main properties of a normal curve are: (a) the mean, median, and mode are nearly identical; and (b) the data are grouped very symmetrically about the mean. It has been determined that approximately 68% of the data lies within one standard deviation of the mean; approximately 96% of the data lies within two standard deviations of the mean; and nearly all the data lies within three standard deviations of the mean.

It should be noted that theoretically this graph never intersects the *x*-axis. In reality, no group of data can actually represent a true normal distribution. However, the normal curve can be used as a very accurate approximation for many groups of data. Often, the amount of data is so large that we use a continuous curve to replace the series of rectangular bars, as shown below.

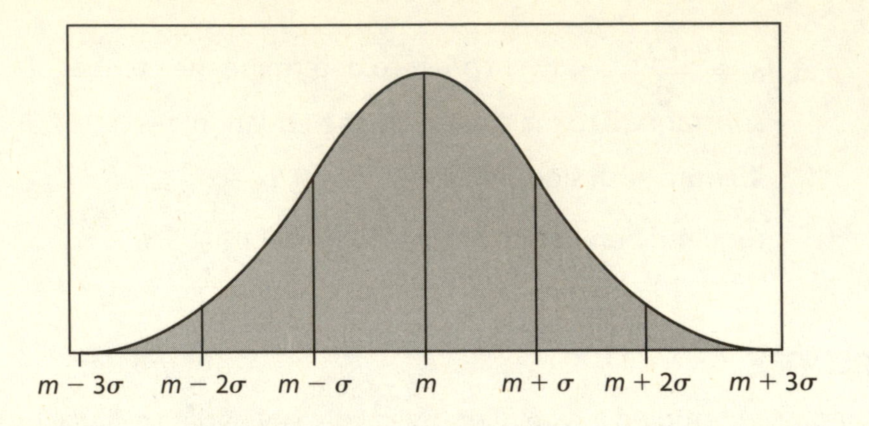

The values of the mean and the standard deviation of a normal distribution will affect its location and "width." In the figure below, the means (μ_1 and μ_2) are identical but the standard deviation of curve 1 (σ_1) is larger than that of curve 2 (σ_2).

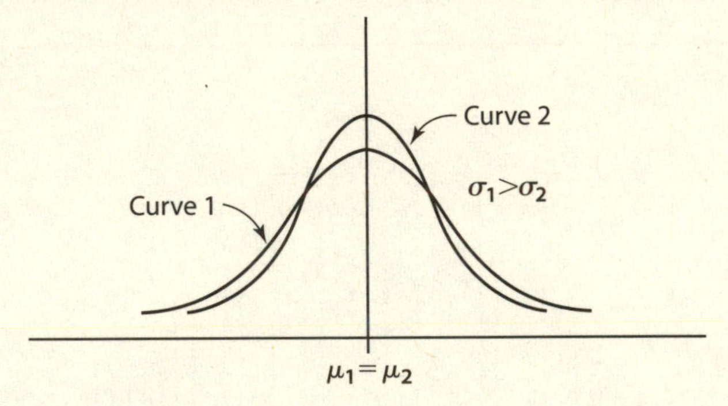

In some instances, the means are different but the standard deviations are identical, as shown below.

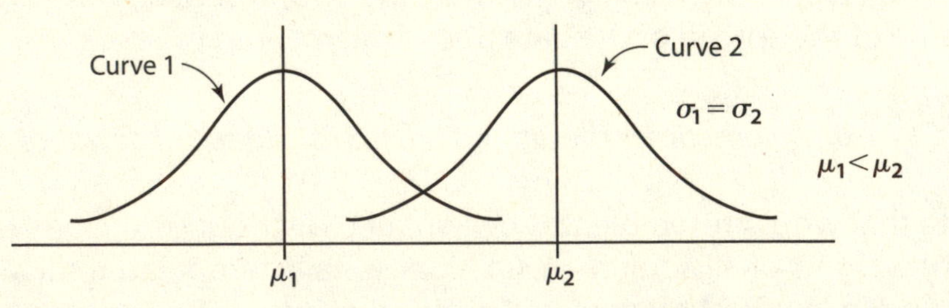

Of course, we recognize that it is possible for neither the means nor the standard deviations to be identical for two normal distributions. This is illustrated below.

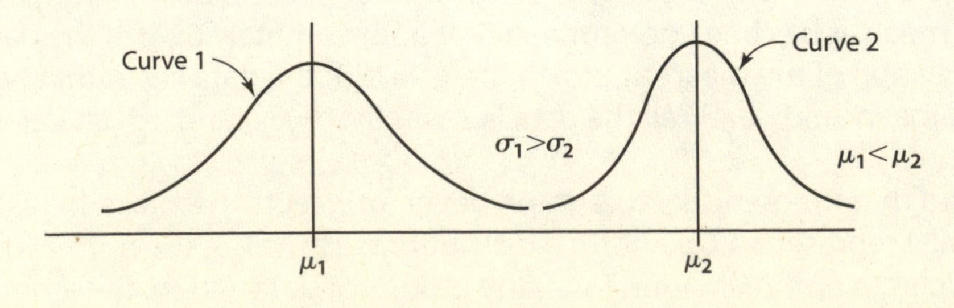

In order to apply the properties of a normal distribution to practical applications, the **standard normal distribution** is used. For a standard normal distribution, the mean equals zero and the standard deviation equals 1. Conversion to a standard normal distribution can be performed on any normal distribution by using the formula $z = \frac{x - \mu}{\sigma}$, where z is called a **standard score** (also called a z-score). The variable x is called the **raw score**. A raw score is a value found in the original distribution (one of the data points). The standard score is a measure of how many standard deviations that score is from the mean.

Example 42: A normal distribution has a mean of 20 and a standard deviation of 4. Change the x scores of 16 and 30 to z-scores.

Solution: The x-value 16 has a z-score of $\frac{16 - 20}{4} = -1$, and the x value 30 has a z-score of $\frac{30 - 20}{4} = 2.5$. So 16 is one standard deviation below the mean, and 30 is 2.5 standard deviations above the mean.

Example 43: A normal distribution has a mean of 100 and a standard deviation of 15. A standard score of -1.4 corresponds to what raw score?

Solution: The answer is 79. By substitution, $-1.4 = \frac{x - 100}{15}$. Multiply both sides by 15 to get $-21 = x - 100$. Thus, $x = 100 - 21 = 79$.

Example 44: In a particular normal distribution, a raw score of 60 corresponds to a standard score of 0. What is the mean raw score?

Solution: The answer is 60. By substitution, we have $0 = \frac{60 - \mu}{\sigma}$. Notice that we do not know the value of the standard deviation of the given data (σ), but it will not be needed. Assuming that $\sigma \neq 0$ (which can occur only if all the data are the same), multiply both sides of the equation by σ. Then $(0)(\sigma) = 0 = 60 - \mu$, so $\mu = 60$.

For Examples 39–42, use the following graph of a normal distribution. This graph represents the heights of 5,000 adult women. Assume that their mean height is 65 inches, with a standard deviation of 2.4 inches.

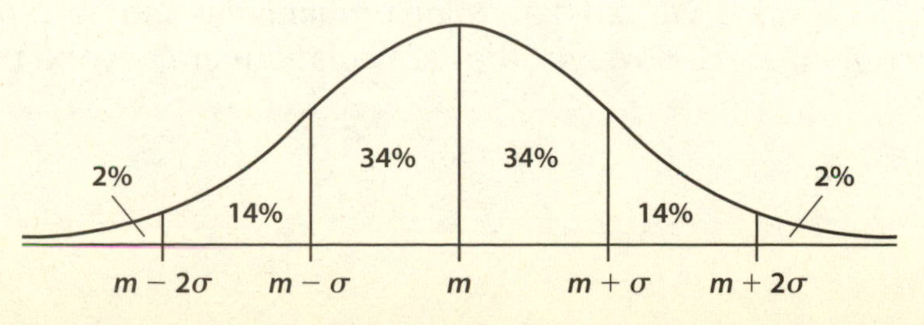

Example 45: How many women are taller than 67.4 inches?

Solution: The answer is 800 Change 67.4 into its standard score, which is $\frac{67.4 - 65}{2.4} = 1$. The percentage of data that are greater than 1 standard deviation from the mean ($m + \sigma$) is 14% + 2% = 16%. Thus, the answer is (0.16)(5,000) = 800.

Example 46: How many women are shorter than 69.8 inches?

Solution: The answer is 4,900. Change 69.8 into its *z*-score, which is $\frac{69.8 - 65}{2.4} = 2$. Instead of adding the percentages that lie to the left of 2 standard deviations ($m + 2\sigma$), we note that only 2% lies to its right. Therefore, we know that 100% − 2% = 98% of the data lies to the left of a *z*-score of 2. Thus, the required number of women is (0.98)(5,000) = 4,900.

Example 47: How many women are between 62.6 inches and 67.4 inches tall?

Solution: The answer is 3,400. We have already changed 67.4 to its *z*-score of 1. Change 62.6 into its *z*-score, which is $\frac{62.6 - 65}{2.4} = -1$. The percentage of data that lies between *z*-scores of −1 and 1 is 34% + 34% = 68%. Thus, the answer is (0.68)(5,000) = 3,400.

Example 48: What is the probability that the height of a randomly chosen woman is less than 62.6 inches?

Solution: The answer is 0.16. The concept of probability is parallel to that of percent. We only need to find the percentage of the data that is less than the *z*-score for 62.6. In Example 47, we identified the *z*-score of 62.6 to be −1. The corresponding probability matches the percentage of data that lies to the left of −1, which is 2% + 14% = 16%. Since probability is usually presented as a decimal (or fraction), our answer can be expressed as 0.16.

In full-year statistics courses, we can determine probabilities and percents that correspond to *z*-scores that are not integers. However, these calculations are beyond the scope of the GRE.

Let's try some exercises on the normal distribution.

For Exercises 61–64, use the following information.

In a town of 45,000 adults, the number of times they eat at a fast-food restaurant per year represents a normal distribution with a mean of 29 and a standard deviation of 8.

Below is the graph of normal distribution and specific percents.

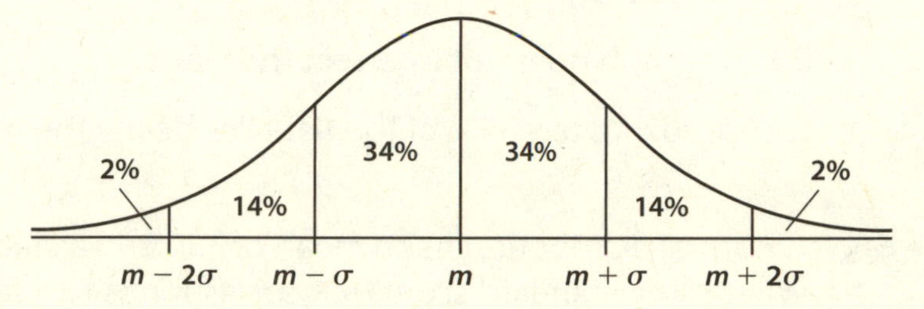

Exercise 61: How many adults in this town eat between 37 and 45 times per year at a fast-food restaurant?

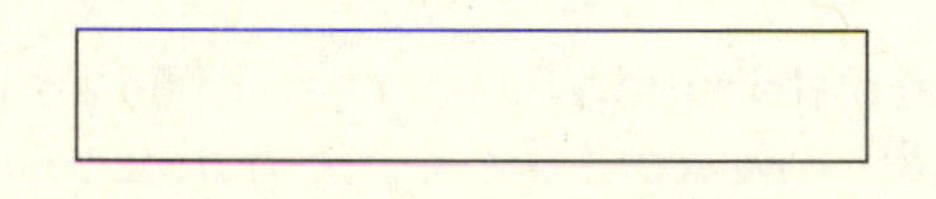

Exercise 62: How many adults in this town eat more than 29 times per year at a fast-food restaurant?

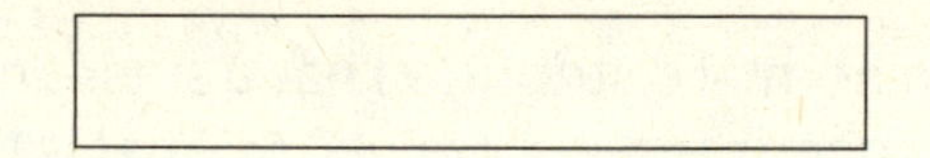

Exercise 63: What is the probability that a randomly chosen adult in this town eats at a fast-food restaurant fewer than 13 times per year?

A. 0.13
B. 0.09
C. 0.07
D. 0.04
E. 0.02

Exercise 64: What is the probability that a randomly chosen adult in this town eats at a fast-food restaurant between 13 times per year and 37 times per year?

A. 0.98
B. 0.88
C. 0.82
D. 0.72
E. 0.68

Exercise 65: Which of the following are true regarding any normal distribution? Indicate *all* correct answers.

A. The mean equals the median.

B. The mode does not exist.

C. The standard deviation is 1.

D. Approximately 68% of all the data lies within one standard deviation of the mean.

E. The graph does not intersect the *x*-axis.

F. Approximately 34% of the data lies below the mean.

Exercise 66: A normal distribution has a mean of 150 and a standard deviation of 6. What is the standard score that corresponds to a raw score of 139.2?

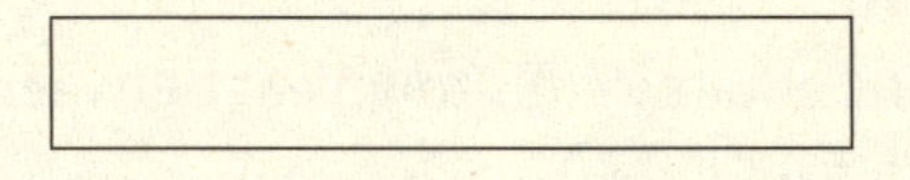

Exercise 67: A normal distribution has a mean of 84 and a standard deviation of 8. What is the raw score that corresponds to a standard score of 2.2?

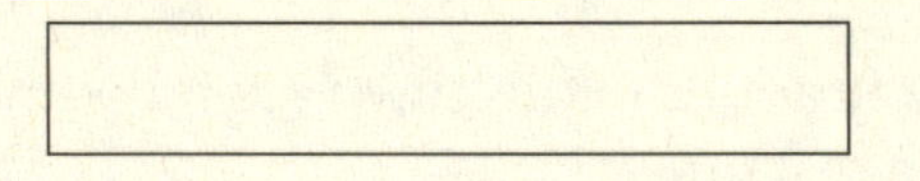

Exercise 68: A certain normal distribution has a standard deviation of 5. An *x*-score of 30 corresponds to a *z*-score of 0.6. What is the value of the mean?

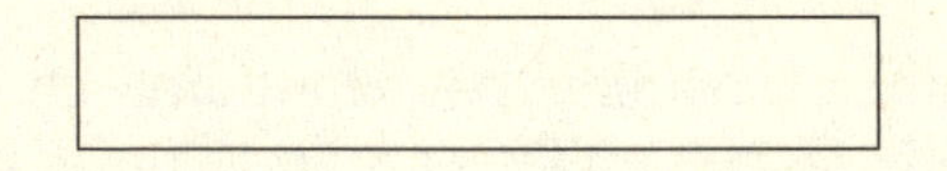

Let's look at the answers.

Answer 61: The correct answer is 6,300. The *z*-score for 37 is $\frac{37-29}{8}=1$ and the *z*-score for 45 is $\frac{45-29}{8}=2$. We find that 14% of the data lies between 1 standard deviation and 2 standard deviations. Thus, $(0.14)(45{,}000) = 6{,}300$.

Answer 62: The correct answer is 22,500. Since 29 is the mean, its corresponding *z*-score is zero. Half the data lies to the right of the mean, so $(0.50)(45{,}000) = 22{,}500$.

Answer 63: The correct answer is (E). Change 13 to its *z*-score of $\frac{13-29}{8} = -2$. For the normal distribution, only 2% lies to the left of a standard score of -2.

Answer 64: The correct answer is (C). We have already changed 13 to its *z*-score of -2. Change 37 to its *z*-score of $\frac{37-29}{8} = 1$. Then 14% + 34% + 34% = 82% of the data lies between *z*-scores of -2 and 1. This means that the correct probability is 0.82.

Answer 65: The correct answers are (A), (D), and (E). Choice (B) is wrong because the mode does exist, and has the same value as the mean and the median. Choice (C) is wrong because the standard deviation can be any non-negative number. For a *standard* normal distribution, the standard deviation is always 1. Answer choice (F) is wrong because approximately 50% of the data lies below the mean.

Answer 66: The correct answer is -1.8. The standard score is computed as $\frac{139.2-150}{6} = \frac{-10.8}{6} = -1.8$.

Answer 67: The correct answer is 101.6. By substitution, $2.2 = \frac{x-84}{8}$. Multiply both sides by 8 to get $17.6 = x - 84$. Thus, $x = 17.6 + 84 = 101.6$.

Answer 68: The correct answer is 27. By substitution, $0.6 = \frac{30-\mu}{5}$. Multiply both sides by 5 to get $3 = 30 - \mu$. Thus, $\mu = 30 - 3 = 27$.

Now we are ready for the practice tests.

Practice Test 1 — Section 1

Directions: Each of Questions 1–9 consists of two quantities. Compare the quantities in Quantities A and B and choose

(A) if Quantity A is greater.
(B) if Quantity B is greater.
(C) if the two quantities are equal.
(D) if the relationship cannot be determined from the information given.

	Quantity A	Quantity B
1. $3 < m < 8$	$\left(\frac{m}{8}\right)^2$	$\left(\frac{m}{0.08}\right)^2$

For Questions 2 and 3, use the following graph:

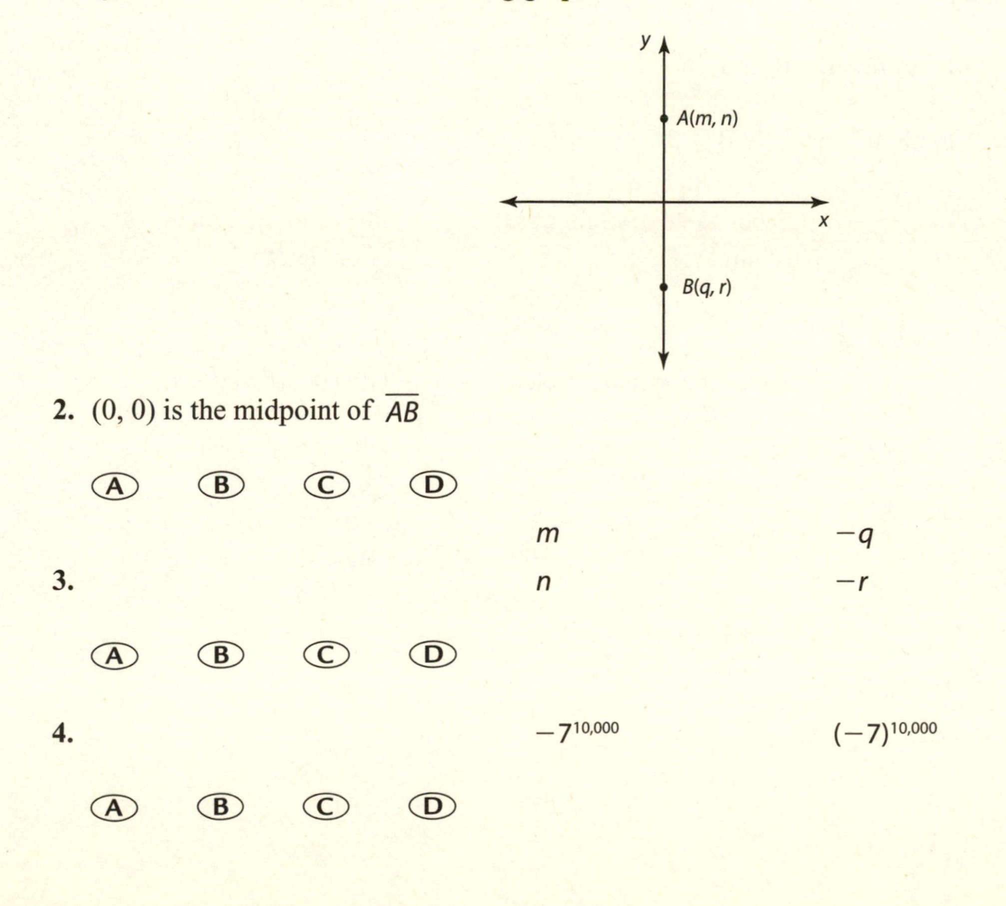

2. (0, 0) is the midpoint of $\overline{AB}$

(A) (B) (C) (D)

	Quantity A	Quantity B
3.	$\frac{m}{n}$	$\frac{-q}{-r}$

(A) (B) (C) (D)

	Quantity A	Quantity B
4.	$-7^{10{,}000}$	$(-7)^{10{,}000}$

(A) (B) (C) (D)

For Questions 5 and 6, use the following diagram:

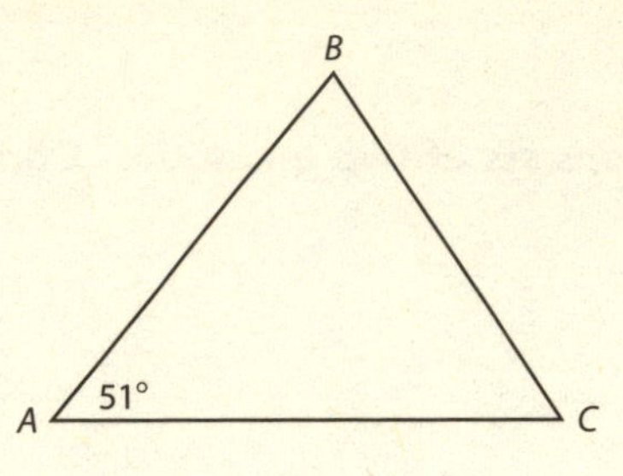

Triangle ABC is isosceles with base $\overline{AC}$. (Note: The triangle is not drawn to scale)

	Quantity A	**Quantity B**
5.	$m\angle B$	68°

Ⓐ Ⓑ Ⓒ Ⓓ

	Quantity A	**Quantity B**
6.	$\dfrac{AB}{AC}$	1

Ⓐ Ⓑ Ⓒ Ⓓ

For Questions 7 and 8, use the following information:

The radius of circle A is x. The radius of circle B is $2x$.

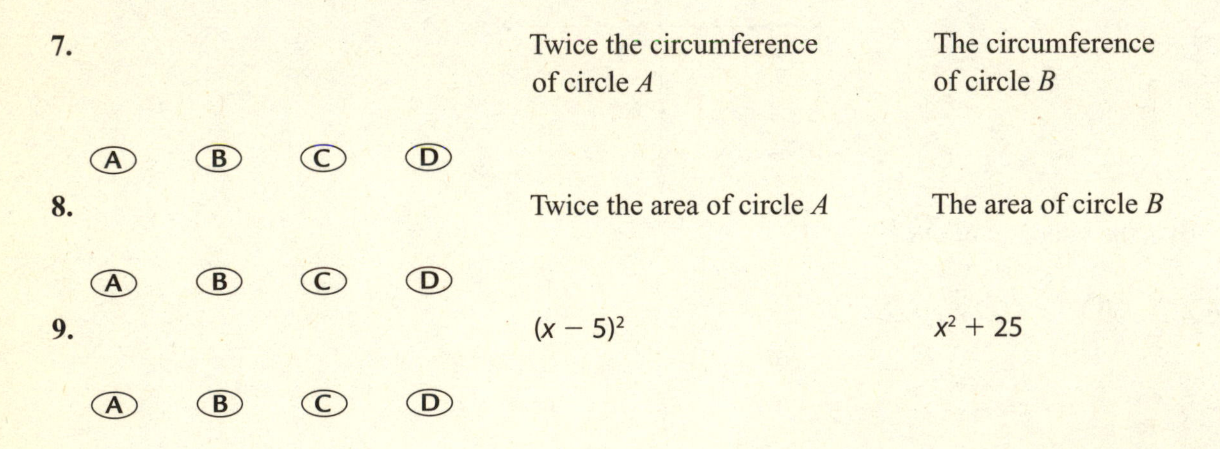

	Quantity A	**Quantity B**
7.	Twice the circumference of circle *A*	The circumference of circle *B*

Ⓐ Ⓑ Ⓒ Ⓓ

	Quantity A	**Quantity B**
8.	Twice the area of circle *A*	The area of circle *B*

Ⓐ Ⓑ Ⓒ Ⓓ

	Quantity A	**Quantity B**
9.	$(x - 5)^2$	$x^2 + 25$

Ⓐ Ⓑ Ⓒ Ⓓ

Directions: Questions 10–25 have several different formats. Unless otherwise indicated, select a single answer choice. For numeric entry questions, follow the instructions below.

Numeric Entry Questions

Enter your answer in the answer box(es) below the question.

- Your answer may be an integer, a decimal, or a fraction, and it may be negative.
- If a question asks for a fraction, there will be two boxes—one for the numerator and one for the denominator.
- Equivalent forms of the correct answer, such as 2.5 or 2.50, are all correct. Fractions do not need to be reduced to lowest terms.
- Enter the exact answer unless the question asks you to round your answer.

10. If $2a = 3b = 4c = 20$, what is the value of $9abc$?

Ⓐ 1,000
Ⓑ 2,000
Ⓒ 3,000
Ⓓ 8,000
Ⓔ 9,000

11. If y is four less than the square root of x, then which of the following is the expression for x?

Ⓐ $4 + y^2$
Ⓑ $4 - y^2$
Ⓒ $y^2 - 4$
Ⓓ $(4 - y)^2$
Ⓔ $(4 + y)^2$

12. Let a, b represent positive odd integers, with $b > 4$. Which of the following expressions *must* be odd? Indicate *all* correct answers.

[A] a^{b+1}
[B] $ab + a + b$
[C] $(a - 2)^{b-4}$
[D] $(a + 1)(b + 2)(b^a)$

13. For which of the following would the values of one base and the height to this base be sufficient to determine the area? Indicate *all* correct answers.

A Triangle
B Square
C Trapezoid
D Parallelogram
E Kite

14. A jar has 7 red balls and 3 orange balls. Two balls are drawn, one at a time, without replacement. What is the probability of selecting two red balls? Write your answer as a fraction.

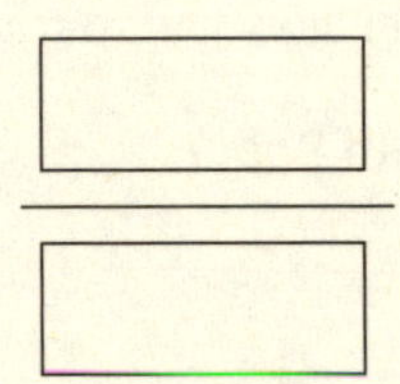

15. A holiday sale on a sweater offers a 40% discount, followed by a 30% discount, followed by a 50% discount. The final price is what percent of the original price?

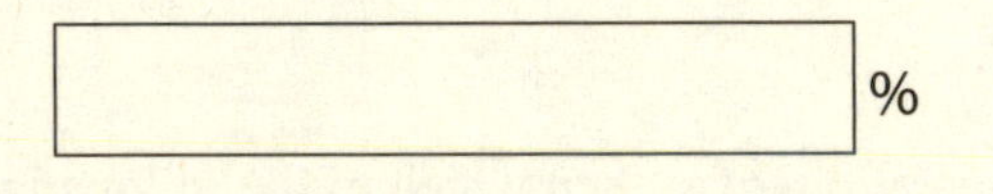

For Questions 16,17, and 18, use the following chart.

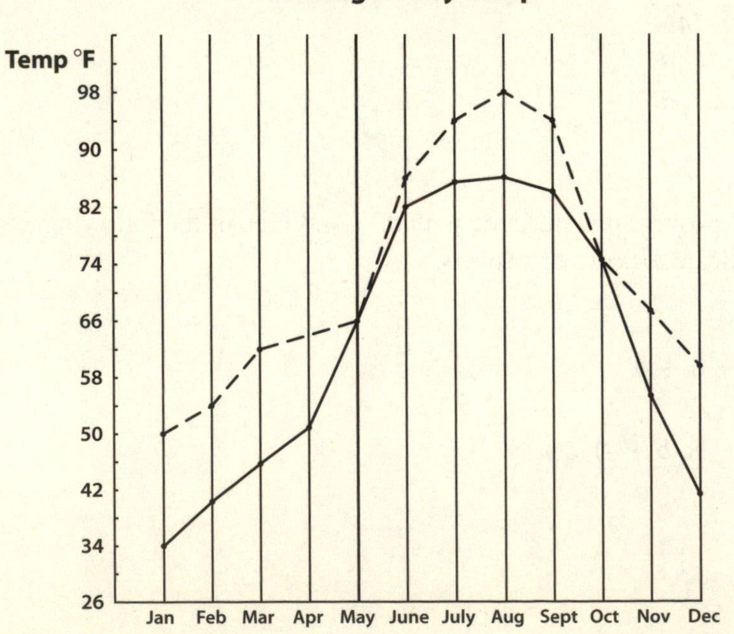

City A is represented by the solid line and city B is represented by the dashed line.

16. For which month is the difference in temperatures greatest?

(A) January
(B) February
(C) March
(D) August
(E) December

17. What is the average (mean) of the differences of the temperatures between the two cities for the months of June, July, August, and September?

(A) 5.7°
(B) 6.8°
(C) 8.5°
(D) 14°
(E) 32°

18. For the month of January, the temperature of city B is what percent higher than the temperature of city A? Write your answer to the nearest whole number.

%

19. What is the value of the interquartile range for the following boxplot?

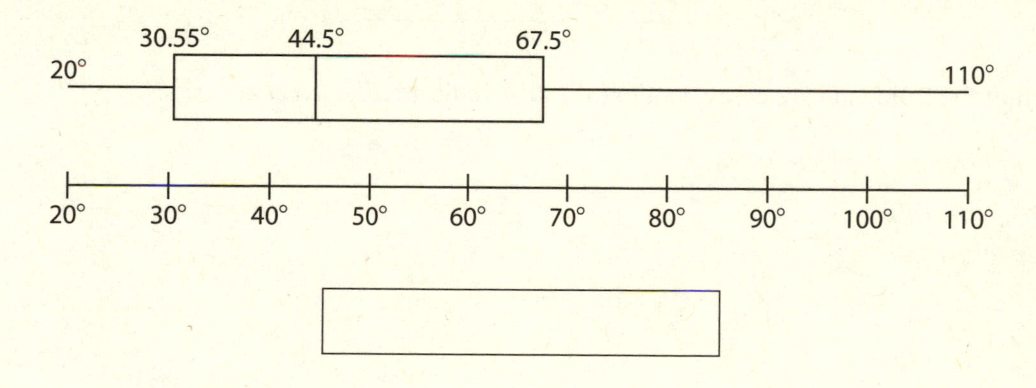

20. Six people, including Alex, are to be seated in a straight line at a table. If Alex is not seated at either end of this table, in how many ways can the six people be seated?

(A) 120
(B) 240
(C) 480
(D) 600
(E) 720

21. What is the solution for x in the equation $\frac{x}{2} + \frac{x}{3} = 1$?

(A) $\frac{2}{3}$
(B) $\frac{11}{10}$
(C) $\frac{6}{5}$
(D) $\frac{3}{2}$
(E) $\frac{9}{4}$

22. If $5a + 4b = 3$ and $2a + 3b = 46$, what is the value of $a + b$?

23. Which of the following are equivalent to $(a^{11})(a^7)$? Indicate *all* correct answers.

[A] $a^{11} + a^7$
[B] $(a^9)^2$
[C] $a^{21} - a^3$
[D] $\frac{a^{36}}{a^2}$
[E] $\frac{\sqrt{a^{54}}}{a^9}$

24. Which of the following values of x satisfy the inequality $|2x - 7| \leq 11$? Indicate *all* correct answers.

[A] -7
[B] 0
[C] 7
[D] 9
[E] 11

25. If $5 + n + n^2 + n^3 = 84$, what is the arithmetic mean of n, n^2, n^3, and n^4?

(A) $10n$
(B) $20n$
(C) $30n$
(D) $35n$
(E) $40n$

ANSWERS AND EXPLANATIONS

1. (B) For $3 < m < 8$, $\frac{m}{8}$ has a value less than 1. Squaring this value decreases it. However, for $3 < m < 8$, $\frac{m}{0.08}$ has a value greater than 1. Squaring this value increases it.

2. (C) Since points A and B lie on the y-axis, $m = q = 0$.

3. (C) Since (0, 0) is the midpoint of $\overline{AB}$, r is the additive opposite of n. Thus, $n = -r$.

4. (B) The number -7^{10000} is a negative number. However, $(-7)^{10000}$ represents an even power of a negative number, which must be positive.

5. (A) Since $\overline{AC}$ is the base, $m\angle C = m\angle A = 51°$. Thus, $m\angle B = 180° - 51° - 51° = 78°$.

6. (B) In any triangle, the larger the angle, the larger the side opposite this angle. Since $m\angle B > m\angle C$, $AC > AB$. This implies that $\frac{AB}{AC}$ represents a fraction less than 1.

7. (C) The circumference of circle A is $2\pi x$, and twice this value is $4\pi x$. The circumference of circle B is $(2\pi)(2x) = 4\pi x$.

8. (B) Twice the area of circle A is $2\pi x^2$, whereas the area of circle B is $(\pi)(2x)^2 = 4\pi x^2$.

9. (D) $(x-5)^2 = x^2 - 10x + 25$. But without knowing the value of x, we cannot determine whether $-10x$ is negative ($x > 0$), zero ($x = 0$), or positive ($x < 0$).

10. (C) $(2a)(3b)(4c) = 24abc = (20)^3 = 8{,}000$. Then $abc = \frac{8{,}000}{24} = 333\frac{1}{3}$. Thus, $9abc = (9)(333\frac{1}{3}) = 3{,}000$.

11. (E) $y = \sqrt{x} - 4$ Add 4 to both sides to get $4 + y = \sqrt{x}$. Then square both sides to get $(4+y)^2 = \left(\sqrt{x}\right)^2 = x$.

12. (A, B, C) Choices (A) and (C) each represent an odd integer raised to an odd power, which must be odd. Choice (B) represents the sum of three odd integers, which must be odd. For choice (D), the quantity $(a + 1)$ is an even integer. If any factor of a multiplication is even, the product must be even.

13. (A, B, D) The area of triangle, square, and parallelogram can be determined from one base and the height to this base. Choice (C) is wrong because a trapezoid has two unequal bases. Choice (E) is wrong because a kite does not have a base.

14. $\frac{7}{15}$ The probability for selecting the first red ball is $\frac{7}{10}$. For the second selection, there are nine balls left, of which six are red. So the probability of selecting a second red ball is $\frac{6}{9} = \frac{2}{3}$. Therefore, the required probability is $\frac{7}{10} \times \frac{2}{3} = \frac{14}{30} = \frac{7}{15}$. (Examples of other acceptable answers are $\frac{14}{30}$ and $\frac{42}{90}$.)

15. 21 After the first discount of 40%, the price becomes 100% − 40% = 60% of its original price. A second discount of 30% means that the price becomes (0.60)(100% − 30%) = (0.60)(70%) = 42% of the original price. Thus, after the third discount of 50%, the final price becomes (0.42)(100% − 50%) = (0.42)(50%) = 21% of the original price.

16. (E) For December, the difference in average daily temperatures is 60° − 40° = 20°. The differences for average temperatures in January, February, March, and August are 16°, 14°, 16°, and 12°, respectively.

17. (C) The differences for average temperatures in June, July, August, and September are 4°, 8°, 12°, and 10°, respectively. Thus, the mean of these numbers is $\frac{4° + 8° + 12° + 10°}{4} = 8.5°$.

18. 47 50° − 34° = 16°. Then the required percent is $\frac{16°}{34°} \times 100\% \approx 47\%$.

19. 36.95 The interquartile range is the difference between the third quartile and the first quartile, which is 67.5 − 30.55.

20. (C) The number of ways to seat Alex is four, since he cannot be seated on either of the two end seats. Once Alex is seated, there are no further restrictions. So, there are 5! = 120 ways to seat the other five people. Therefore, there are (4)(5!) = 480 ways to seat all six people.

21. (C) Multiply each term by 6 to get $3x + 2x = 6$. Then $5x = 6$, so $x = \frac{6}{5}$.

22. 7 Adding the equations, we get $7a + 7b = 49$. Then divide each term by 7 to get $a + b = 7$.

23. (B, E) $(a^{11})(a^{7}) = a^{18}$. Each of $(a^{9})^{2}$ and $\frac{\sqrt{a^{54}}}{a^{9}}$ simplifies to a^{18}. (Remember that $\sqrt{a^{54}} = a^{27}$.) Choices (A) and (C) cannot be simplified to one term, although they can be factored. Choice (D) simplifies to a^{34}.

24. (B, C, D) $|2x - 7| \le 11$ is equivalent to $-11 \le 2x - 7 \le 11$. Add 7 to each part to get $-4 \le 2x \le 18$. Dividing each part by 2 yields $-2 \le x \le 9$. Thus, each of 0, 7, and 9 satisfies this inequality. The numbers −7 and 11 do not satisfy this inequality.

25. (B) Subtract 5 from each side of $5 + n + n^2 + n^3 = 84$ to get $n + n^2 + n^3 = 79$. Multiply this equation by n to get $n^2 + n^3 + n^4 = 79n$. Then $n + n^2 + n^3 + n^4 = 79n + n = 80n$.

Thus, the arithmetic mean of $n + n^2 + n^3 + n^4$ is $\frac{n + n^2 + n^3 + n^4}{4} = \frac{80n}{4} = 20n$.

Practice Test 1 — Section 2

Directions: Each of Questions 1–9 consists of two quantities. Compare the quantities in Quantities A and B and choose

Ⓐ if Quantity A is greater.
Ⓑ if Quantity B is greater.
Ⓒ if the two quantities are equal.
Ⓓ if the relationship cannot be determined from the information given.

	Quantity A	Quantity B
1. M is the mean of 5, x, and 7	M	$\frac{5+x+M+7}{4}$

Ⓐ Ⓑ Ⓒ Ⓓ

	Quantity A	Quantity B
2. Equation of line 1: $y = mx + b$; Equation of line 2: $y = -\frac{1}{m}x + b$	Slope of line 1	Slope of line 2

Ⓐ Ⓑ Ⓒ Ⓓ

	Quantity A	Quantity B
3. $y > x > N > 2$ and $N = y - x$	N^2	$x^2 + y^2$

Ⓐ Ⓑ Ⓒ Ⓓ

	Quantity A	Quantity B
4. q represents a probability value and $q \neq 0$	$(q)(1 - q)$	0.1

Ⓐ Ⓑ Ⓒ Ⓓ

	Quantity A	Quantity B
5. $2^{m-n} = 2$	m	n

Ⓐ Ⓑ Ⓒ Ⓓ

	Quantity A	Quantity B
6. Define $a \circ b = b^2 - ab$. Then for $2 \circ y = -1$	y	1

Ⓐ Ⓑ Ⓒ Ⓓ

Questions 7–9 use the following inequality: $-15 < x < -11$

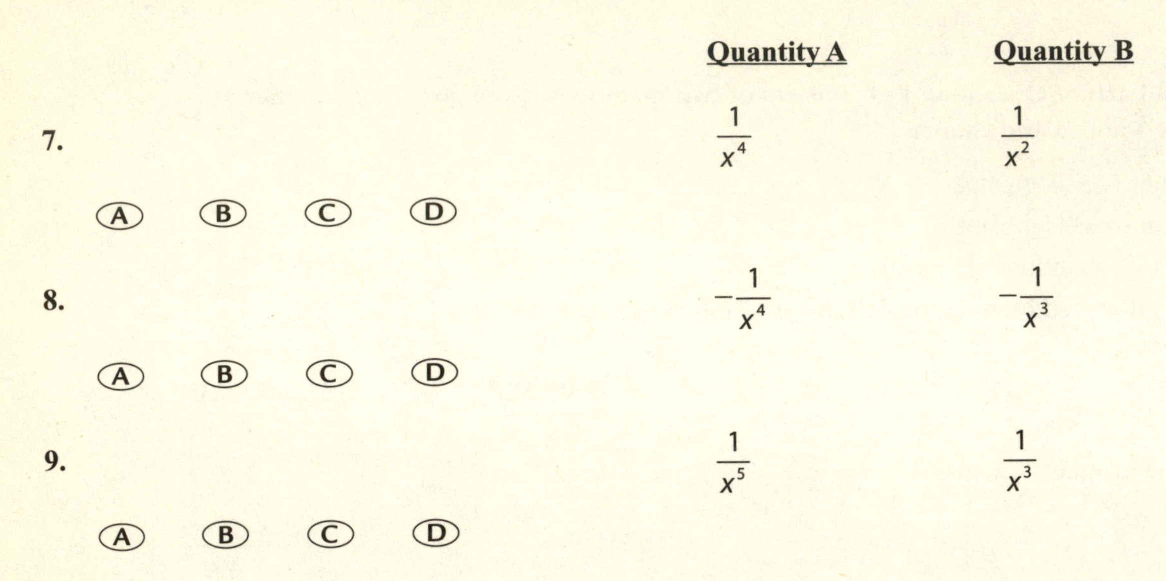

	Quantity A	Quantity B
7.	$\frac{1}{x^4}$	$\frac{1}{x^2}$
8.	$-\frac{1}{x^4}$	$-\frac{1}{x^3}$
9.	$\frac{1}{x^5}$	$\frac{1}{x^3}$

7. (A) (B) (C) (D)

8. (A) (B) (C) (D)

9. (A) (B) (C) (D)

Directions: Questions 10–25 have several different formats. Unless otherwise indicated, select a single answer choice. For numeric entry questions, follow the instructions below.

Numeric Entry Questions

Enter your answer in the answer box(es) below the question.

- Your answer may be an integer, a decimal, or a fraction, and it may be negative.
- If a question asks for a fraction, there will be two boxes—one for the numerator and one for the denominator.
- Equivalent forms of the correct answer, such as 2.5 or 2.50, are all correct. Fractions do not need to be reduced to lowest terms.
- Enter the exact answer unless the question asks you to round your answer.

10. In a large lecture hall, the ratio of men to women is 2:3. If there are 365 people in the lecture hall, how many women are there?

(A) 73
(B) 105
(C) 126
(D) 219
(E) 257

11. The area of a circle is 1. What is the length of its diameter?

Ⓐ $\frac{1}{\pi}$

Ⓑ $\frac{1}{\sqrt{\pi}}$

Ⓒ $\frac{2}{\pi}$

Ⓓ $\frac{2}{\sqrt{\pi}}$

Ⓔ π

12. Look at the following diagram of a rectangular solid:

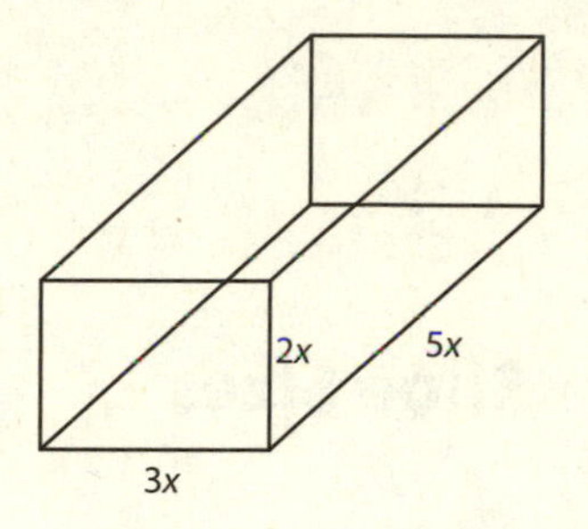

What is the surface area?

Ⓐ $30x^3$

Ⓑ $31x^2$

Ⓒ $50x^2$

Ⓓ $60x^3$

Ⓔ $62x^2$

13. Which of the following are sufficient to determine that the slope of a line is positive? Indicate *all* correct answers.

[A] The x-intercept is five times the y-intercept.

[B] The line contains the point (3, 2) and the x-intercept is positive.

[C] The x-intercept is the negative reciprocal of the y-intercept.

[D] The line is perpendicular to one of the axes.

[E] The sign of the slope and the y-intercept are identical.

[F] The line contains the origin.

14. Which of the following are equivalent to $(x + 10)^2$? Indicate *all* correct answers.

[A] $x^2 + 100$
[B] $(x - 10)^2 + 40x$
[C] $(x)(x + 5) + (5)(x + 5)$
[D] $(x - 5)(x + 5) + (5)(4x + 25)$
[E] $(x + 5)(x + 5) + (10)(x + 8)$

15. The expression $2^n + 2^n$ is equivalent to which one of the following?

(A) 2^{n+1}
(B) 2^{n+2}
(C) 2^{n+3}
(D) 4^n
(E) 2^{n^2}

For Questions 16, 17, and 18, use the following chart.

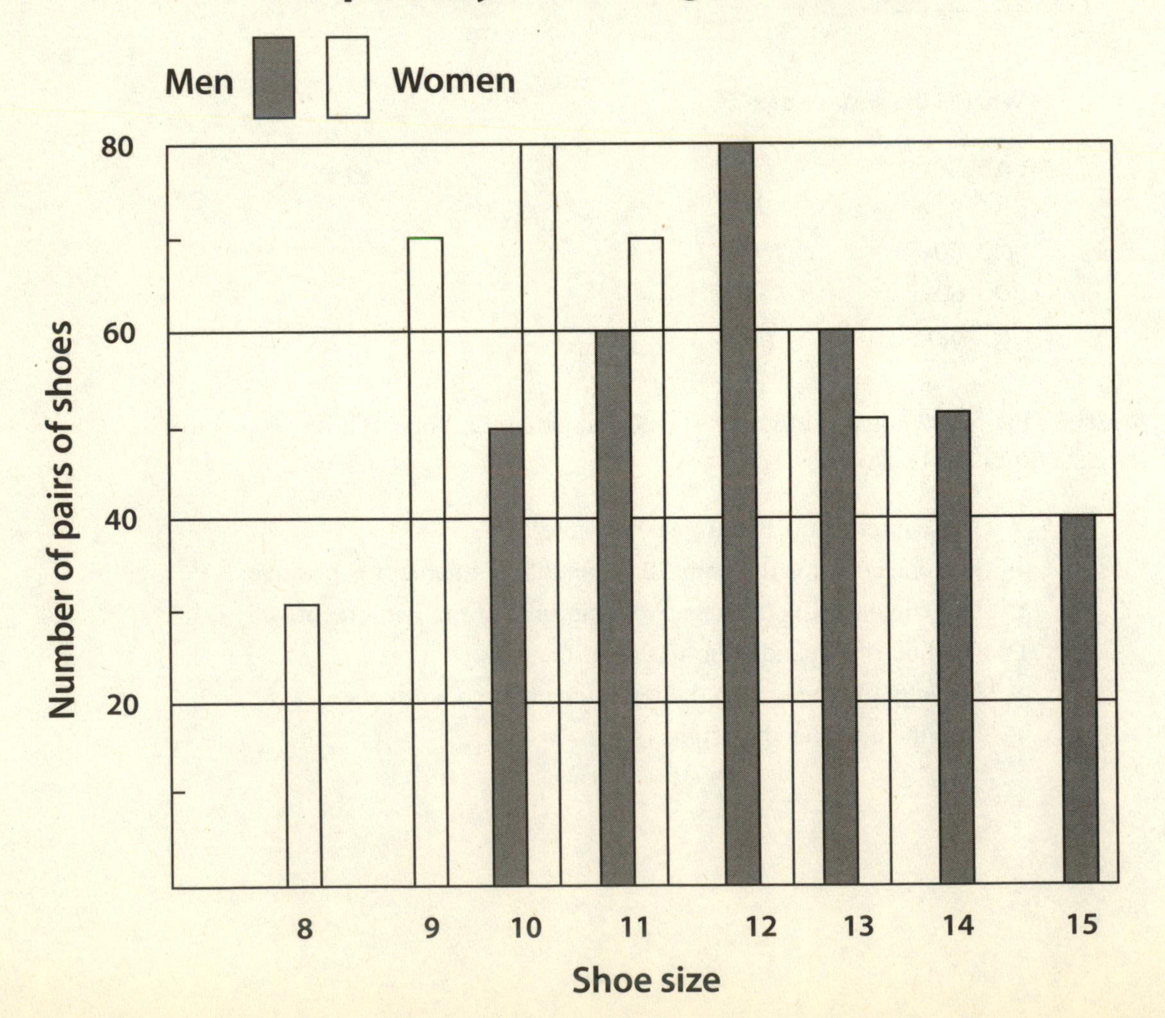

16. If 40% of the women's size 12 shoes are black, and 25% of these black shoes have high heels, how many women's size 12 black shoes do not have high heels?

- (A) 52
- (B) 32
- (C) 28
- (D) 24
- (E) 18

17. The number of pairs of men's shoes that are larger than size 13 is what percent of the total number of pairs of shoes in the store? Write your answer to the nearest whole number.

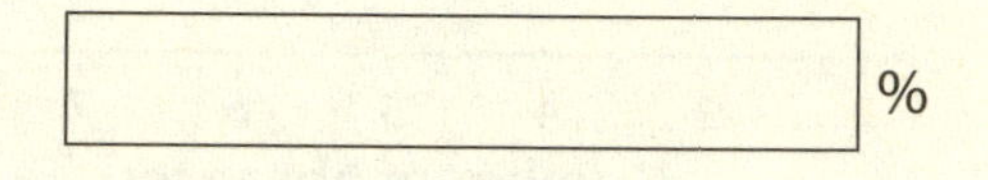 %

18. For women's shoes, the average price for any given size is 10% higher than the average price for the next smallest size. Suppose that the average price for a pair of women's shoes of size 8 is $200. Then the selling price for all women's shoes of size 10 would be how much greater than the selling price for all women's shoes of size 8?

$ [ ]

19. There are seven men and nine women in a room. A committee of five people is to be chosen. If the committee has three men and two women, how many different committees are possible?

- (A) 1,260
- (B) 1,250
- (C) 1,245
- (D) 1,240
- (E) 1,225

20. Look at the following diagram.

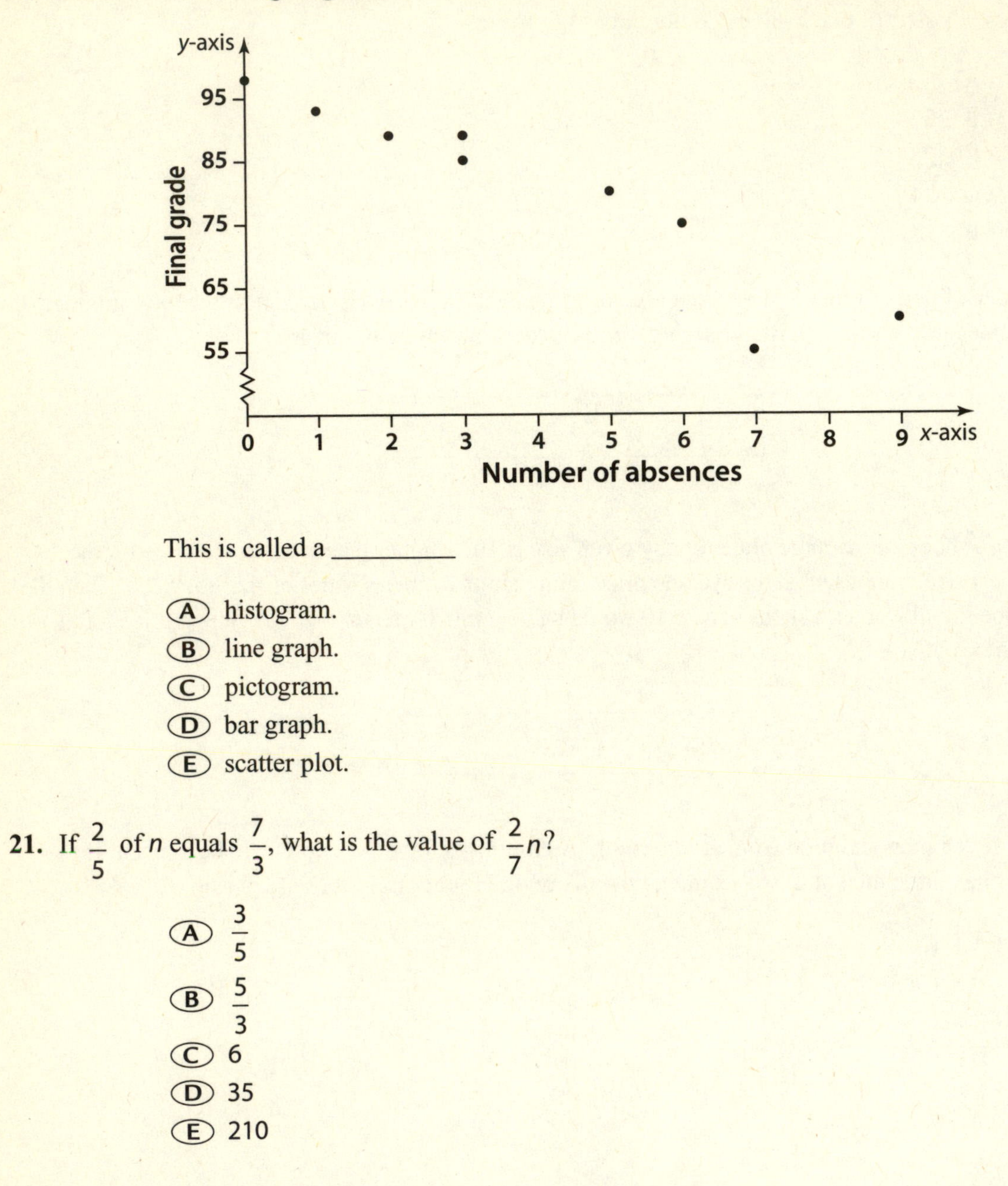

This is called a ________

Ⓐ histogram.
Ⓑ line graph.
Ⓒ pictogram.
Ⓓ bar graph.
Ⓔ scatter plot.

21. If $\frac{2}{5}$ of n equals $\frac{7}{3}$, what is the value of $\frac{2}{7}n$?

Ⓐ $\frac{3}{5}$
Ⓑ $\frac{5}{3}$
Ⓒ 6
Ⓓ 35
Ⓔ 210

22. If $\frac{x-6}{y-4} = 0$, which of the following is true?

(A) $x = 0$ and $y \neq 0$
(B) $x = 6$ and $y = 4$
(C) $x \neq 6$ and $y \neq 4$
(D) $x = 6$ and $y \neq 4$
(E) $x \neq 6$ and $y = 4$

For Questions 23 and 24, use the following diagram of a Norman window, which consists of a rectangle surmounted by a semicircle.

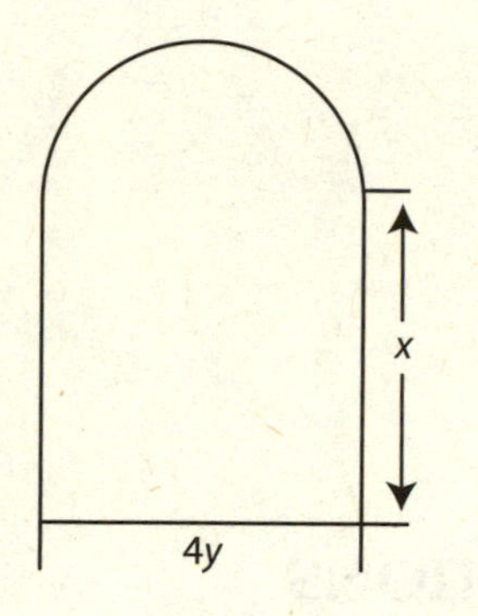

23. What is the perimeter of this figure?

(A) $2x + 8y + 4\pi y$
(B) $2x + 4y + 4\pi y$
(C) $2x + 4y + 2\pi y$
(D) $2x + 4y + \pi y$
(E) $2x + y + \frac{\pi y}{2}$

24. What is the area of this figure?

(A) $xy + \frac{\pi y^2}{2}$
(B) $4xy + 4\pi y^2$
(C) $4xy + 2\pi y^2$
(D) $4xy + \pi y^2$
(E) $4xy + \frac{\pi y^2}{4}$

25. The figure below shows equilateral triangle ABC inscribed in a circle. If $AB = 6$, what is the combined area of the shaded regions?

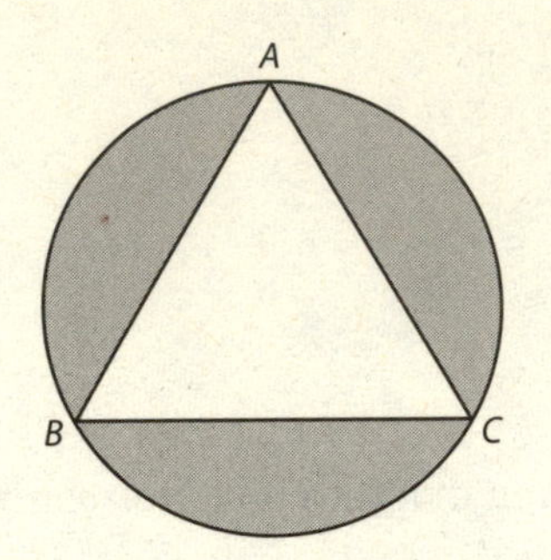

Ⓐ $4\pi - \sqrt{3}$
Ⓑ $6\pi - 4\sqrt{3}$
Ⓒ $9\pi - 4\sqrt{3}$
Ⓓ $12\pi - 9\sqrt{3}$
Ⓔ $18\pi - 16\sqrt{3}$

ANSWERS AND EXPLANATIONS

1. (C) $M = \frac{5 + x + 7}{3}$, which means that $3M = 5 + x + 7$. Then

$$\frac{5 + x + M + 7}{4} = \frac{3M + M}{4} = \frac{4M}{4} = M.$$

2. (D) Either of m and $-\frac{1}{m}$ can be positive and the other will be negative.

3. (B) $N^2 = (y - x)^2 = y^2 - 2xy + x^2$. Since $x, y > 2$, both x, y are positive. Thus, $y^2 - 2xy + x^2$ must be less than $x^2 + y^2$.

4. (D) The value of q is unknown. If $q = \frac{1}{2}$, then $(q)(1 - q) = \left(\frac{1}{2}\right)\left(\frac{1}{2}\right) = \frac{1}{4} > 0.1$.
If $q = 0.1$, then $(q)(1 - q) = (0.1)(0.9) = 0.09 < 0.1$.

5. (A) Since $2^1 = 2$, $m - n = 1$. Thus, $m = n + 1$, which means that $m > n$.

6. (C) By definition, $2 \circ y = y^2 - 2y$. Then $y^2 - 2y = -1$, which can be written as $y^2 - 2y + 1 = 0$. Factor the left side to get $(y - 1)(y - 1) = 0$. Thus, $y = 1$.

7. (B) For $-15 < x < -11$, $x^2 < x^4$. If the reciprocal of each quantity is used, the inequality sign is reversed. Thus, $\frac{1}{x^2} > \frac{1}{x^4}$.

8. (B) For a negative value of x, $-\frac{1}{x^4}$ has a negative value and $-\frac{1}{x^3}$ has a positive value.

9. (A) For $-15 < x < -11$, $x^5 < x^3$. By taking the reciprocal of each quantity, the inequality sign is reversed. Thus, $\frac{1}{x^5} > \frac{1}{x^3}$.

10. (D) Let $2x$ represent the number of men and $3x$ represent the number of women. Then $2x + 3x = 365$, which becomes $5x = 365$. This means that $x = 73$. Thus, the number of women is (3)(73) = 219.

11. (D) $1 = \pi r^2$, so $r = \sqrt{\frac{1}{\pi}} = \frac{1}{\sqrt{\pi}}$. Then the diameter must be $(2)\left(\frac{1}{\sqrt{\pi}}\right) = \frac{2}{\sqrt{\pi}}$.

12. (E) The surface area is $(2)(2)(3x) + (2)(2x)(5x) + (2)(3x)(5x) = 12x^2 + 20x^2 + 30x^2 = 62x^2$.

13. (C) If the x-intercept is the negative reciprocal of the y-intercept, then one of x and y is negative and the other is positive. A line containing these two intercepts must be positive. None of the other answer choices gives sufficient information for determining a positive slope.

14. (B, D) $(x + 10)^2 = x^2 + 20x + 100$. For choice (B), $(x - 10)^2 + 40x = x^2 - 20x + 100 + 40x = x^2 + 20x + 100$. For choice (D), $(x - 5)(x + 5) + (5)(4x + 25) = x^2 - 25 + 20x + 125 = x^2 + 20x + 100$. Choice (A) is obviously incorrect. The simplified expressions for choices (C) and (E) are $x^2 + 10x + 25$ and $x^2 + 20x + 105$.

15. (A) $2^n + 2^n = (2)(2^n) = (2^1)(2^n) = 2^{n+1}$.

16. (E) There are 60 pairs of women's shoes in size 12. Then (0.40)(60) = 24 pairs of size 12 are black. Of these, 100% – 25% = 75% do not have high heels. Thus, the required number is (0.75)(24) = 18.

17. 13 There are 340 pairs of men's shoes and 360 pairs of women's shoes. The number of pairs of men's shoes that are larger than size 13 is 90. Thus, the required percent is

$$\frac{90}{700} \times 100\% \approx 13\%.$$

18. 13,360 There are 30 pairs of size 8 shoes, for which the total selling price is (30($200) = $6,000. The average price of each pair of size 9 shoes is ($200)(1.10) = $220, and the average price of each size 10 shoes is ($220)(1.10) = $242. Since there are 80 pairs of size 10 shoes, the total selling price is (80)($242) = $19,360. Thus, the difference in total price is $19,360 – $6,000 = $13,360.

19. (A) The number of ways to choose three men is ${}_7C_3 = \frac{7 \times 6 \times 5}{3 \times 2 \times 1} = 35$. The number of ways to choose two women is ${}_9C_2 = \frac{9 \times 8}{2 \times 1} = 36$. Therefore, the number of different committees is (35)(36) = 1,260.

20. (E) A scatter plot is a graph of points that represent ordered pairs of variables.

21. (B) We are given that $\frac{2}{5}n = \frac{7}{3}$, so $n = \frac{7}{3} \times \frac{5}{2} = \frac{35}{6}$. Thus, $\frac{2}{7} \times \frac{35}{6} = \frac{70}{42} = \frac{5}{3}$.

22. (D) Whenever a fraction has a value of zero, the numerator must equal zero and the denominator must not equal zero. Then $x - 6 = 0$ and $y - 4 \neq 0$, which means that $x = 6$ and $y \neq 4$.

23. (C) The base of the rectangle is $4y$ and there are two heights whose combined lengths are $2x$. The semicircle at the top contains a diameter of length $4y$, so its length is $\left(\frac{1}{2}\pi\right)(4y) = 2\pi y$. Thus, the perimeter is $2x + 4y + 2\pi y$.

24. (C) The area of the rectangular portion is the product of the base and height, which is $4xy$. For the semicircle, its radius is $\left(\frac{1}{2}\right)(4y) = 2y$. Then the area of the semicircle is $\left(\frac{1}{2}\pi\right)(2y)^2 = \left(\frac{1}{2}\pi\right)(4y^2) = 2\pi y^2$. Thus, the area of the figure is $4xy + 2\pi y^2$.

25. (D) Redraw the figure and connect the center of the circle (point O) with points B and C. Also, draw $\overline{OE}$ perpendicular to $\overline{BC}$ at point E.

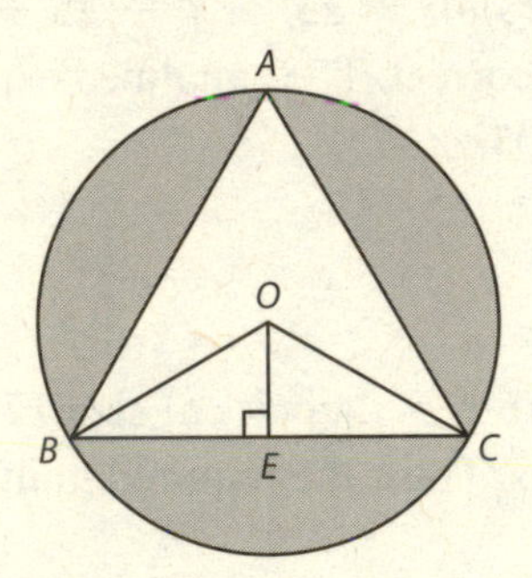

We know that $m\angle ABC = 60°$ and it can be proven that $\overline{OB}$ bisects $\angle ABC$. This means that ΔBOE is a 30°-60°-90° right triangle, with $m\angle OBE = 30°$. It can be shown that E is the midpoint of $\overline{BC}$, so $BE = 3$. $\overline{OB}$ is a radius and also the hypotenuse of ΔBOE. We determine that $m\angle BOE = 60°$ and since $BE = 3$, $OB = \left(\frac{3}{\sqrt{3}}\right)(2) = \frac{6}{\sqrt{3}} = \frac{6}{\sqrt{3}} \times \frac{\sqrt{3}}{\sqrt{3}} = \frac{6\sqrt{3}}{3} = 2\sqrt{3}$. Then the area of the circle is $(\pi)(2\sqrt{3})^2 = 12\pi$. The area of ΔABC is $\frac{6^2}{4}\sqrt{3} = 9\sqrt{3}$. The area of the combined shaded regions is the difference between the areas of the circle and the triangle, which is $12\pi - 9\sqrt{3}$.

Practice Test 2

Section 1

Directions: Each of Questions 1–9 consists of two quantities. Compare the quantities in Quantities A and B and choose

(A) if Quantity A is greater.
(B) if Quantity B is greater.
(C) if the two quantities are equal.
(D) if the relationship cannot be determined from the information given.

	Quantity A	Quantity B
1. $c^2 = 16$ and $d^2 = 25$	c	d

(A) (B) (C) (D)

	Quantity A	Quantity B
2. Look at the following diagram	c	$180 - c$

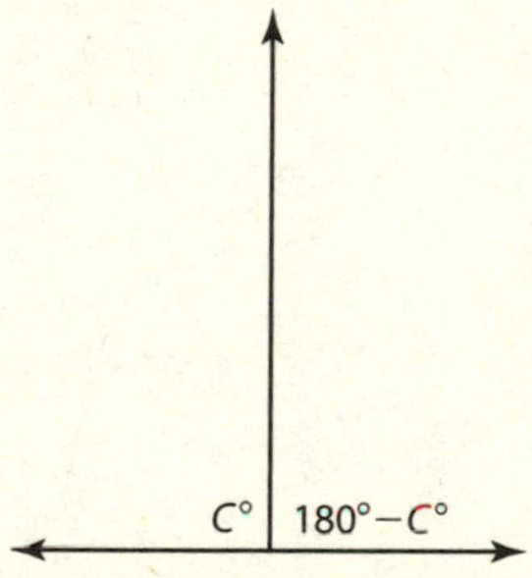

$c°$ | $180° - c°$

(A) (B) (C) (D)

	Quantity A	Quantity B
3.	$\frac{2^{102} - 2^{101}}{2}$	2^{100}

(A) (B) (C) (D)

	Quantity A	Quantity B
4. $2x - 5 = 10$	$(2x - 7)^2$	64

(A) (B) (C) (D)

5. Look at the following graph, in which the equation of line L is $y = mx + b$.

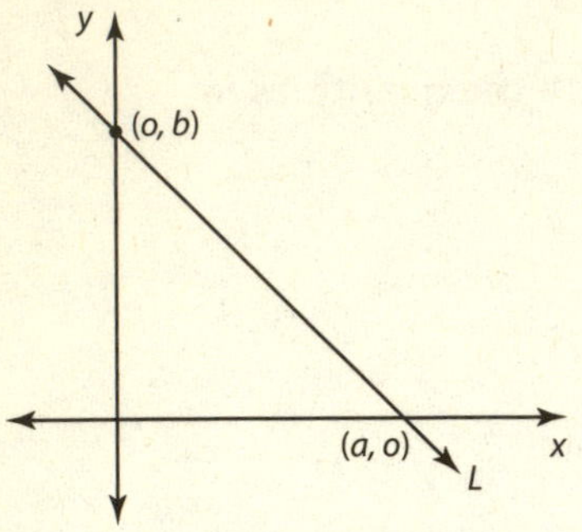

	Quantity A	Quantity B
	m	$\frac{b}{a}$

Ⓐ Ⓑ Ⓒ Ⓓ

	Quantity A	Quantity B
6. $m > 100$ and $n > 100$	$\frac{1}{1/m + 1/n}$	$\frac{1}{m} + \frac{1}{n}$

Ⓐ Ⓑ Ⓒ Ⓓ

	Quantity A	Quantity B
7.	$(-9{,}999)^{9{,}998}$	$(-9{,}998)^{9{,}999}$

Ⓐ Ⓑ Ⓒ Ⓓ

	Quantity A	Quantity B
8.	Ratio of 2 inches to 5 feet	$\frac{2}{5}$

Ⓐ Ⓑ Ⓒ Ⓓ

9. Test scores are normally distributed. A score of 1,400 lies in the 80th percentile and a score of 1,500 lies in the 90th percentile.

Quantity A	Quantity B
The value of the 85th percentile	1,450

Ⓐ Ⓑ Ⓒ Ⓓ

Directions: Questions 10–25 have several different formats. Unless otherwise indicated, select a single answer choice. For numeric entry questions, follow the instructions below.

Numeric Entry Questions

Enter your answer in the answer box(es) below the question.

- Your answer may be an integer, a decimal, or a fraction, and it may be negative.
- If a question asks for a fraction, there will be two boxes—one for the numerator and one for the denominator.
- Equivalent forms of the correct answer, such as 2.5 or 2.50, are all correct. Fractions do not need to be reduced to lowest terms.
- Enter the exact answer unless the question asks you to round your answer.

10. You are reading a book from the top of page 222 through the bottom of page 358. How many pages have you read?

Ⓐ 136
Ⓑ 137
Ⓒ 138
Ⓓ 579
Ⓔ 580

11. Define the symbol □ as follows: $a \square b = ab^2 - b$. What is the value of $-5 \square 3$?

Ⓐ 222
Ⓑ −5
Ⓒ −30
Ⓓ −35
Ⓔ −48

12. For a given rectangle, which of the following changes would *not* affect the value of the area? Indicate *all* correct answers.

[A] Increase the length by 10% and decrease the width by 10%.
[B] Decrease the length by 20% and increase the width by 25%.
[C] Increase the length by 20% and decrease the width by 25%.
[D] Increase the length by 50% and decrease the width by $33\frac{1}{3}$%.
[E] Increase the length by 100% and decrease the width by 50%.
[F] Decrease the length by 50% and increase the width by 50%.

13. Select *two* numbers whose product is greater than 55.

[A] 6
[B] 8
[C] -5
[D] -7
[E] -9

14. If $3x + 5$ is an odd integer, what is the sum of the next two consecutive odd integers?

(A) $6x + 13$
(B) $6x + 14$
(C) $6x + 15$
(D) $6x + 16$
(E) $6x + 17$

15. If x pounds of fruit cost c cents, how many pounds of fruit can be bought for d dollars?

(A) $\frac{100dx}{c}$
(B) $100cdx$
(C) $\frac{100c}{dx}$
(D) $\frac{cx}{100d}$
(E) $\frac{1}{100cdx}$

For Questions 16, 17, and 18, use the following chart.

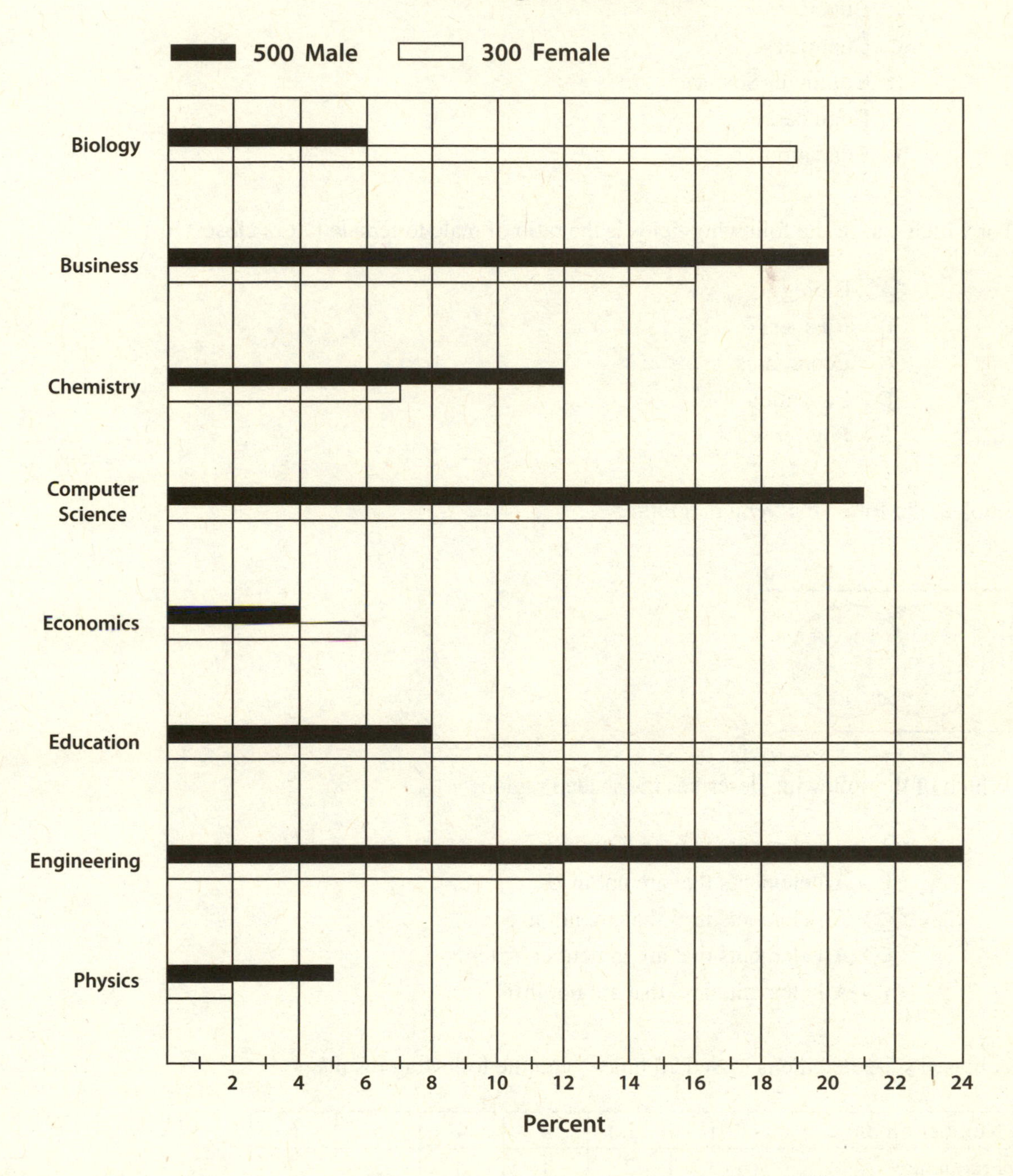

16. For the field of computer science, the number of male tutors is how much larger than the number of female tutors?

17. For which of the following fields does the number of female tutors exceed 7% of all tutors? Indicate *all* correct answers.

- [A] Biology
- [B] Business
- [C] Chemistry
- [D] Computer Science
- [E] Engineering
- [F] Education

18. For which one of the following fields is the ratio of male to female tutors closest to 1:1?

- (A) Biology
- (B) Business
- (C) Economics
- (D) Education
- (E) Physics

19. Look at the following Venn diagram:

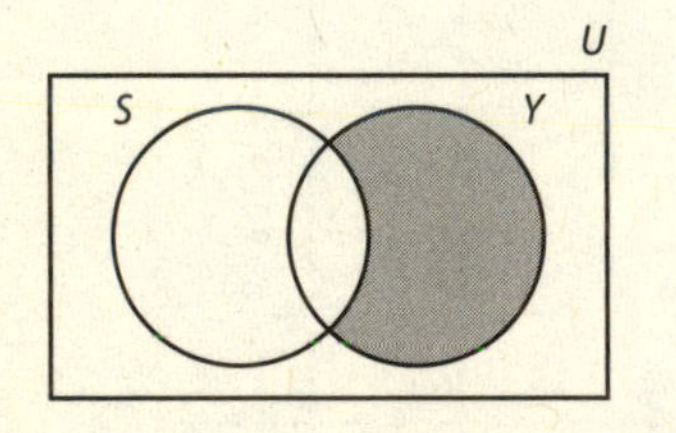

Which of the following describes the shaded region?

- (A) All elements in both Y and S
- (B) All elements that are not in U
- (C) All elements in Y that are not in S
- (D) All elements that are in neither Y nor S
- (E) All elements in S that are not in Y

20. A biased six-sided die is tossed 20 times, with the following results.

Number on die	1	2	3	4	5	6
Frequency	3	2	1	8	2	4

What is the expected value?

[ ]

21. If $x + y = 12$, what is the value of $\left(x+\frac{y}{3}\right)+\left(y+\frac{x}{3}\right)$?

(A) 20
(B) 16
(C) 15
(D) 12
(E) 10

22. The following figure is a rectangular solid.

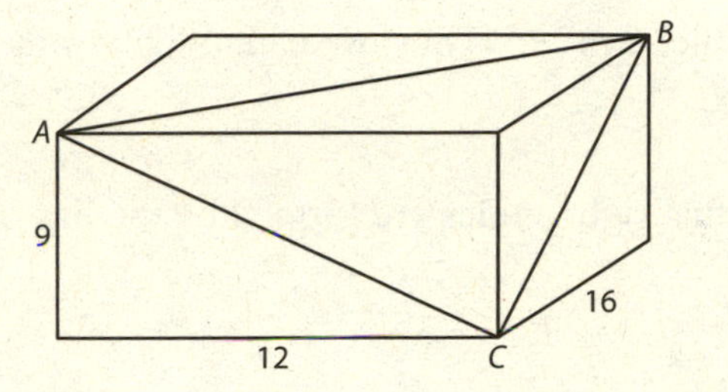

To the nearest integer, what is the perimeter of ΔABC?

(A) 74
(B) 53
(C) 42
(D) 37
(E) 32

23. What is the smallest number such that when it is divided by each of 3, 5, and 7, the remainder is 2?

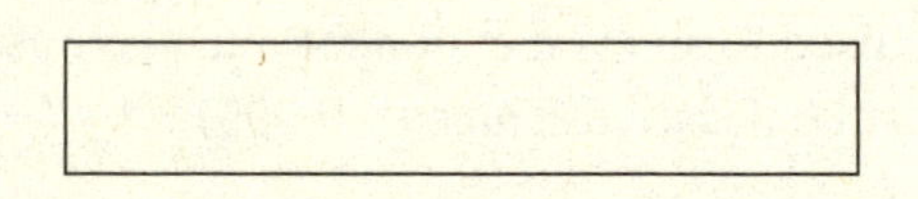

24. If $\sqrt{x-3} = 5$ and $\sqrt{2y-3} = 9$, what is the sum of x and y?

(A) 46
(B) 52
(C) 59
(D) 65
(E) 70

25. Which one of the following is *not* a factor of $2^6 \times 7^5 \times 11^4$?

(A) $2^4 \times 11^3$
(B) $7^4 \times 11^4$
(C) 11^2
(D) 7^3
(E) $2^5 \times 7^6$

ANSWERS AND EXPLANATIONS

1. **(D)** The value of c is either 4 or -4. The value of d is either 5 or -5. Thus, we cannot determine which of c or d is larger.

2. **(D)** Although it appears as if c is 90, we cannot assume that right angles are formed by the line and ray. Thus we cannot determine the value of c.

3. **(C)** $\frac{2^{102} - 2^{101}}{2} = \frac{2^{101}(2-1)}{2} = \frac{2^{101}}{2} = 2^{100}$.

4. **(C)** $2x - 5 = 10$ becomes $2x = 15$. Then $2x - 7 = 15 - 7 = 8$, and $8^2 = 64$.

5. **(B)** From the diagram, both $a > 0$ and $b > 0$. The value of the slope, identified as m, is $\frac{0-b}{a-0} = -\frac{b}{a}$. Then m is negative, whereas $\frac{b}{a}$ is positive. Thus, $\frac{b}{a} > m$.

6. **(A)** Let $m, n = 1{,}000$. Then $\frac{1}{1/m + 1/n} = \frac{1}{1/1{,}000 + 1/1{,}000} = \frac{1}{1/500} = 500$. This value is much larger than $\frac{1}{1{,}000} + \frac{1}{1{,}000}$. Any values of $m, n > 100$ would produce similar results.

7. **(A)** Any negative number raised to an even exponent must be positive. Any negative number raised to an odd exponent must be negative. Thus, $(-9{,}999)^{9{,}998} > (-9{,}998)^{9{,}999}$.

8. **(B)** Change 5 feet to 60 inches. Then the ratio of 2 inches to 60 inches is equivalent to $\frac{2}{60} = \frac{1}{30}$, which is less than $\frac{2}{5}$.

9. **(B)** Both 1,400 and 1,500 lie above the mean. Consider the following diagram of the normal distribution.

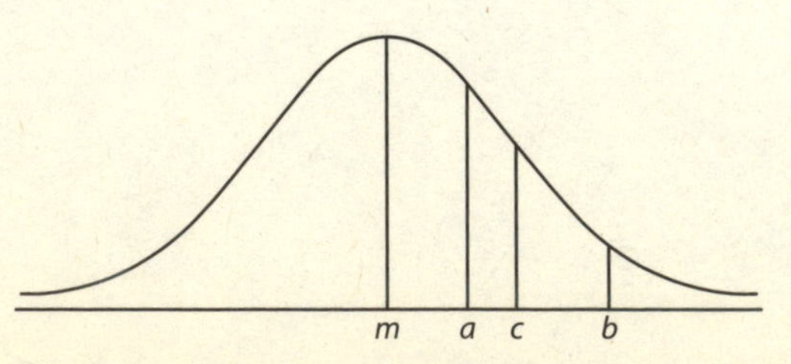

Let a represent 1,400 (80th percentile) and b represent 1,500 (90th percentile). The area of the graph between the 85th percentile and the 80th percentile is equal to the area between the 85th percentile and the 90th percentile. This means that the area between a and c must equal the area between c and b. But the curve drops sharply as the raw score greater than the mean increases. In order for these areas to be equal, c must lie closer to a than to b. Then the 85th percentile must be less than the average (mean) of a and b. Thus, the 85th percentile is less than $\frac{1,400+1,500}{2} = 1,450$.

10. (B) You must count the first page, which is page 222. Then the number of additional pages is $358 - 222 = 136$. Thus, there is a total of 137 pages read.

11. (E) $(-5)(3)(3) - 3 = -45 - 3 = -48$.

12. (B, D, E) The area of the original rectangle is ℓw, where ℓ represents the length and w represents the width. For choice (B), the area is $(0.80)(1.25w) = \ell w$. For choice (D), the area is $(1.50\ell l)\left(\frac{2}{3}w\right) = \ell w$. For choice (E), the area is $(2\ell)(0.50w) = \ell w$. Choice (A) is wrong because $(1.10\ell)(0.90w) = 0.99\ell w \neq \ell w$. Choice (C) is wrong because $(1.20\ell)(0.75w) = 0.90\ell w \neq \ell w$. Choice (F) is wrong because $(0.50\ell)(1.50w) = 0.75\ell w \neq \ell w$.

13. (D, E) We must have either two positive numbers or two negative numbers. The only two available positive numbers are 6 and 8, but their product (48) is less than 55. Using choices D and E, their product is $(-7)(-9) = 63$, which is greater than 55. None of the other two combinations of negative numbers has a product greater than 55.

14. (D) The next two consecutive odd integers are $3x + 7$ and $3x + 9$. Then $(3x + 7) + (3x + 9) = 6x + 16$.

15. (A) Change d dollars to $100d$ cents. Let p represent the number of pounds of fruit. Then $\frac{x}{c} = \frac{p}{100d}$. Cross-multiply to get $pc = 100dx$. Thus, by dividing both sides by c, we get $p = \frac{100dx}{c}$.

16. 63 The number of male tutors in computer science is $(0.21)(500) = 105$. The number of female tutors in computer science is $(0.14)(300) = 42$. Thus, their difference is 63.

17. (A, F) Seven percent of all tutors is $(0.07)(800) = 56$. The number of female tutors in biology is $(0.19)(300) = 57$. The number of female tutors in education is $(0.24)(300) = 72$. The number of female tutors in each of the other fields is less than 56. The number of female tutors in business, chemistry, computer science, and engineering is 48, 21, 42, and 36, respectively.

Another way to do question 17: 7% of the entire faculty is $(.07)(800) = 56$. Then find the fields for which the percentage of women is greater than 56/300, or 18.6%. This is true only for A and F. You don't have to go through the calculations for all the choices.

18. (C) In the field of economics, there are $(0.04)(500) = 20$ male tutors and $(0.06)(300) = 18$ female tutors. This ratio of 20:18 is closest to 1:1 than the ratio of male to female tutors for any other field.

Three of the choices can be eliminated by recognizing that for a 1:1 ratio, the number of females must be close to the number of males, and this is true only for Economics (C) and Physics (E), and then choose the correct one by doing the calculations for them.

19. (C) The shaded region lies inside circle Y but not inside circle S. Thus, it represents elements that belong to Y but not to S.

20. 3.8 Change each frequency to a ratio by dividing the given frequency by 20. Then the expected value is the sum of the products of each number on the die by its respective ratio. Thus, the expected value is

$$(1)\left(\frac{3}{20}\right) + (2)\left(\frac{2}{20}\right) + (3)\left(\frac{1}{20}\right) + (4)\left(\frac{8}{20}\right) + (5)\left(\frac{2}{20}\right) + (6)\left(\frac{4}{20}\right) = \frac{76}{20} = 3.8.$$

21. (B) $\left(x + \frac{y}{3}\right) + \left(y + \frac{x}{3}\right) = (x + y) + \left(\frac{x}{3} + \frac{y}{3}\right) = (x + y) + \left(\frac{x + y}{3}\right) = 12 + \frac{12}{3} = 12 + 4 = 16.$

22. (B) $AC = \sqrt{9^2 + 12^2} = \sqrt{81 + 144} = \sqrt{225} = 15.$

$BC = \sqrt{9^2 + 16^2} = \sqrt{81 + 256} = \sqrt{337}.$

$AB = \sqrt{12^2 + 16^2} = \sqrt{144 + 256} = \sqrt{400} = 20.$

Therefore, the perimeter of ΔABC is $35 + \sqrt{337} \approx 53$.

23. 107 The least common multiple of 3, 5, and 7 is $(3)(5)(7) = 105$. Thus, the smallest number for which there would be a remainder of 2 when dividing by each of 3, 5, and 7 is $105 + 2 = 107$.

24. (E) Squaring each side of the equation $\sqrt{x - 3} = 5$ leads to $x - 3 = 25$, so $x = 28$. Squaring each side of the equation $\sqrt{2y - 3} = 9$ leads to $2y - 3 = 81$. Then $2y = 84$, so $y = 42$. Thus, the sum of x and y is 70.

25. (E) When a number is expressed in prime factorization form, each of its factors must contain only the given prime factor(s), and the exponents of these factor(s) must be less than or equal to the corresponding exponents of the prime factors of the number. Note that a prime factor need not contain each prime factor of the given number. The number $2^5 \times 7^6$ is not a factor of $2^6 \times 7^5 \times 11^4$ because 7^6 contains a higher exponent than 7^5.

Practice Test 2 — Section 2

Directions: Each of Questions 1–9 consists of two quantities. Compare the quantities in Quantities A and B and choose

Ⓐ if Quantity A is greater.
Ⓑ if Quantity B is greater.
Ⓒ if the two quantities are equal.
Ⓓ if the relationship cannot be determined from the information given.

	Quantity A	Quantity B
1. Look at the following diagram:	x	y
2. $-110 < x < -101$	$2x$	$\frac{1}{x}$
3. Circle A has an area of 4π and circle B has a circumference of 4π.	The radius of circle A	The radius of circle B
4.	$4(2x + 2y)$	$2(4x + 4y)$

1. Look at the following diagram:

45°
70°
$y°$
$x°$

Quantity A	Quantity B
x	y

Ⓐ Ⓑ Ⓒ Ⓓ

2. $-110 < x < -101$

Quantity A	Quantity B
$2x$	$\frac{1}{x}$

Ⓐ Ⓑ Ⓒ Ⓓ

3. Circle A has an area of 4π and circle B has a circumference of 4π.

Quantity A	Quantity B
The radius of circle A	The radius of circle B

Ⓐ Ⓑ Ⓒ Ⓓ

4.

Quantity A	Quantity B
$4(2x + 2y)$	$2(4x + 4y)$

Ⓐ Ⓑ Ⓒ Ⓓ

5. Look at the following diagram, in which line L_1 is parallel to line L_2.

	Quantity A	**Quantity B**
	50	$2x - 200$

Ⓐ Ⓑ Ⓒ Ⓓ

6. Car *A* is traveling at 60 miles per hour for one mile. Car *B* is traveling at 50 miles per hour for one and one-half miles.

	Number of minutes for car *A*	Number of minutes for car *B*

Ⓐ Ⓑ Ⓒ Ⓓ

7. $x^4 = y^4$	x	y

Ⓐ Ⓑ Ⓒ Ⓓ

8. $b > 0$	$\sqrt{b^2 + 4}$	$b + 2$

Ⓐ Ⓑ Ⓒ Ⓓ

9. *WXYZ* is a square, as shown below:

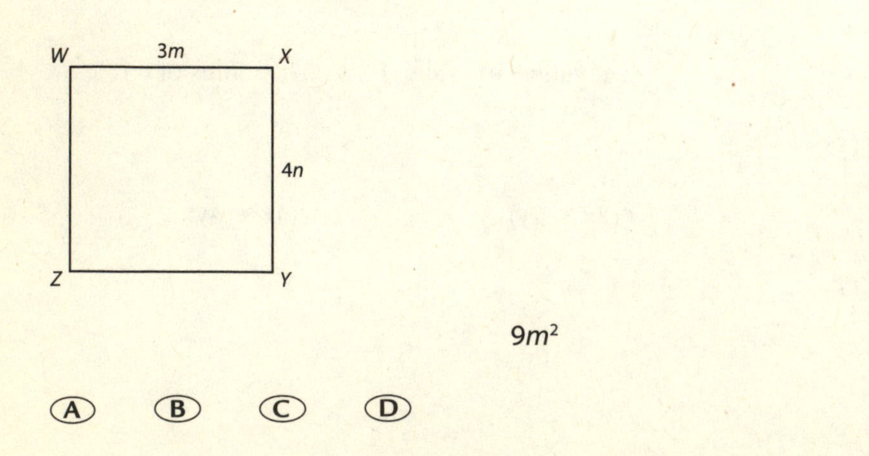

	$9m^2$	$16n^2$

Ⓐ Ⓑ Ⓒ Ⓓ

Directions: Questions 10–25 have several different formats. Unless otherwise indicated, select a single answer choice. For numeric entry questions, follow the instructions below.

Numeric Entry Questions

Enter your answer in the answer box(es) below the question.

- Your answer may be an integer, a decimal, or a fraction, and it may be negative.
- If a question asks for a fraction, there will be two boxes—one for the numerator and one for the denominator.
- Equivalent forms of the correct answer, such as 2.5 or 2.50, are all correct. Fractions do not need to be reduced to lowest terms.
- Enter the exact answer unless the question asks you to round your answer.

10. Look at the following figure. *Note:* The figure is *not* drawn to scale.

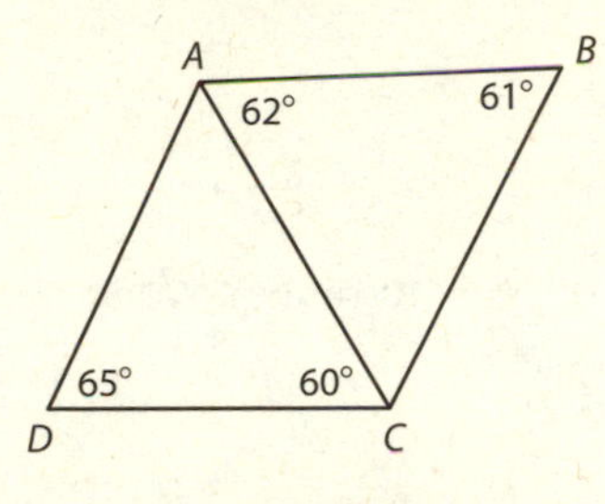

Which is the largest side?

Ⓐ $\overline{AD}$

Ⓑ $\overline{DC}$

Ⓒ $\overline{AC}$

Ⓓ $\overline{AB}$

Ⓔ $\overline{BC}$

11. If $3(2x - 1) + 4 = 2x$, what is the value of x?

Ⓐ $-\frac{1}{8}$

Ⓑ $-\frac{1}{4}$

Ⓒ $-\frac{1}{2}$

Ⓓ $\frac{1}{4}$

Ⓔ $\frac{1}{2}$

12. In a small group of children, one girl who is looking at all the other children sees an equal number of boys and girls. One boy who is looking at all the other children sees twice as many girls as boys. Which of the following is the correct composition of this group?

Ⓐ 3 boys and 4 girls
Ⓑ 3 boys and 3 girls
Ⓒ 4 boys and 3 girls
Ⓓ 4 boys and 5 girls
Ⓔ 5 boys and 4 girls

13. Currently, John is 16 years old and his father is 50 years old. In how many years will John be half as old as his father?

Ⓐ 10
Ⓑ 12
Ⓒ 16
Ⓓ 18
Ⓔ 20

14. If 3 bligs equals 5 bloogs and 7 bloogs equals 8 blugs, what is the ratio of bligs to blugs? Write your answer as a fraction.

15. The figure shown below is a kite, for which $AC > BD$.

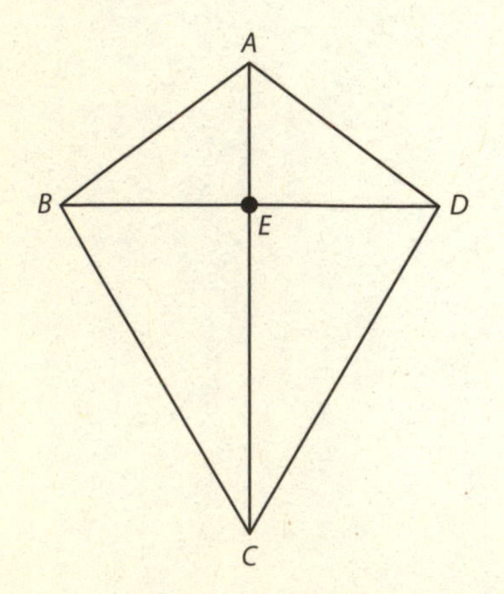

If $AB = 10$, $AE = 6$, and $BC = 17$, what is the product of BD and AC?

For Questions 16–20, use the following circle graphs. There are a total of 2,000 employees.

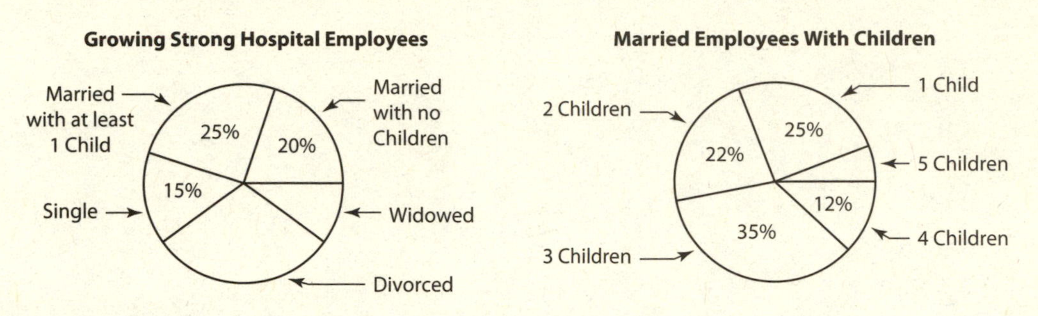

16. The number of divorced employees is three times the number of widowed employees. How many divorced employees are there?

Ⓐ 200
Ⓑ 300
Ⓒ 400
Ⓓ 500
Ⓔ 600

17. How many employees are married and have five children?

Ⓐ 75
Ⓑ 60
Ⓒ 54
Ⓓ 45
Ⓔ 30

18. What is the combined total of the number of employees who are either single or married with at least 3 children?

19. Of the employees who are married with just one child, there are four times as many of them who work full-time as work part-time. Assuming that all employees of this hospital work either full-time or part-time, the number of full-time employees who are married with just one child represent what percent of the entire number of employees?

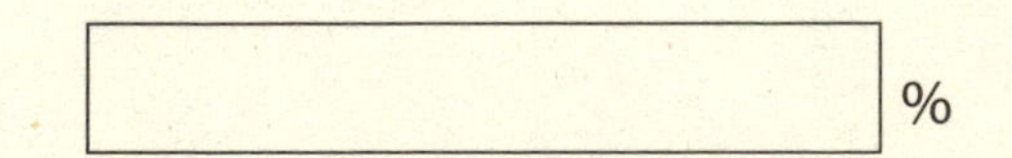 %

20. Next year, the Growing Strong Hospital plans to increase its staff by 10%. If all the new employees happen to be single, then the number of single employees will increase by what percent?

(A) $66\frac{2}{3}\%$
(B) 40%
(C) $33\frac{1}{3}\%$
(D) 20%
(E) 10%

21. Which of the following is equivalent to $\frac{(5x^4)^2(x^3)}{5x^4}$?

(A) x^3
(B) $5x^3$
(C) x^7
(D) $5x^7$
(E) $5x^{15}$

22. Given the data, 2, 2, 5, 7, 9, and 17, what is the sum of the mean, median, and mode?

(A) 13
(B) 14
(C) 15
(D) 16
(E) 17

23. In a group of 35 students, all of them take at least one of the subjects French and Spanish. If 25 students take Spanish and 10 students take both languages, how many students take French but not Spanish?

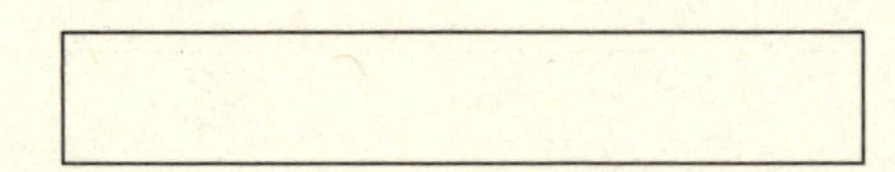

24. A radio that usually sells for $60 is discounted 25% on Monday. On Wednesday, the price is further discounted another 10% from Monday' s price. If there is a state sales tax of 4%, what would be the final price of this radio? Round off your answer to the nearest dollar.

$ 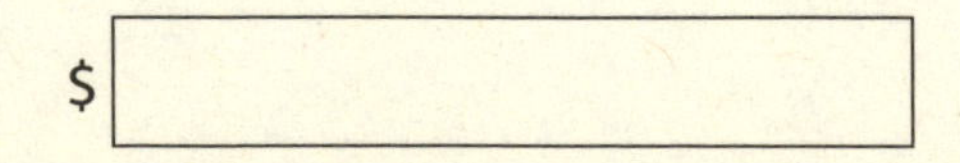

25. If $x^6 = m$ and $x^5 = \frac{n}{2}$, which of the following expressions is equivalent to x?

(A) $2mn$

(B) $\frac{2}{mn}$

(C) $\frac{mn}{2}$

(D) $\frac{2m}{n}$

(E) $\frac{2n}{m}$

ANSWERS AND EXPLANATIONS

1. **(A)** The missing angle in the triangle is $180° - 45° - 70° = 65°$. Then $x = 180 - 65 = 115$ and $y = 180 - 70 = 110$.

2. **(B)** The value of $2x$ is less than -200, whereas the value of $\frac{1}{x}$ is between -1 and 0.

3. **(C)** Let r represent the radius of circle A. Since the area is 4π, $\pi r^2 = 4\pi$. Then $r^2 = 4$, so $r = 2$. Let R represent the radius of circle B. Since the circumference of circle B is 4π, $2\pi R = 4\pi$. Then $2R = 4$, so $R = 2$.

4. **(C)** Using the distributive property, each expression is equivalent to $8x + 8y$.

5. **(B)** Since the lines are parallel, interior angles on the same side of the transversal are supplementary. Then $x = 180 - 50 = 130$. Thus, $2x - 200 = (2)(130) - 200 = 60$.

6. **(B)** Car A is traveling at 60 miles per hour, so the time needed to travel one mile is $\left(\frac{60}{60}\right)(1) = 1$ minute. Car B is traveling at 50 miles per hour, so the time needed to travel one and one-half miles is $\left(\frac{60}{50}\right)(1.5) = 1.8$ minutes.

7. **(D)** If $x^4 = y^4$, then $x = y$ or $x = -y$. Therefore, we cannot determine which of x and y is larger.

8. **(B)** By squaring both sides, $\sqrt{b^2 + 4}$ becomes $b^2 + 4$ and $b + 2$ becomes $(b + 2)^2 = b^2 + 4b + 4$. Since $b > 0$, $b^2 + 4b + 4$ is larger than $b^2 + 4$.

9. **(C)** Since the figure is a square, $3m = 4n$. Thus, the area of the square can be expressed as either $(3m)^2 = 9m^2$ or $(4n)^2 = 16n^2$.

10. (E) In any triangle, the largest side is opposite the largest angle. In ΔADC, $m\angle DAC = 180° - 65° - 60° = 55°$. This means that $\overline{AC}$ is the largest side of ΔADC. In ΔBAC, $m\angle BCA = 180° - 62° - 61° = 57°$. This means that $\overline{BC}$ is the largest side of ΔBAC. Since $\overline{AC}$ is part of ΔBAC, we can claim that $BC > AC$. Thus, $\overline{BC}$ must be the largest of the segments for both triangles.

11. (B) Using the distributive property, the equation becomes $6x - 3 + 4 = 2x$. Then $6x + 1 = 2x$, which simplifies to $1 = -4x$. Thus, $x = -\frac{1}{4}$.

12. (A) Let x represent the number of boys and y represent the number of girls. Then one girl is looking at x boys and $y - 1$ girls. Since she sees an equal number of girls and boys, $x = y - 1$, which can be written as $y = x + 1$. At this point, the only two possible answer choices for which $y = x + 1$ are A and D. We also know that one boy is looking at $x - 1$ boys and y girls. Since he sees twice as many girls as boys, $y = 2(x - 1)$. By substitution, we can write $x + 1 = 2(x - 1)$. This equation simplifies to $x + 1 = 2x - 2$. Then $1 = x - 2$, so $x = 3$. Consequently, $y = 4$, which means there are 3 boys and 4 girls.

13. (D) Let x represent the required number of years. Then $\frac{16 + x}{50 + x} = \frac{1}{2}$. Cross-multiply to get $(2)(16 + x) = (1)(50 + x)$, which simplifies to $32 + 2x = 50 + x$. Then $32 + x = 50$, so $x = 18$.

14. $\frac{40}{21}$ Since 3 bligs equals 5 bloogs, 1 blig is equivalent to $\frac{5}{3}$ bloogs. Likewise, since 8 blugs equals 7 bloogs, 1 blug is equivalent to $\frac{7}{8}$ bloog. Thus, the ratio of 1 blig to 1 blug can be expressed as $\frac{\frac{5}{3}}{\frac{7}{8}}$, which becomes $\frac{5}{3} \times \frac{8}{7} = \frac{40}{21}$.

15. 336 For a kite, the diagonals are perpendicular to each other and the longer diagonal bisects the shorter diagonal. Using the Pythagorean theorem for ΔABE, $(BE)^2 + 6^2 = 10^2$. So, $BE = \sqrt{10^2 - 6^2} = \sqrt{100 - 36} = \sqrt{64} = 8$. Since E is the midpoint of $\overline{BD}$, $BD = 16$. Using the Pythagorean theorem for ΔBEC, $(EC)^2 + 8^2 = 17^2$. So, $EC = \sqrt{17^2 - 8^2} = \sqrt{289 - 64} = \sqrt{225} = 15$. Then $AC = 6 + 15 = 21$. Finally, the product of BD and AC is $(16)(21) = 336$.

16. (E) The combined percent of the number of widowed and divorced employees is $100\% - 20\% - 25\% - 15\% = 40\%$. Let x represent the percent of widowed employees and let $3x$ represent the percent of divorced employees. Then $x + 3x = 40$, which becomes $4x = 40$. So $x = 10$ and $3x = 30$. Thus, the number of divorced employees is $(0.30)(2{,}000) = 600$.

17. (E) The number of employees who are married with at least one child is (0.25)(2,000) = 500. Of these 500 employees, 100% − 25% − 22% − 35% − 12% = 6% of them have five children. Therefore, the required number is (0.06)(500) = 30.

18. 565 The number of single employees is (0.15)(2,000) = 300. We have already determined that the number of married employees with at least one child is 500. Of these 500 employees, 35% + 12% + 6% = 53% have at least 3 children. This means that (0.53)(500) = 265 employees are married with at least 3 children. Therefore, the required number is 300 + 265 = 565.

19. 5 Of the 500 employees who are married with children, (0.25)(500) = 125 of them have just one child. For this group of employees, let x represent the number of part-time workers and let $4x$ represent the number of full-time workers. Then $x + 4x = 125$, which becomes $5x = 125$. We find that $x = 25$, so the number of full-time workers in this group is (4)(25) = 100. Thus, the required percent is $\left(\frac{100}{2,000}\right)(100\%) = 5\%$.

20. (A) The number of employees who will be hired next year is (2,000)(0.10) = 200. Currently, there are (0.15)(2,000) = 300 single employees. If all the new employees are single, this will raise the number of single employees to 500. The percent increase is $\left(\frac{200}{300}\right)(100\%) = 66\frac{2}{3}\%$.

21. (D) $\frac{(5x^4)^2(x^3)}{5x^4} = (5x^4)(x^3) = 5x^7$.

22. (C) The mean is $\frac{42}{6} = 7$, the median is $\frac{5+7}{2} = 6$, and the mode is 2. Thus, the required sum is 15.

23. 10 Let $n(F)$ represent the number of students who take French and let $n(S)$ represent the number of students who take Spanish. Then $n(F \text{ or } S) = n(F) + n(S) - n(F \text{ and } S)$. So, $35 = n(F) + 25 - 10$, which simplifies to $35 = n(F) + 15$. Then $n(F) = 20$. Thus, the number of students who take French but not Spanish is 20 − 10 = 10.

Alternative solution (using simple math): Since the number who take Spanish is 25 and the number who take both French and Spanish is 10, then 25 − 10 = 15 is the number who take only Spanish. Of the remaining students, we then know that 35 − 15 = 20 take French, and since 10 take both languages, 10 take French only.

24. 42 After Monday' s discount, the price of the radio becomes, ($60)(0.75) = $45. Following Wednesday's discount, the price becomes ($45)(0.90) = $40.50. Finally, we include the sales tax so that the final price is ($40.50)(1.04) = $42.12 ≈ $42.

25. (D) $x = \frac{x^6}{x^5} = m \div \frac{n}{2} = \frac{2m}{n}$.

Practice Test 3 Section 1

Directions: Each of Questions 1–9 consists of two quantities. Compare the quantities in Quantities A and B and choose

Ⓐ if Quantity A is greater.
Ⓑ if Quantity B is greater.
Ⓒ if the two quantities are equal.
Ⓓ if the relationship cannot be determined from the information given.

	Quantity A	Quantity B
1. $x^2 = 49$	x	$\frac{1}{x}$

Ⓐ Ⓑ Ⓒ Ⓓ

	Quantity A	Quantity B
2.	$\frac{1}{3} \div 2 + 2 \times \frac{1}{3}$	$\frac{1}{2} \div 3 + 3 \times \frac{1}{2}$

Ⓐ Ⓑ Ⓒ Ⓓ

	Quantity A	Quantity B
3. $\frac{1}{x} > 1$	x	1

Ⓐ Ⓑ Ⓒ Ⓓ

	Quantity A	Quantity B
4. $a \neq b$	$\frac{a^2 - b^2}{a - b}$	$\frac{a^3 + b^3}{a^2 - ab + b^2}$

Ⓐ Ⓑ Ⓒ Ⓓ

	Quantity A	Quantity B
5. $4y^2 + 3y + 6y^2 + 5y = 2y^2 + 6y + 8y^2 + 5$	y^2	6

Ⓐ Ⓑ Ⓒ Ⓓ

	Quantity A	Quantity B
6. $4a = 5b = 6c = 7d$ and $d > 0$	a	d

Ⓐ Ⓑ Ⓒ Ⓓ

	Quantity A	Quantity B
7.	$a \times 3 \times 3$	$a + 3 + 3$

Ⓐ Ⓑ Ⓒ Ⓓ

	Quantity A	Quantity B
8. $x < 0$	$(x^3)^7$	$(x^3)(x^7)$

Ⓐ Ⓑ Ⓒ Ⓓ

	Quantity A	Quantity B
9. $a \otimes b = \frac{b+a}{7ab}$	$7 \otimes 9$	$9 \otimes 7$

(A) (B) (C) (D)

Directions: Questions 10–25 have several different formats. Unless otherwise indicated, select a single answer choice. For numeric entry questions, follow the instructions below.

Numeric Entry Questions

Enter your answer in the answer box(es) below the question.

- Your answer may be an integer, a decimal, or a fraction, and it may be negative.
- If a question asks for a fraction, there will be two boxes—one for the numerator and one for the denominator.
- Equivalent forms of the correct answer, such as 2.5 or 2.50, are all correct. Fractions do not need to be reduced to lowest terms.
- Enter the exact answer unless the question asks you to round your answer.

10. After a 25% discount, the price of an item is \$600. What is the price of this item before the discount?

(A) \$150
(B) \$200
(C) \$700
(D) \$750
(E) \$800

11. In the figure below, point A is the center of two concentric circles. Also, A, B, and C are collinear.

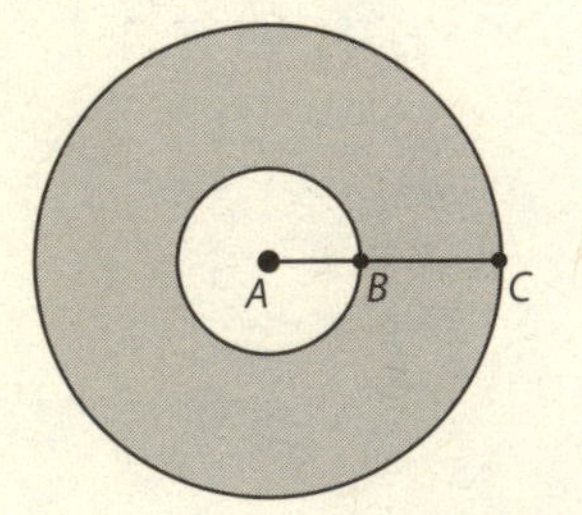

If $AB = 4$ and $BC = 7$, what is the area of the shaded region?

(A) 9π
(B) 16π
(C) 33π
(D) 105π
(E) 121π

12. Events F and G are independent. If $Pr(F \text{ or } G) = 0.9$ and $Pr(F) = 0.4$, what is the value of $Pr(G)$? Write your answer as a fraction.

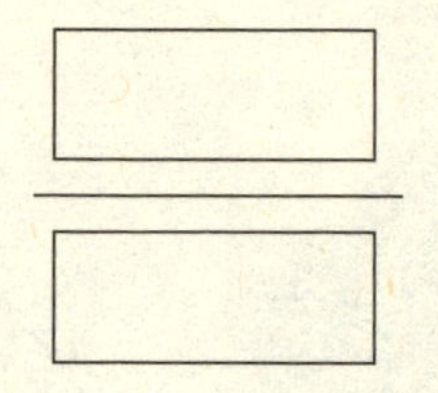

13. Points A and B (not shown) lie on opposite sides of point P on the following line.

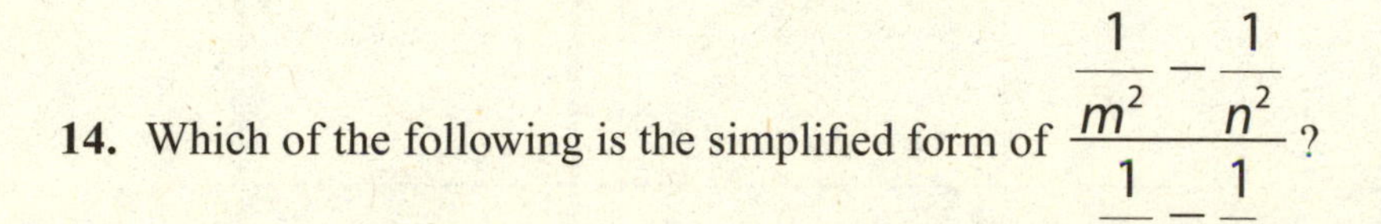

If $(3)(AP) = (4)(PB)$ and M is the midpoint of $\overline{AP}$, what is the value of $\frac{AM}{MB}$? Write your answer as a fraction.

14. Which of the following is the simplified form of $\dfrac{\frac{1}{m^2} - \frac{1}{n^2}}{\frac{1}{m} - \frac{1}{n}}$?

Ⓐ 1

Ⓑ $\frac{1}{mn}$

Ⓒ $\frac{n+m}{mn}$

Ⓓ $mn + 1$

Ⓔ $\frac{1}{mn+1}$

15. If $(9)^{x^2} = \left(\frac{1}{27}\right)^x$ and $x \neq 0$, what is the value of x?

Ⓐ -3

Ⓑ $-\frac{3}{2}$

Ⓒ $-\frac{2}{3}$

Ⓓ $\frac{1}{3}$

Ⓔ $\frac{2}{3}$

For Questions 16–20, use the following graphs. There are a total of 2,000 high school students.

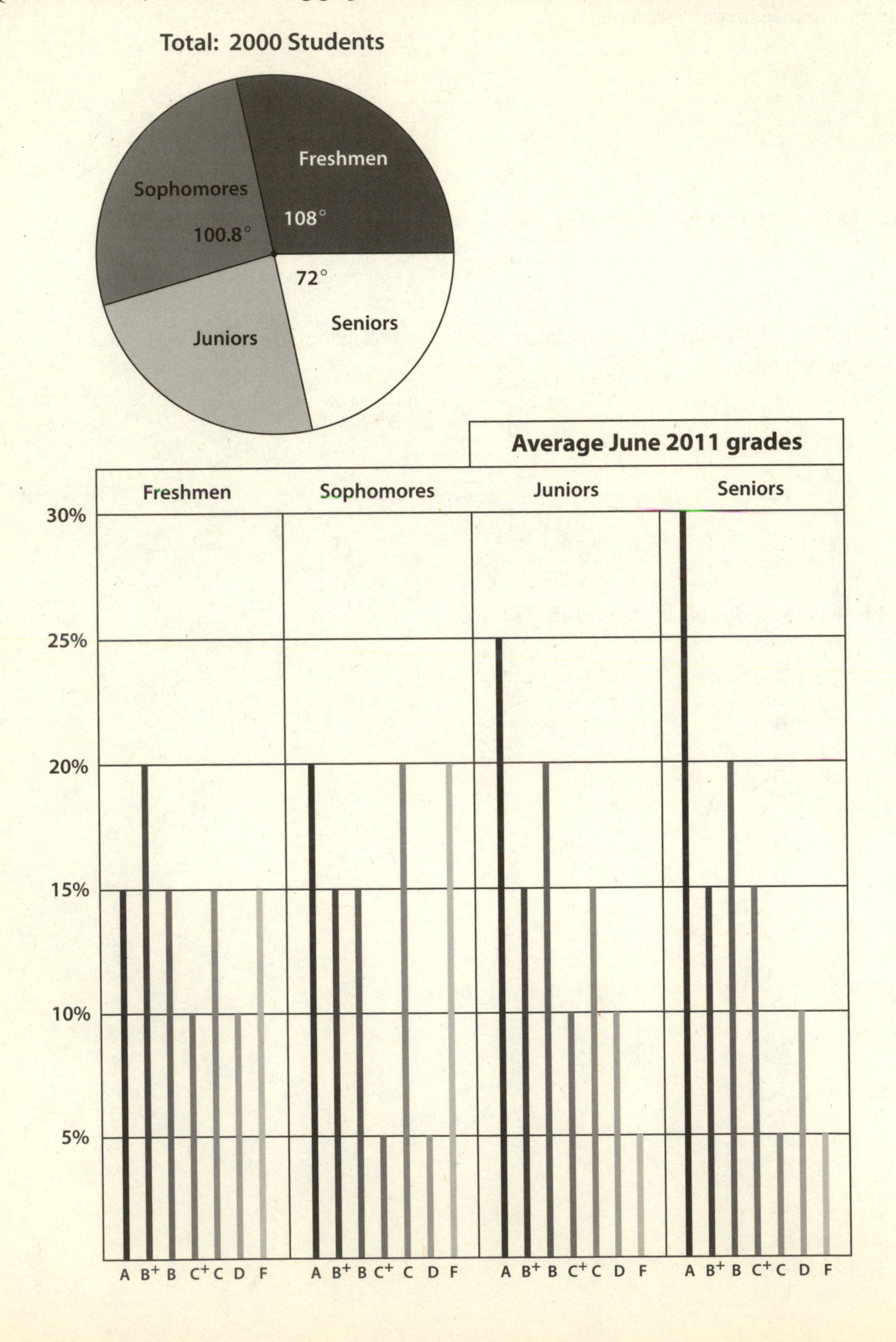

16. What is the combined number of sophomores who received a grade of B or B+?

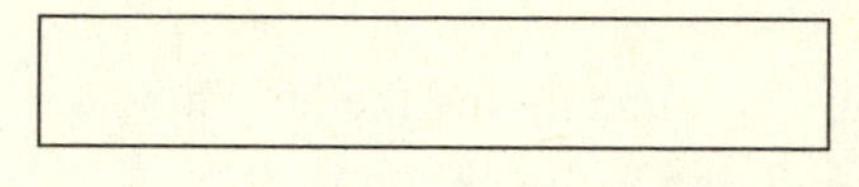

17. The number of seniors whose grade was A is how much greater than the number of juniors whose grade was D?

18. How many freshmen did not earn a grade of either A or F?

19. It was discovered that 10% of the juniors had part-time jobs in June 2011. If one-fourth of these students earned a grade of B+, how many juniors earned a grade of B+ and did *not* work part-time?

20. The minimum grade for a student to graduate is a C. What is the ratio of the number of seniors who did not graduate to the number of sophomores who received a grade of F? Write your answer as a fraction.

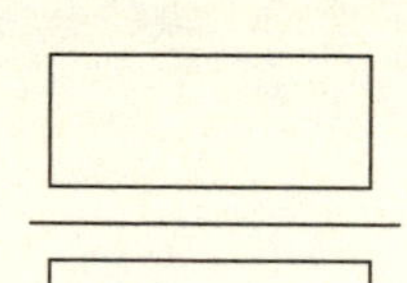

21. The square of the difference between x and 7 is equal to the square of the difference between x and 19. What is the cube of the difference between x and 6?

(A) 13
(B) 49
(C) 64
(D) 125
(E) 343

22. Cylinder P has a given height (h) and a given radius (r). Which of the following changes would yield the same volume as cylinder P? Indicate *all* correct answers.

- [A] Multiply the radius by 4 and divide the height by 4.
- [B] Triple the radius and divide the height by 9.
- [C] Triple the height and divide the radius by 3.
- [D] Double the height and divide the radius by $\sqrt{2}$.
- [E] Multiply both the radius and the height by a factor of 5.

23. At which of the following points do the graphs of $3x^2 + 4y^2 = 91$ and $x^2 + y^2 = 25$ intersect? Indicate *all* correct answers.

- [A] (3, 4)
- [B] (4, 3)
- [C] (−3, 4)
- [D] (3, −4)
- [E] (−4, −3)
- [F] (−3, −4)
- [G] (4, −3)

24. On a number line, which numbers lie twice as far from 20 as they lie from 30? Indicate *all* correct answers.

- [A] 10
- [B] $23\frac{1}{3}$
- [C] 25
- [D] $26\frac{2}{3}$
- [E] 40
- [F] $45\frac{1}{3}$

25. Look at the diagram below.

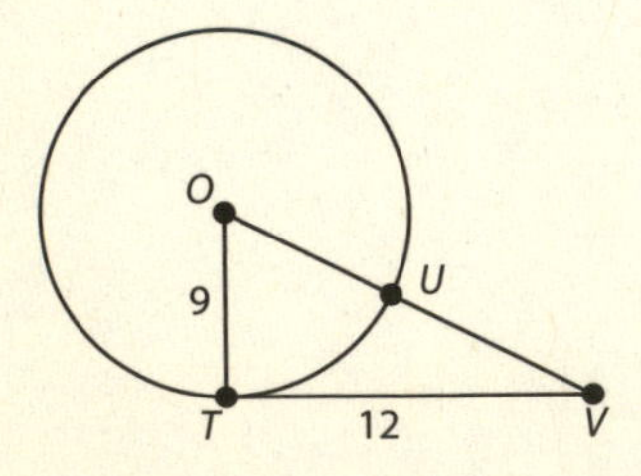

$\overline{VT}$ is tangent to circle O at point T. What is the length of $\overline{UV}$?

[ ]

ANSWERS AND EXPLANATIONS

1. (D) If $x^2 = 49$, then $x = 7$ or -7. If $x = 7$, then $x > \frac{1}{x}$. If $x = -7$, then $x < \frac{1}{x}$.

2. (B) $\frac{1}{3} \div 2 + 2 \times \frac{1}{3} = \frac{1}{6} + \frac{2}{3} = \frac{5}{6}$. $\frac{1}{2} \div 3 + 3 \times \frac{1}{2} = \frac{1}{6} + \frac{3}{2} = \frac{10}{6} = \frac{5}{3}$. We note that $\frac{5}{3} > \frac{5}{6}$.

3. (B) If $\frac{1}{x} > 1$, then x must be positive. Multiply each side of the inequality by x to get $1 > x$.

4. (C) $\frac{a^2 - b^2}{a - b} = \frac{(a+b)(a-b)}{a-b} = a + b$.

$\frac{a^3 + b^3}{a^2 - ab + b^2} = \frac{(a+b)(a^2 - ab + b^2)}{a^2 - ab + b^2} = a + b$.

5. (A) $4y^2 + 3y + 6y^2 + 5y = 2y^2 + 6y + 8y^2 + 5$ simplifies to $10y^2 + 8y = 10y^2 + 6y + 5$. This equation can now be written as $8y = 6y + 5$. Then $2y = 5$, so $y = 2.5$. Finally, $(2.5)^2 = 6.25 > 6$.

6. (A) $4a = 7d$ means that $a = \frac{7}{4}d$. Since $d > 0$, a must be greater than d.

7. (D) $a \times 3 \times 3 = 9a$ and $a + 3 + 3 = a + 6$. Since we do not know the value of a, either of $9a$ or $a + 6$ could be the larger quantity. For example, if $a = -1$, $a + 6$ would be the larger quantity. But if $a = 10$, $9a$ would be the larger quantity.

8. (B) $(x^3)^7 = x^{21}$ and $(x^3)(x^7) = x^{10}$. Since $x < 0$, x^{21} must be a negative number, whereas x^{10} must be a positive number.

9. (C) $7 \otimes 9 = \frac{9+7}{(7)(7)(9)} = \frac{16}{441}$ and $9 \otimes 7 = \frac{7+9}{(7)(9)(7)} = \frac{16}{441}$.

Another way to look at this question is to recognize that addition and multiplication are commutative, so the two values must be equal. No math required.

10. (E) Let x represent the price before the discount. Then $x - 0.25x = \$600$. This equation simplifies to $0.75x = \$600$. Thus, $x = \frac{\$600}{0.75} = \$800$.

11. (D) The radius of the larger circle is 11, so its area is $(\pi)(11^2) = 121\pi$. The area of the smaller circle is $(\pi)(4^2) = 16\pi$. Thus, the area of the shaded region is $121\pi - 16\pi = 105\pi$.

12. $\frac{5}{6}$ $Pr(F \text{ or } G) = Pr(F) + Pr(G) - Pr(F \text{ and } G)$. Since events F and G are independent, $Pr(F \text{ and } G) = [Pr(F)][Pr(G)]$. Let $x = Pr(G)$. Then, by substitution, $0.9 = 0.4 + x - (0.4)(x)$. This equation simplifies to $0.9 = 0.4 + 0.6x$. Then $0.5 = 0.6x$, so $x = \frac{0.5}{0.6} = \frac{5}{6}$.

13. $\frac{2}{5}$ The equation $(3)(AP) = (4)(PB)$ is equivalent to the proportion $\frac{AP}{PB} = \frac{4}{3}$. Insert the points A and B such that $AP = 4$ units and $PB = 3$ units. Then place point M midway between A and P. Here is how the line with points A, M, P, and B should appear.

A M P B

Thus, $AM = 2$ and $MB = 5$, which means that $\frac{AM}{MB} = \frac{2}{5}$.

14. (C) Multiply both numerator and denominator by m^2n^2 to clear them of fractions. Then

$$\left(\frac{m^2n^2}{m^2n^2}\right)\left(\frac{1/m^2 - 1/n^2}{1/m - 1/n}\right) = \frac{n^2 - m^2}{mn^2 - m^2n} = \frac{(n-m)(n+m)}{(mn)(n-m)} = \frac{n+m}{mn}.$$

15. (B) $(9)^{x^2} = (3^2)^{x^2} = 3^{2x^2}$ and $\left(\frac{1}{27}\right)^x = (3^{-3})^x = 3^{-3x}$. By equating exponents, we get $2x^2 = -3x$. Then $2x^2 + 3x = 0$, which can be factored as $(x)(2x + 3) = 0$. Either $x = 0$ or $2x + 3 = 0$. Since we are given that $x \neq 0$, the only solution comes from $2x + 3 = 0$. Solving, $x = -\frac{3}{2}$.

16. 168 The total number of sophomores is $\left(\frac{100.8°}{360°}\right)(2{,}000) = 560$. Of these, 15% + 15% = 30% earned a grade of B or B+. Thus, the required number is (0.30)(560) = 168.

17. 76 The total number of seniors is $\left(\frac{72°}{360°}\right)(2{,}000) = 400$. Of these, (0.30)(400) = 120 earned a grade of A. The central angle that corresponds to the number of juniors is 360° − 108° − 100.8° − 72° = 79.2°. This means that there are a total of $\left(\frac{79.2°}{360°}\right)(2{,}000) = 440$ juniors. Of these, (0.10)(440) = 44 earned a grade of D. Thus, the required number is 120 − 44 = 76.

18. 420 The total number of freshmen is $\left(\frac{108°}{360°}\right)(2{,}000) = 600$. We find that the combined percent of freshmen who did not get an A or F is 100% − 15% − 15% = 70%. Thus, the required number is (0.70)(600) = 420.

19. 55 From the explanation to question 17, we know that there are a total of 440 juniors. There were (0.10)(440) = 44 juniors who had part-time jobs as of June 2010.

Of these, $\left(\frac{1}{4}\right)(44) = 11$ earned a grade of B+. The total number of juniors who earned a grade of B+ was (0.15)(440) = 66. Therefore, the number of juniors who earned a grade of B+ and did not have a part-time job was 66 − 11 = 55.

20. $\frac{15}{28}$ Of the 400 seniors, there were 10% + 5% = 15% who earned a grade below C. This means that (0.15)(400) = 60 seniors did not graduate. Of the 560 sophomores, 20% earned a grade of F. This means that (0.20)(560) = 112 sophomores received a grade of F. Thus, the required ratio is $\frac{60}{112}$, which reduces to $\frac{15}{28}$.

21. (E) The first sentence leads to the equation $(x - 7)^2 = (x - 19)^2$. Then $x^2 - 14x + 49 = x^2 - 38x + 361$. This equation simplifies to $38x - 14x = 361 - 49$, which becomes $24x = 312$. So, $x = 13$. Thus, the required number is $(13 - 6)^3 = 7^3 = 343$.

22. (B, D) The volume of cylinder P is $\pi r^2 h$. By tripling the radius and dividing the height by 9, the volume is $\pi(3r)^2\left(\frac{h}{9}\right) = (\pi)(9r^2)\left(\frac{h}{9}\right) = \pi r^2 h$, which matches the volume of cylinder P. By doubling the height and dividing the radius by $\sqrt{2}$, the volume is $\pi\left(\frac{r}{\sqrt{2}}\right)^2(2h) = (\pi)\left(\frac{r^2}{2}\right)(2h) = \pi r^2 h$. Choice (A) is wrong because the volume would change to $\pi(4r)^2\left(\frac{h}{4}\right) = (\pi)(16r^2)\left(\frac{h}{4}\right) = 4\pi r^2 h$. Choice (C) is wrong because the volume would change to $\pi\left(\frac{r}{3}\right)^2(3h) = (\pi)\left(\frac{r^2}{9}\right)(3h) = \frac{1}{3}\pi r^2 h$. Choice (E) is wrong because the volume would change to $\pi(5r)^2(5h) = (\pi)(25r^2)(5h) = 125\,\pi r^2 h$.

23. (A, C, D, F) Multiply the first equation by 4 to get $4x^2 + 4y^2 = 100$. Now, by subtracting the equation $3x^2 + 4y^2 = 91$, we get $x^2 = 9$. So, $x = \pm 3$. Now replacing either 3 or -3 into the equation $x^2 + y^2 = 25$, we find that $9 + y^2 = 25$. This means that $y^2 = 16$, so $y = \pm 4$. The four answers are (3, 4), (3, −4), (−3, −4), and (−3, 4).

24. (D, E) Let x represent the unknown number(s). The distance between x and 20 is written as $|x - 20|$ and the distance between x and 30 is written as $|x - 30|$. Then the problem is to find x such that $|x - 20| = (2)(|x - 30|)$. This absolute value equation is equivalent to $x - 20 = (2)(x - 30)$ or to $x - 20 = (2)(30 - x)$. The first equation simplifies to $x - 20 = 2x - 60$, which becomes $-20 = x - 60$. Thus, $x = 40$. The second equation simplifies to $x - 20 = 60 - 2x$, which becomes $3x - 20 = 60$.

Then $3x = 80$, so $x = 26\frac{2}{3}$.

25. 6 A tangent to a circle forms a right angle at the point of tangency. By the Pythagorean theorem, $OV = \sqrt{9^2 + 12^2} = \sqrt{81 + 144} = \sqrt{225} = 15$. Also, $OU = OT = 9$. Thus, $UV = OV - OU = 6$.

Practice Test 3

Section 2

Directions: Each of Questions 1–9 consists of two quantities. Compare the quantities in Quantities A and B and choose

Ⓐ if Quantity A is greater.
Ⓑ if Quantity B is greater.
Ⓒ if the two quantities are equal.
Ⓓ if the relationship cannot be determined from the information given.

	Quantity A	Quantity B
1.	$a(a + b)$	$3(a^2 + ab) - 2a(a + b)$

Ⓐ Ⓑ Ⓒ Ⓓ

2. Look at the following diagram:

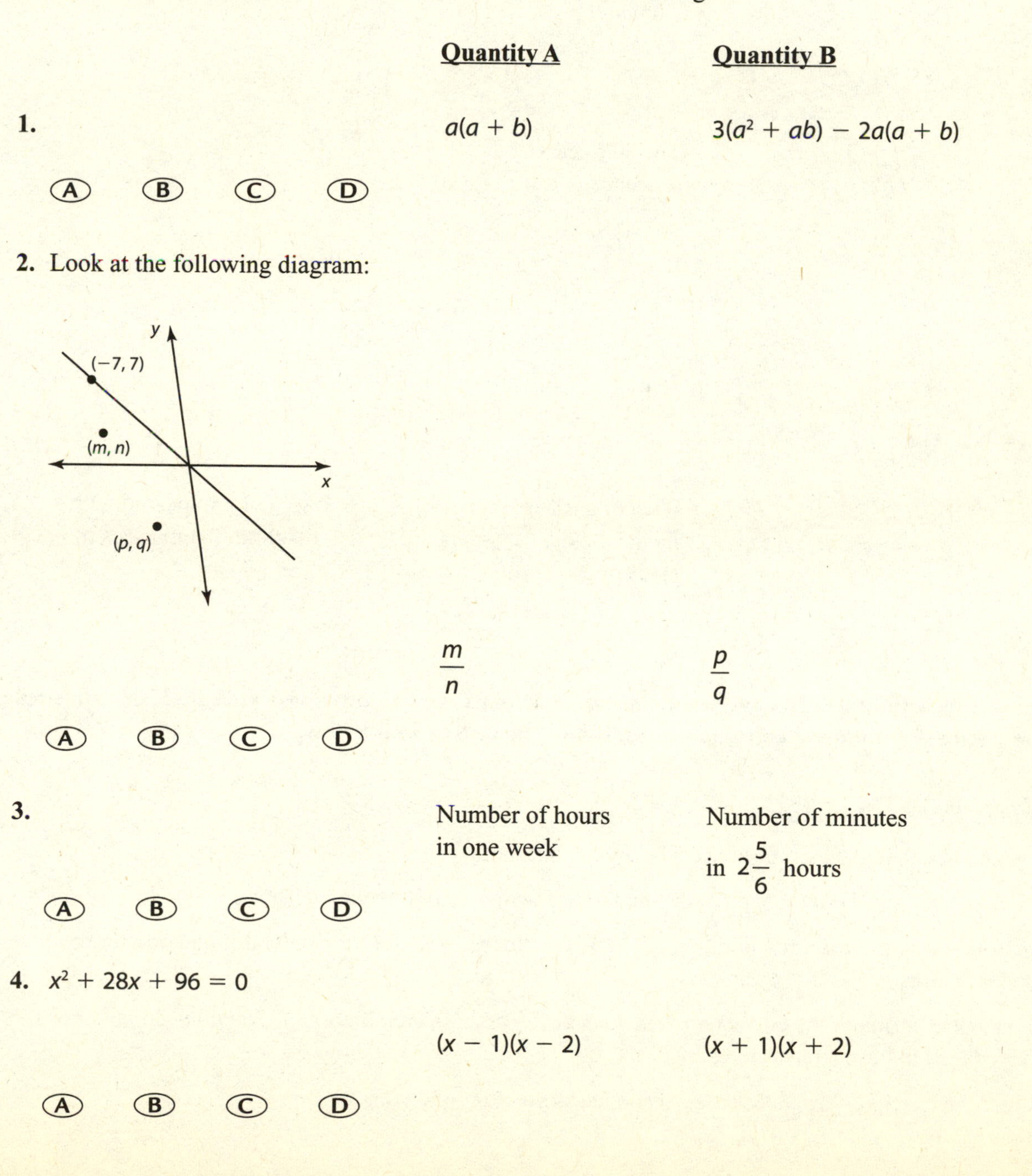

Quantity A	Quantity B
$\frac{m}{n}$	$\frac{p}{q}$

Ⓐ Ⓑ Ⓒ Ⓓ

	Quantity A	Quantity B
3.	Number of hours in one week	Number of minutes in $2\frac{5}{6}$ hours

Ⓐ Ⓑ Ⓒ Ⓓ

4. $x^2 + 28x + 96 = 0$

Quantity A	Quantity B
$(x - 1)(x - 2)$	$(x + 1)(x + 2)$

Ⓐ Ⓑ Ⓒ Ⓓ

	Quantity A	Quantity B
5. Each of $a, b, c, d, e > 1$ and $abc = bcde$		
	a	d
(A) (B) (C) (D)		
6.	Area of an equilateral triangle with a side of 6 units	Area of a square with a side of 4 units
(A) (B) (C) (D)		
7.	The 86th term of the sequence $-1, 0\ 1, -1, 0\ 1, \ldots$	0
(A) (B) (C) (D)		
8. $y = 4x$		
	$3y - 1$	y
(A) (B) (C) (D)		
9.	Area of a triangle formed by the x-axis, the y-axis and $y = 2x + 10$	Area of a trapezoid with a height of 3 and bases of 7 and 9
(A) (B) (C) (D)		

Directions: Questions 10-25 have several different formats. Unless otherwise indicated, select a single answer choice. For numeric entry questions, follow the instructions below.

Numeric Entry Questions

Enter your answer in the answer box(es) below the question.

- Your answer may be an integer, a decimal, or a fraction, and it may be negative.
- If a question asks for a fraction, there will be two boxes—one for the numerator and one for the denominator.
- Equivalent forms of the correct answer, such as 2.5 or 2.50, are all correct. Fractions do not need to be reduced to lowest terms.
- Enter the exact answer unless the question asks you to round your answer.

10. Two letters are randomly selected from the 26 letters of the English alphabet, one at a time, with no replacement. What is the probability that both selections are vowels? Write your answer as a fraction. (There are a total of 5 vowels.)

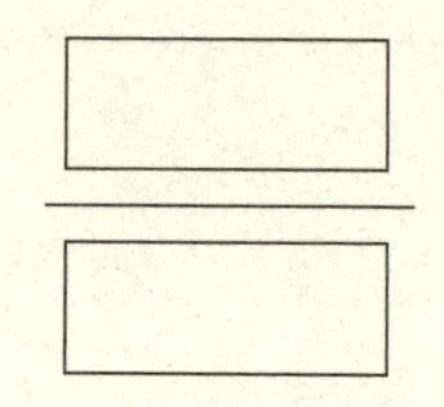

11. What is the value of $\frac{200!}{198!}$?

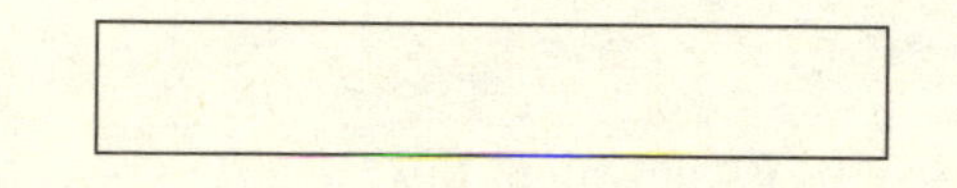

12. Define $a \oplus b$ as $b + a^3$. If $2 \oplus x^2 = 9x$, what are the solutions for x? Indicate *all* correct answers.

[A] -8
[B] -3
[C] -1
[D] 0
[E] 1
[F] 3
[G] 8

13. Look at the following diagram on the xy-coordinate axis.

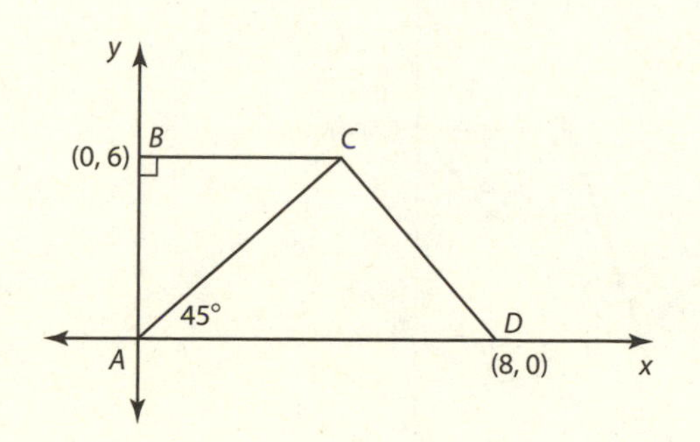

What is the area of $ABCD$?

(A) 24
(B) 36
(C) 42
(D) 48
(E) 54

14. The sum of seven consecutive odd integers is -105. What is the product of the two largest of these integers?

15. Look at the following triangle.

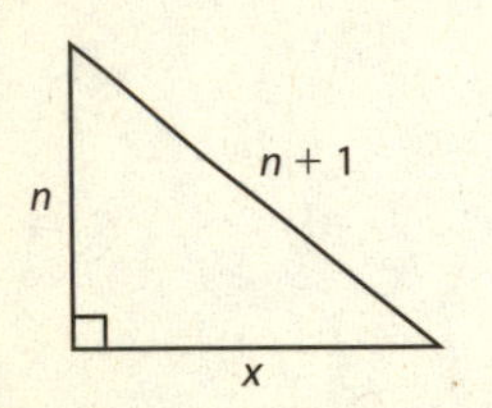

Which of the following expressions is equivalent to x?

(A) $n^2 + n$

(B) $2n + 1$

(C) $\sqrt{2n+1}$

(D) $\sqrt{2n^2+2n+1}$

(E) $\sqrt{n+1}$

For Questions 16–18, use the following line graph.

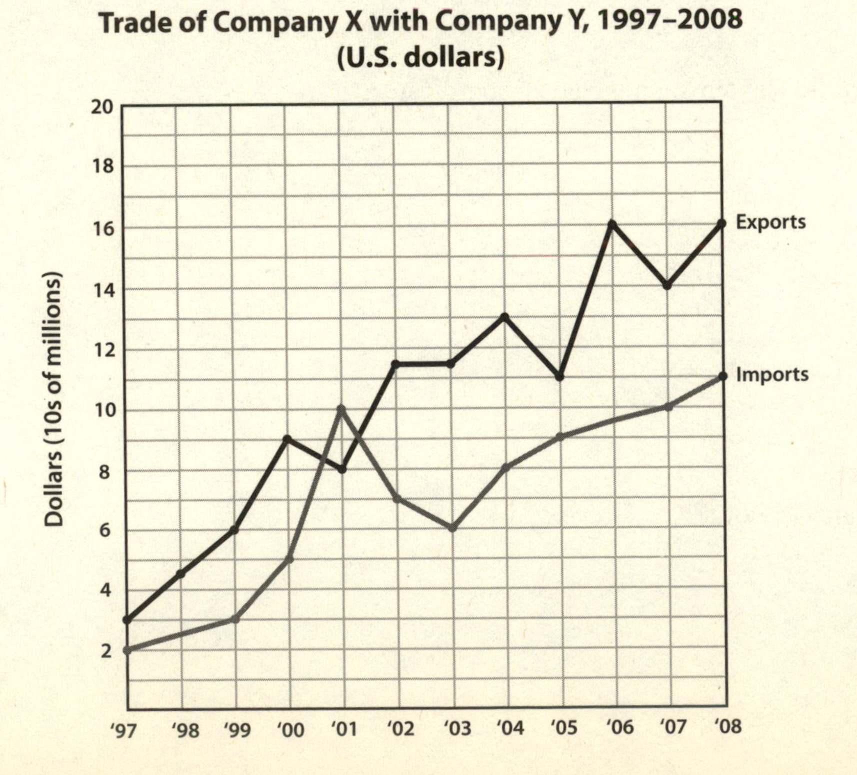

16. For the year 2003, exports represent what percent of imports? Round off your answer to the nearest whole number percent.

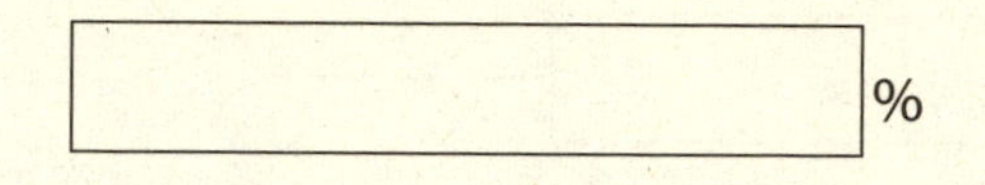

17. Which of the following time periods shows the largest percent decrease in exports?

(A) 2000 to 2001
(B) 2002 to 2003
(C) 2004 to 2005
(D) 2006 to 2007
(E) Both 2004 to 2005 and 2006 to 2007

18. The rise in imports between 2004 to 2008 was how much greater than the rise in imports between 2003 to 2004?

(A) $1,000,000
(B) $1,500,000
(C) $2,000,000
(D) $10,000,000
(E) $20,000,000

19. The probability that Nancy will go shopping today is 0.3 and the probability that it will rain today is 0.6. Assuming that these events are independent, what is the probability that at least one of these events will occur?

(A) 0.18
(B) 0.3
(C) 0.45
(D) 0.72
(E) 0.9

20. Look at the following boxplot.

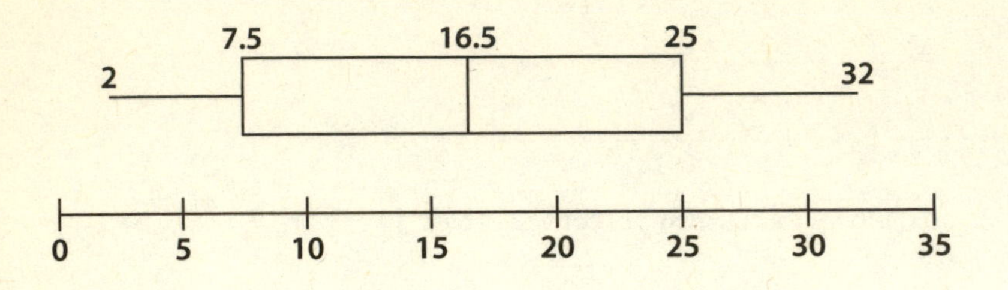

What is the difference between the mean and the range?

Ⓐ 30
Ⓑ 22.5
Ⓒ 13.5
Ⓓ 5
Ⓔ It cannot be determined.

21. If $M = 2^r$, which one of the following is equivalent to $8M$?

Ⓐ 16^r
Ⓑ 64^r
Ⓒ $(2^r)^3$
Ⓓ 2^{r+1}
Ⓔ 2^{r+3}

22. If $m = \frac{p^6}{q^5}$, which one of the following is equivalent to $\frac{qm}{p}$?

Ⓐ $\frac{p^5}{q^4}$

Ⓑ $\frac{p^7}{q^6}$

Ⓒ $\frac{p^8}{q^7}$

Ⓓ $\frac{p^9}{q^3}$

Ⓔ $\frac{p^{10}}{q^2}$

23. If $8 \leq m \leq 10$ and $4 \leq n \leq 6$, what is the maximum value of $\frac{m}{n}$?

24. If $0 < m < 1$, which of the following *must* be true? Indicate *all* correct answers.

A $m < \frac{1}{\sqrt{m}}$

B $\frac{1}{m} < \frac{1}{m^2}$

C $1 - m < m$

D $\frac{1}{m^3} < m$

E $\sqrt[3]{m} < \sqrt{m}$

25. If $\frac{x+1}{x-1} = \frac{x-1}{x+1}$, which of the following are solutions for x? Indicate *all* correct answers.

A 2

B 1

C 0

D − 1

E − 2

ANSWERS AND EXPLANATIONS

1. (C) $a(a + b) = a^2 + ab$ and $3(a^2 + ab) - 2a(a + b) = 3a^2 + 3ab - 2a^2 - 2ab = a^2 + ab$.

2. (B) The point (m, n) lies in the second quadrant, so $m < 0$ and $n > 0$. Then $\frac{m}{n} < 0$.

The point (p, q) lies in the third quadrant, so $p < 0$ and $q < 0$. Then $\frac{p}{q} > 0$.

Therefore, $\frac{p}{q} > \frac{m}{n}$.

3. (B) The number of hours in one week is (7)(24) = 168, whereas the number of minutes in $2\frac{5}{6}$ hours is $(60)(2\frac{5}{6}) = 170$.

4. (A) The equation $x^2 + 28x + 96 = 0$ can be factored as $(x + 24)(x + 4) = 0$. So, $x = -24$ or $x = -4$. Let $x = -24$. Then $(x - 1)(x - 2) = (-25)(-26) = 650$, whereas $(x + 1)(x + 2) = (-23)(-22) = 506$. If $x = -4$, then $(x - 1)(x - 2) = (-5)(-6) = 30$, whereas $(x + 1)(x + 2) = (-3)(-2) = 6$. In either case, Quantity A has the larger value.

5. (A) $abc = bcde$ implies that $a = de$. Since each variable has a value greater than 1, it follows that $a > d$ and $a > e$.

6. (B) The area of the equilateral triangle is $\frac{6^2}{4}\sqrt{3} = 9\sqrt{3} \approx 15.6$ square units. The area of the square is $4^2 = 16$ square units.

7. (C) The terms that are 0 are the 2nd, 5th, 8th,... Each of these term numbers, when divided by 3, leaves a remainder of 2. Note that when 86 is divided by 3, the remainder is also 2. Therefore, the 86th term is 0.

8. (D) By substitution, the expression in Quantity A becomes $(3)(4x) - 1 = 12x - 1$. Likewise, the expression in Quantity B becomes $4x$. Either of $12x - 1$ or $4x$ may be the larger expression. For example, if $x = 1$, $12x - 1$ is larger than $4x$. But if $x = -1$, $4x$ is larger than $12x - 1$.

9. (A) We need to find the x- and y-intercepts for the line $y = 2x + 10$. The x-intercept is found by the equation $0 = 2x + 10$, which means that $x = -5$. The y-intercept is found by the equation $y = (2)(0) + 10 = 10$. So, the triangle has vertices of (0, 0), (−5, 0), and (0, 10). Its area is $\left(\frac{1}{2}\right)(5)(10) = 25$. The area of the trapezoid is $\left(\frac{1}{2}\right)(3)(7+9) = \left(\frac{1}{2}\right)(48) = 24$.

10. $\frac{2}{65}$ The probability of getting a vowel on the first selection is $\frac{5}{26}$. For the second selection, 25 letters remain, of which 4 are vowels. So, the probability of getting a vowel on the second selection is $\frac{4}{25}$. Thus, the required probability is

$\frac{5}{26} \times \frac{4}{25} = \frac{20}{650}$, which reduces to $\frac{2}{65}$.

11. 39,800 $\frac{200!}{198!} = \frac{(200)(199)(198)(197)\cdots(2)(1)}{(198)(197)(196)(195)\cdots(2)(1)}$. By canceling all common factors of both numerator and denominator, the result is (200)(199) = 39,800.

12. (E, G) $2 \oplus x^2 = 9x$ becomes $x^2 + 8 = 9x$. Then $x^2 - 9x + 8 = 0$ can be factored as $(x - 1)(x - 8) = 0$. Thus, $x = 1$ or $x = 8$.

13. (C) Since BC is parallel to AD, this is a trapezoid, so we need to find the height (AB) and the bases (BC and AD). Based on the diagram, ABC is a 45°-45°-90° right triangle. Then AB = BC = 6. Since AD = 8, we can compute the area of the trapezoid to be

$\left(\frac{1}{2}\right)(6)(8+6) = \left(\frac{1}{2}\right)(84) = 42$.

14. 99 Let the seven numbers be represented by $x, x + 2, x + 4, x + 6, x + 8, x + 10$, and $x + 12$. Then $7x + 42 = -105$. So, $7x = -147$, which means that $x = -21$. The seven numbers are $-21, -19, -17, -15, -13, -11$, and -9. The two largest numbers are -11 and -9. Thus the required product is 99.

15. (C) Using the Pythagorean theorem, $x^2 + n^2 = (n + 1)^2$. Then $x^2 = (n + 1)^2 - n^2 = n^2 + 2n + 1 - n^2 = 2n + 1$. Thus, $x = \sqrt{2n+1}$.

16. 192 The required percent is $\frac{11.5}{5} \times 100\% \approx 192\%$.

17. (C) Although the dollar drop was the same for both periods 2004 to 2005 and 2006 to 2007, the percents are different. The percent drop for 2004 to 2005 was $\frac{13-11}{13} \times 100\% \approx 15.4\%$. The percent drop for 2006 to 2007 was $\frac{16-14}{16} \times 100\% = 12.5\%$. The percent drop for 2000 to 2001 was $\frac{9-8}{9} = 11.1\%$. For the period 2002 to 2003, there was a 0% drop.

18. (D) Be aware that the unit on the vertical axis is \$10,000,000. The rise in imports from 2004 to 2008 was \$110,000,000 – \$80,000,000 = \$30,000,000. The rise in imports from 2003 to 2004 was \$80,000,000 – \$60,000,000 = \$20,000,000. Thus, the required difference is \$10,000,000.

19. (D) The probability that at least one event occurs is the sum of the individual probabilities of each event subtracted by the product of their individual probabilities. Thus, the required probability is 0.3 + 0.6 – (0.3)(0.6) = 0.72.

20. (E) A boxplot shows the lowest and highest numbers, but does not show the mean. Therefore, the required difference cannot be determined.

21. (E) $8M = (8)(2^r) = (2^3)(2^r) = 2^{r+3}$.

22. (A) $\frac{qm}{p} = \left(\frac{q}{p}\right)(m) = \left(\frac{q}{p}\right)\left(\frac{p^6}{q^5}\right) = \frac{p^5}{q^4}$.

23. 2.5 The maximum value of $\frac{m}{n}$ is attained by using the highest value of m and the lowest value of n. Thus, the maximum value is $\frac{10}{4} = 2.5$.

24. (A, B) Choice (A) is correct because $\sqrt{m}$ must lie between 0 and 1, so its reciprocal must be greater than 1. Choice (B) is correct because $m^2 < m$ whenever $0 < m < 1$. This means that $\frac{1}{m^2} > \frac{1}{m}$. Each of choices (C), (D), and (E) can be shown false with a numerical example. Let $m = \frac{1}{2}$. Then choice (C) states that $1 - \frac{1}{2} < \frac{1}{2}$, which is false. Choice (D) states that $\frac{1}{\left(\frac{1}{2}\right)^3} < \frac{1}{2}$. But $\frac{1}{\left(\frac{1}{2}\right)^3} = \frac{1}{\frac{1}{8}} = 8$, so choice (E) is false.

Choice (E) states that $\sqrt[3]{\frac{1}{2}} < \sqrt{\frac{1}{2}}$. But $\sqrt[3]{\frac{1}{2}} \approx 0.79$ and $\sqrt{\frac{1}{2}} \approx 0.71$, so choice (E) is false.

25. (C) Cross-multiply to get $(x + 1)^2 = (x - 1)^2$. By expanding both sides, we get $x^2 + 2x + 1 = x^2 - 2x + 1$. Then $2x = -2x$, which becomes $4x = 0$, Thus, the only solution is $x = 0$. (Note that the value of x cannot be -1 or 1 because one denominator will be zero, which means that the fraction would be undefined.)

EPILOGUE

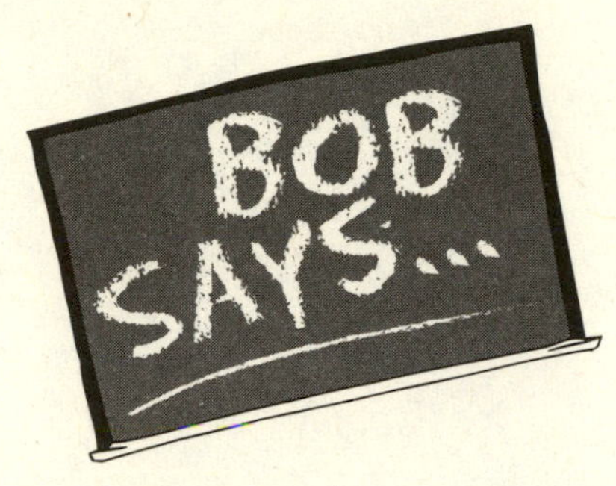

"If you feel more is needed, you may need a little more for your confidence. But if our journey together has been complete, you have all you need for success."

Again, congratulations. Now that you've finished the book, you should review any section that has caused you difficulty.

Remember, again, that you do not need a perfect score. You need only a score that will get you into the graduate school of your choice.

Good luck with the rest of your college education and your chosen career.

INDEX

INDEX

A

B

C

D

E

Q

R

S

T

V

W

NOTES

NOTES

NOTES

NOTES

NOTES

NOTES

NOTES

NOTES

NOTES